Making War, Not Love

Other Books by Emil Draitser

Forbidden Laughter: Soviet Underground Jokes
The Fun House (in Russian)
The Lost Boy and Other Stories (in Russian)
Techniques of Satire: The Case of Saltykov–Shchedrin
Taking Penguins to the Movies: Ethnic Humor in Russia

Making War, Not Love

Gender and Sexuality in Russian Humor

Emil A. Draitser

St. Martin's Press
New York

ISBN 0-312-22129-0

Library of Congress Cataloging-in-Publication Data
Draitser, Emil, 1937-
  Making war, not love : gender and sexuality in Russian humor / by
Emil A. Draitser.
      p.   cm.
  Includes bibliographical references and index.
  ISBN 0-312-22129-0
  1. Russian wit and humor—History and criticism.   2. Sex—Humor.
  I. Title.
PG3099.W5D7   1999
891.77'009—dc21   99–19094
                                                                          CIP

Book design by Letra Libre Inc.

First edition: September, 1999
10 9 8 7 6 5 4 3 2 1

Contents

Author's Note

Since humor is deeply embedded in a culture, it presents problems for the outsider. My own background in Russia should help in understanding the intricacies of Russian humor. Having lived in Russia until I was in my late thirties, and later trained in the West as a scholar, I offer an insider's knowledge from an outsider's vantage point. This study is a natural extension of my lifelong involvement with and interest in the phenomenon of laughter. From 1964 to 1974, under my pen name Emil Abramov, I contributed satirical columns and humorous short stories to *Krokodil* (The Crocodile), "The Club of Twelve Chairs" in *Literaturnaia gazeta,* and other major Russian publications. In the United States, I have published a number of satirical sketches and humorous essays in the *Los Angeles Times,* the *San Francisco Chronicle,* the *Los Angeles Herald Examiner, Studies in Contemporary Satire, Confrontation, New Press Literary Quarterly,* and several other American periodicals as well as in many Russian émigré publications.

My research in Russian sexual humor has evolved from my study of Soviet underground humor. After publishing a small collection of Soviet underground jokes, *Forbidden Laughter,* I followed it up with analytical work on the subject. My next book-length effort resulted in *Taking Penguins to the Movies: Ethnic Humor in Russia.* As the first extensive work on the subject, it attempts to offer to the Western reader not only a comprehensive collection of Russian ethnic humor of the second half of this century but its interpretation in sociopolitical and psychological terms.

The current study is devoted to another large area of Russian oral jokelore—gender-related matters. I hope it will interest scholars and students of folklore, gender studies, sociology, political science, cultural history, literature, sociolinguistics, and cultural anthropology, and the general reader will gain an understanding of Russia as a male-dominant society.

Although I cite a number of sociological research findings, this book is a study of folk humor. Therefore, references to Russians (and occasionally to other ethnic groups) are primarily concerned with their image as it is portrayed or transpires in this humor. A comic stereotype is invoked, foreknowledge of which for both the teller and the hearer is a necessary condition for a joke's success.

I should also warn readers who may prefer to skip the analysis and read only the jokes that, while some Russian jokes make for an unpleasant (and even at times disturbing) reading, I have approached the selection of jokes solely on the basis of their analytical interest, choosing not the funniest (or tasteful) samples but those most representative of the variants and richest in texture. Note that reading jokes in a book is not the same as hearing them in an actual setting and in a certain mood. Even if this were possible, Westerners may lack something in order to appreciate them fully, something that French philosopher Henri Bergson considers a requirement for laughter—a "secret freemasonry . . . with laughers."

Acknowledgments

I am grateful for research grants by the Research Foundation of the City University of New York; beginning in 1990, I made four field trips to Russia, where I have had an opportunity to update my research database. The collection of a Muscovite (who chose to remain anonymous) helped me to fill the gap of fifteen years in my private collection (I emigrated to the United States in 1974), for which I am deeply thankful.

Professor Daniel Rancour-Laferriere of the University of California at Davis read the first draft of this book, has given my project steady encouragement, and offered his valuable insights. I also thank Professor Boris Gasparov of Columbia University for his criticism of the manuscript. My colleagues Professors Alex Alexander, Elizabeth Beaujour, Tamara Green, and Gregory Massell have provided continuing moral support. I am grateful to Norman Clarius of Hunter College Interlibrary Loan Department. My loyal friend Dr. Anthony Saidy has assisted me in staying abreast of press coverage of latest developments in Russia, and another friend, Martin Weiss, has helped me to get a better grasp of American slang and jokelore. I am grateful to Ruth Mathewson not only for her editing of the manuscript but for many valuable suggestions. Sylvia Berger's aid and encouragement over the past four years has been invaluable.

I would also like to express my appreciation for the benefit I received from the questions and encouragement of many participants in the following scholarly meetings at which parts of this book were presented in their initial form: annual meetings of the American Association for Advanced Slavic Studies and the American Association of Teachers of Slavic and East European Languages, the Conference on Post-Soviet Cultural Studies at the Columbia University, the International Conference on Humor Research in Ithaca, New York, and the International Conference on Russian Pornography at the University of Southern California.

Special thanks go to my brother, Vladimir Draitser, who provided me with personalized technical support and who, with his inimitable sense of humor, has helped me to remember many jokes we exchanged in our youth.

A Note on Transliteration
and Translation

I have used the Library of Congress System of transliteration throughout this book, except for certain well-known Russian names that are traditionally spelled differently, such as Dostoevsky, Tolstoy, Yeltsyn, Khrushchev, and Sinyavsky. Unless otherwise noted, all translations from Russian are my own.

To two beautiful ladies: Ruth Mathewson, for her expert editorial help and long friendship, and Sylvia Berger, for many years of moral support and gracious goodwill

Humor . . . is impregnated with the convictions, customs, and associations of a nation. . . . The humor of a people is their institutions, laws, customs, manners, habits, characters, convictions—their scenery whether of the sea, the city, or the hills—expressed in the language of the ludicrous.

—Westminster Review, *December 1838*

Not a Dostoevsky but a simple, uncomplicated joke will open for us all the nooks and crannies of the mysterious Russian soul.

—Efraim Sevela, Russian writer

The level of a culture is measured by its attitudes toward women.

—Maxim Gorky

There is often anger in a laugh.

—Old Irish proverb

Beware of jokes . . . we go away hollow and ashamed.

—Emerson

Sex is a great human comedy where the joke is always on us.

—Camille Paglia, American scholar

Introduction

Learning about Russians as a people is important now as never before. Russian society is undergoing tremendous political and social changes. To deal successfully with the new Russia that is gradually emerging from the rubble of totalitarianism, we must know as much as we can about the world individual Russians inhabit, his or her attitudes and customs, beliefs, and idiosyncrasies, and the inter- and intragroup relationships of this complex society.

Although entertainment is the primary—the recognized—goal of telling jokes, the subjects they are related to are usually those that are most important to the tellers, even if they don't realize it. Humor expresses serious anxieties in lighter terms; it is this capacity to relieve frustration that makes laughter so attractive.

Properly analyzed, folk humor can help make visible areas of unacknowledged attitudes and behaviors in private, unofficial realms. Therefore, rendering tacit culture explicit is at the core of my analysis. What makes such analysis possible is the awareness that a joke dies as a bit of communication unless the teller and the hearer share common ground. Thus the implicit assumptions of the culture form the foundation of a joke. Analyzing and interpreting jokes make it possible to deduce certain behavioral patterns based on deeply held popular beliefs, the hidden underpinnings of a culture. In *The Silent Language,* anthropologist Edward Hall (1973) stresses the importance of understanding a people's sense of humor as one key to the structure of that society: "People laugh and tell jokes, and if you can learn the humor of a people and really control it you know that you are also in control of nearly everything else" (52).

Jokes, then, can give us clues to what people think about their lives; we learn by studying the way they verbalize their thoughts and feelings. Such lore is widespread among many people in Russia and elsewhere, although its degree of visibility and its meaning in every society must be determined separately for every group and for individuals within the groups. But its widespread presence and persistence cannot be denied.

Jokelore as part of everyday discourse is important not only because it reflects prevailing attitudes and mores but also because it reaffirms and sustains them. In *Russian Talk: Culture and Conversation During Perestroika,* Nancy Ries (1997, 75) shows that everyday discourse, even when it "mourns or mocks" a certain norm, is instrumental in "its reproduction over time." Thus repeated and continuous joke-telling, no matter how biting the jokes may be, assures one result: validation of the norm in the consciousness of the listeners. From this vantage point, jokes are masked contributors to the status quo. As British social psychologist Christopher Wilson (1979, 228) points out, "though jokes feed on subversive thought, on deviations from the normal and expected, they reinforce established views of the world."

Jokes that Russians exchange with each other are most often called *anek-doty,*[1] from the Greek *anekdota,* meaning "unpublished things." The Russians' resort to humor in daily life when other avenues of expression are closed has long been begging for exploration and interpretation. The only contemporary Russian jokelore that has been systematically collected by Westerners is political humor. Sovietologists and American media observers sporadically attempted to analyze this material primarily to better understand Soviet society.

The Russian culture of popular laughter, however, is a much broader phenomenon than is generally believed in the West. Coming from a rich tradition of oral literature and folk tales, contemporary Russian popular laughter contains a wealth of sociological, anthropological, ethnographic, and other material. The data for such inquiry into this resource has not been sufficiently collected and analyzed, probably because of language and cultural barriers and the disregard of some scholars for contemporary folklore as an important expression of a people's cognitive and emotional life.

At the same time, in recent years Western scholars have shown a growing interest in Russian sex- and gender-related issues. Among these studies are Igor Kon's and James Riordan's *Sex and Russian Society* (1993); Eve Levin's *Sex and Society in the World of the Orthodox Slavs, 900–1700* (1989); Jane Costlow's, Stephanie Sandler's, and Judith Vowles's *Sexuality and the Body in Russian Culture* (1993); Laura Engelstein's *The Keys to Happiness: Sex and Search of Modernity in Fin-de-Siècle Russia* (1992); and Barbara Heldt's *Terrible Perfection: Women and Russian Literature* (1989). Igor Kon's *The Sexual Revolution in Russia* (1995) was also published in the West.

Although some of these studies address Russian popular views on gender and sexuality (e.g., Catriona Kelly's 1993 work on the popular puppet street show, "Petrushka," a Russian variant of "Punch and Judy"), most of these scholarly works are devoted to high culture. In his otherwise exhaustive two-volume studies, *Rationale of the Dirty Joke: An Analysis of Sexual Humor* (1968, 1975), Gershon Legman makes sporadic use of Russian samples, referring primarily to Alexander Afanasiev's nineteenth-century collection of Russian folk erotica, *Secret Tales.* Little contemporary Russian sexual material has been collected in the West; the field is, by and large, untouched by Western scholarly inquiry. Only a handful of sex- and gender-related jokes is included in such collections as *Russia Dies Laughing* by Zhanna Dolgopolova (1982) or my book *Forbidden Laughter.*

In those rare instances when Russian sexual jokelore has been analyzed in the West, it has almost never been approached from the anthropological, sociological, or psychological vantage point. Thus in his *Semantic Mechanisms of Humor* (1985), Victor Raskin scrutinizes samples of Russian sexual jokes as well as of ribald popular rhymes (chastushkas), but he does so only in the context of his linguistic theory of humor. Raskin was not interested in studying the material as it relates to Russian culture—behavioral patterns, customs, folk beliefs, and tacit assumptions held by various population groups.

With glasnost and perestroika and the lifting of official taboos on the publication of folk humor, the streets of Russian cities were soon flooded with hastily published books and booklets of current sexual jokes. However, a number of works devoted to the erotic in Russian culture published in recent years by Russian scholars—*Russkii eroticheskii fol'klor* (Russian erotic folklore) (1995), *Seks i erotika v russkoi traditsionnoi kul'ture* (Sex and eroticism in Russian traditional culture) (1996), both edited by Andrey Toporkov, and *Antimir russkoi kul'tury* (The anti-world of Russian culture), edited by Nikolai Bogomolov (1996)—concentrate on ancient erotic folklore. As Toporkov (1995, 9) points out, while the main avenue of interpretation of erotic folklore in current Russian scholarship is "establishing traces of agrarian magic or attempting hypothetical reconstruction of institutions of primordial society," these studies shy away from any sociological and psychological analysis of the functions of erotic folklore today. My work is intended to fill this gap.

Sexual jokes abound in many societies. In most cultures, sexuality represents an important feature of human life as well as one of its most volatile and emotionally charged aspects. Since "the subject of sex and sex roles is a great reservoir of fears, resentments, defenses, projections of the repressed, displacement of emotions, myth, pure fabrication, and arrant nonsense" (Murphy 1989, 65) and straightforward discourse is often inhibited by almost universally imposed societal taboos, humor serves as a natural vehicle of expression of the whole array of human emotions related to these topics. As Michael Mulkay (1988, 9) shows, the sex-related joke, while frequently told to amuse and entertain, not only benefits by bypassing the taboos but often exists solely because such taboos exist.

Western readers may recognize some of the jokes analyzed in this book as variants of jokes they have perceived as belonging to their own culture, past or present. (This proves that popular laughter is able to cross both spatial and temporal borders.) Since many Russian sexual jokes are similar to those of other peoples, it may seem that analysis of their "Russianness" presents a special problem of cultural identification.

Indeed, it would seem difficult to tag some of the jokes as being truly Russian. American society of the early 1970s was undergoing "sweeping changes in public attitude toward things erotic in almost every facet of daily life, from serious reading matter, to movie fare, to television commercials or magazine advertisements" (Hoffmann 1973, 9). Russian society is experiencing similar changes today.

In Russia, as in most Western societies, ribaldry is "accepted as a part of social contact and communication on every level," and sexual jokes are also perpetuated "in almost ritual manner" (Hoffmann 1973, 9). Even a brief look at the types of erotic folk tales (160–83) and the motif index of erotic folk literature (184–288) is enough to show that Russian Eros follows world patterns. A popular Russian series of jokes about "little Vova" is akin to Western jokes based on the mock sexual ignorance of children recorded and analyzed by Legman (1968, 65–72).[2]

However, the origin of a joke is much less important than its social/cultural/symbolic/communicative and context-summarizing functions as well as its emotional/psychological ones. These jokes are pulled from a vast reservoir of available material, not completely at random, but recurrently in direct correspondence to the emotional, often unconscious, needs of the teller and his intended audience. Therefore, for the purpose of this study, it is important to establish not so much the origins as the kinds of jokes that circulate most frequently.

Thus the effort to acquaint Western readers with samples of Russian humor makes this study comparative. Whenever possible, I cite similar American jokes. From this standpoint, the absence of Russian jokes on certain subjects found in American humor is sometimes telling. And when the jokes are similar, they operate in different cultural contexts, with different connotations. Accordingly, I have attempted to interpret the Russians' erotic folklore in terms of their everyday life, customs, and popular beliefs.

Although many folklore genres, like many works of high literature and art, provide entertainment, jokelore (especially sexual) seems to possess this capacity in the highest degree; it is often assumed that a joke is told for its own sake. There exists, however, a scholarly tradition of serious interpretations of seemingly nonserious material, Sigmund Freud's classic *Jokes and Their Relation to the Unconscious* (1960; originally published in German in 1905) chief among them. Russian folklore itself often looks beyond its text for deeper meanings and implications. Russian proverbs and sayings have long been considered "age-old people's wisdom" *(vekovaia narodnaia mudrost'),* and many fairy tales end in this way: "A fairy tale's a lie, but it has a clue in it and a lesson for all good fellows" *(skazka—lozh', da v nei namek, dobrym molodtsam urok).*

As for the modern Russian joke, which in part derives from the "everyday tale" *(bytovaia skazka),* Russians often point out that it is not just, as the saying goes, "There's some truth in every joke" *(V kazhdoi shutke dolia pravdy)* but "Only part of a joke is a joke" *(V kazhdoi shutke dolia shutki).* This saying captures the fact that it is conventionally often overlooked that humor, in fact, has no substance on its own; most of the time it is only a *mode* of expression, a shell charged with a serious substance (often objectionable, especially when it comes to sexual matters).

Thus I pay attention not to the comic techniques (unless they contribute to the content analysis) but to what jokelore's cleverness and wit try to render as merely amusing and entertaining.

Freud finds a similarity between jokes and dreams in their defiance of logic and reality. Since this book is about Russian humor, another similarity comes to mind, that between alcohol and humor. Russian scholar Zara Abdulaeva (1996, 211–212) makes much of the connection between Russians' love for the bottle and their country's turbulent history. Humor, like alcohol, has helped the Russians to cope with the unbearable reality of their country's cruel history. It is not by chance that in the Soviet years waves of jokes washed every man's shore with the constancy of daily tides. Both alcohol and humor help to blur a sense of reality and give the speaker a temporary license to suspend the conventions and proprieties of ordinary speech. Without much exaggeration, a Russian expression "What's on a sober man's mind is what's on a drunkard's tongue" *(chto u trezvogo na ume, to u p'ianogo na izyke)* may be paraphrased as: "What's on a serious man's mind is what's on a humorous man's tongue."

Humor's licensing of speech about the unspeakable often is used in the most exploitative genre of public communications—advertisements. Not only are sexual messages camouflaged but non-sexual ones are as well. For example, in the journal *Popular Photography* (October 1997, 35), aiming evidently at a younger buying public, the Nikon company has placed an ad for their "Advanced Simple" camera N50 model. Here is the ad in its entirety under the caption: "You Point it, You Shoot It":

When we say the N50 is easy to use, we don't mean "easy for people who've won Pulitzers for Photography." We mean seriously *simple* as in, hand it to an average dad and say "push here." In Simple Mode, you can literally point the N50, shoot it, and capture frame worthy, SLR-quality images like this. The camera is positively fool proof. Or more to the point, dad proof.

It is clear that the company is using humor to avoid a counterproductive, thus unspeakable, message. If the company could talk to every prospective buyer in private, the message of this ad would most likely sound something like: "Even an idiot can take good pictures with this camera." To make the same message publicly acceptable, humor and skill with words come into play. Thanks to this advertisement, the impossible in a serious mode became possible in a humorous one. It is set up by a reference to the mundane taking of a snapshot ("hand it to an average dad and say 'push here'") and reinforced with a parallel construction: ". . . fool proof. Or more to the point, dad proof." Thus the ad triggers a stereotypical image of an "average dad" as an aging man who is either "losing it" or just falling behind the times, overwhelmed by modern technology that is too sophisticated for him to handle.

Advertising copy provides insight into a people's psyche, but folk humor sometimes is the only source of inquiry. Although it relies on established stereotypes and misses all the oscillations, nuances, and subtleties of an ongoing social process, humor, due to its ability to handle the most emotionally charged and sensitive areas of human existence, gives voice, if only opaquely, to the usually unspoken aspects of a culture.

However, in using such an approach, caution has to be exercised. A treatment of folk material at its face value may be misleading because folklore in general can be as contradictory as life itself. For instance, readers of Vladimir Dahl's (1879) nineteenth-century collection of Russian proverbs and sayings may find in it pronouncements that show diametrically opposed attitudes toward various human values. Thus one proverb may praise love ("There is no value higher than love") and another one may condemn it ("Where there is one's love, there is one's woe"). One proverb shows disdain for a bachelor's life ("A bachelor is like a mad man. A bachelor is half of a human being"). Others find a married life not much better ("A bachelor may as well drown himself. A married man may as well hang himself").

What is a constant in my study is the context of the jokes and their point of view, almost all, throughout this text, a male one. As a rule, these jokes are exchanged in male company—in groups and man to man—in smoking areas, army barracks, factory shops, offices, while riding in train compartments or cabs, during drinking parties (there are no other kinds in Russia), and the like. The tellers are Russian men of all walks of life—soldiers, students, taxi drivers, businessmen, petty and high officials, journalists, scholars, street sweepers, and so on.

Therefore, this work is a study of Russian masculinity as it expresses itself through humorous venues. While there is a growing literature on masculinity in gender studies (e.g., one about Andalusian culture: Brandes 1980), there has been very little research done on Russian masculinity. This study of the dominant masculinity structure and of the gender relations and gender structures shaped by it attempts to fill the void, at least in part. The humorous database of this study, seemingly casual, recreational, and entertaining by nature, should not be dismissed as insignificant; moreover, thanks to its inconspicuous nature, such a mode of men's self-discourse is highly effective in reproducing male behavioral patterns and reaffirming prevailing attitudes. The power of laughter as a corrective and instructive force is well known.

While the male-dominant point of view is expressed in many sex jokes, I do not agree with George Fine's view (1981, 11) that most of these jokes are "the product of male chauvinism." In his *On Humor,* Michael Mulkay (1988, 137) also argues that that "dirty jokes depict the relationship between men and women in terms of a radical form of sexual, social and linguistic domination of women by men." These statements make it look as if male dominance is unshakable and not threatened, void of any dynamics. Although most male jokes are undoubtedly misogynist, the picture is more complicated. While most humor in this study is male-centric and indicative of the male dominance in Russian culture, this humor not only asserts such dominance but also deals with dominance anxiety as well as other issues of gender hierarchy in a distinctly masculine culture.

Although sex jokes make "most clearly visible . . . men's most basic, serious assumptions regarding women and sexuality" (Mulkay 1988, 142), too literal a reading is misleading; humor by its very nature needs to exaggerate and simplify "elements that are already pronounced within serious discourse" making "in the domain of humor men's control over and sexual domination of women . . . exceptionally stark and unrestricted" (Mulkay 1988, 141). The true distribution of power in a given social grouping or unit, such as a family, may prove to be much more complex, as it is examined in chapter 6 devoted to marriage jokes.

A study of sex humor also may give some sexological insights, shedding some light on the most intimate aspects of gender relationships. However, by no means do I see jokes as a substitute for a scientific study of a nation's sexuality—the kind of project undertaken by Dr. Alfred Kinsey in the

United States. Sex jokes reflect sexual reality only to a degree; they constitute a *discourse* on the topic of gender relations and sex. While some jokes provide a truthful commentary, others seemingly contradict life, often fulfilling a wish or a fantasy. Therefore, it would be a mistake to depend on sex humor alone to understand Russian sexual practices. Humor is a specific discourse, often shaped around anxieties and insecurities, and therefore it cannot be relied on without reservations. To support my observations, whenever possible, I draw on sociological surveys, psychological and psychoanalytical studies, literature, and other evidence as well as on interviews with informants of both genders. I also make use of my personal observations of life in Russia, the country in which I spent most of my life.

The reader should bear in mind that, because humor is by nature aggressive, it often addresses the negative, troublesome aspects of a relationship. After all, the misogynist attitude, as expressed in jokes, has not deterred men all over the world from falling in love time and again. And despite the proliferation of antimarriage jokelore, most people continue to value the institution of marriage in deed, if not in word.

And tellers of dirty jokes need not subscribe fully to the opinions expressed. While some men may tell jokes that quite accurately reflect their views, some do not. Joke telling may serve as a mythmaking process and as a case of self-construction, as are other conversations reported by Nancy Ries (1997, 77). Men may tell jokes in order to come across as virile to themselves and to other men.

While male jokes are indicative of prevailing attitudes toward women, it would be wrong to assume that a man telling these jokes fully subscribes to the stereotypes he plays with. Thus Kevin Pollack, an American stand-up comedian, concedes that when he uses antiwomen jokes in his routines, "as a guy, [his] right brain laughs. But [his] left brain is horrified."[3]

In fact, men may use customary male jokes to cover up their deviance from the pressure group. Laughter may constitute conformity, a sign that the teller and his listener(s) stand on the same ground. It is not by chance that the Russians call joke-telling sessions, which spring up during parties and other informal gatherings, *travit' anekdoty,* which, in this context, has two meanings borrowed from slang: "to let the jokes out [one by one]" and "to lie" [to make them up].

Jokes can be highly ambivalent. As American scholar Elliott Oring (1993, 31) argues, "like a proverb, a joke has specific performance meanings that are only discernible in situations of performance in relation to particular tellers, audiences, settings, and interactions." These meanings, though they may be "innumerable," are restricted, because otherwise "any joke would be appropriate for any situation, and this is certainly not the case." In psycho-analytical terms, psychologists Renatus Hartogs and Hans Fantel (1967, 170) also find that jokes have "multiple goals: seduction, aggression, or release from sexual anxiety, depending on the story and the teller."

What seems to be the unifying property of all plausible "performance meanings" is their reliance on the instantaneously recognizable stereotypical images or attitudes the joke triggers. Because humor works by playing with the most deeply seated, well-established stereotypes in a group conscious-ness, it lends itself to studies of mass stereotypes in a given cultural context and historical moment.[4]

In his example of a joke about a businessman's decision to hire a secretary based not on her honesty but on her sexual appeal, Oring offers four "plau-sible performance meanings" (1992, 29–30): treatment of women as sexual objects, an attempt at sexual arousal, ridiculing men "who allow sexual im-pulses to overpower critical reason and judgment," and celebration of "male sexuality . . . in all circumstances . . . no matter how unsuitable" (31). These meanings do not really contradict one another, rather, they all correspond to the recognizable stereotype: Men see women as sexual beings first and fore-most. What's more, one can imagine that all of Oring's four possible mean-ings are offered to a woman listener, to test her response and make her choose. She may be insulted by the joke's treatment of women as sex objects or aroused by its sexually explicit content; she may agree with the ridicule of male's self-destructive sexual drive or enjoy being the all-important object of men's desire. Folklorist Carol Mitchell's (1977, 329) study proves that joke appreciation gender-wise not only could be uneven but may depend on dif-ferent elements of the joke.

The reader may find in these pages a number of jokes that seemingly at-tack not women's shortcomings but men's: womanizing, the double stan-dard, a tendency to shirk domestic chores, and so on. These may seem to be women's jokes about men, but that is seldom the case. Russian female jokelore has a very limited coinage and circulation, and stand-up comedi-ennes, as we know them in America, are yet to appear in Russian nightclubs or on TV. Feminism has not made much headway in Russian society.[5]

The existence of jokes ridiculing males, although they may reflect ac-knowledgment of their own faults, can be understood as part of the usual dynamics of satire. For instance, an ethnic joke that may sound self-effacing often is meant not as an attack on the teller's own ethnicity but on a subset of it from which he wants to distance himself.[6]

In the same vein, a man telling a joke that ridicules male behavior also may make a sincere attempt to distance himself (and his fellow listeners whose agreement is often taken for granted) from "that kind of man." The joke teller may refuse to see himself as the target and assume that the joke is about someone else. As Russians say, "This is not about me but about my next-door neighbor" *(Eto ne pro menia, a pro moego soseda).*

A clash of traditional and changing cultural pressures may account for the male jokes ridiculing men. On one hand, Russian everyday culture shows all the signs of preserving the traditional male dominance over women. On the other hand, many educated Russians feel the need to Westernize this attitude and to recognize women's equality. These opposing cultural tendencies produce a conflict which is reflected in the jokes ridiculing males.

If the reader allows for the exaggerations, ambiguities and contradictions of the genre, he or she will find these jokes quite telling with respect to Russian sexual behavior and gender relations. As Kon (1995, 271) notes, "Russia's current sexual attitudes and practices are . . . highly diversified according to age; gender; education; regional, ethnic, and social background; generational cohort, and religious affiliation." In this respect, sexual jokelore is an equalizer. It appeals to a common denominator in all these diverse attitudes, shows what opinions and attitudes are shared by many groups that are otherwise heterogeneous in their makeup. By its very nature, a joke cannot be told to a listener who does not understand and appreciate the teller's position. In this respect, jokelore is indispensable as an instrument of analysis and elucidation of the national stereotypes of attitudes and behavior, for discovering the anxieties expressed behind what Legman calls "the bravado of laughter."

Using the methodology of content analysis, I examine Russian jokes of the Soviet and post-Soviet periods as well as other relevant material such as proverbs, sayings, catch phrases, chastushkas, folk parodies, and toasts, all of them, as a rule, of oral nature. They have been recorded in my private collection and in several of the Russian joke books I have consulted. While versions of some of the jokes analyzed in this work may be found in some English-language compilations, almost all my entries appear in English for the first time and are my translations. (I find a number of these jokes offensive to women and to my own taste, but I have included them on the grounds that a researcher cannot be a censor.)

Among the most comprehensive sources of sexual jokelore are O. Ivanova's *Anekdoty i tosty* (Jokes and toasts) (1994 and 1996 editions), Iosif Raskin's *Entsiklopediia khuliganstvuiushchego ortodoksa* (Encyclopedia of a rowdy Orthodox man; 1995), L. A. Barsky's *Eto prosto smeshno ili zerkalo krivogo korolevstva* (This is just funny, or the mirror of the crooked kingdom; 1994), Yury Nikulin's *Anekdoty ot Nikulina* (Jokes from Nikulin; 1997), and Victor Kulikov's *Anekdoty pro novykh russkikh i drugikh zhitelei zemli* (Jokes about the New Russians and other inhabitants of the Earth). Recently I also have made use of Internet postings of "Jokes from Russia" (//www.anekdot.ru//); I denoted these jokes in the text with the abbreviation (JFR) and the date of an entry's posting. Wherever possible, I have provided bibliographical data about versions of the jokes analyzed. (Often, to convey the flavor of a saying, a rhyme, a slang expression to readers who know Russian, I have provided the transliteration.)

Chapter 1 addresses the historical origins of the phenomenon of Russian sexual humor. It also discusses the idiosyncratic nature of Russian sex appeal, which is still deeply connected to the agrarian roots of Russian everyday culture, as it is expressed in painting and folklore—numerous folk rhymes (chastushkas), proverbs, sayings, nicknames, and slang expressions.

Chapters 2 and 3 explore the key issue of male/female relationships—the ways in which gender roles are defined in the folk consciousness as they are enacted in oral humor. Contemporary jokelore affords ample evidence of the pervasiveness of the traditional view of gender roles in Russia and the tension it creates and sustains. Showing how sexist vocabulary, denigrating nicknames, and obscenities function to maintain male control, I analyze representative samples of jokes that treat women solely as objects of male desire as well as those that at the same time portray them as fools or as wanton. In contrast to such disparagement, numerous jokes approvingly portray the male as sexual predator and favorably contrast male camaraderie with female lack of gender solidarity. I address such male attitudes as they derive from cultural customs and the effects of upbringing in a country with a volatile historical background.

Chapter 4 is devoted to jokelore dealing with the most intimate part of the male/female relationship—courtship and lovemaking. I discuss these jokes in terms of recent studies of Russian sexuality and show the semiotic significance of certain sexual practices of Russian men as they are reflected in jokelore.

Chapter 5 analyzes various humorous folkloric material related to violence toward women. As wife-beating has been a frequent feature of everyday life, through analysis of the dynamics of the peasant family I attempt to give a new reading of the seemingly bizarre proverbs collected by Vladimir Dahl that treat the attacker's violence as an expression of his love (e. g., "I beat the one I love," *kogo liubliu, togo i b'iu*). I also address contemporary male jokelore related to rape and the myth that women always welcome it that these jokes help to perpetuate.

Chapter 6 explores contemporary Russian attitudes toward various aspects of married life as they are reflected in the jokelore and analyzes psychological and sociological reasons for the savagery of jokes about mothers-in-law, contrasting it with the milder treatment of them in other cultures.

Chapter 7 treats the ways in which contemporary Russian jokes help Russian men deal with the most painful issues for the male ego—impotence and women's infidelity. Since the excessive consumption of alcohol plays a large part in these problems, I include jokes about drunken males.

While ribald chastushkas are discussed throughout in various contexts, chapter 8 considers the genre separately, relating it to agrarian pagan fertility rites and asking why women often sing these bawdy misogynist songs. As a way of understanding the function of this festive genre in rural areas, I examine the role of these performances in creating a sexually suggestive atmosphere sought after by both males and females. Finally, I examine the chastushka texts as verbal pranks, part of the entertainment of rural Russians.

Any folkloric material, especially of such a delicate nature, should be discussed not only with reference to text and texture (rhyming patterns, rhythm, alliterations, various tropes, etc.) but in terms of its context. Who is performing?[7] Is the audience male or female or both? What is the age range of the audience? What is the occasion of the gathering, the mood? As folklorist Alan Dundes (1980, 24) points out, a context can not only interpret the text but explain its very raison d'être. However, researchers have yet to collect contextual information; without it, a chastushka's text may be misinterpreted. Therefore, my inquiry in this area must be considered a preliminary one.

CHAPTER 1

"The More of the Beloved's Body the Better": Jokelore of Russian Sex Appeal

The proliferation of sexual jokes in Russia has been a marked feature of daily discourse because sexuality has been a forbidden topic for long periods of modern history. Even before open discussion of sexual matters was considered politically undesirable under the Soviet regime in the 1930s, Russia was primarily a Victorian country in terms of sexual mores (Kon 1993, 19–20). For a long time, Russian literature and art avoided venturing into the realm of sex. Although much of nineteenth-century literature focuses on love and passion (in works of Pushkin, Lermontov, Turgenev, and many other Russian writers), it never actually developed an erotic literary tradition.[1] Sex was totally avoided or trivialized and deeroticized in Barkovian verses (named after Ivan Barkov, an eighteenth-century Russian poet), or treated in its medieval ecclesiastic interpretation—as an evil to be condemned and confronted. (Tolstoy's late-period *Kreutzer Sonata* and *Father Sergius* are especially indicative of this attitude.) The first growths of refined erotic culture, cultivated by artists, poets, and prose writers around the turn of the twentieth century, were eventually destroyed by the sweeping social changes of the Russian revolution of 1917.

Sexuality as "a culturally constructed phenomenon" (Highwater 1990, 11) is temporal, and its history often corresponds to the history of political doctrines. The history of ideology in the Soviet Union paralleled fairly closely the history of Communist sexual politics. As a rule, the most forceful political suppression was accompanied by the imposition of strict control in the sexual sphere as well. After brief experimentation with the idea of "free love" in the 1920s, the Soviet authorities expurgated (for ideological reasons) any manifestation of sexuality. The strictly individual, private value of sexuality, in the party view, contradicted and endangered the collective cause to which people should devote their lives.

As the body serves as "a metaphor of society" (Highwater 1990, 11), bodily purity can symbolize the purity of ideology. Anthropologist Mary Douglas notes: "Societies, like other bounded groups, are vulnerable at their intersection with other groups. Thus much attention is paid in many societies to the orifices of the human body, for here matter passes from outside to inside, and vice versa. Societies which deem it important to maintain their separateness will also guard their [cultural boundaries or margins] against intrusion and pollution . . . and this may be symbolized through taboos on food and sex" (quoted in Highwater 1990, 11–12).

In the 1920s, when foreign specialists were invited to help build the new Socialist industry, attitudes toward sex had been fairly liberal. When Joseph Stalin consolidated his power in the late 1920s, borders were sealed and strict rules were imposed regarding sexual behavior.[2] At this particular juncture of Russian history, when the "iron curtain" was lowered to isolate the country from Western influence, foreigners in Russia discovered that the nation's body wore a symbolic iron "chastity belt."[3] It was then that marriages with foreigners were strongly discouraged, if not altogether forbidden.

The late 1940s, marked by the further tightening of ideological controls, saw a new reinforcement of so-called Socialist morality which remained virtually unchanged until the introduction of Mikhail Gorbachev's glasnost and perestroika policies in the late 1980s.

Of course, the ideological pressure greatly damaged people's personal lives, but it failed to completely subjugate them, to strictly fit the party line(s). During most of Soviet time, sexual love was "a refuge for Soviet people from the harshness of life" (Shlapentokh 1989, 177). Premarital and extramarital love and sexual activity have never ceased to exist despite the great chances taken by lovers. Sexual jokes, therefore, with their aggressive, intentionally iconoclastic, often primitive and crudely biological nature, represented a defiance of the officially proclaimed "happy Soviet family." In the post-Stalin period love, sex, and lovers increasingly grew into "private institutions."

The collapse of totalitarianism brought a drastic turnaround in the sphere of open sexual expression. The works of Henry Miller, D. H. Lawrence, and other Western authors that discussed sex became available to Russian readers for the first time. With this revival, all the negative aspects of this new freedom became the subject of heated public debates. In a few years an officially asexual country became a country flooded with sexually oriented material available literally on every corner. These developments notwithstanding, Russian gender-related folklore has hardly changed; recent samples of sexual jokes collected in Russia express the same emotions and attitudes, still deeply ingrained in the folk mind.

Sources of Russian Bawdy Jokelore

The Russians' bawdy jokes show a substantial connection with the international body of Indo-European folklore. Some motifs, themes, and uses of language are similar to those appearing in subliterary forms in contemporary Western collections. The evidence drawn from the enormous body of ever-present and popular jokes [anekdoty] challenges those Russian nationalists who insist that their sexual traditions differ from those in the West—that they are purer, cleaner. Most Russian sex jokes are not cleaner (and not much dirtier) than their Western counterparts. But some issues touched upon by this folkloric genre not only assert their importance—in their frequency—but are quite different; they are intrinsic to Russian conditions with deep roots in national history and culture.

The resemblance of Russian sexual jokelore to that circulating elsewhere is the result of direct borrowing and the fact that much sexual humor has common sources traceable to time immemorial. Sexual tales of ancient Eastern origin were carried by the Arabs to Spain and then to Italy, spreading throughout the whole of Western Europe; the same tales penetrated Russian folk culture via Byzantium, through Greek religious literature. The *Lives* (*Zhitii*) of the saints sometimes contained racy descriptions of the future saint's sinful life prior to his conversion. (What is less known, and perhaps worth exploring, is the contribution of Tartar and Mongolian tales to the Russian repertoire of sexual folklore. Taking into consideration a rather long stretch of Russian history when both peoples were closely interconnected and cohabitation, often forceful, sometimes voluntary, between Tartar men and Russian women was common [Popovsky 1985, 434], such an influence is quite possible.)

In the second part of the seventeenth century, with the beginning of the orientation of Russian statesmen toward Europe, European jokelore entered Russian culture via translations from the Polish; in this period Poland's own jocular literature was also translated into Russian (Dolgopolova 1983, 12). Thus the collection of tales of everyday life, *Fatsetsii* (Facetiae), widely known to educated Russians of the time, contained a number of sexually colored stories that were, in turn, a product of Western literature of the same sort. The most notable was the Italian collection of tales by Poggo Braccolini. Probably the seventeenth-century Russian courtiers observed by the European diplomat Adam Olearius (Kon 1995, 11) were telling stories from this risqué miscellany.

However, the Russians have their own rich tradition of erotic humor. Erotic material was part of several pagan fertility rites, such as harvest celebrations, weddings, and the rites of spring [maslenitsa]. The Russian ribald folk tales and erotic proverbs and sayings collected by Alexander Afanasiev and Vladimir Dahl in the nineteenth century also can be traced back to pagan times and had long been part of Russian everyday discourse. (These collections could not appear in Russia, only abroad—evidence of the state of public mores.) Many popular rhymes and ditties of Russian medieval street entertainers [skomorokhi] contained salacious humor. Throughout the nineteenth century there circulated a Russian folk artifact known as lubok—cheap prints made from linden bark, many of them licentious (Farrel 1991).

Developed around the 1870s (Keldysh 1991, 621), short rural popular rhymes (chastushkas)—which later, with the influx of peasants to the burgeoning industrial centers, also became part of nascent urban folklore—often have been concerned with sexual matters as well. Displaced from their traditional way of life, Russian peasants became factory workers; they used this rhyming medium to deal with unfamiliar and often uncomfortable social reality. Jokes, however, are a genre of urban folklore, beginning in the late seventeenth century (Dolgopolova 1983, 10).

Two Cultural Standards Clash

Of course, jokes that address phenomena peculiar to Russians are among those for which it is hard to find Western counterparts. Among them are those concerned with Russian sex appeal. While Russian standards of beauty are one-sided and chauvinistic—a Russian saying collected by Dahl (1879, I: 455) postulates: "If a man looks a bit better than the Devil, he's a handsome fellow"—there is one aspect of Russian sex appeal in which both sexes are about equal—the shape of their bodies. Westerners traveling through Russia notice that both Russian men and women are often rather overweight. One explanation lies in their diet, which lacks those foods that help Westerners keep themselves in shape—fresh vegetables year-round, lean meats and poultry, and so on. These foods appeared on the average Russian's table only sporadically through most of the Soviet regime. These and other factors contributed to unhealthy Russian diets, rich in starches and carbohydrates.[4]

However, one glance at the portraits of the Soviet leaders (Khrushchev, Brezhnev, Gorbachev, Yeltsin) should convince us that portliness results not only from the lack of fresh vegetables (at least these leaders could have access to them) but from something else.

One of my Moscow informants, a female artist in her early 40s, expressed her conviction that a man is more attractive when he is corpulent. For her, a man should be "solid, have a sizable body" [*solidnyi, v tele,* cf. Ukrainian for a fat person—"a smooth one," *gladkii*]. The Russian word for "a fat man" literally means "a complete man" [*polnyi*] and that for "a bad man" means also "skinny" [*khudoi*]. The word "healthy" [*zdorovyi*] in Russian has a colloquial meaning "big," as in: "Look how healthy [read: big] your boy has grown!" [*smotri, kakoi zdorovyi tvoi mal'chik stal!*]. In his article "It's Not Hunger That Kills You. It's Food," Russian doctor, V. D. Silantiev, notes that part of the problem of overeating in today's Russia is following eating habits deeply imbedded in Russian consciousness of which "our beloved sayings, such as 'our mouth is rejoicing when having a big bite' [*bol'shomu kusku rot raduetsia*], 'there should be a lot of a good person' [*khoroshego cheloveka dolzhno byt' mnogo*] are emblematic" (1997, 21).

Such attitudes may be accounted for by the deep-seated conviction of a culture that, because of the tardiness of the industrial revolution, is still predominantly rural in its world outlook. As "no society entirely escapes its past" and "there are always elements that persist from prior conditions" (Barret 1984, 114), while Russia has made great strides in the direction of industrialization and urbanization throughout this century, in their habits and customs, the Russians are still in the process of cultural acclimatization.

The enormous cultural chasm between the intelligentsia with its European-level education and the mostly illiterate peasant masses (80 percent of total population; cited in Aileen Kelly 1999, 7) that existed before revolution of 1917 was closed only on the surface. A great many Russians from humble stations in life advanced to positions of power and control willfully and forcefully. According to Kon (1997), "as a result of the industrialization and collectivization of the country, as well as political repressions, in the beginning of the 1930s the social make-up of the leading cadres of the party and the state changed. More often than not, yesterday's peasants took the place of intelligentsia and blue-collar workers by birth, a 'villagization of the cities' [*oderevenshchivanie gorodov*] occurred" (162).

Although with lesser vigor, this practice continued in the post-Stalin era as well. In Russia, having a college degree (especially in a technical field) and keeping a high position in society do not necessarily indicate civility and cultural awareness that the higher education seems to signify. Alexander Solzhenitsyn (1975, 242) only touches upon this phenomenon, talking primarily about this kind of people's ideological complacency about the Soviet regime: "Although the polish we have acquired is rather third-rate, it will be entirely in the spirit of the Russian language and will probably convey the right sense if we refer to this 'polished' and 'schooled' stratum, all those who nowadays falsely and rashly style themselves as 'intelligentsia,' as the *obrazovanshchina*—the semi-educated estate—the 'smatterers.'"

As often happens with many issues that are publicly by and large unacknowledged, this cultural tension between refined Russian intelligentsia and unpolished, hastily promoted villagers in commanding positions is expressed in jokes:

> (1.1)   A radio broadcast. The year is 1966.
>
> Radio announcer (joyfully): "Good morning, comrades. We begin our concert on listeners' requests. A boy called Vanya from the village of Godforsaken asks us to play for him his favorite song 'Felt Boots' *[valenki]*. You're welcome, Vanya. Listen to your favorite song 'Felt Boots.'"
>
> 1976. Radio announcer (joyfully): "Good morning, comrades. We begin our concert composed of listeners' requests. A student of an agricultural trade school of the town of Remoteville, Vanya Petrov, writes to us asking to play for him his favorite song 'Felt Boots'. You're welcome, Vanya. Here is your favorite song 'Felt Boots.'"
>
> 1986. Radio announcer (joyfully): "Good morning, comrades. We begin our concert composed of listeners' requests. The Director of the Patrice Lumumba kolkhoz of the Godforsaken village Ivan Petrov asks us to play for him his favorite song 'Felt Boots'. You're welcome, Ivan. Here is your favorite song 'Felt Boots.'"
>
> 1996. Radio announcer (joyfully): "Good morning, ladies and gentlemen. We begin our concert composed of listeners' requests. A State Duma Deputy, Academician of the Russian Agricultural Academy, Ivan Sidorovich Petrov asks us to play for him a piece by Johann Sebastian Bach, 'Toccata and Fugue E-minor.' (Even more joyfully). Dear Ivan Sidorovich, please DON'T SHOW OFF[5] and listen to your favorite song 'Felt Boots.'" (JFR 2/14/98)

In jokes of this kind, the artistic need to underscore the difference between the two disparate cultural standards coexisting in the Russian cities makes it necessary to use shocking words or urgent situations. Thus a museum is a place of worship of beauty for one Russian and for another, due to the notorious shortage of public toilets in the cities,[6] just a place where a rest room could be found. The vulgar synonym for the imperative form of the verb "urinate"—"piss" [*ssy* or *stsy*] used by one of the characters in the following joke betrays his low-class (peasant) background:

(1.2) On a St. Petersburg street, one man asks another:
       "Can you tell me how to get to the Hermitage?"
       "What do you need it for? Piss right here." (Private collection)

The clash of two cultures often is expressed as a linguistic contrast between crude street vernacular and educated Russian. A subtitle of a recent collection of jokes *Dinner Is Served. Pig Out Please [Kushat' podano. Sadites' zhrat', pozhaluista]* (Sonin 1995) is one example of this kind of humor.

(1.3) One man complains to anther:
       "The cultural level in our city has drastically plummeted."
       "Yeah? How did you figure that out?"
       "Well, recently I came out of the joint—not that late, around 1 a.m.—
       and some kind of swine stepped on my ear." (Private collection)

Much humor in the modern-day Venedikt Erofeev's classic "Moscow Stations" (Moskva-Petushki) derives from this tension between the high and the low, or, to be exact, from degradation of the high by associating it with the low. Often such dissimilar cultural standards are combined in one person. Venichka, the narrator of "Moscow Stations," demonstrates a formidable knowledge of Russian and world culture—he is equally versed in modern and ancient history and literature; quotes by heart many biblical passages; shows an admirable acquaintance with sophisticated musical terminology—and at the same time lacks a sense of elementary hygiene, undoubtedly a remnant of old peasant lifestyle.[7]

Peasant folklore and folk life still show their strong presence in Russian everyday life. Superstitions, fortune-telling (not strictly commercial, as in the West), love potions, folk remedies, and many other popular forms of pagan culture are widespread among college-educated Russian city dwellers of today. This lingering peasant mentality and system of values manifests itself in the great proliferation of village folklore in everyday speech. Numerous proverbs and sayings of peasant origin expressing peasant values, points of reference, and outlook still permeate Russian speech. Not only are these idioms saturated with images from rural life, they often make judgments from the peasants' points of reference.[8] Urban Russians still often address the sun and rain, the two most important natural phenomena in peasant life, with endearing diminutive suffixes—"the little sun" *[solnyshko]*, "the little rain" *[dozhdichek]*. To underscore a person's physical strength, a Russian often says: "You can hitch him [her] to a plow" *[na nem (nei) pakhat' mozhno]*.

While American folklore, as folklore in general, also shows traces of its rural roots, the Russian is firmly anchored in it. It often features not only the hut [*izba;* as in the expression "to sweep out the dirt out of one's own hut" (to expose family dirty secrets) *vynosit' sor iz izby*] but many elements of flora and fauna, closely familiar to a peasant of which modern Russian city dwellers have no immediate knowledge. For example, everyday expressions contain images of a black grouse ["as deaf as a black grouse," *glukh kak teteria;* Krylov 1973, 36], a woodgrouse [as in: "he's like wood grouse at its place of mating," *kak glukhar' na toku,* meaning "When his mouth is open his ears are shut"; Krylov 1973, 36], a snipe [*kulik;* as in "Every snipe praises his own swamp," *vsiak kulik svoe boloto khvalit,* equivalent to the American "Every cook praises his own broth"; Krylov 1973, 12], or a poisonous grass *belena,* as in a question asked about someone suddenly enraged: "What's it with you? Have you eaten 'belena' or what?" [*Ty chto, beleny ob"elsia?"*].

Many Russian sayings not only metaphorically involve the peasant's helper ["An old horse won't spoil the furrows," *Staryi kon' borozdy ne portit;* meaning "old hands are most reliable"; "A horse has four legs, and even he stumbles" meaning "nobody's perfect"; *kon' na chetyrekh nogakh, da i to spotykaetsia,* Krylov 1973, 90], but they feature many details of harnessing equipment about which many of today's urbanites have only a vague idea. Often-cited proverbs and sayings involve a horse-collar, reins, a shaft-bow, a pole, blinders, and the like.[9]

Food and Sex Appeal

Perhaps the most convincing evidence of the closeness of Russian everyday culture to peasant culture can be seen in Russian eating habits. Peasant food, porridge *[kasha],* and *kvas* [a fermented drink brewed from bread crusts] are still popular among city residents, and many old Russian proverbs and sayings still currently in wide use reflect the villagers' old ways of life. Not only does bread still occupy a central place in the Russian diet, but it has managed to preserve its traditional symbolism of emotional life. A Russian would say about loneliness: "There is no one to break bread with" *[ne s kem khleb perelomit'];* about one's own state of depression: "a piece of bread gets stuck in my throat" *[kusok khleba v gorle zastrevaet].* To indicate that someone is really involved in something, bread is used as the yardstick. A woman may say about her teenage son: "The Internet is his bread" *[ego khlebom ne kormi, dai poigrat' s internetom].* To say that someone has a one-track mind, a Russian may say: "All that hungry godmother is preoccupied with is bread" *[golodnoi kume khleb na ume].*

In peasant Russia, a meal, often as much as he could eat, was the only pay that a hired hand *[batrak]* would get for his labor. Thus the quantity of food consumed was the measure of these people's well-being, a notion expressed in such sayings as "A big bite [of food] makes one's mouth happy" *[Bol'shomu kusku rot raduetsia]* or "Eat till you get sweaty, work till you get chilly" *[esh' poka ne vspoteesh'—rabotai poka ne oziabnesh']* A verb denoting living too luxuriously—*zazhrat'sia*—means literally "to overfeed oneself."[10]

The presence of fat, usually in the form of butter or cheese, in a peasant's food used to carry a socioeconomic significance. If a peasant could add butter to his kasha, it meant his household had a cow, and that often spelled prosperity for poverty-ridden serfs. (Traces of this rural mentality are seen in the name of the Western carnival Mardi Gras—Fat Tuesday with its license of indulgence in bodily pleasures, including eating; fat and oils traditionally were assumed to be the food of the rich.) Etymologist Max Vasmer (1986, II: 56) suggests that the Russian word "fat" *[zhir]* probably has its roots in the old Russian word meaning "food" and, thus, is connected to the old Russian word "to live" *[zhiti]*. A number of Russian sayings and proverbs reflect this peasant attitude toward food: "You can't spoil kasha with too much butter" *[Maslom kashu ne isportish']* meaning "You can't have enough of a good thing." A man with an extravagance of fat in his food was an object of envy. The verb that literally means "to lead fat life" *[zhirovat']* means "to live luxuriously, to carouse, to go on the buying spree" (Vasmer II: 56; cf. American "fat cats"). Of someone who really has all the luxuries, a Russian may say: "He rolls around like cheese in butter" *[kataetsia, kak syr v masle]*. When a Russian says about somebody "he's gone mad from fat" *[s zhiru besitsia]* he basically means: "Who does this guy think he is? Is his diet so rich that he can treat everyone like a vassal?" (Specter 1997, 7). Numerous other expressions also point to fat as a signifier of opulence. To describe his desperate state of affairs, a Russian may say: "Getting fat is not even on my mind; I'm lucky if I survive" *[ne do zhiru—byt' by zhivu]*. To reprimand someone for greediness, a Russian may say: "Would it be too fat [read: good] for you?" *[Ne slishkom li zhirno budet?]* (Smirnitsky 1992, 175).

> (1.4) A grandma boards a bus. A plump youngster offers his seat to her right away.
>
> The grandma sits down, looks at him, and says: "What a good boy!"
>
> "Well, it's nothing, it's not worth talking about. . . ."
>
> "But what a good boy, after all. . . . A nice plump one." (JFR 2/3/98)

The joke is funny for Russians because of the difference in cultural points of reference. The old woman thanks the boy for a good deed by praising his plumpness, which in the up-and-coming culture of Western standards, sounds like an insult.

When the French word "bourgeois" entered Russian political vocabulary in the years preceding the Russian revolution, the Bolshevik propagandists spelled the word in a way that would make it comprehensible for the illiterate masses, fitting their associations of abundant and varied food consumption with wealth. The resulting word—*burzhui*—has as its ending an imperative form of the verb "to chew" *[zhui]*, which associates prosperity with eating. Vladimir Mayakovsky's famous lines rhyming these two words—*burzhui* and *zhui*—in a poem that promises the end of the bourgeois makes this association explicit:

Esh' ananasy,   Eat pineapples,
riabchikov zhui!   chew hazel-hens!
Den' tvoi poslednii   Your last day's
prikhodit, burzhui!   coming, you the bourgeois!

Thus *burzhui* became for the Russian masses a symbol of gluttons, rich fellows in peasant terms. From the early days of the October revolution through Leonid Brezhnev's time, Soviet political posters invariably depicted capitalists as fat men with big stomachs, and their profits were shown in the form of bursting grain sacks. Undoubtedly the red propaganda took into consideration the peasant conception of what a rich man should look like.

Childhood and adolescent socialization of urbanites of peasant origin shaped their view of sexuality and resulted in sexual conservatism and low sexual tolerance (Kon 1995, 271). This tension between two value systems finds its expression in jokes, many of which are a verbalized reaction to expressions of sexuality that do not fit in with predominantly peasant attitudes and customs and from which the jokes derive their sense of ludicrous. Many jokes play on the incongruity of having two, often opposite, standards of behavior and value systems.

In 1990, the majority of adults living in the cities (83 to 85 percent among sixty-year-old Russians, 60 percent among forty-year-olds, and about 50 percent of the twenty-year-olds) were born in the countryside (Kon 1995, 271). Their strong peasant heritage shapes their views on gender relations and on sex and sexuality. It is no wonder that Russians still use the words "a male peasant" *[muzhik]* and "a peasant woman" *[baba]* colloquially

to denote any man or woman. Today these words either carry a slightly jocular tone, implying a person's provinciality, or may be used approvingly; in
contemporary Russian, the word *muzhik* carries a connotation of ragged,
raw masculinity. About a "true man" a Russian would say: "He's a true
muzhik," a "go-getter." Consider the following statement of well-known
Russian actor Evgeny Menshov: "It seemed to me: If you are a man, you
should play serious parts, important ones, and not occupy yourself with zany
antics. If there are no such parts—then be a true muzhik *[bud' po-nas-
toiashchemu muzhikom]*, take your fate in your own hands and get yourself
involved in some other serious business, and do not keep swimming at the
will of [life's] waves" (quoted in Sekridova 1998, 49). A Russian may also say
about an admired woman: "She is a high-class baba" *[klassnaia baba]*. (For
another treatment of the word *baba,* see chapter 2.)

In many societies today, slenderness is likely to suggest affluence—the
ability to afford a special diet, membership in a health club, possession of exercise machines, etc. In a country in which the availability of food has been
linked directly to weather conditions and in which periods of food scarcity
have occurred often, indulgence in food is perceived as life-affirming, compensating for periods of hunger.

As Jamake Highwater (1990, 157) points out, people tend to view the
human body as "a metaphor for nature." Hence in the peasant culture,
abundance of food has served as a signifier of fertility and full-figured bodies have spelled prosperity, just as an expensive automobile signifies affluence
in contemporary American culture. The Russian association of a full body
with wealth can be seen in one of the old Muscovite bathhouse attendants'
sayings as a customer leaves the public baths: "May you be happy, keep getting rich and keep gaining weight!" *[Schastlivo ostavat'sia, bogatet' vam i tol-
stet'!;* Ivanov 1986, 300]. An old Russian riddle about a wealthy family
clearly shows what is the measure of their well-being: "The husband's [body]
is thick, the wife's is wide" (Sadovnikov 1986, 511).[11]

Current Russian oral humor continues this folkloric tradition. There is a
popular series of jokes about the Russian parvenu of the 1990s—the so-
called New Russian, the obscenely wealthy man, usually a lawbreaker, who
drives the latest model Mercedes and owns a toilet made of gold. He is a
"husky lad with a bull's neck" *[detina s bych'ei sheei]*. His acquisitiveness is
still associated with eating:

(1.5)   A young lady says to a New Russian:
        "You know, I have seen you before somewhere. . . . I've got it: on
        a can of Spam." (Erokaev 1997, 90)

(1.6)   A New Russian comes to a restaurant. After he is seated at his reserved table, he says to the waiter: "Please make me a cake with 'To
dear Vassya' written on the icing."

In half an hour, the waiter comes with the cake and asks: "Do
you want me to pack it for you?"

"Why bother? I'll eat it here." (Erokaev 1997, 46)

Although real "New Russians" tend to surround themselves with long-
legged, slim, attractive females, in folklore the wives of these *nouveaux riches*
are also portrayed as heavy:

(1.7)   A grossly fat wife of a New Russian asks a furniture salesman: "Are
you sure that beds made by this company are truly reliable?"

"Oh yes, lady, this is a very solid firm. They test every new model
of their beds by borrowing a hippo from a zoo. However, in your
case, I'd recommend 'proceed with care.'" (Erokaev 1997, 86)

As a man's worth has subconsciously been judged by how well he feeds
himself and his family ["What's honor if you have nothing to eat?" *chto i
chest', kogda nechego est';* Krylov 1973, 244], rounded bodies, male and female, have long been the Russian standard of beauty. The most vivid illustration of this standard of female attractiveness comes from the paintings of
Boris Kustodiev (1878–1927). In a series of his works devoted to merchants'
wives, middle-class *[meshchanstvo]* women who, by and large, came from the
peasantry, one can see fleshy females. To underscore the national character
of this beauty pageant, Kustodiev named some of these portraits "Belle"
(1915) and "The Russian Venus" (1925–1926). In two paintings, both entitled "A Merchant's Wife Sipping Tea" (1918 and 1920), the well-endowed
female body and the luxurious food on her table are rendered as one and the
same appetizing item, rich and sweet.

No wonder, then, that in the peasant folklore one finds numerous
proverbs, sayings, chastushkas, and jokes that promote images of portly
women as sexually appealing. As a folk saying from Dahl's collection attests, a girl should be "round and plump, and white [of skin] and rosy-
cheeked, blood with milk" (1879, II: 311) (cf. the English expression
"peaches and cream"). This equation of sex and eating can also be seen in
parallel images, as in an ancient Russian song: "A gray duck is my meal,
a beautiful girl is my bride" [*Sera utitsa estva moia, krasna devitsa nevesta
moia;* cited in Pyliaev 1992, 38] and in a Russian riddle about a bride: "In
the evening a little white hare jumps at will, after midnight it lies on a

plate" *[So vechera bel zaiushka po privol'iu skachet, so polunochi na bliude lezhit].*[12]

In a current attempt to revive the ancient wedding ritual of "bargaining for a bride" *[vykup nevesty]*, a girl is also described in terms of delicious food: "our bride is made of rich dough . . . her little shoulders are made of cottage cheese, her little hands are tarts" *[Kak u nas nevesta iz sdobnogo testa . . . plechiki tvorozhnye, ruchen'ki pirozhnye]* (Starinskaia 1996, 186).

The connection between food and sex is also suggested by the name of a famous Russian dish—*rastegai,* "a pie with a slit in the crust through which its fish stuffing is seen" (Vasmer 1986, III: 445). According to Dahl, the same word in a local Volga dialect also means a seductive "silk sleeveless summer dress *[sarafan]* with cutouts" (literally, *rastegai* is the imperative "unbutton" in this dialect). This kind of pie came into fashion in 1807 when Styosha, a gypsy singer, sang a hit song entitled "My Little Summer Dress That Can Be Unbuttoned" *[Sarafanchik-rasteganchik];* the pie was named to commemorate this song (Pyliaev 1992, 45). In a contemporary satirical commentary on declining public morals, the original meaning of this dish is made explicit: "Russian cuisine: *rastegai* with striptease (payment in hard currency only)" (Berezin 1994, 17). Contemporary metaphors for a girl or a young woman include mostly flour products—"a freshly baked roll" *[pampushka],* "thick pan-cake" *[olad'ia],* "puff" *[pyshka]* (Elistratov 1994, 314), "bun" *[pliushka]* (337).

Changing Beauty Standards

Predictably, a skinny woman is an object of scorn and even contempt: "A bony girl is a *vobla*" [a flat Caspian fish consumed usually dried] (Dahl 1879, 1). A typical saying succinctly expresses her lack of appeal: "[She has] neither face (read: an attractive one), nor skin (read: not enough of it, i.e., not fleshy)" *[Ni rozhi, ni kozhi].* Contemporary urban slang has a number of scornful names for a thin woman: "a soup mix" [usually consisting of bones; *supovoi nabor*] (Elistratov 1994, 260), "a hanger" *[veshalka];* a little thin woman is called "a toothpick" *[zubochistka].*

   (1.8)   "Dear, you're like a radiator . . ."
           "What, that warm?"
           "No. That ribbed." (Private collection)

Also predictably, the popular rural chastushkas express the Russian taste for fleshy women. For example (Starshinov 1992a, I: 136):

(1.9)   Uprekaiu teshchu ia: I reproach my mother-in-law
           "Tvoia dochka toshchaia.   "Your daughter is skinny.
           Nachinaiu ee miat'—   As soon as I begin to knead her,
           Tol'ko kostochki gremiat'."   Her little bones begin to clatter."

(1.10)   Moiu milku zvat' Marinka,   My darling's name is Marinka,
           Ruchki, nozhki—kak   Her little limbs like blades of grass.
              bylinka,
           Ia ebu ee na dache,   I fuck her in the summerhouse
           Chut' ot zhalosti ne   And almost weep with pity for her.
              plachu.   (Kozlovsky 1982, 78)

In yet another chastushka (Starshinov 1992a, I: 30), a woman addresses her man:

(1.11)   Esli ia tebe ne nravlius',   If you don't like me,
           Kormi luchshe—ia   Feed me better—and I'll grow
              popravlius'.   plumper.

In Russian, the verb for gaining weight *[popravliat'sia]* has another meaning—"to correct oneself," that is, "to look better."

As a line of defense for being slender, the female narrator of the following four-line poem by Igor Guberman (1978, 164), fashioned in chastushka form, cheers up her thin girlfriend, who is too timid with men: She can compensate with sexual abandon:

(1.12)   Ty, podruzhka dorogaia,   You, my dear girlfriend,
           Zria takaia robkaia.   Shouldn't be so shy.
           Lichno ia khot' i khudaia   I'm thin myself
           No uzhasno ebkaia.   But I'm terribly hot.

As we have noted, urban jokelore reflects the same preference for corpulent females. In fact, one of my Moscow informants, an intellectual in his late fifties, believes that a woman cannot be too plump. Numerous proverbs, sayings, and quips echo this conviction.

(1.13)   "What is the correlation between a woman's endowment and love?
           "The more of the beloved's body the better." (Private collection)

(1.14)   "If you like a person, you want to have more [of her]." (Private collection)

In the late Soviet period, Western culture (as conveyed by foreign films and occasional fashion shows) had some influence on sexual tastes. However, trimness as the new standard of female beauty has by and large been met with skepticism and resistance on the part of the male population. Addressing this Western fad, a Russian proverb collected in the early 1970s makes it clear that, as the idea of moderate alcohol consumption is foreign to a Russian man, so is Western men's sexual taste: "Men only pretend that they like light wine and thin women." Along the same lines, a joke collected in the early 1990s talks about a fictitious magazine, "The Russian Woman," which asks 100 Russian men:

(1.15)   "What kind of women do you like, full-figured or thin?"
         "Ninety six men answer 'full-figured' and four—'very full-figured.'"
         (Smetanin and Donskaia 1992, 60).

In this sex-appeal humor, Westerners are actually pitied for having thin wives:

(1.16)   An Englishman, a Frenchman, and a Russian boast about their wives.
         The Englishman: "My wife is trim as a blade of grass."
         The Frenchman: "And mine is slim as a straw."
         The Russian sneers: "Poor you! What kind of wives do you have?
         To find them in bed, you have to use rakes." (Private collection)

It is noteworthy that all three images played with in this joke are rural. A contemporary take-off from a Russian proverb: "Don't be born beautiful, be born lucky" [Ne rodis' krasivoi, a rodis' schastlivoi] reveals the sexual taste of the nation: "Don't be born beautiful, but be born massive." (There is a rhyme in the Russian original: ne rodis' krasivoi, a rodis' massivnoi.) In Moscow slang, a fat wife is called "real estate" [nedvizhimost'; Elistratov 1994, 277].[13] In the following male toast, the same idea of the desirability of an oversized woman is rendered a bit more elaborately:

(1.17)   "I have an African toast: 'To women, in whose shadow we feel so
         good!'" (Starinskaia 1996, 55)[14]

In the post-Soviet period, when European and American television broadcasts, magazine and billboard ads, and all other media flooded the country with images of slim, even near-emaciated young women, genuinely rural folklore (primarily chastushkas) still expresses the old male sexual preference. Urban folklore on the same subject reveals a certain tension between true sexual taste and the fear of being accused of falling behind the times. Some jokes manifest this dilemma:

(1.18) Two friends meet.
"Why haven't I seen you on fishing trips for a long while?"
"I have a new love. She won't let me go no matter what."
"Quarrel with her."
"How?"
"Tear the blanket off her and say: 'You're so fat!' She'll be offended, and you'll go fishing."
The man decides to follow this advice.
He lies down with his love, peeks under the blanket and thinks: "Why the hell do I need that fishing trip!" (Nikulin 1997, 157)

A strategy frequently used in recent jokelore to relieve this tension transfers the desire for corpulent women to other ethnic groups, mostly southerners, such as Ukrainians, Georgians, Armenians, and Jews. The first of the following items usually is told in a distorted variant of the Ukrainian language:

(1.19) "A woman should have enough body to give you something to hold on to." (Private collection)

(1.20) A Russian says to a Georgian: "You know, my wife has such an ass that she's not allowed to enter the subway. They say that with such an ass she can't fit into the train."
The Georgian says: "And my wife has such an ass that when she takes clothes to the laundry, they throw her underpants back at her and say: 'We don't accept tank-covers.'" (Private collection)

(1.21) A Georgian comes to a lingerie shop.
"Show me please the largest panties you have," he says to the salesperson. "Excellent! Here is my telephone number. When someone buys them, have the store call me." (Private collection)

Another joke about the Georgians actually addresses Russians' uneasiness with the notion that a modern "cultured women" should be thin. Here it is a Georgian who speaks for a Russian:

(1.22) Two Caucasian men talk:
"Listen, is your wife a cultured woman?"
"Cultured, my foot! She's as thin as a chip of wood." (Nikulin 1997, 370)

The fictitious Armenian Radio, known for its sly and subtle humor, is asked why men (all men, not only Russian, assumed here) don't like spare women. The answer is uncharacteristically straightforward, even angry: It seems that the very thought of an unappetizing sex partner enrages the Armenian males behind the joke: "Because a man is not a dog. He wouldn't throw himself on a bone." Another question to Armenian Radio:

(1.23) "What do people call a small, but disgustingly fat, woman?"
        "God's little cow." (Milgram 1985, 83)

(1.24) Question: "What's do happiness [*nakhes* in Yiddish] and an ass [*tukhes*] have in common?"
        Answer: "A good [read: big] ass is also happiness" [*khoroshii tukhes— eto tozhe nakhes*]. (Milgram 1985, 74)

With this geographical alignment of Russian jokelore's preference for fat women, it is no wonder that the farther South a nationality lives, the more a desirable woman weighs:

(1.25) They ask Armenian Radio: "What should a full-figured lady do to lose weight?"
        "She should twist in a hula-hoop," Armenian Radio answers.
        "And what if she is so fat that she can't get into the hoop?"
        At this point, a Turkish radio interferes: "For God's sake, don't spoil a beautiful woman!" (Nikulin 1997, 158)

The Breast Fetish

The breast is the main attraction in Russian sexual folklore, as it is the principal fetish for Western males (Legman 1968, 242; Nilsen and Nilsen 1987, 73). However, the Russians' obsession with breasts is extraordinary. A woman with small breasts is a total disappointment:

(1.26) A man is waltzing with a woman he recently met.
        "Excuse me," says the woman, "what are you fumbling about on my back?"
        "I'm looking for your breasts."
        "But they're in my front, aren't they!"
        "Well, I have already looked for them there." (Private collection)

A flat-chested woman is labeled "a scow" [*ploskodonka*]. In Moscow slang, breasts are nicknamed "pineapples" (Elistratov 1994, 23), and a contemporary humorous saying concludes that "a [real] broad should be one with good [read: big] breasts" (255). A jocular blessing says: "May God give you a wife with three breasts!" (134). A take-off of a current saying "Happiness is not in the money, but in its quantity" reads "Happiness is not in the breasts, but in their volume" [*Ne v grudiakh schast'e, a v ikh kolichestve;* JFR 2/4/98]. A womanizer is called a "tit-catcher" [*sis'kolov*] and a "tit-grabber" [*sis'kokhvat*] (Elistratov 1994, 430).

(1.27) "What's most precious about a woman's milk?"
"Packaging." (Nikulin 1997, 193)

(1.28) "What's the difference between a breast and a toy train?"
"Both are made for children, but it is daddy who plays with them." (Private collection)

(1.29) A husband and his wife are in bed resting after sex.
"Listen," the wife says, "if I die, will you sleep with another woman?"
"Well . . ." says her husband. "You should understand, I'm a man, I need it sometimes. Also somebody should help me around the house. . . . Well, in general most likely I will be with another woman. . . ."
"And what will you give her? My fur coat?"
"Well, probably. You can't sell it so easy. It's expensive, and anyway I would have to buy one for that other woman . . ."
"Then you'll give her my bras as well?"
"You're joking! Her breasts are twice as big as yours." (Kulikov 1997, 320)

In fact, the following repartee suggests the only good reason for men to have hands:

(1.30) "Why don't cockerels have hands?"
"Because chickens don't have breasts." (Private collection)

With the new freedom to express sexual desires, Russians have held American-style beauty contests and "sponsored a Miss Breast contest, replete with photographed contestants in national news publications" (Costlow 1993; note 291). Popular journals, such as *Ogonyok*, have regularly shown "tit shots."[15]

This overwhelming breast fixation, undoubtedly the result of strong peasant sensibilities, still alive in many Russians—the same word is used to denote the "nurturing earth" *[zemlia-kormilitsa]* and a nursing woman—is responsible for contemporary expressions in which a woman is totally identified with breasts, as in "Breasts is a woman's face" (JFR 3/2/98) or in the following popular rhyme:

(1.31) Khodiat po ulitse grudi,   Breasts are strolling along the street.
        Nosiat ikh zhenskie liudi.   Female people are wearing them.
                                          (JFR 2/8/98)

Not only the breast but every protrusion of the female body seems to appeal to a Russian man:

(1.32) "A woman without a belly is like a mattress without springs" (Kozlovsky 1982, 229)

(1.33) Question to Armenian Radio: "Is a woman's belly becoming?"
        "Yes! A woman without a belly is a mare without a tail." (Milgram 1985, 90).

(1.34) "A broad without an ass is the same as a ship without sails." (Kozlovsky 1982, 230).

Although all parts of the female anatomy are admired in their bulkier versions, the woman's buttocks are often featured in these appeal jokes:

(1.35) Three man argue about whose wife has the biggest ass.
        "My wife's ass can't sit on two chairs," brags one.
        "And my wife has such an ass that on leaving for work in the morning I give it a flick, and when I return in the evening it is still vibrating," says the second man.
        "And my wife has such light blue eyes!" says the third man dreamily.
        "What do her eyes have to do with it?" the others ask.
        "And the rest of her is her ass." (Private collection)

In Russian sexual humor, these jokes are the most good-natured; by and large, they do not express negative emotions (as long, of course, as women do not offend male taste by being too spare). However, humorous material that touches any other aspect of male/female relations presents a different, much less cheerful picture.

CHAPTER 2

"I'll Call You Boeing 'Cause You're My 747th": Female Roles in Russian Male Jokelore

If we compare the treatment of women in Russian sexual jokelore with that in Russian literature, we can add one more contradiction to the list of the highly polarized qualities of the Russian character. Together with the tradition of the high idealization of women in literature, there exists a most appalling denigration of them in the vast realm of private oral folklore—jokes, proverbs, sayings, catch phrases, and everyday expressions. This sphere of verbally expressed deeply embedded beliefs and tacit cultural assumptions provides unequivocal evidence of misogyny.

Indeed, unlike Western literature, which often has subjected women to ridicule and offense, Russian literature from its very beginnings has created powerful images of worthy women who are not only loving, kind, and devoted to their beloved but who also possess extraordinary intelligence, wisdom, and strength of character.[1] There is Yaroslavna, the ardent wife of the ill-fated hero of the Russian medieval tale *The Lay of the Host of Igor,* who pleads movingly for the prince's release from captivity. There is the princess of Murom, Fevronia, of the fifteenth-century *Tale of Peter and Fevronia* who, while morally and intellectually superior to her husband, Peter, still cherishes him. When forced by her enemies to leave town, allowed to take only what is the most valuable to her, she chooses to take Peter. She remains attached to him even after their deaths. Despite the townspeople's attempts to separate them, her dead body miraculously makes its way inside her husband's coffin.

There is also Yuliania Lazarevskaia in the seventeenth-century tale of the same name, a married gentlewoman whose energy, intelligence, sense of duty, and ability to endure misfortunes bring her sainthood. In *The Life of Avvakum,* the same qualities are attributed to the Archpriest Avvakum's wife, Anastasia Markovna, who stoically shares with her husband all of his sufferings. In an act of self-sacrifice, she forgoes her own interests and blesses her husband's decision to leave his family to continue to preach and stand for his beliefs.

Beginning with Pushkin's Tatiana in *Eugene Onegin,* Lermontov, Turgenev, Dostoevsky, Tolstoy, Leskov, and Chekhov created a splendid succession of proud, beautiful, and spiritually endowed heroines who often show more integrity and will than the men in their lives. Nikolai Nekrasov's series of images of virtuous Russian women runs the spectrum from a simple peasant who freezes to death in the forest while burying her husband ("The Red-Nosed Frost" *Moroz Krasnyi Nos*), to the aristocratic wives of the Decembrists who followed their beloved to the place of exile and hard labor (in his epic poems "Princess Trubetskaia" and "Princess Volkonskaia").

This is the literary tradition that shaped the poet and philosopher Vladimir Soloviev's vision of "Eternal Femininity" as the moral ideal of the future of mankind. It is the tradition that fosters the myth of Russian women as the most beautiful and faithful in the world. Russians associate the very name of their country with the image of a woman worthy of worship: "Oh my Russia! My wife!" exclaims Alexander Blok in his poem "The Scythians." It is this piety toward Russian womanhood that sustained the proverbial age-old cult of Holy Mother Russia; with this name on their banners, companies of the White Army fought and died during the Civil War.[2]

Another, quite opposite view of women is clearly evident in the oral culture of everyday speech. Many Russian proverbs, sayings, jokes, set expressions, foul words, and other utterances portray women as stupid, promiscuous, treacherous, and unfaithful. American scholar Bonnie Marshall (1992, 118) bases this stereotypical image of the Russian female on an analysis of a sample of contemporary Russian jokes: She is "desperate for a man, sexually ambivalent, childish, unprincipled, masochistic, vain, lazy, bitchy, frigid and undiscriminating in her choice of partner."[3]

Why is such a portrayal of women found in contemporary Russian male jokelore? First of all, this kind of depiction of women is not new. In fact, in the culture of everyday speech, a tradition of condescension, neglect, and denigration can be traced back to time immemorial. In part, it echoes the misogyny of medieval Orthodox Christianity. Analyzing the sexual vocabulary of medieval Russia, Eve Levin (1993, 52) supports the view of such scholars as Michel Foucault and Helena Michie that "the language used to talk about sexuality embodies attitudes about sex and about women, the 'other' in the perspective of male-centered culture" and that "language not only reflects attitudes but also shapes, defines and ultimately dictates them."

Sexist Vocabulary

If language reflects and dictates a people's mentality then it is worth exploring the most frequently used Russian word for a woman—*baba*. S. I. Ozhegov's dictionary (1964, 31) gives several meanings. While the first, referring to a married peasant woman or a woman who comes from the uneducated, underprivileged classes, is outdated and emotionally neutral, all the others express a condescending (and often denigrating) attitude toward women in general.[4] Today the word is used to put down both females (e.g., in the expression "She is not a woman but a *baba*," meaning "a primitive being") and males (to mock a weak-willed man, a Russian may say: "He whines and moans like a woman" *[razniunilsia, kak baba]*).[5] In conjunction with several adjectives, *baba* connotes not even a human being, as a direct translation into English suggests, but a number of *things* having qualities similar to the qualities popularly attributed to a female.

Since the stereotypical image of a *baba* is of a fat, shapeless, and mindless old (or not so old) woman, an amorphous archeological artifact is named "a stone woman" *[kamennaia baba]*. This same shapelessness also defines the "snow woman" *[snezhnaia baba]* (as distinguished from "snowman" in English) and "rum cake." *[romovaia baba]*. With the adjective "cast iron" *[chugunnaia]* the word *baba* refers to a very heavy solid part of a giant hammer that drives metallic piles down into the ground during construction work.

Elistratov's dictionary (1994) contains many derogatory nicknames for a woman; whether she is a stranger or a wife or a girlfriend makes little difference. Thus the word "sledgehammer" *[kuvalda]* denotes both a woman (girl, wife, or girlfriend) and a fool and uneducated man in contemporary Moscow argot (218). Some nicknames refer to a female as a "heifer" *[telka]*[6] or "a sheep" *[ovtsa]* (292); others as a beast of prey ("an anaconda," *anakonda*) (22) or "a latch" *[shchekolda]* (583), suggesting that a woman limits male freedom.

A number of insults reify a woman as "a string-bag" *[avos'ka]* (Elistratov 1994, 17), "a cutlet" *[kotleta]* (211), "a yashmak" *[parandzha]* (315), "a rattle" *[pogremushka]* (338), "sour clotted milk" *[prostokvasha]* (379), and "a mop" *[shvabra]* (565). Some nicknames are direct insults, such as "human trash" *[shushera]* (582), "pestilence" *[iazva]* (590, and "a hole" *[dyrka]* (Shlyakhov and Adler, 1995, 57).

Obscenity: *Mat*

In many cultures foul language, although used discreetly by many, is assumed to belong to the lower stratum, to outcasts. But it permeates the everyday speech of virtually all layers of contemporary Russian society,[7] and it is especially infected with negative attitudes toward females. The most insulting obscenities in Russian are women-oriented. In fact, because "mother" *[mat']* is the key word, the collective name for Russian foul language is *mat* or *matershchina* ("mother-related").

Many Russians attribute the appearance of foul words to the (bad) influence of the Tartar-Mongolian yoke (1237–1480) (Kolesov 1991, 77). However, an analysis of the roots of key Russian words in these obscenities clearly indicates much earlier origins in the common Slavic language. Kolesov suggests that usage of these words as insults began with the advent of serfdom, that is, in the beginning of the seventeenth century.

As recent folklore studies seem to indicate, the pervasiveness of such language among Russians may well be related to the agrarian origins of their folk consciousness. The use of foul language has deep ritual pagan roots. Among young male villagers, this language was used to prove their maturity, that is, their ability to perform sexually and to join the adults in reproductive functions. (See, for example, T. G. Ivanova 1995, 536).[8]

In Afro-American culture[9] the archetypal insult represents a violation of an ancient taboo against incest (Legman 1968, 782); a similar Russian one has a more complex cultural origin. In the Russian language, the identity of the actor in the Russian obscenity "I [or: you] fucked your mother" *[eb tvoiu mat']* is not clear: Is it the speaker (the phrase is used by males exclusively) or the object of his insult (as a rule, also a male)? The current linguistic confusion about the actor (the first or second person singular) may be attributed to historical shifts of the phrase's meaning. According to Russian scholar, Boris Uspensky (1988, 248), the expression was an oath derived from the ritualistic expression related to the myth about the sacred marriage of Heaven and Earth (Mother Earth).

Whatever its linguistic origins,[10] in its contemporary usage the generic insult *eb tvoiu mat'* is invariably misogynist in sociolinguistic terms. One of the two possible meanings ("I fucked your mother") is that the attacked man's mother is promiscuous. The other ("You fucked your mother") is an accusation of incest. As Renatus Hartogs and Hans Fantel (1967, 60–61) show, a similar African American insult "mother fucker!" is especially insulting to a man of a deprived social group for, due to cramped living conditions, sleeping in the same bed with the mother can evoke suppressed desires in the male child.

Although in man-to-man company *mat* was used even by Russian aristo-
crats (e.g., by Tolstoy; see Gorky 1990, 366), it was considered totally unacceptable for use in public and in mixed company; foul language of that sort
was unprintable. Thus there was an uproar when in the beginning of the
twentieth century a well-known Russian linguist, Baudouin de Courtenay,
for the first time included foul words in the third edition of Dahl's dictionary of the Russian language (Vladimir Kolesov 1991, 77).

Russian scholar L. Zakharova (1994, 292–293) cites such political and
social roots of the proliferation of *mat* in today's Russia as "permanent fear,
unsettled social conditions, existence of the lumpen-proletariat, aggressiveness in combination with illiteracy"; she considers the widespread use of foul
language the result of "the cultural, and consequently lingual, illness of the
society." This illness is not of recent origin, however.

The tremendous social upheavals of twentieth-century Russia were conducive to the widespread use of *mat*. The mass influx of peasants into industrial centers with the abolition of serfdom in the second half of the
nineteenth century and the increasing criminalization of urban populations
as an aftermath of the revolution and the Civil War were instrumental in the
pollution of everyday language. In the 1920s, for instance, thieves' argot became part of the vocabulary of popular entertainment, as seen, for example,
in the repertory of the immensely popular singer, Leonid Utesov, whose career started at that time.

Foul language often serves as a means of meta-communication—that is,
when regular words fail to express the intensity of emotions that cannot be
discharged by other means (cf. the use of the word "fuck" in American culture). As linguists Felix Dreizin and Tom Priestly (1982) show, due to linguistic properties of Russian, the core Russian obscenities can express a wide
range of feelings and notions, as the following items amply illustrate:

(2.1) A trade union meeting. They discuss agenda item: the working conditions in a plant.
A locksmith Ivanov has the floor: "Mother fuckers! . . . Go fuck
yourself! . . . Fuck you and fuck you again!"
A voice from the audience: "That's right, Vassya, we won't work
without work robes!!!" (Private collection)

(2.2) A man returns from a trip to Paris and shares his impressions with
his wife:
"Well, Mania, Paris is one mother-fucking town! You climb on
the Eiffel Tower, and—Manya, fuck your mother! You look to the
left—mother fucker! You look to your right—Manya, fuck your

> mother! You look forward and backward—it's just one mother fuck-
> ing! . . . Why do you cry, Manya?"
> "What stupendous beauty!" *[Krasotishcha-to kakaia!]* (Private
> collection)

It is understandable that, due to this expressive quality, the use of *mat* became especially widespread during the extreme harshness and inhuman conditions of the Great Patriotic War. It was further facilitated in the late 1950s
and early 1960s by the mass release of gulag prisoners for whom it had been
the only means available to express suffering (Vishnevskaia 1984, 284–285).
Judging from statistical data, the influx of former inmates was considerable.
In 1981 every sixty-seventh Soviet citizen was a former labor-camp inmate
(Timroth 1986, 97).[11]

During the last three decades of the Soviet regime, the use of obscene language became increasingly widespread, even ubiquitous (Cherednichenko
1994, 26). This is recognized in the following joke. Even babies use dirty curses:

> (2.3) A young mother with a baby buggy comes to a store, leaves it at the
> entrance and goes inside.
>
> From the carriage, a little boy cries out: "What a bitch! Left me
> alone. What if I couldn't hold it and piss into my pants? Then again,
> somebody could steal me . . ."
>
> A man passes by, hears the boy, and comes up to the carriage,
> flabbergasted. "You're so little. You probably can't walk yet, and there
> you go—swearing like that!
>
> "And you, Mister, can you walk?"
>
> "Of course, I'm a grown-up, and I can walk."
>
> "Well, then hit the road and fuck yourself." (JFR 2/17/98)

In fact, current Russian jokelore treats the use of foul language (together
with the lack of manners) as a matter of national identification.

> (2.4) A man is fishing at the beach. Suddenly an American submarine sur-
> faces. A captain appears on the top deck: "Where are we, my friend?"
>
> "Go fuck yourself" *[Poshel na khui]*
>
> The captain shouts down to his crew: "Fellows! We're in Russia!"
> (Nikulin 1997, 181)

The following popular rhyme is a take-off on Mayakovsky's famous lines
glorifying the Russian language as the language of the great Soviet leader,
Vladimir Lenin:

(2.5) Da bud' ia i negrom   Even if I were a Negro of old age
       preklonnykh godov,
       Indeitsem is shtata Aidakho   Or an Indian from the state of Idaho,
       Ia russkii by vyuchil tol'ko za I'd learn Russian if only to suggest that
       to,
       Chtob vsekh vas poslat' na   All of you go to fuck yourself! (JFR
       khui!   2/7/98)

Another popular rhyme acknowledges that the use of dirty language is the Russian way of alleviating life's harshness:

(2.6) "Ebena mat'" dlia russkogo   For the Russian people "fucked
       naroda,   mother" is
       Kak miaso v shchakh, kak   Like meat in our cabbage soup, like
       maslo v kashe!   butter in porridge!
       S nim nasha zhizn' stanovitsia   With it, our life becomes brighter
       svetlei
       I mysli skazannye krashe!   And our thoughts more beautiful!
                                        (Private collection)

Today *mat* has permeated Russian life to such an extent, filling every pore of it, that one aspect of it—the degradation of women—is taken for granted, ignored even by many sophisticated members of the intelligentsia.[12] While Dostoevsky and Gorky opposed *mat* [the former considered it an extremely primitive language of drunkards;[13] the latter found it totally unacceptable for its degradation of women[14]], foul language has gained a higher status now, not only in popular culture but also in literature. The ubiquity of *mat* in contemporary Russian culture, especially evident in the post-Soviet period when official taboos on vulgar language were lifted, has even found numerous defenders. Defying Mikhail Bakhtin's (1986, 34) assessment of contemporary Russian obscenity, in which "almost nothing is left of carnival ambivalence besides bare negation, pure cynicism and insults," Elistratov (1994, 654–671) sees in today's Russian *mat* the last true features of the "Golden Age" of medieval carnival worth preserving. Writer and poet Igor Guberman (1993, 109) also reveres it as the "national pride of Great Russians."

At the same time, many other members of the Russian intelligentsia view the proliferation of foul language as a negative phenomenon that bears witness to a cultural crisis of alarming proportions. It is noteworthy, however, that although in many cultures invectives may be used for positive ends (e.g., to reduce stressful and emotionally charged situations) (Zhelvis 1991, 317), in Russian culture such relief is achieved primarily at the expense of women. In his 1911 article, psychoanalyst Sandor Ferenczi addresses the "visual imperative" of obscene words, the fact that they "force the person hearing them to visualize the anatomic parts or the physical action referred to. . . . Because of the visual explicitness attached to four-letter language, obscene whispers addressed to a woman are psychologically equivalent to removing her clothes. Again there is the implied suggestion of violence and dominance" (quoted in Hartogs and Fantel 1967, 85).

The notion that *mat* is offensive to women and that children should not be exposed to it is well understood by Russian men, as the following jokes testify:

(2.7) "What's the difference between a woman and glass?
"When glass is covered with *mat* [frost], it becomes white. When a woman is covered with *mat* [foul words], she becomes red [she blushes]. (Barsky 1994, 189).

(2.8) A group of hunters entered a forest. A hare began to cover his children's ears.
"What are you doing?" his wife asked indignantly. "We have to hide, or they'll kill us."
"Maybe they'll kill us, but now the kids won't have to hear foul language." (Repina and Rostovtsev 1995, 22: 51)

It is exactly due to the fact that, in the Russian folk consciousness, the usage of *mat* is considered incompatible with the image of people of high culture that the following jokes (and many similar ones) derive their humor:

(2.9) At the Bolshoi Theater, an aged couple comes up to the manager's window. The man says:
"Excuse me please! You see, I'm a professor, and my wife's a professor. We are in Moscow for the first time, and we want to attend the Bolshoi Theater."
"Sorry, but I don't have any tickets left."
"You see, but I'm a professor, and my wife's a professor. We've dreamt about seeing this performance for such a long time!"
"Sorry, but I can't be of any help!"
"Yes, but, you see, I'm a professor, and my wife's a professor. We would like very much to see this ballet. May we have a pass?"
His wife interrupts him: "Let's go, Boris! Don't degrade yourself!"

"Get lost!" [literally: "Go to your fucked mother!" *Poshla k ebanoi materi!*], he says to her. Then, turning to the manager: "You see, I'm a professor, and my wife's a professor . . ." (I. Raskin 1995, 338)

(2.10)   In the Great Hall of the Moscow Conservatory, somebody whispers: "Excuse me, have you said 'mother fucker' right now?"
"No."
"Excuse me then. It's Beethoven's music must have evoked it."
(Private collection)

(2.11)   A young lady in a hat walks on the street. Suddenly a strong gust of wind blows her hat to the ground.
A man passes by, picks up the hat, and gives it to the lady.
She thanks him: "You're such a gentleman!"
"Well, I'll be fucked, of course, I am." (Private collection)

(2.12)   "After all, we are cultured people, aren't we, you shit eater!" (JFR 2/21/98)

In many cultures, the use of words related to the lower body is intentionally offensive, but the gender asymmetry in Russian culture is all too obvious. While the strongest American insult directed at a female, the metonymical word "cunt," implies her sexual looseness, reducing her whole being to her sexual organ (Jay 1992, 180), the Russians use this word [*pizda*] when attacking members of both sexes.[15]

As the very nature of foul language is to serve as word magic that aims to provoke a negative reaction in the verbally attacked person, the similar reduction of a man to his sexual organ ["dick" in Russian: *khui*] is infinitely less offensive in the Russian language than the same kind of insult drawing on its female counterpart.[16]

What linguist Adam Jaworski (1984–1985, 91–92) writes about the asymmetry of insults in Polish applies equally to Russian. Referring to the insult "You cunt!" [*Ty pizdo* in Polish], he notes: "This implies that if insulting is connected with the downgrading of one's status a man can be downgraded by two means: first, he (his ego) may be equated with his sex organ, and secondly he can be leveled to the status of the female sex organ. Because women's status is lower than men's their downgrading (in the way of obscene insults) can be achieved by identifying them with the female organ."

In Russian, the word *pizda* (and its derivatives) consistently carries a heavily negative connotation well beyond the American accusation of sexual looseness. Directed at males, the word serves as a strong insult, conveying such meanings as "you betrayed me" and "you're scum." The word usually functions as an ultimate insult that aims to provoke a fistfight (unless the verbally assaulted man chooses to retreat).

Verbs that derive from the word *pizda*, with several prefixes, describe actions that are invariably negative and evoke such feelings as condescension and contempt. For example, they could mean "to beat somebody up" *[otpizdit', dat' pizdy]*, "to steal" *[spizdit']*,[17] "to engage in idle talk" *[popizdet']*, "to lie" *[pizdet'; especially in negative form, ne pizdi*—"don't bullshit me"], or "to be out of one's mind" *[opizdenet']*. Correspondingly, all the set expressions containing the word *pizda* have a strong degrading coloring, such as "to get in a big trouble," [*ia v pizde*; literally: "I'm in a cunt"] or "to abandon one's hope" ["*nakryt'sia pizdoi*," literally: "to cover oneself with a cunt."]

In addressing the issue of carnivalian popular culture in his book on Rabelais, Bakhtin was not writing about Russian curses, but he may well have had in mind the Russian expression *poshel v pizdu* [a shortened form of the full expression *poshel by ty v pizdu* "Why don't you go (back) into the cunt you came from!"]; sometimes it is followed with: "for a remake" *[na peredelku]*, to demonstrate what he called "ambivalence." As with other carnival curses Bakhtin (1986, 33–34) discusses elsewhere, in modern times not a trace has remained of the ambivalent nature—death and rebirth—of this curse.[18] This expression is used in its denigrating meaning only—as a wish that the person to whom it is addressed would vanish from the face of the earth (something like the English curse "May your stinking bones never be found").[19]

Hartogs and Fantel's observation (1967, 29) that "While obscenity appears to be universal, each culture has its own patterns of obscenity reflecting its own conflicts and preoccupations" can be illustrated by citing certain American and Russian obscenities that show a slight but telling linguistic difference. These authors attribute Americans' use of the word "fucking" regarding inanimate objects to the "intensified sexual imagination characteristic of many Americans—reacting against the Puritan tradition" (26). In this respect it is interesting to note that in Russian everyday discourse, a passive form of the same participle is widely used ["fucked," *ebanyi*] with all three gender endings of the modified noun. Whereas an American would say, for instance: "Where is that fuck*ing* hammer?" *[Kuda devalsia etot ebushchii molotok?]*, a Russian would say: "Where is that fuck*ed* hammer?" *[Kuda devalsia etot ebanyi molotok?]*.

Thus, while the American scolds the "misbehaving" object, degrading it from the position of puritanical morality, the Russian's scolding has a different underpinning. When, under similar circumstances, a Russian uses the word "fucked" *[ebanyi]* in his sexualization of objects, his outrage and disparagement is based on the fact that the unruly thing disobeys its master, who reminds it that it had been sexually conquered and therefore fully subjugated; it should not have a will of its own. As the same epithet is applied to people as well, it sheds light on the principle underlying Russian attitudes toward women.[20]

Misogynist Folklore

As separate words and everyday expressions mercilessly slander women, so do many Russian proverbs and sayings. In them, a Russian woman is not given credit for any of the virtues that are so highly praised in literary works. The female image is that of a mindless chatterbox. Why solicit a woman's opinion, since she doesn't have one? Thus one of the ancient Russian proverbs cited in the thirteenth-century tale "The Prayer of Daniil Zatochnik" *[Molenie Daniila Zatochnika]* says that "a husband (man) is not a husband if he listens to his wife" *[ni muzh v muzhekh, kto zheny slushaet]*.

The proverbs and sayings of the Dahl collection are no more respectful toward women. In them, Russian men often see a woman *[baba]* as a heavy burden. Not only is she a mindless creature, but her very membership in the human race is not even questioned; it is flatly denied:

(2.13)   When a woman's off the cart, the horse has it easier. *[Baba s vozu, kobyle legche.]*

A woman has long hair but a short mind. *[U babu volos dolog, a um korotok.]*

She hallucinates; who would believe her! *[Baba bredit, da kto ei verit!]*

A woman should know her place. *[Znai baba svoe vereteno.]*

A hen is not a bird, a woman is not a human being. *[Kuritsa ne ptitsa, baba ne chelovek.]*

If you give a woman freedom to do what she wants, you won't stop her. *[Babe voliu dat'—ne uniat'].*

A woman is precious twice: when she is carried across your threshold [that is, after the wedding] and when she is carried out. *[Dvazhdy zhena mila byvaet: kogda v izbu vedut, da kogda iz izby nesut].*[21]

Contemporary folkloric material is not very different. In these proverbs, sayings, and jokes, a woman is under the strict control and supervision of her man. An echo of the notorious sixteenth-century household manual, *Domostroi,* can be heard in such current male sayings as "He who lets a cunt [read: a woman] get away with anything is a 'cunt' [read: a despicable underling] himself" [*Kto pizde spustil, tot sam pizda budet;* Armalinskii 1992, 35],[22] or in a satirical barb directed at a man: "Where there had once been a conscience in him, there grew a cunt" [*Gde ran'she byla sovest', tam pizda vyrosla;* 37], that is, the man has become morally corrupted, shameless. Everything that is most despicable is given a name commonly associated with females, as in the Armenian Radio's answer to the question:

(2.14) "What's your philosophical credo?"
   "The whole world is a whorehouse and everyone in it is a whore" (Milgram 1985, 39; Iliiasov 1994, 188).

(2.15) A racketeer rings up his client, a New Russian: "Petrovich, happy March 8th!" [International Women's Day]
   "What? Are you calling me a *baba* [a broad] or what?"
   "Well, broad or not, you're quite a bitch. You're behind in the payments you owe." (Eroshkin et al. 1997, 88)

(2.16) "A man is such a scum, the only thing worse is . . . a woman." (JFR 9/14/97)

Bitchiness is a common theme:

(2.17) "Of two lovers one always turns out to be a bitch." (JFR 2/12/98)

(2.18) "Are women really kind and good?"
   "Only when they sleep with their teeth toward the wall." (Milgram 1985, 41)

(2.19) A Russian, an Englishman, and a Frenchman get together and discuss their wives.
   The Englishman begins praising his wife: "She is as light and fast as a wolfhound."
   The Frenchman: "And mine is tender and soft as a Pekinese."
   The Russian: "Mine's also a bitch. I just don't know which breed." (Anon. 1994, 266)

(2.20) During a public meeting in a theater, an angry feminist says: "Well, tell me what would you men do without women? I'm asking you, what! What!"
   A voice comes from the gallery: "We would still be getting high in paradise!" (Anon. 1990, 3)

A male learns about the evil nature of women early, in elementary school:

(2.21) A class in ancient history. A teachers asks a pupil: "Tell me, who was the first man on earth?"
"Adam."
"And what horrible disaster did God visit on him?"
"Eve." (Anon. 1990, 20)

(2.22) Everybody in the world had been brothers to each other, until the sisters appeared. (JFR 3/20/98)

In the following popular rhyme, a woman is held responsible for the country's downfall:

(2.23) Strana nuzhdaetsia v geroiakh,   The country needs heroes,
Pizda rozhaet durakov . . .   And the cunt keeps giving birth to
                                     fools. (JFR 2/15/98)

The deadly threat of a woman is the subtext of the following rhyme. It plays with the double meaning of the word *kosa,* which means in Russian both "braid" and "scythe," and the fact that in Russian language the word "death" is feminine:

(2.24) Goda prokhodiat cheredoi,   Your years are passing in a row,
A zhenskii pol vsegda s toboi,   And the female gender is always with
                                     you:
To pod toboi lezhit s kosoi,   One time she's lying under you with
                                     her braid
To nad toboi stoit s kosoi.   Another time she stands over you with
                                     a scythe. (JFR 2/11/98)

In the humorous meditation on aging of the famous Russian cabaret singer, Leonid Utesov, death appears as a woman:

(2.25) Mashina podana.   A car is rolled up.
Voditel'—baba zlitsia.   Its driver—a broad—is angry.
V rukakh ee kosa.   She has a scythe in her hands.
Sud'by ne izmenit'.   You can't change your fate.
Net, ia ne vyzyval,   No, I didn't call for her,
No znal, ona primchitsia   But I knew she'll rush to me
I skazhet: "Ia za vami,   And say: "I'm after you.
Khvatit zhit'."   You've lived enough." (Utesov 1995, 232)

In the following joke, rated by Russian Internet readers among the 100 best for 1997, the fact that in Russian "Indian summer" is called "a woman's summer" *[bab'e leto]*, let the men express their misogyny:

(2.26) Two men are talking: "How disgusting—cold, muddy, and dirty— the woman's summer is this year!"

"Like woman, like summer." *[Kakie baby, takoe leto].* (Private collection)

In the following joke, the sadistic attitude toward women found new images of expression in the reality of post-Communist Russian life: the conversion of Soviet military industry to the production of everyday items and the appearance of Western TV ads of feminine hygiene aids.

(2.27) Taiga. Deep snow around a rocket installation. A smart-looking officer begins countdown. The rocket launches. It's on its orbit. The mother warhead slowly separates onto its components. A little dot passes through the atmosphere. It flies fast toward the earth. It flies in into somebody's window. A wild female shriek is heard. The officer with a tender and caring face turns toward the viewers:

"Tampax conversion! Up to a millimeter precision." (Private collection)

The following recent joke is a travesty of the much-celebrated image of a Russian woman in Russian high culture as one who, as the famous lines of Nekrasov have it, is able "to stop a stallion on his run and walk into a burning hut."

(2.28) A man crosses a street and gets run over by a car. For two days he is in a coma, but then comes back to his consciousness. He opens his eyes and sees his wife next to him.

"Oh, my dear!" the man whispers. " You're always next to me. Do you remember, when I was at the university and was failing one exam after another, you were always next to me and cheered me up."

His wife presses his hand in understanding, and he continues: "And do you remember how I was rushing around looking for work? Nobody even wanted to talk to me, and you kept searching for new and new ads in the papers. Then I found after all a job in that tiny company and turned it into a successful enterprise. If it weren't for that tiny mistake, all would be well. We got bankrupt, but you were always next to me.

"Then I found another job. And though no matter how hard I worked, the bosses didn't promote me on the job and all these years I worked for the same salary, you have always been next to me."

Upon hearing all this, tears of tender emotion appear in the wife's eyes, but her husband continues: "And now here this, this horrible accident, and you're again next to me. . . . You know, my dear, I want to tell you something very important. . . ."

His wife embraces him overcome with emotion.

"I think," the man says, "I think that you bring me only bad luck." (JFR 2/2/98)

Woman as Object of Male Desire

The following joke succinctly expresses the ambivalence of men's feelings toward women:

(2.29)   "What's the difference between female sex organs and a cunt?"
"Female sex organs are soft, moist, and appealing. A cunt is the one who owns them." (Private collection)

But more often there is no conflict between desire and hatred; a desirable woman is treated as no more than a sexual plaything, on the woman-as-object principle of male jokes formulated by sociologist Michael Mulkay (1988, 136). Such an attitude toward women can be traced back to an earlier period. Commenting on the street puppet show, "Petrushka" (a Russian variety of the "Punch and Judy" show) popular in Russia throughout the nineteenth century and up to the 1930s, American Slavist Catriona Kelly (1993, 74) notes that "the presentation of women in the Petrushka texts as passive objects of male desire has been regarded by many commentators as . . . a time-honored and inevitable phenomenon." The following joke is especially indicative of this attitude:

(2.30)   While having intercourse, a girl coyly asks her boyfriend:
"Tell me, is there anything good in me?"
"Yes, there is," the boy answers. "But right now I am going to withdraw it, and there won't be any good in you anymore." (Private collection)

While the boy's narcissistic penis fixation and adoration of the sexual self have little to do with lovemaking, from sociological point of view, his total self-absorption is just another manifestation of the phallocentrism embedded in Russian popular culture. The woman-as-object theme is sometimes expressed in even cruder and more cynical forms.

(2.31) "A woman is a can: One opens it and all others use it." (JFR 3/8/98).[23]

(2.32) Two men are walking along the railroad tracks. One says to another: "Listen, I'm the luckiest man in this godforsaken little town!"
"How come?"
"You see, last week I was walking on this very spot and all of a sudden I spotted a $20 bill! Well, I returned to town, bought myself a whole pack of Thunderbird wine and was drunk for three days!"
"That's nothing! " the other one says. "I was walking two weeks ago over this same very place and all of a sudden I see—a naked broad! I picked her up, dragged her under that tree, and banged her for two days in a row."
"Wow!" the first man says. "And you . . . and she . . . Did she . . . give you a blow job?"
"Well, not quite. . . . You see, I didn't find her head." (JFR 3/11/98)

If in the preceding two items woman-as-object motif is reduced to its logical absurdity—to the treatment of a woman as inanimate (with the forbidden delight of necrophilia in 2.32), in other jokes the same motif is present in a more subtle ways.

The following jokes mock artificial insemination. Bypassing a husband or a lover is ridiculed as a fruitless attempt to dethrone the male. As these jokes imply, the man is still in charge and the woman's wishes are still gibberish:

(2.33) A woman comes into a clinic for artificial insemination.
A huge, burly man is sitting behind the desk.
"What kind of baby do you want to conceive?" asks the man.
"We can fulfill your wishes. Do you want a boy or a girl?"
"A boy."
"Blond or brunette?
"Brunette."
The man reaches for a tube and pours some liquid into a glass.
"Tall or medium height?"
"Tall."
The man reaches for another tube. "IQ score 100, 120, or 150?"
"150."

The man adds liquid from another tube.

"And also, I'd like my boy to look like the French actor Jean-Paul Belmondo. Can you do that?"

"No, problem, dear lady."

He gives her a glass with the liquid to drink, puts her on a sofa. When she falls asleep, he unzips his fly and murmurs: "Belmondo, Belmondo . . . Whatever comes out comes out." (Private collection)

The source of the teller's delight in the following item with the same premise is the fact that the woman had been "had," in both figurative and direct meanings of the term:

(2.34)   An artificial insemination clinic. An outraged woman bursts into the director's office:

"I wanted to get pregnant without having sex with a man. And your doctor fucked me in an old-fashioned way and, on top of that, took my money."

"Well, you know, the complicated imported equipment is often out of order. We are forced to turn to the methods of folk medicine." (JFR 1/28/98).

In the following item, a woman is rendered not simply as an object but a dangerous one. There is no shortage of jokes elaborating this point.

(2.35)   After a passionate night of love, a girl asks a young man:

"Listen, do you have a certificate that you don't have AIDS?"

"I do."

"Well, then, here is the thing: You can tear it up now." (Private collection)

(2.36)   Two bolts stroll along and spot a nut.

"Hey, how about screwing her?" says one bolt.

"To hell with her," another bolt says. "She might give us rust." (Private collection)

(2.37)   She has nothing positive in her . . . besides her reaction to Wassermann test. (JFR 3/4/98)

The treatment of a woman as an object becomes especially transparent when she is sick or has lost her sexual appeal, as is the case in the following two items, involving the same characters:

(2.38) A husband brings his wife for a check up. After numerous tests, the doctor tells the husband: "You wife has either sclerosis or gonorrhea."

The husband asks: "And how can I find out which one of them she has?"

The doctor says: "Throw her out from your car on the way home. If she returns, do not have intercourse with her no matter what." (JFR 3/2/98)

(2.39) A man comes to a doctor: "Doctor, when I look at my wife, I can't get it up."

"Tomorrow come with your wife."

Next day, the man enters the doctor's office with his wife.

"Wait behind the door," the doctor tells him. Then he says to the wife sitting on the chair:

"Get undressed! Yes, yes . . . completely. Well . . . turn around. . . . Well. Now bend. . . . Well, lie down on a bed. . . . Well . . . turn on your stomach. . . . Well, now go down on all fours. . . . That's all, you may dress and leave. Call your husband on your way out."

The husband comes in.

Doctor: "Don't worry, nothing is wrong with you, my friend! I couldn't get it up either." (Private collection)

The not-so-obvious source of delight of the tellers of these jokes is the fact that a man exposes his own wife to another man, in fact, offering her to him. He readily shares his disgust with her with another man, an act of male solidarity, in which the women is left humiliated and estranged.

In the post-Soviet period, the treatment of women as objects of monetary value appears in the jokelore about those who are strapped for cash and those for whom money is not a problem, the Russian newly rich:

(2.40) Kak deneg net—okhota babu.
When I don't have money, I feel like having (sex with) a woman

Kak den'gi est'—stremlius' propit'.
When I have the money, I strive to drink it off.

Vopros takoi—a mozhet srazu
Here's the question: How about

S den'gami bab ob"edinit'?
Combining money and woman into one?

Zarplatu chtob davali baboi.
My salary would be paid in women.

Prikin': prikhodish' v magazin,
Imagine: You come to a store

I ei oplachivaesh' razom
And pay with her for all your stuff:

Vinishko, krabov il' benzin.	Your little wine, and lobsters, or gasoline.
Potom domoi prikhodish' p'ianyi,	Then you're coming home drunk,
A tam i baba i eda,	And there they are both—woman and food,
Poesh' i vyp'esh' polstakana	You eat a bit, you drink half glass of vodka,
I tra-ta-ta, i trata-ta . . .	And bang-bang-bang, and bang-bang-bang . . . (Private collection)

(2.41)   A New Russian comes home in the morning and says to his wife: "I'm very sorry, dear, but you'll have to move to another man. I've lost you to him in a game of cards."

"You lost me?! Oh God, how could you!!!"

"How, how! . . . Very simply: I didn't notice his king of spades." (Private collection)

Woman as Fool

Unlike the clever wives encountered in Alexander Afanasiev's *Secret Tales* (1991), the women in contemporary male jokelore are stupid and lacking in common sense. In the following item, a take-off of *Lysistrata*, women, vain and shallow, are unable to realize their own intentions:

(2.42)   The Third World War is coming. All women of the world decide to gather at a World Congress to work out a resolution that would put an end to the coming disaster. For three days they discuss the text of a resolution to be approved by all the women of the planet. The resolution consists of two items:
1. All men are bastards.
2. There is absolutely nothing to wear. (JFR 3/5/98)

In the following jibe, the teller plays on the Russian name for "marrow," which in this context literally means "bone brain" *[kostnyi mozg]*:

(2.43)   As known, God created a woman from a man's rib. It's not a secret to anyone that a rib is the only bone that doesn't have a marrow. (JFR 9/22/96)

(2.44)   A TV ad for Tampax. A voice over: "What unites millions of women all over the world?"

A man watching the ad interjects: "The fact that they are brain-less fools." (JFR 2/14/98)

In the following popular rhyme, the senseless first two lines are there only to amplify through rhyme the main message—female mental inferiority:

(2.45) Zhenshchiny nosiat chulki i kolgotki,

Women are wearing stockings and pantyhose,

Vovse ne znaia nashei kul'tury:

They don't know our culture at all:

Piat'desiat protsentov iz nikh idiotki,

Fifty percent of them are idiots

Piat'desiat protsentov polnye dury.

And fifty percent are complete fools. (JFR 3/9/98)

The popular stand-up comedian Mikhail Zhvanetsky summed up the male view of female intelligence in one of his monologues: "There are no in-telligent women. There are only charmingly foolish *[ocharovatel'no-glu-pen'kie]* and horrifyingly stupid" (quoted in I. Raskin 1995, 204). As the diminutive-endearing suffix *-en'k* suggests, a softer kind of stupidity is re-served for a sexually appealing female. A contemporary chastushka contrasts male intelligence and higher aspirations with female carnal nature, which makes brains unnecessary:

(2.46) Vzorom muzhchina sledit za zvezdoi,

A man follows a star with his sight,

Zhenshchina mir postigaet pizdoi.

A woman takes in the world with her cunt. (I. Raskin 1995, 230)

In the post-Soviet era, with more automobiles on city streets, woman-driver jokes began to circulate. Some are mild, recalling similar jokes told in the 1930s in America:

(2.47) Two women are driving. Suddenly—bang!—one tire got busted.
The women get out of the car. One of them says to another: "Well, here it is. All the air's out."
The other says: "Well, not quite. There's some of it left on the top." (JFR 3/7/98)

Others are full of misogynist spite:

(2.48)   "A woman behind the wheel is like a monkey with a hand grenade: You never know where she's going to throw it." (JFR 2/20/98)

(2.49)   "A woman behind the wheel's like a fascist in a tank." (JFR 2/20/98)

At first glance, such treatment of Russian women is especially odd in view of the fact that more Russian women than men hold university degrees.[24] There is, however, a hidden agenda of dominant masculinity in jokes characterizing women as fools. The Russian frequently refer to women as "the weaker sex" [slabyi pol]. While currently "half of all working women are still engaged in manual physical labor" (Voronina 1993, 101), it is clear that the expression refers to their mental, not their physical, inferiority. It reflects a patronizing attitude: "What can you ask from her? She's just a weak woman" [chto s nee vziat'—ona vsego lish' slabaia zhenshchina]. Current Russian jokes about stupid females are, then, just a modern rendering of the same attitudes expressed in proverbs collected by Dahl: "A woman's hair is long, but her mind is short."

(2.50)   A girl says to her mother: "Mom, why does daddy have no hair on his head?"
"Because our daddy thinks a lot. . . ."
"And why do you have lots and lots of them?"
"Shut up and keep eating!" (JFR 3/27/98)

In her article "Soviet Patriarchy: Past and Present," Russian sociologist Olga Voronina (1993, 108) notes that, in the Soviet period, misogyny had the same sociological roots as xenophobia, racism, and other forms of discrimination—the fight for survival and privileges: "In a totalitarian state, having no rights one can assert oneself only at the cost of suppressing those weaker, and for this reason the masculinist stereotype of 'the weaker sex' was strengthened."

The woman-as-fool motif is also used in a large number jokes about so-called female logic portraying women as odd creatures to whom normal (meaning men's) logic does not apply. To understand their true psychological meaning, it is necessary to analyze those aspects of female behavior male joke tellers find lacking in intelligence.

Female characters act stupidly under specific circumstances: Attempting to hide their promiscuity, they offer ludicrous—and therefore transparent— excuses for their licentious behavior. The jokes, then, aim to underscore the futility of feigning innocence. The women's attempts to cover up their indiscreet behavior are clumsy, left-handed, and all too obvious; the men see through them easily. For example:

(2.51) A Russian woman gives birth to a black baby. She says to her girl-friend: "My husband is awful! He sleeps around so much that I don't know anymore whom my children resemble." (Private collection)

(2.52) A white woman gives birth to a black baby. She says to her surprised husband:
"See what your idiotic habit of switching off the lights has led to?" (Kulikov 1997, 328)

(2.53) "What a horror! Every year I give birth to a baby."
"Did you try to stop making love to your husband for two years?"
"I've tried. It hasn't helped." (I. Raskin 1995, 205)

(2.54) A divorce hearing is in progress. Says the judge: "Tell us, Comrade Ivanov, why do you want to divorce your wife?"
"She doesn't suit me as a woman."
His wife shouts: "Look at that prince! I suit every man in town, but I don't suit him!" (Private collection)

(2.55) A female fox married a crocodile. Piglets were born. Her conclusion: All men are pigs. (Private collection)

These Russian jokes are quite akin to American "dumb blonde" jokes, which are also based on female attempts to seduce and appear innocent at the same time.

Woman as Wanton

The message of "female logic" jokes is that, despite their education, women are all the same, that is, oversexed creatures, so unable to control themselves that they fail every time to cover their tracks. Invariably full of unbearable sexual desires, they hide them to invite men's pursuit. Their sexual urges are so strong that an experienced man need only have enough patience and wait—and the "ripe fruit would fall into his lap."

(2.56) A train compartment for two. A man takes place on the upper berth and a woman on the lower. After a while a woman says: "How can you lie there quietly when there is a woman with you in the same compartment?"

Descending from the upper berth, a man says: "You know, I prefer to wait for half an hour rather than keep talking a woman into it
for two hours." (JFR 1/28/98)

Female loose behavior is a topic found in the male jokes in many cultures
(e.g., an American item: "She submits to sexual acts only within limits—
state and national"; Fine 1991, 97). It is not incidental that the word "slut"
[bliad'] used by many Russian men in many nonsexual contexts and situations has no male counterpart.[25] Moreover, "slut" is used to connote not only
a prostitute or a loose woman but *any* woman or girl (Iliiasov 1994, 22). It
is used in nonsexual contexts for emphatic purposes in constructions like *vo,
bliad'!; nu, bliad'!, akh, bliad'!* (marginally they can be translated, as "fucking
good," "well, fuck!" and "Oh, fuck!"). The word so contaminates everyday
speech that often its shortened form *blia* is mechanically used as mere inter-
jection, a fact acknowledged and addressed in the following item:

(2.57)   After a crash course in Russian, a teacher says to her American stu-
         dents: "Now you know enough Russian for everyday use. Do you
         have any questions?"
             One student raises his hand: "There is one thing I can't compre-
         hend. In the phrase 'Who's last in line for vodka?' does the indefinite
         article *blia* come in the beginning or at the end of the phrase?" (For
         another version of this joke, see I. Raskin 1995, 91–92)

A woman's sexual attractiveness is her fault. If she is approached by a
man, it is always she who is to blame. She is accused of encouraging men to
pursue her sexually by sending alluring messages through body language or
wearing especially seductive makeup. Even members of the Russian intelligentsia are known to reproach their wives for paying too much attention to
their appearance. "Don't act like a whore" goes the saying.

Preoccupation with sex is so much a part of women that even the epitome of ugliness in Russian popular culture, the Boney Legged Baba Yaga
[Baba Iaga Kostianaia noga] of fairy tales, prefers it to food:

(2.58)   Baba Yaga catches Prince Ivan *[Ivan-tsarevich]* and says: "I'll give you
         a riddle. If you guess it right, I'll give myself to you; if not I'll eat you
         alive."
             Prince Ivan agrees. Baba Yaga asks him, "What is this: It's a little
         one, it's green, it jumps, and it's name starts with 'fr' and ends with
         'og'"? [in Russian *lia* and *gushka*].
             "A grasshopper," Prince Ivan says.
             "You got it, you little playboy!" (Private collection)

There is an abundance of jokes in which the storytellers make one and the same point—wantonness is inherent in female nature. In these jokes, a woman is invariably portrayed as treacherous, inherently unfaithful, and promiscuous:

(2.59) "Did Eve cheat on Adam?"
        "We don't know for sure. But scientists insist that humans came from apes." (Kulikov 1997, 353)

That a woman is sexually indiscreet and promiscuous is taken for granted.

(2.60) Preparing for her vacation trip to the South, a wife says to her husband: "Dear, what do you want me to bring for you from the trip?"
        "Bring whatever you want. Nowadays they cure everything." (JFR 2/25/98)

(2.61) A gynecologist asks his patient: "With how many men have you had a relationship?"
        "Five or six."
        "Well, it's not that many, after all."
        "Yes, the week wasn't that good." (JFR 2/21/98)

(N.B.: This echoes Andrey Sinyavsky's [Abram Tertz 1980, 25] remark: "Women are more sinful than we [men] are. . . ." Sex is always on a female's mind):

(2.62) An attractive young woman dresses before a visit to a dentist. Her husband asks her: "Why do you change your underwear?"
        "What if the doctor is too forward?" (JFR 2/19/98)

(2.63) "Lady, may I buy you a cup of coffee?"
        "Only no smoking in bed!" (McLovsky, Klyne, and Chtchuplov 1997, 143)

In the following item, a subliminally romantic man is contrasted with a woman with a carnal appetite:

(2.64) "What would you think about me, oh mysterious female stranger, if I blew you a kiss?"
        "That you're a sluggard who avoids the real work." (JFR 3/8/98)

A line from a famous anonymous Russian erotic tale about a sexual superman, Luka Mudishchev: "All women are weak in front" *[Na peredok vse baby slaby]* serves as the leitmotif of many sexual references. In school-age children's folklore, while males are disparaged as stupid, females are ridiculed for their sexual looseness: "All the boys are fools, all the girls are sluts" [*Vse mal'chishki—duraki, vse devchonki—bliadi;* Iliiasov 1994, 229]. The same message is repeated in contemporary college students' graffiti: "All women are sluts" (Shumov 1996, 465).

(2.65) Khodiat po ulitse teti i diadi,   Aunts and uncles are walking the
                                                                streets.
          Diadi khoroshie, teti vse   All uncles are good and all aunts are
              bliadi.   whores. (2/11/98 JFR)

Utilizing the aural resemblance of the English word "ladies" spelled in Russian both in singular and plural forms as *ledi* and the Russian *bliadi* (sluts), the following joke makes female looseness specifically Russian.

(2.66) "What do they usually call women in England and Russia?"
          "In England, they call them *ledi* (ladies), in Russia *bliadi*. (Kulikov 1997, 391)

From a popular joke series about the Civil War hero Vasily Ivanovich Chapaev:

(2.67) [Chapaev's orderly] Petka comes to Vasily Ivanovich: "I'd like to get married. But I don't want my future wife to be a slut."
          Chapaev lines up all the women in his regiment. "Those of you who are sluts, step forward!"
          Only one woman doesn't move.
          Later Vasily Ivanovich asks Petka: "So, how's your new wife doing?"
          "She's also a slut, Vasily Ivanovich. Only she's a deaf one." (I. Raskin 1995, 93; for a version with Archangel Michael and women to be admitted to paradise, see Smetanin and Donskaia 1992, 23)

An abundance of jokes are based on the stereotype of a female of *any* age as sexually loose:

(2.68) A little girl runs into the kitchen and pulls her mother by the skirt: "Mummy, tell me, can I have children?"
          "What are you saying, my dear! After all, you're still quite little."
          The girl runs out of the kitchen and shouts joyfully: "All right, little Vova! Let's do it." (Private collection)

(2.69)   A pedophile sneaks up on two girls near their school and says to one
         of them: "Let me touch your little breasts. I'll give you some candy."
             The girl agrees. Then he asks again: "Do you want more candy?
         I'll touch your little tushi."
             The girl agrees again.
             The pedophile: "And do you want another candy? I'll touch."
             The girl says to her girlfriend: "Till this dummy finally bangs me,
         I may get diabetes." (JFR 3/31/98)

(2.70)   A mother says to her school-age daughter: "When I was your age, I
         kept a diary."
             "You're so behind the times, Mom! I'm keeping a card file." (Pri-
         vate collection)

(2.71)   On a business trip, a man picks up a girl on the street and takes her
         to his hotel room. When she starts to undress, he becomes a bit
         suspicious.
             "How old are you?" he asks.
             "Thirteen."
             "Are you out of your mind! Get dressed and get out of here!"
             The girl picks up her clothes and says: "How could I know you're
         superstitious!"
             (Private collection; for an American version, see Fine 1981, 146).

(2.72)   A high school girl asks her classmates: "Girls, do you know the signs
         of pregnancy?"
             "Headache and no wish to go to school." (I. Raskin 1995, 23)

(2.73)   In a sanatorium, an old lady of eighty speaks to the doctor: "Doctor,
         I'm taking sulfur baths and I'm taking physiotherapy. Assign me to
         'bush therapy' [kustoterapiia, a slang word for outdoor sex]
             "What's with you, old lady! You're barely keeping yourself on
         your feet!"
             "But I can still lie on my back, can't I?" (Petrosian 1994, 166)

Especially conspicuous is the woman-as-wanton principle in a popular series
about "little Vova" [Vovochka], a sexually precocious spoiled brat. Here is one
joke in this series.

(2.74)   Little Masha brags to little Vova about her jump rope. Little Vova
         teases her:
             "I have a pee-pee, and you don't have one and never will."

Little Masha runs home to her mother crying but soon comes back quite content.

"I have a pee-pee!" little Vova says again.

"So what! Mommy told me that when I grow up I'll have a hundred like that." (Klimkovich 1990, 6–7)

It is obvious that the joketeller puts even a little girl's innocence in question, asserting that she will be what all other women are—that is, promiscuous. (By implication, her mother speaks from her own experience.) To have as many men as possible is part and parcel of being a woman. In complete reversal of real Russian life, many Russian jokes ceaselessly underscore the female's much greater sexual experience, no matter how young she is:

(2.75)   A young man makes love to his sweetheart for the first time.

"My dear, I know your name is Marina. But I'll call you Eve from now on," he says.

Sitting in the chair and smoking, his beloved asks: "Why?"

"Because you're the first woman in my life, as Eve was for Adam."

"Then I'll be calling you Boeing."

"Why?"

"Because you're my 747th." (Private collection; for a variant playing on a Russian-brand car, Muscovite–412, see O. Ivanova 1996, 487)

(In Andrey Sinyavsky [Abram Tertz 1980, 7], the same perception of a woman as a more sexually experienced is, in fact, a moderate version of the joke: "I was her 67th, she was my 44th.")

Needless to say, Russian women's perpetual promiscuity is nothing but a male fantasy, a product of wishful thinking. True, occasionally the jokes acknowledge an actual situation. The women are not wanton but tired and overworked, forced to carry the burden of both homemaking and working for a second wage, often lacking the simplest conveniences available to Western women; many are sexually dysfunctional, as several sociological studies have shown.[26] But this can become another male complaint:

(2.76)   A female train conductor returned from her trip. All day she had also taken care of the laundry, cleaned the apartment, cooked. And, of course, got tired. At night she made it finally to bed.

Her husband said to her impatiently: "Well, let's do it."

Falling asleep, the conductor murmured with her eyes closed: "Can't you wait awhile? Let the train begin moving, then . . . then . . ." (Private collection)

(2.77) An executive *[otvetsvennyi rabotnik]* comes to Moscow on business. He checks in at a hotel and calls a female acquaintance.

"Come on over, I'm settled here in a luxurious double."

The woman drops by after work, says hello, and then says: "Forgive me, but I'm a bit pooped. Give me a chance to rest a bit."

And she lies on the sofa. The man covers her with a comforter. She falls asleep. She wakes up in the morning, grabs her purse, kisses the man good-bye, and heads for the door: "Don't think there's anything's wrong with me. I'm very sexy. I simply have no time." (Anon. 1994, 225)

(2.78) Work had made a man out of an ape and a horse out of a woman. (JFR 12/10/97)

An interesting reversal of roles that underscores the same point is used in the following item:

(2.79) On March 8, International Women's Day, a husband gets up early in the morning and prepares breakfast for his wife. Then he cleans the apartment, runs out to many stores, stands for hours in many lines, prepares a festive dinner, and, late at night, totally exhausted, falls into bed and thinks in horror: "Is it possible that I am also going to be fucked now?!" (O. Ivanova 1996, 519)

Nevertheless, in most Russian jokes, women are not merely eager to engage in sex, but are insatiable:

(2.80) In ancient times, a pharaoh was put to sleep. He could wake up only if a beautiful young girl kissed him.

Many years passed. One day Masha Kolokolchikova was strolling in the forest and saw the beautiful young man. She kissed him, and woke him up.

"Because you gave me my life back," said the pharaoh, "I must fulfill twelve of your wishes."

Masha thought a bit and said: "There is no need to fulfill twelve wishes. Instead, fulfill one of my wishes twelve times."

The pharaoh could not endure the task and died. (Anon. 1990, 5)

Several elements in this story are chosen for the sole purpose of underscoring the point of the joke—the female sexual appetite is larger than life. First, it is not a mature woman, but a young girl, Masha, who acts in the story; despite her tender age, she is already able to exhaust a man to death. The implication here is that a grown woman is even more sexually inexhaustible and demanding. Second, if a man of great power (read: sexual potency), the pharaoh, is unable to meet the female's needs, what then can be expected from a common man? And the plot is also a significant reversal of the "Tale of the Sleeping Beauty." It is no longer a man who is in the position of power through his kiss but a female. The message is that the world of intimate relationships belongs to a woman, and she is merciless in her sexual demands. These jokes lead to the conclusion that only a machine can satisfy her; and even that will eventually fail, so great is her sexual appetite:

(2.81)   A machine to replace a man is invented. To test it, women of different nationalities gather.
        An American comes into a room with the automaton and spends fifteen minutes. "Time is money," she says as she leaves.
        A French woman goes into the room for half an hour. She tries all the ways of lovemaking and teaches the machine some more that it was not programmed for.
        An English woman spends an hour and leaves quite pleased. "A real gentleman," she says. "It does everything you ask."
        A Russian woman enters. One hour passes, two . . . Suddenly the door opens. The automaton crawls out, pushed by the Russian woman with a broom: "A likely story—your batteries are worn out!" *[Ia tebe dam—batareiki seli!]* (Private collection)

It is noteworthy that it is the Russian woman who turns out to be insatiable, which signifies that nothing would be wrong with Russian men if they could deal with Western—that is, more civilized, not so savagely sexual—women. The threat to masculinity is right there, at home, from those overly demanding Russian females.

A charge that a woman is sexually undiscriminating is sometimes combined with a conviction that she is treacherous, tending to betray not only her mate but also her country. In the years immediately following World War II, the following joke, playing on wartime propaganda clichés, circulated in Russia:

(2.82)   Victorious Soviet troops liberate one of the Russian towns held by Germans. As the soldiers proceed through streets filled with cheering crowds welcoming the liberators, they see a young woman who is hitting her big stomach with her fists.
        "What are you doing?" shouts one of the soldiers.
        "I am finishing off the fascist beast in its own lair."

"What were you doing under the Germans?"
"I was exhausting the enemy's forces." (Private collection)

(This joke gradually faded away, not because of a change of heart on the part of Russian males but because with time these propaganda clichés gradually ceased making rounds.)

Sexism is so deeply ingrained in the Russian mind that it is often revealed when there is a need for a metaphor for anything that can be stereotyped as female. Such an attitude remains for those who have left Russia. Thus, during the Gorbachev era, one émigré commentator in broadcasts over Radio Free Europe made the point that perestroika's whimsical and often ambivalent and inconsistent character directly corresponded to the feminine gender of the word itself.

The Controlling Functions of Male Jokes

The males' perception of sex as a threat accounts for their use of jokes as a means of mutual support and reassurance that they still control the situation, that they are still in charge. A comparison of two kinds of male jokes shows that these jokes constitute a trap of sorts from which a woman cannot escape. The treatment of women as sexual beings is strikingly ambivalent; a number of jokes show the highly conflicting demands imposed on them. On one hand, sexual adventurousness is a sign of a woman's true femininity. Spinsters are laughed at mercilessly:

(2.83) Two old maids sit on the steps and watch a chicken trying to escape a rooster. He has circled the house twice without catching her. She runs into the street and is run over by a car. One of the old maids says loftily: "She preferred death!" (Private collection; for American jokes about spinsters, see Fine 1981, 229)

A woman's fertility is often her only gender identification, as the following joke suggests obliquely, putting the message in the mouths of children:

(2.84) A boy and a girl are leafing through a book entitled *Animal Life* and arguing:
"She can."
"No, I tell you, she can't."
"She can."
"Let's go to Grandma and ask her."
They go to the kitchen and ask: "Grandma, can you have children?"

"What are you saying, grandchildren, of course not."
"I told you she's a male." (Private collection)

For all the emphasis on sluttishness, a woman's refusal to please a man sexually is treated in many jokes as inhuman, as showing a lack of compassion for his sexual needs, which are often rendered as essential to his health and even survival. The following parable succinctly presents this idea; the sexual connotation is revealed only in its punch line, where the key slang term "to put out" *[davat']* (connoting a woman's submission in the sexual act) is used.

(2.85) A rich man rides a camel across a desert. As he moves along, he sees a dying man who begs: "Give me water!"

The rich man thinks: "I'd have to unsaddle, I'd lose time, and I have to get to town while it's still daylight."

"I don't have water," he says and moves on.

He rides for some time and thinks: "What a bastard I am! How inhuman I am! So what if I don't make it to town in daylight! A man is dying!"

He turns back. And the man has died.

The moral: "You have to give ('put out') not when you want to but when you are asked." (I. Raskin 1995, 167)

A woman who not only does not say no but is insatiable is a man's dream come true, as is seen in the following statement by a Russian joke collector, I. Raskin (1995, 84), about nymphomania: "For me, [it] is the state of a normal healthy woman without any complexes." (A term for nymphomania, "madness of the womb" *[beshenstvo matki],* is still in use clinically; it is also colloquial.) Elsewhere the same author supports his view with an attempt to challenge the standard pejorative meaning of the word "slut" *[bliad']:* "In my view, the word is always a compliment to a woman, not an insult at all. I give my own meaning to this word. A slut is a woman who is born to be a woman, who feels herself a woman and doesn't forget for a second that she's a woman" (90). The following joke of the Soviet period makes women indispensable to men's health:

(2.86) "What qualities should an ideal woman have?"
"She should be like a polyclinic—clean, available to the public, and free of charge." (Kulikov 1997, 356)

The following toast extols sexually enterprising women, even if they're married.

(2.87) A woman cheated on her husband once, and a brick fell out of the wall. She did it again, and another brick fell out. Let us drink to women walls crumble for. (I. Raskin 1995, 417)

On the other hand, a woman's alleged promiscuity is scorned and infidelity is attacked:

(2.88) A judge: "Why did you decide to divorce your husband?"
"I can't live with him. He treats me like a dog."
"How?"
"He demands fidelity." (I. Raskin 1995, 349)

The next joke implies that all married women cheat on their husbands. A "slut" differs from a "decent" woman because she does it openly:

(2.89) "Can you imagine, I'm returning from my business trip and catch my wife in the arms of her lover. What a slut! After all, I sent her a telegram to tell her I was coming back."
"Maybe she's not a slut, after all! Maybe she simply didn't get your telegram?" (Barsky 1994, 273)

What evidently makes a difference is whether a woman is somebody else's wife or one's own, an attitude familiar in other cultures. Italian scholar and writer Umberto Eco (1989, 9) notes of his compatriots: "It's OK to say that all our women are sluts, except our mothers and sisters." The message of many Russian male jokes is that a woman cheats on her husband no matter how cultured she happens to be, even if she is an embodiment of refinement as is the Queen of England:

(2.90) They conducted a competition among English school students for the shortest composition on the topic: "God, the Queen, Sex, and a Bit of Mystery."
The first prize was won by a student who wrote the following composition: "Oh, God," exclaimed the Queen. "I'm pregnant again! And again I don't know by whom!'" (Private collection)

In a number of jokes, these contradictory demands on a woman are compressed and put her in a no-win situation:

(2.91) Riding in a bus filled with women, a drunkard suddenly announces: "Those in front of me are fools. Those behind me are sluts."

Silence. After another bus stop he announces again: "Those in front of me are fools. Those behind me are sluts."

After another stop, he repeats: "Those in front of me are fools. Those behind me are sluts."

Finally one woman can't stand it any longer and says: "How can you say such a thing! I have lived with my husband for twenty years and have never slept with another man."

"Well, then you're a fool. Move to the front of the bus." (For a variant, see O. Ivanova 1996, 83.)

In this joke, it is hard to see any humor because of the overwhelming hatred that fills the man. He insults women, giving them no chance to defend themselves since they are just women and, by definition, are worthy of contempt. The fact that he is drunk is not meant to ridicule his attitude or make the joke milder. The teller's ploy here is different. In Russian folklore (and often in real life as well), a drunkard enjoys the status of a "holy fool" who is allowed to tell the truth that others do not dare to say. That is, he acts on the principle of the saying "What is on a sober man's mind is on the drunkard's tongue" [chto u trezvogo na ume, to u pianogo na iazyke].

The message in jokes of this kind is that the world still belongs to men and it is useless for a woman to fight it. She is wrong even when she is right just because she is a woman. Subject to a double standard, she is guilty even when found innocent. As a way of convincing themselves that they still have power over women, men readily find a woman at fault even if she is virtuous, for her main function is to be always available for the males:

(2.92) Three men are discussing women. "Hey, Vasily," says one, "did Manya put out for you?"
"No."
"And for you, Vanya?"
"No."
"What about you, Kolya?"
"Also no."
"What a slut!" (Private collection)

(2.93) "What's the difference between a pessimist and an optimist?"
"A pessimist is sure that all women are sluts, and an optimist hopes they are." (Kulikov 1997, 385)

(2.94) A husband comes home from a business trip. Outside of his apartment, he sees his neighbor and asks: "Well, how was it? Have many men come to my wife?"

"None, really. Nobody came."
"Well, then I won't go either." (JFR 2/1/98)

As Catriona Kelly's (1992, 6) study of Russian popular entertainment of
1870 to 1910 shows, the portrayal of a woman's sexuality as dependent on
man's is one "important central assumption of [the] jocular representation of
marital and extra-marital relations." The following two items of current
jokelore indicate that this tradition does not show any signs of fading away.
In the first, a woman is denied the right to her own sexual self; her sense of
sexual fulfillment is defined only through a sexual experience with a man:

(2.95)   An elderly couple is having breakfast. Suddenly, out of the blue, the
          old woman smashes her man right in his face.
              "What have I done wrong?"
              "Our whole married life you've been a poor fucker."
              In a few minutes, the old man gives a tremendous blow to his
          wife's head.
              "What's that for?"
              "For knowing the difference." (Private collection)

The next joke mocks any attempts to avoid sexual dependence on a man:

(2.96)   At a flea market, a man sells a mosquito in a jar: "A mosquito that
          can fulfill any woman's desire! Full satisfaction guaranteed, or your
          money back."
              A woman asks: "How does it work?"
              "Very simply, lady. You just lie down, undress, open the jar. The
          mosquito is specially trained to do the job. If there is any problem,
          here's my phone."
              The woman brings the jar home, undresses, and lies down on a
          bed. She opens the jar, and the mosquito flies away, landing on the
          wall, ignoring the woman.
              She calls the man.
              "I'll be right there."
              Soon he comes in and says to the mosquito while unzipping his
          fly: "Okay, buddy. I'll show it to you for the very last time." (Private
          collection)

The next joke makes an even more striking point: The world belongs to
men, and a woman is absolutely helpless in it. Nothing, including conforming to men's demands, can improve her lot. Even yielding to a man's sexual
coercion does not protect her:

(2.97) The outskirts of Moscow. It's after midnight and terribly cold. A woman is waiting for a cab. Finally one arrives. As is the custom, the woman asks about the fare. The cabman says: "Five rubles."

"Are you out of your mind!" the woman says. "That's twice as much as usual."

The cab leaves without her. Another hour passes. A new cab arrives. The half-frozen woman says: "Okay, I'll give five rubles. Just take me out of here. I'm freezing."

"Five rubles and I get to sleep with you," says the cab driver.

"You're crazy," screams the woman, and slams the door of the cab.

Another hour passes. Half dead from cold, the woman throws herself at the next passing taxicab.

"Please, I'll give you five rubles and you can sleep with me if you want. Just take me out of here."

"Okay," says the cabman. "Five rubles and sex with perversions."

"I'd rather freeze to death," says the woman and slams the door of the cab.

Another hour passes. The woman is barely alive. When the next cab appears, she opens the door and gasps: "Okay, have it your way. Five rubles and sex with all the perversions."

The cabman pushes her out of the car, slams the door and as he drives away shouts through the open window: "We don't transport sluts." (Private collection)

Sex for Money

Finally, there are a number of jokes in which women are desexualized. Their interest in men has nothing to do with their sexual needs; it is purely mercenary.[27] "The idea of the venal susceptibility of females to male financial largesse" (Kelly 1992, 6) is a traditionally "important central assumption" of the jocular representation of marital and extramarital relations in Russian popular entertainment of the past. Every collection carries a number of jokes about women engaging in sex for money either professionally or whenever there is an opportunity, in and outside of marriage, whether young or old:

(2.98) "Mommy, I found a three-ruble bill on the road."

"Brush off your back, stupid. When I was your age, I kept finding twenty-five-ruble notes."

(O. Ivanova 1996, 488; for a variant, see V. Raskin 1985, 159)

(2.99) "I gave myself to him out of love. You wouldn't call 100 rubles money." (Private collection)

(2.100) She married him on the third day of acquaintance with his savings
account. (Kharkover 1993, 1: 5).

(2.101) Two friends are talking.
"Can you imagine, I get so carried away these days. Yesterday in
bed I gave my wife twenty five rubles."
"You don't say! And how did she react to that?"
"She took it." (Private collection)

(2.102) "Dad, what's love?"
"The Russians invented it so that they won't have to pay for it."
(Barsky 1994, 288)

(2.103) A women's motto: "Men are like linoleum. If you lay *[postelit']* them
well for the first time, you can walk on them for twenty years" (JFR
2/15/98)

In the post-Soviet period, prostitution jokes have a somewhat different
motif—lack of money—reflecting the impoverishment of the population
under the new turbulent economic conditions. The following joke is a reflection of the fact that the standard of living of once well-off professors,
male and female, has been sharply reduced:

(2.104) "Maria Ivanovna, how did it happen that you, a professor's daughter, a Ph.D. in science yourself, became a hard-currency prostitute?"
Maria Ivanovna shrugs her shoulders: "Just lucky, I guess." (Private collection; for an American version, see Fine 1981, 145.)

In the following joke, a male's lament about the impossibility of sup-
porting a family under the new, post-Communist conditions is a natural extension of the general conception of a female as a whore. As he has suspected
all along, his wife and his daughter would not long resist the temptation to
get paid for sex:

(2.105) A father of a family asks his wife: "Could you give yourself to some-
one for money?"
"Why talk such nonsense! I'm a decent woman."
"And what if it would be for a hundred dollars?"
"Well, you know, a hundred dollars is a lot. You would under-
stand me."
"And what about you, daughter, could you do it for money?"

"Never!" answers his daughter. "How could you, my father, think about me this way?"

"Okay, Okay," he cries out. "And for a hundred dollars could you?"

"Well, Daddy, you and Mom earn so little . . . Perhaps, you would understand me."

"O Lord!" The husband sits down on a chair and covers his head with his hands. "Two whores in the house, and we live like beggars!" (Barsky 1994, 290)

If an American one-liner "A man with money can't buy just any woman, but he has a wider choice" (Fine 1981, 139) assumes at least some incorruptible women, the message of Russian jokes is that *all* females are the same—ready to sell sex for money no matter how respectable they happen to be:

(2.106) They reported to the Queen of England that a Jew had claimed that practically every woman can be bought.

"And the English queen as well?"

"Yes, Your Majesty."

"Bring him in."

They brought the Jew to the queen, and she asked him: "Tell me, do you really believe that one can buy any woman?"

"Yes, Your Majesty."

"And even me, the Queen of England?"

"Yes, Your Majesty."

"And how much would you find me worth?"

"Seven thousand pounds."

"Is it possible that you can set a price of seven thousand pounds on the Queen of England herself?"

"Your Majesty," the Jew replied, "it seems to me that you're beginning to bargain." (Private collection)

In this joke, the message is conveniently put in the mouth of a folkloric Jew, here serving as a spokesman for Russian men. The joke suggests that the queen just pretends to be outraged by the idea of taking money, whereas, in fact, she shows her interest in the possibility.

Although the target of the following joke is the Russian parvenu of the 1990s, the so-called New Russian, what is taken for granted is that no matter how innocent and pure a woman may appear, she is corrupted, ready to sell herself to the highest bidder:

(2.107) A New Russian wakes up with a hangover after a drinking party and finds a girl—a miracle, a queen, "a genius of pure beauty" [from Pushkin's famous poem "To Kern"], pure innocence itself and enchantment—next to him in bed.

He tears himself off the sticky sheets, drags himself to the mirror, and examines himself. A crushed ugly face . . . His little piglet eyes . . . His low forehead, covered with pimples . . . His yellow teeth . . . His flabby paunch . . . His bowed legs . . .

He again looks at the girl and grabs his head in horror: "O Lord! What people will do for money!" (JFR 1/3/1998)

Stalking women is all right, for they just pretend that they do not appreciate it. It all depends how much a man can offer. In the following joke, the inexpensive Russian-made subcompact car, Zhiguli, in comparison with foreign-made Mercedeses and Jaguars driven by the newly rich, precipitates the woman's response: She finds the man's pursuit of her outrageous only because the man who does it does not have much to offer:

(2.108) Two girlfriends are talking: "Yesterday, as I was walking on the street, a Zhuguli stops nearby, and a stranger invites me for a ride. Can you imagine, such an insolent type!"

"What's so insolent about him?"

"O Lord! You should have seen his apartment!" (JFR 2/18/98)

A number of jokes target a specific group of women who are invariably portrayed as harlots—female secretaries. In contemporary Russian vernacular, they received a telling nickname—"secretute" [*sekretutka,* on the pattern of "prostitute," *prostitutka;* in Russian both words are used exclusively in reference to females]. This term (and the phenomenon it denotes) originated in the 1920s (Corten 1992, 128), when the mass involvement of women in the Soviet workforce began.

As in American culture observed by Legman (1968, 253), the modern Russian female office worker is subject to sexual exploitation. In the Soviet period, male jokelore reflected the real-life situation when many women were sexually exploited and a secretarial job often combined business duties and sexual services for the boss. Many jokes had the same motif: A secretary was primarily her employer's sexual plaything:

(2.109) A wife: "They say you have a new secretary. Is she young?"

Her husband: "Twenty years old."

"How's she at work?"

"More or less okay."

"Is she beautiful?"
"She's okay."
"And how does she dress?"
"Quickly." (Barsky 1994, 275)

(2.110) A secretary comes in one morning and finds the couch gone.
"Where is it?" she asks her boss.
"Oh, it takes up too much space. I ordered it thrown out."
"Does that mean that I'm fired too?" (Private collection)

(2.111) A young woman comes for a job interview. She admits that she doesn't
know how to type or take shorthand. Her handwriting is also illegible.
The manager asks her: "What business skills do you have then?"
"I never get pregnant." (I. Raskin 1995, 365)

(2.112) A young woman comes for a job interview. The director of the plant
explains her duties.
"And your salary will be three hundred rubles," he says.
"Are you joking?"
"And how much would you want?"
"Five hundred rubles. At the very least."
"Our chief engineer gets that much money."
"Then go and fuck your chief engineer." (Private collection)

(2.113) "Boss! I have good news and bad news for you."
"Tell me the good news first."
"You don't suffer from sterility." (I. Raskin 1995, 365; for an
American version involving a kindergarten teacher and a school
principal, see Fine 1981, 147).

The following joke reflects the occasional requirement that a secretary
serve more than one boss:

(2.114) Being a lover of both the director and his deputy, a secretary got
pregnant and was due to give birth shortly. To conceal this fact, it
was decided that she and the deputy would leave for a business trip
in another city and she would give birth there.
After a while, the director received the following telegram from
his deputy: "She's had twins STOP mine died STOP telegraph what
to do with yours STOP." (Smetanin and Donskaia 1992, 26)

Although sexual harassment is currently rampant (Powell and Palchikoff
1997, 52), policies to fight it have yet to make their way to Russia, where

any working woman is still considered a sex object for any man, as she was in the Soviet period:

> (2.115) "Comrade Director! The bookkeeper kissed me."
> "I'm very sorry, Comrade Ivanova, but our department is very big, and I can't do everything by myself." (Repina and Rostovtsev 1995, 90)

Old stereotypes (and attitudes) die hard. The advance of the market economy has been especially traumatic for women. In 1993 they constituted up to 73 percent of the unemployed (cited in Meshkova 1997, 82). Hiring a secretary still means getting on-the-job sexual services. This old tradition has become an open secret today. American journalist Vanora Bennett (Dec. 6, A10) reports from Russia: "No one raises an eyebrow at job ads for women stipulating that only young need apply, and even then only those who're leggy, scantily clad and *bez kompleksov*—without hang-ups, [and] willing to have sex with the boss. Women who prefer to work at their work places must specify *bez intima*—without intimacy—and face the consequences." Many jokes about the so-called New Russians testify to the longevity of this traditional exploitation:

> (2.116) They ask a New Russian, "What's the difference between a good female secretary and a very good one?"
> "It's very simple," he says. "A good secretary every morning says 'Good morning, boss!' And a very good one tenderly whispers in your ear: 'It's already morning, boss.'" (Erokaev 1997, 85)

> (2.117) Two New Russians meet on a beach.
> "What's going on? Are you going to swim in the middle of a working day? What about your business?"
> "Well, buddy, I'm here on a business matter."
> "What kind?"
> "I'm choosing a new secretary." (Private collection)

(Cf. an American joke about female stenographers: "Why did your sister lose her job as a stenographer?" "Her boss was so bowlegged she fell through his lap"; Meiers and Knapp 1986, 536.)

Jokelore reveals another side of this ugly practice—the complacency of husbands regarding the sexual exploitation of their wives on the job:

> (2.118) A terribly jealous man looks at his young wife as she undresses and suddenly notices blue spots on her thigh.

"And who has been feeling you over?" he shouts, beside himself.
"My director," she answers, "before giving me a raise."
"It's okay if it was that way," says the jealous man, quieting down.
"Well, I thought some hoodlum molested you in the subway." (Kulikov 1997, 305)

Almost every collection of jokes published in recent years in Russia includes the same joke in which a woman who is paid for her sexual services is cheated and robbed.

(2.119)   A Frenchman, an Englishman, an American, and a Russian discuss how to bring a woman to ecstasy.
The Frenchman tells about his lovemaking secrets, an Englishman about the signs of devotion he bestows on his woman, an American about expensive gifts.
A Russian says: "It's much simpler for me. I take a woman off the streets, give her a three-ruble bill, take her to a dark hallway, fuck her, and snatch the three-ruble bill away from her. And here she reaches her ecstasy!" (Popovsky 1985, 431; for versions, see Anon. 1994, 262–263, 275)

It is clear that while the word "ecstasy" in the punch line is used ironically, it correctly describes the feeling of the male protagonist and the tellers of this joke about what constitutes total triumph over a woman. This joke is an example of not only reproducing the status quo but also functioning as an instrument for naturalizing and normalizing it; it reassures men that women, whether they want it or not, accept a status that is defined for them by men.

All this contempt for women notwithstanding, in some items another spectrum of feelings toward women can be sensed—that of fear and mortal dread, based in part on a folk script about emasculating power of women (cf. in Andalusian folklore, Brandes 1980).

(2.120)   Question to Armenian Radio:
"Is it true that if a man drinks imported beer preserved with female hormones, he can't get it up?"
"He can but it'll stick . . . inward" (JFR 2/21/98)

Commenting on the cult of mother in Russian folk cultures—complete with reference to the whole country *[Rossia-mat']*, to its nursing Mother Earth *[zemlia-matushka kormilitsa]*, and its rivers [Mother Volga in particular; *Volga-matushka*], American writer Francine du Plessix Gray (1990, 115) notes, citing American Slavist Joanna Hubbs's study, *Mother Russia* (1988), that

> Yet there are few cultures in which sentiment of heterosexual love, on men's part, has been so admixed with dread. The very word for "passion," *strast'*, also means "horror, terror"; men's apprehension of women, and the exacerbated tension between sexes particular to the Russian heritage, remains explicit in the lines of the popular song "*Ochi Chernye,*" "Dark Eyes": "*kak liubliu ia vas, kak boius' ia vas,*" "How I love you, how I fear you." This blend of awe and aversion may well be rooted in an archaic terror of the forceful female's sexual powers, a terror which the Orthodox church fully exploited when Christianity finally came to Russia in the tenth century.

This unconscious perception of women as charged with mystical power is clearly expressed in the ambivalent Russian males' attitude toward sex. Russian perception seems to consider regular intercourse as an immoral abnormality: "Here the desire is built on the notion that it is forbidden to do it, and the more it is forbidden the more one wants to do it," Andrey Sinyavsky (Abram Tertz 1980, 20–21) writes. "Anatomy is elementary. . . . Something of a black mass is always present in a sexual act. The enjoyment one gets with it is deeper and more horrific than with usual bodily pleasures. In a great degree it is based on the fact that you are engaged in a sacrilegious act."

In the following joke, the female world is presented as enviable, full of luxuries a man can't even dream of, and yet ultimately dangerous. To step into this world means to wander on unknown, treacherous, and emasculating territory.

(2.121) During a flight, a man wants urgently to use the toilet. The trouble is that every time he approaches the men's room, it's occupied. He sits in his seat and nervously taps with his foot. The flight attendant takes pity on him and advises him to go to the ladies' room. She warns him, however, not to push buttons marked "WW," "HA," "TP," and "ATE."

The man goes to the room, does his business, and, understandably, can't resist pushing the buttons. With caution, he pushes the first button—"WW"—and his behind gets washed over with warm water.

"Well, well, you don't say, damn broads!" he thinks with delight.

Burning with curiosity, he pushes the "HA" button, and a light stream of hot air dries his buttocks. "Wonderful!" the man thinks.

The "TP" button powders his behind with talcum. Well, naturally, he can't resist pushing the last button—"ATE."

He comes to his senses in a hospital. Scared, he calls the nurse. When she comes, he asks: "What's happened to me? I remember only that I used the plane's ladies room for my needs. Then I don't remember anything."

The nurse tells him: "Of course, everything was all right until you hit the ATE button—the one that performs automatic tampon extraction. Your member is under your pillow." (JFR 1/7/1998)

Even in a different folkloric genre—not "for men only" but for mixed company—the woman, customarily showered with compliments, still appears as an ambivalently dangerous creature, the source of uncertainty, horror, and destruction. The following toast, raised by males, suggests that danger for men is an inalienable part of what constitutes a woman; the suffering she causes is also in the nature of the "beast":

(2.122) Once a man appeared before God and asked Him to create a woman. God took a few sunbeams, the moon's pensive melancholy, the chamois' caressing look, the fallow-deer's trepidation, the dove's docility, the swan's beauty, the down's tenderness, the air's lightness, the water's freshness. In order not to make her too sweet, he added the wind's inconstancy, the magpie's chatter, the clouds' fearfulness, and all the horrors of thunder and lightning. He mixed them all. From this mixture, a beautiful woman has emerged. God inspired life in her, gave her to a man, and said: "Take her and suffer! So, let us drink to this beautiful mixture." (O. Ivanova 1994, 467)

CHAPTER 3

"You Can't Do It to All the Women in the World But You Have to Try": The Male Image in Russian Jokelore

The Male as Sexual Predator

The antithetical character of sexual attitudes toward males and females is especially evident in jokes celebrating men's sexual looseness. Many Russian jokes apply a double standard:

(3.1)   A husband says to his wife: "Imagine this situation: You come home, and here I'm lying with a gal in bed. . . ."

His wife: "Imagine this situation: you come home, and here *I* am lying with a guy in bed. . . ."

"Well, no way! Don't confuse a situation with sluttish behavior [*bliadstvo*]!" (O. Ivanova 1996, 506)

Russian folklore has a long tradition of treatment of male sexual indiscretion as forgivable. In one of Afanasiev's (1991, 57) *Secret Tales*, "A Kind Father," in the dark of the night an incestuous act is committed by mistake in a peasant hut. Learning about it in the morning, the father reacts rather nonchalantly, making it clear that it is his daughter's sexuality that got her in trouble in the first place, not his own lack of self-restraint.

While "slut" [*bliad'*], an epithet for a loose woman, invariably carries negative connotations, a semantically comparable word "womanizer" [*babnik*] lacks the disparagement of the word *bliad'*. Moreover, *babnik* often sounds like a compliment. Such treatment of the word has become so widespread that a recent popular song of the same name glorifies the women chaser because his excuse is dear to a woman's heart: It is impossible not to pursue woman after woman, for "so many beautiful ones are around." It is in the spirit of this cultural conditioning that a man's claim to fame as a womanizer can be understood:

(3.2) Ia na kar'eru, byt i veshchi   I didn't spend much thought and effort
      Ne tratil myslei i trudov,   On my career, on everyday living, on
                                             things.
      ia ochen' bab liubil i   I loved all sorts of women very much,
      zhenshchin,
      a takzhe devushek i vdov.   And also girls and widows. (Guberman
                                             1978, 159).

It is not surprising, then, that while Russian jokes presuppose and ridicule every woman's lewdness, they promote and glorify male promiscuity. A contemporary Russian saying underscores the desirability of a man's animal nature and adds the terms well known in the West: "A man should be mean, stinky, and hairy, and a woman knocked up and barefoot in the kitchen" (Elistratov 1994, 256).

Citing a 1994 *Izvestiia* survey, which showed that every other Russian man openly admitted to cheating on his wife, Lynn Visson (1998, 124) concludes that "for Russian men infidelity is the rule rather than exception." Male promiscuity has become such a part of social conditioning that at least some women buy into this male stereotype and consider it attractive. As one of my Russian female informants put it, for her "a true man should smell of tobacco, wine, and the perfume of another woman." Similar qualities are called for in the following toast, composed by a woman and offered for women to make:

(3.3) "To our men, who have a bit of Casanova in them, who are steadfast and durable, elegant and seductive, rich and loving women." (Starinskaia 1996, 175).

The following toast relies on two readings of the Russian word *postoianstvo*, "constancy" and "fidelity," for its comic effect:

(3.4) An old woman goes across a square and sees a young man sitting with a blonde. She goes there the next day and sees the same young man, but with a brunette. Next day, she sees him with a red-haired woman. Let's drink to men's constancy. For, while the women are different every time, he's one and the same. (Starinskaia 1996, 174)

While this toast is somewhat ambiguous (there is a hint of disapproval of a man's promiscuous behavior), the point is made from an old (read: wise) woman's vantage that women have to cherish men as they are; their infidelity is taken for granted.

All transgressions that are on a taboo list for a female are on the "okay" list for a Russian male. Interest in copulation with a female is elevated to a universal law and is an unquestionable, almost imperative mode of male behavior ("the primacy of coitus," as Legman [1968, 236] defines one of the main principles of male jokes). As in other cultures, the Russian man takes pride in the number of women he has seduced as quickly as possible. Faithful to this tradition, the Russian poet Sergey Esenin boasted drunkenly in public that he had three thousand women (cited in Popovsky 1985, 426).

For a Russian man, it is not only all right to be promiscuous; it is the ultimate sign of his masculinity. He considers his promiscuity praiseworthy, whether he is single or married:

(3.5)   "What does a real man do every morning?"
        "He gets up, washes, dresses, and heads for home." (Private collection)

In the following joke, it is not a matter of chance that the man who is faithful to his wife speaks in a "thin voice"; the teller suggests that he acts in an "unmanly" way because he lacks male hormones:

(3.6)   Sailors are gathered on a battleship to hear a lecture on morals: "Unfortunately, spousal infidelity is still a quite frequent phenomenon. According to sociological data, among those who most often cheat on their wives are actors, then sportsmen, and then sailors. You know the reasons well: long separations, constant stress . . . Any questions?"
        "Excuse me," a thin voice pipes up, "I don't know why sailors are on this list. In the thirty years I've been in the navy I have never cheated on my wife."
        And a deep bass comes from the back row: "It's because of such good-for-nothing men like you that the navy lags in third place!" (Private collection)

Not even his poor health or a wife's pregnancy should prevent a man from lovemaking:

(3.7)   A question to Armenian Radio:
        "Can a man with a heart condition make love to a woman?"

Answer: "He can if he smears her nipples with nitroglycerin."
(Private collection)

(3.8)   "How long can a man keep making love to a woman?"
"Until the fetus begins biting it." (Milgram 1985, 6)

The ideal young man ought to be engaged in sexual pursuit all the time. If
he does not obey his sexual drive, he ill serves women, who are always hungry for him.

(3.9)   At a medical lecture the speaker was saying: "A man who wants to,
but is unable, is called 'impotent.' A man who is able but doesn't
want to is called—"
An angry female voice from the audience screamed out "A bastard!" (Draitser 1980, 39).

"I think that a genuine impotent is the kind of man who can do it, but does-
n't want to," writes Iosif Raskin (1995, 228), who includes the following in
his collection:

(3.10)   After making love to all the chickens in a hen house, a young cockerel lies in the dust, his eyes rolling and his wings spread. A crow
flies down from a tree to feast on the cockerel's motionless body. A
turkey says to the cockerel with a air of superiority: "So, you
fucked yourself to death finally, didn't you? And that's it—you've
croaked."
The cockerel opens one eye and hisses angrily: "Get out of the
way, dummy! You'll alert the crow." (Raskin 1995, 318)

The moral of the following joke, rendered in a form of a fable, is that a
man has to be tireless in pursuing sexual pleasure.

(3.11)   One night a sultan called his eunuch: "Bring me my first wife."
The eunuch brought her in. Some time later, the sultan called
him again:
"Bring me the second one."
Again the eunuch did as ordered. The sultan called for the
third, fifth . . . the tenth wife. In short, he made the poor eunuch
run his head off. Just before dawn he called him again: "Bring me
the last one."
"Sultan," the eunuch said. "You're going to die soon."
"What from?"

"From exhaustion. I'm worn out from running after your wives all night long. And you're banging them like a monkey. Your body won't tolerate such a load."

"Remember," the sultan replied. "One can die from a foolish running around, but not from a favorite activity." (JFR 2/22/98)

A quote from the proletarian writer Nikolai Ostrovsky, one that every schoolchild learned by heart, runs: "Life is given to you only once, and you have to live it in such a way that when dying you can tell yourself: 'My whole life was devoted to the happiness of humanity.'" Here is a take-off:

(3.12) Life is given to you only once, and you have to live it in such a way that every baby you encounter could greet you with: "Hi, Daddy!" (Private collection)

In Erofeev's (1997, 87) "Moscow Stations," considered an encyclopedia of contemporary Russian life, a character called the Decembrist claims that "thirty of the worst women *[baba]* is better than one, though [she is] the very best one." Even if a man must pay a high price for it, sexual indiscretion is still praiseworthy:

(3.13) A performer has not shown up for a concert. The theater director calls him up and asks: "What's with you?"

"I've got the flu."

"At your age, young man, I only got sick with the clap." (I. Raskin 1995, 371).

(3.14) "Which is the better way of dying: from syphilis or dysentery?"

"It's better to die a real man than a shitter." (Kulikov 1993, 361)

According to a well-known saying, "You can't fuck all the women of the world but you have to try" (Iliiasov 1994, 189). As a popular toast goes, "To the question 'which does he love—brunettes or blondes?' the answer should be: 'Yes!!!' So, let's drink to real men!" (O. Ivanova 1994, 470). The following joke is a fantastic extension of this principle:

(3.15) A mermaid with a little newborn in her arms swims up to a steamship docked in the harbor and shouts up to the men on board: "Would you please call deep-sea diver Kolya?" (Private collection)

Another joke suggests that when he has the chance to show his manhood, a real man should not be put off by the absence of a woman:

(3.16) "How to achieve superconductivity?"
"By screwing a telephone pole until the telephone operator gets pregnant." (Milgram 1985, 8).

Womanizing is justified as part and parcel of being male, as the Old Testament context of the following item suggests:

(3.17) Moses goes off to talk to God. He is away for a long time. Finally he comes back. People gather around him: "Well, how did it go?"
"I have good news and bad news," Moses says. "The good news is that we struck a bargain on ten commandments. The bad news is that fornication is one of them." (JFR 3/4/98)

If a man is accused of philandering, it is the woman's fault:

(3.18) A young man comes to the office of a female sex consultant.
"Help me, Doctor, my wife is sore at me."
"What's the reason?"
"You know, I'm leaving the house heading to work in the morning, and the neighbor woman asks: 'Kolya, are you going to work or what?' I hop into her bed.
"I get to the factory, and the director's secretary says: 'Are you going straight to your shop or what?' Well, I do it with her. . . . In my shop, there are three beautiful interns. They ask me: 'Are you going over to your machine or what?' Well, I do it with them. . . . When I come home, I do it again with my wife."
The female sex consultant: "Should I give you my prescription right away or what?" (Repina and Rostovtsev 1995, 22: 50)

(3.19) A woman is like a parachute: At any given moment she can refuse you. That's why you have to have a spare. (Private collection)

There are some other justifications for womanizing:

(3.20) S chuzhoi zhenoi delia krovat',
greshu,
No cherv' somnen'ia glozhet moiu dushu:
Ved' esli blizhnemu ia otkazhu,
Druguiu zapoved' narushu.

Sharing a bed with somebody else's wife, I sin.
But a worm of doubt eats my soul:
After all, if I refuse to oblige a fellow human being
I'll break another commandment. (JFR 3/19/98)

(3.21) Esli ty liubov' bol'shuiu   If, no matter how you've tried,
          Otyskat' ne mozhesh',   You can't find a great love
          To naidi sebe skoree   Then find yourself quickly
          Mnogo malen'kikh liuboei   Many little loves. (JFR 3/19/98)

A few jokes express men's weariness with the cultural imperative of women-chasing behavior:

(3.23) "Lady, may I introduce myself?
        "No, you can't."
        "Well, then, thank God!" (JFR 3/19/98)

A take-off of Pushkin's line "The less we love a woman, the more she likes us" runs:

(3.24) "The less we love girls, the more time we have for sleep." (JFR 2/21/98)

(3.25) One man says to another: "Can you imagine, I've recently become impotent, and it turns out that the world is so interesting: there are theaters, cinema, circus, parks . . ." (JFR 1/30/98)

Male Camaraderie and Alcohol

A number of jokes contrast solidarity among men with its absence among women:

(3.26) A conversation about what most pleases a woman. A man who considers himself an expert on the female heart says: "Her own beauty."
        "No," says a beautiful woman. "The ugliness of her girlfriend." (Private collection)

(3.27) One woman says to another: Why are you in such a bad mood? Keep your chin up . . . and now the other one." (Private collection)

How are relationships among Russian males shaped by their relationship to females? Many observers note that Russian men esteem male friends more highly than other cultures do, usually avoiding deep intimacy with women—not just sexual, but also spiritual and emotional. An old Russian saying "An old friend is better than two new friends" [*Staryi drug luchshe novykh dvukh*] now reads: "An old friend is better than two *girl*friends"

[Staryi drug luchshe dvukh podrug] (JFR 2/9/98). Contemporary Russian males tend to gather in all-male groups not only for spectator sports, hunting, and fishing, as their Western counterparts do, but for many other purposes. Lynn Visson (1998, 171) concludes that in Russia "a male friend is a brother, a drinking companion, a soulmate and a bulwark against the outside world."

Drinking with a friend is of a paramount importance to a Russian. The popular understanding that having enough to drink constitutes total bliss is ages old. (On drinking in Russian history, see White 1996, 5–23). In the folk mind, not drinking means missing the first of the two most important things that life has to offer.

(3.28) Akh, kak bystro vpered   Ah, how quickly
        Vremia katitsia!   Time flies forward!
        Kto ne p'et, ne ebet,   One who doesn't drink and doesn't fuck
        Tot spokhvatitsia!   Will live to regret it. (Starshinov 1992b,
                                    152)

It is worth noting that the root of the Russian word denoting extreme enjoyment, ecstasy, rapture, and thrill—*upoenie*—is "to drink" *[pit']*. Vladimir, a grand prince, in the tenth century acknowledged that "Drinking is the joy of the Russes, we cannot do without it" (quoted in White 1996, 3). It follows that a government that sets up artificial obstacles to drinking is playing with fire. In fact, limitations on alcohol sales have invariably created social tensions that find some relief in popular humor. The following chastushka was widely circulated in 1985 when, in the course of fighting widespread alcoholism in the Soviet Union, state prices for a bottle of vodka were raised. (The reference to Poland invokes the confrontation of the Polish Communist regime by the workers' Solidarity movement in 1980–1981.)

(3.29) Bylo shest', a stalo vosem',   It was six rubles, it became eight,
        Vse ravno my pit' ne brosim.   We won't stop drinking, don't you wait.
        Nu, a esli budet bol'she,   And if it costs even more,
        Budet takzhe, kak i v Pol'she.   It will get as bad as in Poland, to be
                                         sure.

        Esli stanet dvadtsat' piat',   If it costs all twenty-five,
        Zimnii budem brat' opiat'.   We'll storm the Winter Palace again.
                                         (Private collection)

This chastushka is a perfect example of the validity of studying popular humor as a gauge of public opinion. The jocular threat of mass revolt was actually realized. Prompted by antialcoholic measures under Gorbachev, "wine" riots did take place in Perm, Cheliabinck, and Moscow (White 1996, 166). Ironically, the historic storming of the Winter Palace was marked by riots of drunken soldiers (18).

Alcohol, because of its centrality in Russian life, has long been associated with the Russians. Russian fairy tales customarily end with a phrase indicating that the story told is a product of sheer fantasy; it has no resemblance to reality. The tale is no more plausible than the story of a Russian man who has alcohol but can't drink it: "And I was there, with wine and beer, it all poured down my mustache, none got into my mouth." There is a modern joke, a take-off on fishing tales, usually told by men:

(3.30) "My husband caught a fish th-a-a-t big!"
        "And mine went on a fishing trip and brought back an unopened bottle of vodka!" (Private collection)

In the paradoxical world of Russian drinkers, excess of alcohol is a norm:

(3.31) What kind of a drinking bout was it if you're not ashamed of it the next day!" (JFR 3/9/98)

(3.32) The problem with drinking is that no matter how much you drink, you'll get sober anyway." [skol'ko ni pei, vse ravno protrezveesh'] (JFR 2/21/98)

(3.33) One should get three bottles at once—so that it won't be necessary to run after the second one. (Private collection)

Russians have long perceived themselves as having a great capacity for drinking; it is a matter of pride of sorts. The narrator of Erofeev's "Moscow Stations" (1997) distinguishes what is Russia and what is not: "On one side of the border they speak Russian and drink more, on the other they drink less and they don't speak Russian" (100). The Russians' own jokelore has always ranked them as the world greatest drinkers. (It is noteworthy that there is no Russian joke involving real competitors—the Irish or the Scots. Those who do feature in international alcoholic competitions are usually defeated without much effort.)

(3.34) A drinking competition is in progress among our uncle Vassya, an American, and a Frenchman.
        The first drinker is the American. He drinks whiskey by the glass. He drinks five of them, twenty—and he folds. While they are

straightening out the American, our uncle Vassya is entertaining himself with red wine.

Then the Frenchman drinks. He drinks cognac by the shot. He drinks ten of them, thirty—and he folds.

While they are straightening out the Frenchman, our uncle Vassya is entertaining himself with red wine.

The last one is our famous uncle Vassya. He drinks pure spirits by the ladle. He drinks 20 of them, 50, 100—and it folds.

While they are straightening out the ladle, our uncle Vassya is entertaining himself with red wine. (Nikulin 1997, 324–325)

(3.35) An Italian in Russia makes entries in his journal: "Yesterday I was drinking with the Russians. I almost died. . . . From early morning, together with the Russians, I've been taking the hair of the dog that bit me. It would be better if I had died yesterday. . . ." (A variant of this joke involves an American pilot; JFR 2/27/98)

In view of this association of "Russian" with alcohol, it is understandable that, in contemporary slang, a newly manufactured product—an alcoholic beverage in a small sealed plastic container—is nicknamed "Russian yogurt." A bottle of vodka offered as a payment is perceived by the accepting party as having much higher value that its nominal cost; vodka is often regarded as "liquid currency" (a take-off on the term "hard currency"). It also has a symbolic value, an extension of a friendly hand. A bottle of vodka can get many jobs done. ("If a mechanic doesn't get a bottle, the elevator stays broken;" Pesmen 1995, 70). In this regard "bottle" is a magic word:

(3.36) In the Chamber of Measurements, a bottle of Russian vodka is guarded as a standard of the unit of measurement of work and pay. (JFR 1/1/98)

Russian drinkers have long created their own idiosyncratic world, an anti-world of sorts that defies common sense and physiological facts. Despite medical evidence to the contrary, they strongly believe in the miraculous healing qualities of vodka. This is not unlike the Irish belief in the numerous healing attributes of whiskey (the English rendition of the Irish word denoting *aqua vitae*).[1] Vodka is widely used for curing all sorts of ailments—from chills (as a popular rhyme has it: "Our little hands are getting cold, our little feet are getting cold—isn't it time for us to have a drink?" *[Ruchki ziabnut, nozhki ziabnut, ne pora li nam deriabnut'?]*, headaches, and upset stomach to depression and other psychological problems when one's "soul aches" *[dusha bolit]*. Some Russians even believe that vodka protects them from the effects of radiation (Pesmen 1995, 72). "Have a drink and everything will go away" *[Vypei—i vse proidet!]* is the popular Russian prescription.

> (3.37) It's late autumn and cold. A shabby alcoholic comes into a bar and asks for a shot of vodka as the hair of the dog that bit him. The bartender says:
> "Instead of drinking all the time, you'd better buy yourself new shoes."
> "What for? Health's more important."[2]

Although it has been established that alcohol intake impedes mental processes, dulls the mind, this jokelore finds not only that it is all right to drink and do business, as the Russian proverb has it ["Drink but keep your wits for business!" *Pei da delo pazumei*], but even beneficial in solving a complicated problem: "You won't figure it out without half a liter of vodka" *[bes pollitra ne razbereshsia]*. This saying may be an exercise in slight exaggeration but it is not ironic: in real life a Russian may respond to a problem with an offer to his companion: "Let's have a drink and put our minds together" *[Davai vyp'em i obmozguem eto delo]*. A student of the Moscow Higher Technological Institute (MVTU) posted the following slogan on the Internet: "Without enough to drink, it's difficult to study" (JFR 2/8/98).

By the same token, a drinking man has his own sense of morality, of what constitutes good and evil, what is humane and inhumane. Consider an item from a widely popular joke series about the Civil War hero Vasily Ivanovich Chapaev:

> (3.38) Chapaev asks his orderly Petka:
> "Well, have you already interrogated the captured White Army officer?"
> "Yes, but he isn't talking."
> "Well, have you beaten him with a ramrod?'
> "And how! But he still doesn't talk.'
> "And have you driven needles under his nails?"
> "We have. Still not a word from him."
> "Hm. . . . And have you tried making him properly drunk, and in the morning denying him an opportunity to take a hair of the dog that bit him. *[opokhmelit'sia]?*"
> "What's with you, Vasily Ivanovich? After all, are we beasts?"
> (Dezhnov 1993, 7)

Alcohol is perceived as a soothing wonder drink that helps to balance the Russian view of life. Like *aqua vitae* in Russian fairy tales, it can restore a man who is on the verge of total collapse:

(3.39) He is in deep trouble. His wife has left him for her lover, his teenage daughter has been knocked up, and he has lost his job. Grieving, he decides to hang himself. He takes a rope and climbs on a stool. And at this moment his eye catches a bottle of vodka.

"I'm going to die anyway. Why should a good product be wasted?"

He pours himself a glass of vodka and drinks it. Then he looks at the rope, looks at the bottle, and pours himself another glass. Without much thought he finishes off the whole bottle. He looks around him, sighs and says to himself:

"Well, it looks like my life has pulled itself together." (JFR 2/11/98)

The soul-healing qualities ascribed to drinking and celebrated in jokes explain the slow progress of the support groups recently set up on the pattern of Alcoholics Anonymous. These programs were allowed to operate in Russia only after long resistance; in 1990 some 200 people attended meetings in Moscow (White 1996, 18), a drop in a bucket for a city with tens of thousands of alcoholics.

The Drinking Ritual

For a Russian not only is alcohol important, but the rituals around drinking are, the most salient of which is drinking in company. Russians distinguish between an alcoholic and a "normal" drinker not on the grounds of frequency and amount of alcohol consumption, but on whether he drinks alone or in company. The lonely drinker is regarded as "truly alcoholic," a pitiable and lost person who has reached a point of no return. American anthropologist Dale Pesmen (1995, 67), who spent some time in a Siberian city, notes: "Drinking is inherently *with others*. I was repeatedly told how offensive it would be to enter a room, pour oneself a drink and not offer one to others present."

Having a conversation, not necessarily profound, with a drinking companion is of utmost importance to the ritual:

(3.40) Two drunks approach an intellectual who has come into a store to buy cigarettes: "Give us a ruble!"

Trying to get rid of them, the man gives them the money and is about to leave the store when the drunks, after splitting a bottle of vodka in thirds, hand him a glass with his share: "Cheers!"

The intellectual swallows the drink and again tries to leave the store only to be grabbed by the drunks:

"Where do you think you're going? And what about shooting the breeze?" (In the original, foul language is used: "*A popizdet?*"; from *pizda* (cunt). For a discussion of this word usage, see chapter 2)

This joke, first recorded in the mid-1960s, became a classic and its punch line became a popular saying; it denotes the need to have someone present merely to have a talk, no matter how trivial it may be. Pesmen (1995, 67) records one Russian's objection to drinking without toasting: "What, now we're drinking silently, like animals?" Since having vodka and a drinking companion provides a Russian drinker with everything that truly matters to him, the locale of the following joke is a case in point:

(3.41)   An American, a Frenchman, and a Russian find themselves on a desert island. They see an ancient bottle in the water, open it, and a genie emerges:

"I'll fulfill two wishes for each of you."

The American: "I want a million dollars and a safe return home."

"Done!" the genie says.

The Frenchman: "Give me a beautiful woman and take me to Paris with her."

"Done!" the genie says.

The Russian scratches the back of his head and says: "Well, I've had good company. Gimme a case of vodka and bring the fellows back." (Kharkover 1993, 3: 40; for another version of this joke, see Pesmen 1995, 72)

In other words, the Russian's sense of home is wherever there is enough drink and company. There is no limit to a drinking man's efforts to find companionship:

(3.42)   A father comes home and sees his aging daughter sitting with a dildo in her hand. "What's this?!"

"Dad, I've lost hope! . . . Here, I bought it in a sex shop."

Next day she comes home and finds her father sitting in the kitchen at a table on which there is an open bottle of vodka and that dildo.

"Dad, what are you doing?"

"Well, don't you get it? . . . I'm having a drink with my son-in-law."

The following item shows what constitutes a truly global catastrophe for a drinking Russian:

(3.43) One drunk asks another: "What is the nitrogen bomb all about?"
"Imagine that in the kitchen faucet it's not water that's running but vodka."
"So?"
"And imagine that, instead of water, all the creeks and rivers are vodka. And the ocean is nothing but vodka."
"So, what's your point?"
"What, don't you get it? There's vodka all around, and there's nobody to drink it with."

Note that the teller assumes that the explosion of the bomb would render all his potential drinking companions dead but not himself. The alcohol makes him feel invincible, which corresponds to the Russian saying "To a drunk, the sea is just knee-deep" *[P'ianomu more po koleno]*. (Vladimir Dahl [1984, 2: 247] registered a variant of this saying with an addendum that shows more realistic attitude toward the drunk's true capabilities: "To a drunk, the sea is just knee-deep, but a puddle is up to his ears [. . . *a luzha po uzhi].*" But this is seldom heard today.)

Other jokes often suggest that having alcohol and a boon companion not only gives a Russian man everything he wants from life but represents the source of his ability to withstand any of life's hardships. In the following item, it is clear that Ivan is able to endure discomfort because he is supplied with both alcohol and company to drink it with:

(3.44) The Japanese invented a freezer that could bring the temperature to minus 1000 degrees Celsius [approx. minus 1970 Fahrenheit]. They announced a prize: Whoever remained in the freezer the longest would be given the island of Hokkaido.
A Frenchman tried first and asked that a woman and a case of wine accompany him. But they didn't last more than a minute when the temperature dropped below 200 degrees.
Then an Englishman tried. He sat with a woman and a case of whisky until the temperature read minus 300 degrees.
The only other contender was Ivan, very drunk. He said to the Japanese: "Give me a milk-can of moonshine and bring in my buddy."
They gave him what he asked for. They shut both men in the freezer and watched the thermometer; the temperature dropped below the limit in an hour. One little Japanese [in Russian: *iapioshka*

both derogatory and condescending] said to another: "Well, let's take these 'icicles' out. They're probably already dead."

The other little Japanese opened the freezer and saw the two friends sitting opposite each other, drinking moonshine.

Suddenly Ivan bashed the Japanese over his head and asked his buddy: "Did I do the right thing?"

"Of course you did the right thing. It's cold in here, and he goes and opens the door." (Draitser 1998, 172)[3]

The Sociology of Drinking

For a Russian, drinking in the company of other men (women are usually excluded) creates a sacred communion among them; it is a sign of trust and spiritual intimacy. One man may refer to another as "our own" *[svoi]* on the grounds that they got drunk together at least once. A Russian saying about a man who can be trusted is "he is tested by pure spirits" *[proverennyi na chistom spirte]*. This means that since they drank together, in a state of intoxication when alcohol "unties tongues" *[razviazyvaet iazyki]*, it was proven that they have nothing to hide from each other. A Russian proverb collected by Dahl (1984, 2: 244) points to drinking as the one and only way of socializing: "Drunkenness accepts you into a company, and no one knows a teetotaler" *[Khmel' v kompaniiu prinimaet, a nep'iushchego nikto ne znaet]*."

By the same token, a man who declines a drink is an object of suspicion. For a Russian, "sober" often means "having in mind some secret designs" *[on trezvyi, sebe na ume]*. A "nondrinking man evokes suspicion on principle" (JFR 3/28/98). One of the reasons for Russian popular resentment toward Jews is that, according to the stereotype,[4] they are teetotalers, and thus cannot be trusted. Pesmen (1995, 72) observes that "in Omsk, if a person leaves a party early or refuses to drink, he may be asked if he is Russian or not." For a Russian the very offer to drink together indicates that friendship is extended.

A man's right to drink in the company of other men finds many defenders on sociological and cultural anthropological grounds. Russian sociologist Vladimir Shlapentokh (1984, 226) believes that, in the Soviet period, drinking with buddies was a Russian man's response to the oppressive regime and an attempt to built a support system for himself: "The importance of a steady drinking companion in the lives of many Soviet men, simple workers and peasants, is so great because drinking in Soviet society is not always simply for the consumption of alcohol. More important, drinking is a social event in which people can release themselves from various fears and troubles and pour out their souls. In fact, in many cases, drinking is an act with strong political overtones, for it involves the release of frustration generated by the strictures of Soviet life. . . ." Pesmen (1995) also notes: "Part of *sitting* and *resting* [while drinking] is feeling that you are together against a greater power, the boss, the System, Fate. *Sitting* must simultaneously be outside and in defiance of contexts of power relations" (1995, 73).[5]

This passive way of relieving frustrations helped the Communist regime to maintain its power for such a long period. The fact that Soviet leaders, from Stalin through Brezhnev, saw to it that inexpensive vodka was available in stores is a sign of their understanding that, despite the obvious negative impact of intoxication on workers' productivity, by providing supplies for alcohol relief they safeguarded themselves against much greater problems.

Elistratov's (1994, 656) treatment of the Russians as the last people of carnival culture adds a dimension of cultural history to the widely recognized phenomenon of Russian drinking:

> One cannot deny that in our time the carnival became part of everyday life *[bytovizirovan]* in the sense that, in comparison with the carnival of Rabelais' time, it is more dispersed in space and time, in everyday life. The modern popular culture of laughter is discrete. It is separated in hundreds of genres of what can be called unofficial socializing. This is especially characteristic for Russia with its unregulated etiquette of socializing in the lower social stratum *[nepredpisannost' etiketa nizovogo obshcheniia]*. Modern Russia knows genres purely medieval in their spirit which the West has long forgotten. Let's take, for example, genres of drinking . . . and brawls with their ramified argot poetics.

In Elistratov's view, "Russian culture of the socially lower stratum preserves in itself a great many medieval traits, and, on the whole, a Russian man preserves a medieval mentality" (656). He compares the elaborate ritual of contemporary Russian drinkers and the medieval "symposium." Every phase of this ritual is strictly observed and tagged with a memorable and colorful nickname or phrase. For example, "recovering money for empty bottles is called 'Operation Crystal,' . . . a way of splitting a bottle is 'by gurgles' *[po bul'kam]*; a mandated toasting; an instruction to drink strictly in line and not to hold up the rest is called 'sticking to the rules' *[sobliudat' reglament]*; the etiquette of having snacks after drinks, as in 'I'm not having a snack after the first shot' *[posle pervoi ne zakusyvaiu]*; the regulating of the time period between alcohol intakes, as in 'Let's have a short break between the first and second shots' *[mezhdu pervoi i vtoroi promezhutok nebol'shoi]*, etc." (Elistartov 1994, 658).[6]

Elistratov concedes, however, that ubiquitous drinking on the streets and often in unsanitary conditions may seem "swinishness to a civilized man," but he tends to qualify it as "purely carnival, purely medieval swinishness." He enlists the writer Ivan Bunin in his camp of admirers of the Russian thirst for carnival life. In his *Life of Arseniev,* Bunin writes:

> In my time, Russia lived an unusually wide and busy life; the number of working people, healthy and strong, kept growing. However, hasn't the age-old Russian dream about the fairy-tale milky rivers, about freedom with no constraints, about a holiday, been one of the most basic reasons for Russian revolutionary character? And what is a Russian protester, a mutineer, a revolutionary in general, always ridiculously estranged from reality and contemptuous toward it, not a bit willing to be subjugated by reason and calculation, by inconspicuous, unhurrying, and gray work! What! To serve in the governor's office, to do some pitiful bit for society! Never! Better to flee from it all! (quoted in Elistratov 1995, 656–657)[7]

In *Russian Talk: Culture and Conversation During Perestroika,* ethnographer Nancy Ries (1997, 69) also sees the drunken mischief-making of Russian men as "a very popular and recognized" behavioral mode of defying the "pragmatism and concerns of everyday life while also mocking the (often absurd) rationalism of [Soviet] state projects and promotions." Ries echoes Bunin's observations: "While alcoholism as a biomedical/social phenomenon is a serious and tragic problem in Russian families, and for the polity as a whole, alcoholism as a performative/narrative phenomenon offers endless possibilities for an elaboration of ironic resistance to the mundane, practical disciplines of family, community, and state."

Russian writer and philosopher Alexander Zinoviev also observes the centrality of drinking in Russian life: "In regard to Russian mentality, the fundamental dilemma 'To be or not to be' amounts to this: 'To drink or not to drink.' The answer is self-evident: 'To drink, of course!'" (quoted in Abdulaeva 1996, 211). The fact that alcohol helps a Russian man to cope with reality is acknowledged in the following joke.

(3.45) "Objective reality is hallucination caused by the lack of alcohol in the blood."(Private collection)

Most Russian alcohol-related jokes, however, focus on less profound topics, such as the misadventures of intoxicated men.

(3.46) A young drunk is lying on a railroad platform and dying of laughter. After about ten minutes, people around him begin to worry and call an ambulance.

He explains to the ambulance crewmen who try to subdue him: "Fellows, fifty people saw me off to the army. They've left on the train, and I stayed." (Private collection)

(3.47) The phone rings in a hospital emergency room.
"Ambulance? Come over right away! Our friend's swallowed a corkscrew. . . ."
Ten minutes later: "Ambulance? Everything is all right. We've found another corkscrew." (I. Raskin 1995, 28)

(3.48) In the evening a drunk crawls around, looking for something. A militiaman approaches him: "What are you looking for?"
"I've lost my keys."
"Where did you lose them?"
"Over there, in the city park."
"Why are you crawling around here?"
"There's more light here."[8] (Private collection)

(3.49) A drunk wakes up on the street and begins to yell: "Where am I? Where am I?"
"On Lenin Street."
"To hell with details! In what city?" (O. Ivanova 1996, 92)

(3.50) From a Russian Telegraph Agency dispatch:
"Today, near the island of Madagascar, the Russian fishing trawler *Unsinkable* has sunk. Its crew, ashore on a drinking bout in Vladivostok, survives." (Private collection)

Other frequently told jokes elaborate on the futility of fighting drinking since virtually everybody drinks:

(3.51) A drunk barges into a photo studio. "Make me a group picture."
"No pro-o-ob-lem! But pl-e-e-e-se," says the photographer, "make a semi-circle." (Efimov 1994, 259–260)

Yet another frequent humorous topic is the pretext and excuse for drinking:

(3.52) A father and son are drinking. When they run out of reasons for raising their glasses, the father catches a cockroach and ties a thread to its leg. Then he pulls the cockroach across the table: "Let's have one for the road!"
Then he pulls the cockroach in the opposite direction: "And now let's drink to the happy homecoming." (Private collection)

Drinking often celebrates a new purchase. A regular Russian word "to wash" *[obmyt']* in Russian slang also means "to wash it with alcohol." (There is also "to sprinkle it [with alcohol]" *[sbryznut']*):

(3.53)   "Let's buy shoe laces."
         "What for?"
         "We'll wash them [with alcohol]" *[obmoem]*. (Private collection)

(Compare an Irish proverb: "The four drinks—the drink of thirst, the drink without thirst, the drink of fear of thirst, and the drink at the door"; McCarthy 1968, 337).

Some alcohol-related jokes reveal the existing tension between the widespread imperative of the "low, carnival culture" and aspirations of "high culture" to comply with Western standards of public and private civility, especially in big cities. The following items ridicule the Russian's street drinking and partying:

(3.54)   It's half an hour before the New Year. A couple rushes down the empty street with shopping bags. They find a drunkard lying on the sidewalk. The wife growls:
         "See—people are already celebrating, and you do everything at the last minute" (Dubovsky 1992, 251)

(3.55)   A policeman caught a well-dressed educated man pissing into his own briefcase.
         "What are you doing, comrade? You're just a few steps from a public toilet. Why would you disgrace yourself? Why would you do a thing like this?"
         "Oh yes, officer. I know. I tried to use the facilities. But I feel it's gross to urinate next to people who are having a good time toasting, drinking, having snacks. . . ." (Private collection)

Even more biting than the satire on the "heartfelt swinishness" that Elistratov admires is the following version of this joke, in which the same situation is viewed from the point of view of a black man, who, in the Russian folk mind, is uncivilized:

(3.56)   Near a public toilet, a black man is urinating. A policeman approaches him:
         "Shame on you! Can't you do it in the toilet?"
         "No, I can't," he replies. "Over there a white gentleman is drinking wine." (Kharkover 1993, 1: 15)

In Georgy Danelia's film *Autumn Marathon,* a scene shows the clash between Western ideas of productivity and rationality (represented by a Danish linguist) and Russian carnival ways of everyday life. The end result is frustration, a ruined work day, and the foreigner's confinement to a sobering-up house.

According to Elistratov, drunken brawls are part and parcel of carnival behavior and thus should be treated as essentially Russian:

> (3.57)   One Russian—a drunkard. Two Russians—a drunken brawl. (Elistratov 1994, 656)

A score of Russian proverbs collected by Dahl (1984, 2: 199) makes violent mischief part and parcel of carousing: "Drink and beat up people so that they know whose son you are;" "We drink and break dishes; and punch those who object," and so on. In fact, a drunken brawl has become a fixture of Russian wedding celebrations:

> (3.58)   A knock on the door. A huge man stands on the threshold: "I'm from the Bureau of Public Services. Have you ordered a brawl for your wedding?" (Private collection)

In the following item, the Russianness of such behavior is underscored by featuring a mythological Russian hero, Ilya Muromets, who, because of his strength, good heart, and wisdom, is considered the embodiment of the Russian national spirit. Another character is also intrinsically a Russian fairytale character, a witch called Baba Yaga, who usually moves around in a giant mortar bowl:

> (3.59)   Ilya Muromets wakes up with an awful hangover and looks around him: Everything is destroyed, trees are wrenched out by their roots. Somebody has pushed Baba Yaga head down into her mortar [*stupa*]. . . . Ilya Muromets gets her out of the mortar and asks: "What bastard did this to you, Grandma?"
> "Oh!" cries Baba Yaga, "Dear little Ilya, what a kind man you are when you're sober!" (Kharkover 1993, 1: 15)

Another joke deromanticizes alcohol-driven abusive behavior while mocking a Soviet political cliché:

> (3.60)   Two drunks are sitting at the table with their heads close together:
> "I love you, Pete, not because your boozing got you fired from your job. . . . And I love you, Pete, not because you beat the hell out

of your wife every night. . . . And I love you, not for chasing your own mother out of your house. . . . But I love you, Pete, for the fact that . . . you are a simple Soviet man! (O. Ivanova 1996, 70)

Although Elistratov (1994, 21) interprets a whole slew of slang names—*alkash, alk, alik, alkonaft, alkmen, alkonoid, alkofan, alkashka*—as denoting alcoholics and drunkards, Iosif Raskin (1995, 27) makes a distinction between "an alcoholic" and *alkash* (roughly: "a boozer"), considering the former a hopeless "goner" and expressing sympathy for the latter, a good fellow driven to alcohol by the women in his life: "A boozer has nothing in common with an alcoholic—a sick man . . . a totally degraded drunkard. And very good people, I'm sure, become boozers—kind, honest, decent, and unhappy. Very often it's the loving women, more often wives, who make men boozers."In other words, a boozer is an alcoholic in the making who is a victim of females (ironically termed "loving") who make his life unhappy: He is a casualty of cruelty, personified by the "women who love him." (Comedian W.C. Fields's comment: "A woman drove me to drink . . . and I never even had the courtesy to thank her" [quoted in Tom Carey 1987, 131] comes to mind here.)

This perception of a drunkard who is driven to drink by repeated misfortune is very strong in Russian lore. Such an attitude creates an atmosphere of compassion toward a drinking man not unlike that felt for a "holy fool" *[iurodivyi]* who suffers for the sins of others.

In his review of Erofeev's "Moscow Stations," Russian writer Zinovy Zinik (1997, 7) notes:

Among the legendary alcohol abusers—such as the Scots and the Irish—the Russians stand out, not merely by virtue of their yearly consumption of vodka, but also because of the special character of their inebriation. In any other country, excessive drinking is a way to overcome shyness or a sense of alienation, to strike up a conversation with strangers, to experience a feeling of unity with the world, of belonging to the same kind.[9] It sometimes ends in a brawl; but then, any search for love and brotherhood is risky. All this could be said of the Russians' way of drinking too, but, as with everything in Russia, there is another dimension. In a country notorious for its intolerance of dissent, for the strict control of its borders, and for the yawning gap between the intelligentsia and the faceless underclass; in this huge, unpredictable prison of a country, heavy drinking is more like an acid trip; a journey to the forbidden "abroad," across the state frontiers, a flight into another reality where different metaphysical laws apply; a warped inside-out version of ordinary life. Getting drunk is like entering a fictional world. . . .

Sinyavsky (Tertz 1980, 41) also stresses the escapist nature of Russian drinking: "Russians drink not from destitution and not from grief, but due to age-old need for the miraculous and extraordinary: they drink, as it were, mystically, aiming to take the soul out of earthly balance and return it into its blissful bodiless state. Vodka is the white magic of a Russian man. . . ." This out-of-this-world euphoria is suggested by the contemporary slang name for a drunkard—"alconaut" *[alkonaft]*, created on the pattern of "cosmonaut" *[kosmonavt]*.

The image of a drunkard often acquires not only cosmic but also metaphysical overtones. Russian proverbs collected by Dahl (1984) treat a drinker as one whom "God protects as he would a raw youth" *[P'ianogo da malogo bog berezhet]*; "He drinks as everybody else but we don't know why God doesn't like him" *[P'et kak liudi, a za chto bog ne miluet ne znaem]* (2: 245). When an American says, "I feel like having a drink," the Russian says with feeling, "My soul's longing for it" *[dusha prosit]*. A Russian's offer of a heart-to-heart talk with someone *[pogovorit' po dusham]* implies having a drink together. If an American refuses a drink because his "stomach can't take it," a Russian would say "My soul doesn't accept it" *[dusha ne prinimaet]*.[10]

> (3.61)   It's early morning. A boozer brings a shot of vodka to his mouth:
> "My soul, will you take it?"
>   His exhausted soul says: "No!"
>   The boozer is surprised: "My soul, will you take it?"
>   "No."
>   "I'm asking you for the last time: Will you take it?"
>   "Nope."
>   "Then move over, otherwise I'll wet you."
>   (Nikulin 1997, 327–328; for another version, see Soloviev 1992, 2: 21)

These "soul talks," together with the Russians' ardent search for drinking companions, the inclination to treat drunks as "holy fools" who tell the truth that the sober do not dare tell ("What's on the sober man's mind is on the drunk man's tongue"),[11] all point to directions other than those of the tradition of the medieval carnival. In fact, in a culture of dual belief (paganism and Christianity, see Sinyavsky 1991, 109), the carnival ritualization of alcohol consumption described by Elistratov does not contradict another possible meaning. While having fun and releasing the tensions of everyday life is the primary motivation of all carnivals, the Russian drinking party with its seemingly endless contemplative conversations about the essence of life *[smysl zhizni]* may have deep religious roots. As one Russian put it: "Drunkenness is so well developed in Russia because we think about the meaning of life too much" (quoted in Pesmen 1995, 69). The Russians indulged in alcohol before the adoption of Christianity in the tenth century. (After all, among other reasons, the religion was chosen over Islam on the grounds that the latter prohibits inebriation.) But the tacit requirement that there be at least one drinking companion, the contemptuous and dismissive attitude toward lonely drinkers, the attention to disabled drunks on the street, and the general veneration of the process of drinking may have something to do with the early Christian rituals of the Eucharist, aimed at creating a sense of Christian community. The view of intoxication as a way of altering a believer's perception in order to reach a certain mental state that would provide a deeper mystical insight of the divine can be traced even further, to the Judaic holiday of Purim. In her "Excerpts from a Teshuva on Sacred Clowning, from Reb Kugel," Judith Kerman (1998, 8) writes:

> Rabbi Michael Strassfeld points out, "the time when all our rules and inhibitions are swept away" is also when we are able "to see how easy it is to change from Mordecai to Haman, from a crusader for justice into simply a crusader." . . . That is why the Talmud says that we fully accept the Torah only on Purim, for only when we can mock the tradition can we fully accept it. Only then are we safe do so; otherwise we make the tradition into an idolatry rather than a smasher of idols. . . . *Adde-to-yada* [drinking until we cannot distinguish between Mordecai and Haman] . . . is not an animalistic state of stupor, but rather a . . . messianic/mystical moment when there is no difference between Haman and Mordecai, good and evil, for both are found in the holy One "who created light and darkness, made peace and created evil" (Isaiah 45.7).

This ancient concept appears to have been acted out in the Russian medieval religious "antibehavior" acts described by Boris Uspensky in his article on Afanasiev's *Secret Tales*. (See chapter 8.) All the talk about "we haven't got enough" or "we overdid it" *[nedobrali, perebrali]* aims not so much at reaching the point of alcoholic oblivion; it attempts to reach the point in which communion with God could be established. A Russian proverb collected by Dahl (1984) makes this explicit: "Though the drunk's in a fog, he still sees God." *[P'ianyi khot' v tumane, a vse vidit Boga]* (2: 245).

The mechanism of this phenomenon is not unlike that in which pagan shamans engage when trying, with the help of intense ritualized dancing and the use of alcohol or other means of altering consciousness, to enter into a state of higher revelations. Statements of Russian drinkers recorded by Pesmen (1995, 69, 73) are indicative of this purpose: "Sitting together occurs according to the principle of spirituality." "We get drunk . . . only in order to open up and feel ourselves brothers." "*The bottle is only a path* . . . the goal is not to get drunk but to communicate, to commune." "Indifference is the greatest sin and drinking talk is not indifferent"—that is, it creates community rather than emphasizing self-interest. The custom of "washing a deal" also has a spiritual side to it; it "'washes,' purifies, a deal between friends [purging] its defiling practical nature, and also often labels as friendship a deal between near strangers" (Pesmen 1995, 71).

There is some literary evidence of drinking to spirituality of this possible link. In the seventeenth-century "Tale about a Carouser" *[Povest' o brazhnike]*, the drinking man eventually earns his place in paradise (and the most honorable place) by reasoning with all the holy fathers of the church that his sin of drinking is infinitely lighter and much more excusable than their own sins. In fact, in the tale his behavior is much less defiant than the term "carouser" suggests. Besides drinking, he prays to God every night. It is no wonder, then, that the hero of "Moscow Stations" talks with angels who advise him when and how much to drink. His intuition tells him that his drinking has a much higher aim than merely reaching an alcoholic stupor (Erofeev 1997, 38).

Since, once some men start drinking they have difficulty stopping, one often hears a proverbial question addressed to a boon companion: "Do you respect me? *[Ty menia uvazhaesh'?].* It serves as a source of many Russian witticisms and jokes.[12] To a Westerner it may seem like a question rooted in the troubled sense of self-worth that many alcoholics suffer from. However, the queries are psychologically more complicated. One explanation is offered by a Russian woman (quoted in 1995, Pesmen 73): "'He [the drinking man] wants to hear that you respect him and he wants proof of it, because—look, he's drunk, but nevertheless he is respected, that means that even in that state he is still *a human being!*'"

Although in recent years Russian women have also indulged in drinking, a drinking company is usually one of men, a communion of sufferers escaping from the sober world. Absent a war, which creates great male bonding, the concept of "sacred male friendship" takes root at such gatherings. In fact, an American observer, Victor Ripp, finds Russian friendship "more similar to war camaraderie than to the Western kind of social friendships—no wonder, because Russian life was always a kind of war" (quoted in Visson 1998, 171). For a Russian male, such friendship often supersedes all other attachments and obligations.[13] In male-to-male private conversations, it is not unusual for a man to brag about his sexual victories, to disclose to another man the most intimate details of his encounters with a woman (Popovsky 1985, 427–428):

(3.62) Two university professors are walking down a corridor talking. Suddenly a student rushes through and almost runs into them. They stop him and demand an explanation of his disrespectful behavior. The student apologizes, explaining that he didn't mean to show any disrespect; he was just late for class.

"It's a poor excuse, young man," says one of the professors. "Here I am trying to convey important scientific information to my colleague, and you rudely interrupt me . . ."

"Please, Professor, accept my apology. I'll never do it again."

"This is absolute insolence and rudeness!"

"Please . . ."

"Okay," says the other professor. "Let him go. I'm dying to hear more."

As soon as the student leaves, the first professor says: "Where did I stop? Oh, yes! As I told you, first I grabbed her breasts, and when she began moaning I ached for her ass . . ." (Private collection)

Implicit in the joke is the recognition that this kind of conversation is part and parcel of Russian male socializing.

Men's faithfulness to a male club often overrules any spousal obligations. A woman's interests, even her life, can be sacrificed just to prove allegiance to the membership. Russian writer Mark Popovsky (1985, 431–432) and American scholar Barbara Heldt (1987, 25) remind us of the popular Russian song about Stenka Razin, sung at the table by tipsy Russians for centuries, "with a tear" of admiration for the strength of male bonding. The folk hero Stepan Razin, reproached by his band for "trading them in for a *baba*," a captured Persian princess, drowns her in the Volga River just to prove his loyalty to his comrades-in-arms.

Russian history provides many horrifying examples of the extent to which male camaraderie can go. In the early 1930s, a Marxist intellectual and one of the organizers of Soviet industry, Georgy Piatakov, was arrested on fabricated charges, typical of the time, of disloyalty and treachery. Piatakov made an offer to Stalin through the secret police chief, Ezhov: Let his, Piatakov's, wife be shot as the ultimate proof of his "advanced commitment to the working class" and personal devotion to the Soviet leader (Maksimov 1991, 5).[14]

The Russian Male's Catch-22

A study of a large body of Russian male jokes indicates that, in their entirety, the jokes show contradictory attitudes toward women. On one hand, many jokes denigrate women both as human beings and as sexual beings; on the other hand, many others promote relentless pursuit of them.

These contradictory tendencies reflect traditional Russian misogyny shaped, in part, by certain conditions of child rearing. As cross-cultural anthropological studies have shown, due to a tradition of strong and overlong attachment to mothers, excessive closeness to the mother in childhood results in a boy's strong psychological identification with the female gender (Rancour-Laferriere 1985, 193). In his book *Fighting for Life: Contest, Sexuality, and Consciousness,* anthropologist Walter Ong (1981, 65), citing Robert Stoller's *Sex and Gender: On the Development of Masculinity and Femininity,* explains: "The young human male is very feminine in significant ways, and necessarily so, because of his earliest maternal environment. After initial identification with the feminine, the boy must grow away from the feminine [gender] identification that resulted from his first encounter with his mother's female body [sex] and feminine qualities [gender]."

As all this holds true for many cultures (cf. the discussion of "momism" in American culture in the 1950s; see also Goldberg 1987, 30), the problem has been exacerbated under Russian conditions, past and present. In the predominantly peasant Russia of the past, a boy grew up in a matrifocal environment. Psychologist Erik Erikson (1950, 367–368) finds that Russian motherhood has traditionally been "divided and diffused" by a whole slew of females—grandmothers, nannies, aunts, neighbors, and so on—"a rich inventory of giving and frustrating mother-images."[15]

Kon (1995, 151) observes that while dependence on the "dominant mother" begins at birth, in the Soviet period in nurseries and schools, most of the authority figures were women: Male teachers were rare. (This is also true in the United States, especially before World War II.) In the Communist youth organizations, the Young Pioneers and the Komsomol, girls generally took the lead. Schoolboys "found kindred spirits only in informal street groups and gangs, where the power and the symbols of power were exclusively male." Throughout the Soviet period this pattern of child rearing persisted, and today, Kon says, there still can be seen the overwhelming role of the mother in a boy's life long after it is truly needed.

With the father frequently absent physically or emotionally, it is the mother who provides stability, but at the same time she creates in her boy a powerful identification with the female. As a consequence, an adult male exhibits "defensive masculinity" (Rancour-Laferierre 1985), that is, he indulges in behavior traditionally ascribed to males—swearing, fighting, smoking, and drinking; he tries thus to disassociate himself from the feminine gender. Ong (1981, 70) explains:

As a boy, the young human male must "prove himself a man," differentiate himself from this given ambiance in which he finds himself. He must prove he is not a "sissy" (sister, girl). It is assumed that he is unless he proves the contrary. Anatomical differences do not suffice, since the fact is that all boys started out in the feminine world. How are they to be psychologically sure, consciously or unconsciously, that they have really ever left that world, that they have really achieved the differentiation that it is every male's business to achieve? They must cut girls out of their lives, scorn feminine sources of comfort and safety, do things that they hope their mothers and sisters cannot do.

The following items perfectly illustrate this psychological pattern:

(3.63) After examining a patient, a doctor says: "You should stop smoking, drinking, and chasing women."
"But, Doc, I'm a man after all!"
"You can keep shaving. . . ." (McLovsky, Klyne, and Chtchuplov 1997, 140)

(3.64) A biology teacher decides to show her pupils the great harm of drinking and smoking. She takes a worm and throws it into a glass of alcohol. The worm croaks.
She throws another worm into a glass of nicotine acid. This worm also croaks.
She throws a worm into a glass filled with egg yolks. And the worm lives!
"Children! What conclusion can we draw from this experiment?" she asks.
Says little Vova: "If you don't drink and smoke, worms will begin to breed in your eggs." [*iaitsa*, a colloquial word for testicles][16] (Private collection)

Here we have a symbolic representation of the clashing behavioral aims of the female and the male. The life-giving and life-supporting female functions of an egg (demonstrated by a woman) are contrasted with a destructive (and self-harming) primary concern with the male's gender identity.

Kon (1995) also offers sociological explanations for Russian men's aggressive behavior in private life. He cites the emasculating role of the "maternal Communist Party," its self-imposed role of all-knowing and all-correcting force in all matters, including personal relations, which the party played for almost seventy-five years. For illustration, it is enough to recall a classic joke about a husband who is questioned by the party committee about his failure to fulfill his spousal duties:

(3.65) "Well," says the man, "it's difficult for me to admit it, but the reason for this is that I'm impotent."

"May we remind you, Comrade Ivanov, that you're first of all a Communist." (Private collection)

As a reaction to party interference with conventional gender socialization, the average Russian man turned to behavior that served as "a psychological compensation and hypercompensation through idealization and imitation of the old, primitive image of a strong and aggressive male" (Kon 1995, 152). The sociologist Olga Voronina notes that the Soviet system endorsed the traditional patriarchy, "the masculinity paradigm, . . . a system of standardization of the individual through gender," and, by doing so, ascribed and prescribed to a person "certain sexual parameters in behavior, thought, feeling and perception" (1993, 111). Thus masculinity became a dominant cultural construct defined as much by gender hierarchy as by developmental male opposition to the maternal.

Jokes that portray women as "unattractive and undesirable" (Marshall 1992, 118) or as depersonalized whores are the direct manifestation of men's need to distance themselves from women that stems from these factors. What American anthropologist Anne Allison (1994, 184) suggests in her discussion of the sex talk in Japanese hostess clubs may apply to misogynist sex jokes told by men—that telling these jokes is "a strategy for constructing gender rather than a sexuality or heterosexual interest *per se*. Because sex talk degrades the woman but not the man, it emphasizes a gender imbalance that gives a man the pleasure of dominating. Putting the woman down is another means of structuring this relationship." In Japanese hostess clubs, "after sufficient inflation of his ego, the man may in fact proceed to a sexual encounter with a woman." At the end of a session of telling women-bashing, male ego-boosting jokes, a Russian man may also call for a similar encounter with a phrase that seemingly qualifies the dismissive attitudes of the talk: "Let's go after the sluts" *[poshli po bliadiam* or *poshli na bliadki]*, meaning ordinary women, not necessarily prostitutes.

This misogynist tendency in a paradoxical way predisposes the male toward developing "a Don Juan complex." As psychologist Legman (1968, 309) notes, "The mating urge, to repeat intercourse as often as possible, usually involves the need for a completely new woman . . . every time," because a man's hostility toward the woman (that is, any woman) "makes it unpalatable or impossible to have intercourse with [her] again." A man's compulsive tendency to look for a new partner comes from his hope that a fresh mate will succeed in sufficiently exciting him, thus enabling him to perform sexually. As a contemporary Russian saying goes, "Every woman deserves sex, but not every woman deserves it twice" [*kazhdaia zhenshchina dostoina seksa, no ne kazhdaia—dvazhdy;* JFR 3/11/98]. In *The Natural History of Love,* cultural historian Mort Hunt (1994, 280) cites modern psychoanalytic findings that commonly explain the Don Juan complex as one that "arises from a deep-lying fear of impotence, which in turn [is] frequently traced to a heavily repressed mother attachment."[17]

Besides the psychoanalytical, there are a number of cultural, biological, psychological, and sociological reasons, each complimenting and reinforcing another, for the pervasiveness of the promiscuity motif in Russian male jokes. First of all, there is a notion, strikingly persistent in many male jokes, that pursuing women, being constantly interested in them, is an inalienable, almost mandatory part of male identity, a mode of behavior that "separates men from boys":

(3.66)   Two toddlers are sitting on their night potties.
"How old are you?"
"I dunno."
"How come you don't know?"
"Well, I dunno. What about you?"
"I'm five. And don't you really know how old you are?"
"Really."
"Well . . . tell me . . . are you interested in women?"
"No . . ."
"Ah . . . Then you're three years old." (JFR 3/2/98)

Thus a womanizer is not so much a man of high virility and sex drive as a cultural self-construct of masculinity. "The more women you bed the more manly you are" is the logic underlying such behavior. Since most often it is a man who is the pursuer and a woman who is the prey, the man is given the appearance of dominance, a notion postulated by the prevalent pattern of gender hierarchy in Russian society. The notion that sexual prowess means social dominance is reflected in the following post-Soviet item:

(3.67)   A rumor is spread in the forest that a tigress is stuck between two trees. Scores of males of various species rush to the scene to take advantage of the situation and fuck her.
A sweating ant rushes in the same direction. A hare stops him: "Hey, ant, where are you running?"
"Haven't you heard? A tigress got stuck in the trees."
"So? What do you have to do with it?"

"I'm a male, am I not?" *[A ia chto, ne muzhik, chto li?"]* (Private collection)

There are also a number of social conditions that promote and facilitate male promiscuity. Popovsky (1985, 426) accounts for a Soviet man's pride in "a number of affairs, a long list of conquered women" by pointing to the availability of women caused by their lower economic status. One of his respondents, an engineer from Riga, formulated his view of gender relationship: "The Soviet Union is a world of men convinced of their irresistibility and [their access to] inexpensive woman" (425). In her paper "Venus in The Looking Glass: The Female Image in 20th Century Russian Painting," commenting on works of Russian-born painter Oscar Rabin, Professor Mary Rossabi concludes: "Taken as a group, Rabin's paintings must be read as a commentary on the lives of Russian women, who, in the twenty five years after the death of Stalin, could be bought cheaply, discarded easily, and finally, like laundry, even hung up on the line to dry."[18] (A crude post-Soviet example of such mores was broadcast on the new Russian TV show *About That [Pro eto]*. One of the show's participants, a man of sixty five, "described how he lures [twenty-five-year-old women] into the bushes behind McDonald's by buying them Big Macs. 'Oh yes,' he chortled happily. 'They all like those American pies'" (quoted in Vanora Bennet, October 10, 1997, 5).

These phenomena are interdependent. Russian men's belief that women will not long resist their advances is based on both the myth that all women are burning with sexual desire and the fact that they are penniless. And economic conditions make the perks of courting quite seductive for a woman, even though the affair is ephemeral. As Popovsky's (1985, 425) respondent explains, "an unmarried Soviet woman would frequently agree to intimacy with a man just because she was very poor. She craved at least two hours spent in a normal, decent environment. If a man had an apartment with a shower, had money to treat her to a restaurant and a ride in a car, a beautiful and intelligent woman would go for it, no matter how physically unattractive the man happened to be."

In his book *Moscow Farewell* (1976), American writer George Feifer estimates that "at least seven out of ten of Moscow's young women are instantly available for bedding by any presentable male. These are respectable girls looking for a little light relief from the drabness of everyday life: they are enthusiastic amateurs, not professionals . . ." (quoted in Hingley 1977, 191). One of my informants, a Russian living in Rome, sharing his first impressions of the West, said with some dismay: "Here in the West, getting a woman is a big problem. In my native Kiev, I see a girl on the street, offer a bottle of vodka for us to drink together, and she's mine. But here—you have to *buy* a woman!" He was discovering that in the West, a woman is used to being protected by law from unwanted advances, from being solicited by men on the street. She expects to be reassured about the depth of a man's interest in her by the duration and the manner of courtship. Because of their unprotected position in the society, Russian women cannot count on anybody's help in getting rid of a street stalker.[19]

Popovsky (1985, 427–428) cites other reasons for the tendency to seduce as many women as possible, such as an opportunity to brag not only to friends but to chance travel companions.[20] Ong (1981, 110) considers such behavior to be a complex, "rather thoroughly masculine": "It is both self-administered public mothering and the oral equivalent of ritual physical combat between males, formalized, serious, and bantering at the same time." Beyond this kind of vain behavior, not completely unknown to males in the West, the braggart's often unconscious need is to reaffirm his masculinity. The following joke shows how important it is for a man to come across as virile—if not in deeds, then at least in words:

(3.68)   A man is at the doctor's office: "Doctor, I have two big problems! . . . I don't know how I can live this way any longer!!"

Doctor: "Well, let's take it one step at a time. What's your first problem?"

The man says: "You know, Doctor, as soon as I wake up in the morning, I have sex with my wife right away. . . . Then I eat my breakfast and can't get hold of myself and I have my wife again. . . . Then I go to work by bus and make love to the female bus driver. . . . At work, I do it with my female secretary. . . . During lunch break, it is the female cook that I am having sex with. . . . Then I do it again with the secretary. . . . I come home in the evening to my wife and keep doing it all night long!!! . . . Doctor, what should I do?"

"Well, well, well . . . and what's your second problem?"

The man: "Doc, I'm a terrible liar!" (JFR 2/20/98)

Womanizing has been further facilitated by perpetual shortages of men due to the Revolution, the Civil War, two world wars, famines, and Stalin's mass terror, which befell the nation over the first half of this century. (For a short account of "the habitual loss and absence" of men throughout Russian history, see Ries 1997, 75.) Some jokes reflect the male perception of an abundance of available women:

(3.69) A woman is like a city bus: It's simpler to wait for the next than run after her." (Private collection)

I would add another psychological factor to these reasons for Russian men's pronounced tendency to promiscuity. The extensive womanizing in the Soviet period can also be explained by the rigidity of the system, with its emotionally dull climate, its utter predictability and monotony. For Russian men caught in this system, chasing women was a sport of sorts, a hobby with challenges and joys not unknown to stamp or butterfly collectors: Both quantity and variety add to the collectors' feeling of pride and accomplishment. Every new woman would present a brand-new challenge of seduction and help to overcome boredom. Ries's Russian informant describes male "mischief"—especially extramarital mischief—as "the zone of freedom, *the only area where one could exercise initiative and [use one's] wits. . . .* This was always regarded as a free zone, even in pre-revolutionary Russia; peasant humor is full of sexual adventures and deceptions. This was always the only place where people could be free, even for an hour, steal some kind of fun which they were not supposed to have. This is how you could get more from life than you are entitled to" (1997, 70–71, emphasis added).

On a smaller scale, this process takes place in the West as well. Some American sociological studies discuss American Don Juans who, working within huge corporate structures with their predictability of promotions and career developments, pension and retirement plans, seek refuge in womanizing, (as exemplified in the recent film *In the Company of Men.* In Japanese culture, seeking the company of women to boost male egos and improve corporate executives' morale by visiting hostess bars has even been institutionalized (Allison 1994).

Approaching a woman out of sheer idleness of the soul is well expressed by Sinyavsky: "Because of the lack of a gesture, an absence of the words, of not having anything better . . . we turn to women and make them different indecent proposals in order to do something and to say something about something" (Tertz 1980, 27).

Stalking women on the streets is not so outrageous for Russians as it is for Westerners; at least some women see nothing wrong with it and buy into the male mode of behavior. One of my female informants explains why she went along with a man who approached her at a bus stop: "I was alone in Moscow. I needed a man. How else would I meet him? The man who approached me seemed okay, well dressed, and so on." Sinayavsky feels that such female behavior is related to a general lack of self-worth: "Women's compliance is saddening. There is something in it of our common, human inferiority" (Tertz 1980, 24). The Russian perception of a woman as some kind of dark pagan goddess, discussed in chapter 2, also contributes to male promiscuity:

> From a strictly physiological point of view, a new love object is not much different from the old one. But that's what the whole thing is all about—that the new object seems "sweeter" beforehand, because with it you overstep the law for the first time and therefore are acting more sacrilegiously. . . . Don Juan's story of the eternal search for The One, still untouched, with whom to do the forbidden is especially pleasurable. In relationship with a woman, it is always more important to remove her pants than to quench your natural need. And the higher the woman is, and the more unapproachable, the more interesting it is. (Tertz 1980, 21–22)

And again, there is the alcohol factor. Since hard liquor is considered "a man's drink," it is often believed to contribute to his physical strength, making him almost a fairy-tale hero who can be revived by drinking the miraculous *aqua vitae* (in Russian fairy-tales, *zhivaia voda*). In the following two items, the Russian's raw power grows with the amount of alcohol consumed. He is able to tear off the bumper from a car and clobber his Japanese adversary:

(3.70)   In the restaurant of an international airport, a Russian drunk bothers a Japanese:
"Let's go out for a man-to-man talk!"
They leave. In a minute the Japanese returns, bows politely to the others, and explains: "There's a little Japanese thing—judo."
The drunk comes in again with a bruise under his eye, drinks another half glass of vodka, and again bothers the Japanese: "Let's get out for a talk!"
They leave. After a time, the Japanese comes back, bows politely and says: "There's a little Japanese thing—judo."
The drunk comes back with two bruises on his face, drinks a bottle of vodka, grabs the Japanese by his jacket: "Let's go for a talk!"
They leave. There is banging behind the walls. The Russian comes back into the restaurant and says: "There's a little Japanese thing—a Toyota bumper." (Anon. 1994, 323–324)

(3.71)   A Russian walks in the desert with a parrot on his shoulder. An Arab with a boa constrictor on his neck comes his way and asks the Russian:
"Is it true that you can drink a glass of vodka without having a snack?"

"Yes," says the Russian, and drinks a glass of vodka.

"Is it true that you can drink another glass of vodka without having a snack?"

"Yes," says the Russian, and drinks another glass of vodka.

"Is it true? . . ."

The parrot: "Yes, we'll drink the third one and the fourth one, and then we'll bang you over your head and eat that worm on your neck." (Efimov 1994, 232–233)

Such jokes have deep roots in Russian folklore, where heroes measure their stamina through drinking contests and gather strength as they drink. The ease with which, in 3.34, a Russian Uncle Vassya beats his puny foreign competitors is based on ancient traditions of national folkloric heroes. In Ivan Goncharov's *Oblomov* (chapter 9, "Oblomov's Dream"; 138–139) a Russian nanny tells heroic ballads *[bylinas]* to the little Oblomov: "She recounted the exploits of our Achilles and Ulysses: of Ilya Muromets, Dobrynya Nikitich, Alyosha Popovich . . . , and of how they traveled throughout Russia, slaying untold hordes of Moslems, how they vied with one another in drinking whole goblets of new wine in a single gulp and without uttering a sound."

The reality is much less cheerful. Today Russia is the country with the highest per-capita alcohol consumption in the world,[21] nearly double the danger level set by the World Health Organization (Specter 1997, 5). Ubiquitously practiced and socially mandated in many nonsexual contexts, heavy consumption of alcohol, which inevitably lowers male sexual prowess, only contributes to the misogynist's fear of sexual inadequacy. Moreover, in Russian culture the amount of hard liquor a man can hold is often used as a measure of his manhood:

(3.72)	Esli vypil khorosho,	If you drank well,
	znachit utrom plokho.	then you feel lousy in the morning.
	Esli utrom khorosho,	If you feel well in the morning,
	znachit vypil plokho.	then it means that you didn't have
		enough to drink. (JFR 2/9/98)

The following joke of 1985 vintage, collected during Gorbachev's unsuccessful attempt to fight alcoholism, features a factory worker who has what it takes—that is, a "man's" stamina—under the influence of alcohol.

(3.73) A delegation led by Gorbachev is walking through a factory. They approach a lathe operator who is cutting a metal part. Gorbachev asks him:

"Excuse me, it interests me. Could you work the way you do now if you had drunk a full glass of vodka?"

"I suppose I could."

"What if you had two glasses?"

"I could."

"And could you work after three glasses?"

"Mikhail Sergeevich, why are you bothering me with these silly questions? Can't you see for yourself? I'm working, am I not?" (Private collection)

The proverbial statement of male pride: "I don't take any snacks after the first shot of vodka" [posle pervoi ne zakusyvaiu], was used in Sergey Bondarchuk's film Fate of a Man, based on Mikhail Sholokhov's story. (During Gorbachev's anti-alchohol campaign this episode was cut from the film before public viewing in reruns; cited in White 1996, 88–89). In fact, a true man takes pride in not having much to eat while drinking:

(3.74)   "What's Russian party time?

"A cart of beer, a couple of bottles of vodka, a stick of sausage, and a dog . . ."

"And what is the dog for?"

"Well, somebody should eat the sausage after all." (JFR 3/6/98)

There is an abundance of folkloric evidence that a Russian man often resorts to drinking to dull his hostility toward women, thus only adding to his problem. A contemporary Russian proverb makes the association of misogyny and alcohol quite clear: "There is no such thing as an ugly woman: There's just not enough vodka on a table."[22] Hard liquor, mostly vodka ("light wine is not a man's drink"), is considered the male aphrodisiac par excellence. But the men keep forgetting that, in Shakespeare's words in Macbeth, drink "provokes the desire but it takes away the performance" (quoted in White 1996, 78).

(3.75)   A man calls his friend:

"Let's party. I'm coming down with my girl and her girlfriend."

"Is she pretty?"

"Well, not very. But don't worry, I'm bringing two bottles of vodka. You'll like her after you've had a drink."

When the company arrives, the man opens the door, looks at the woman intended for him, and says: "Oh, no, Ivan! It won't work. I can't drink that much." (Private collection; for another version, see Anon. 1994, 273)

The motifs of misogyny and alcohol are often interdependent:

(3.76) "Ah, I shouldn't have married," says one man to another. "My wife can't stand me when I'm drunk, and I can't stand her when I'm sober." (Petrosian 1994, 164)

(3.77) A husband comes home drunk and says to his wife: "Kiss me, please."
She hasn't heard this from him for a few years and is therefore terribly surprised: "Are you out of your mind, or what?"
"I beg you—please kiss me."
"What's the matter with you today?"
"Kiss me. Maybe it'll help me to throw up." (Private collection)

In jokes, a woman is represented in two extreme images—a beautiful whore or an ugly asexual housewife; in fact, the "ugly old bag" is traditionally a favorite source of popular humor (Kelly 1992, 16). In the following contemporary item, she is full of hate for her husband, even at the expense of admitting her own unattractiveness:

(3.78) Petrova looks at herself in the mirror and mumbles gloatingly: "That's just what you deserve, Mister Petrov!" (JFR 2/16/98)

In male jokes about an "ugly" woman, fear of women and their power is sublimated. Her "ugliness" is not to be taken literally (there is a popular notion of Russian women as world-renowned beauties); rather, it is a folk way of distancing and estrangement, as the "ugly Jew" notion is in anti-Semitic folklore.

The "ugly woman" theme runs through American jokelore as well (Fine 1981, 214), and alcohol helping men to overcome hostility toward women also appears in American jokes ("Drinking booze makes you beautiful, Lizzie!" "I haven't been drinking." "I have;" Fine 1981, 217.) In Russia, however, a woman's ugliness usually comes up as the last line of defense for a man disparaged for his drunkenness. His excuse, as the following items demonstrate, is that drunkenness is just a temporary impairment of an otherwise admirable fellow, while women's "ugliness" is a permanent quality that she cannot shed. In other words, a woman is always (read: eternally) ugly (read: bad)—a tradition of popular culture, which can be traced back at least to the nineteenth-century Petrushka puppet street show. Petrushka's wife or bride was usually shown as ugly, tastelessly dressed, and speaking in a squeaky voice (Kelly 1993, 79). A number of contemporary jokes about alcoholics delight the listeners with the "wittiness" of a drunk's response to a woman's expression of disgust with his unseemly state of intoxication.

> (3.79) A bus in rush hour. A girl says to a man: "You're drunk, terribly drunk, disgustingly drunk!"
> "And you, young lady, are bowlegged, terribly bowlegged, disgustingly bowlegged! And I'll be sober tomorrow." (O. Ivanova 1996, 77)

In the next item, a woman's ugliness is assumed if she is not young and nubile:

> (3.80) A man wakes up in the morning after a terrible drinking bout. Suddenly, as he turns on his side, he sees that somebody is lying next to him.
> "Who are you?" he asks.
> "I'm your woman."
> "And how old are you?"
> "I'm as old as I look."
> After a few minutes of thought, the man says: "C'mon, people don't live that long!" (JFR 3/2/98)

The following comic Gothic story is a more elaborate variant of the same idea:

> (3.81) A wife decides to give a lesson to her drunkard husband, who always goes through a cemetery after he drinks. She changes to a weird dress and fixes her hair so that she looks like a witch.
> "Stop drinking vodka!" she shouts at him in the cemetery. "Otherwise I'll drag you to hell."
> The husband stares at the witch and says: "Listen, am I married to your sister?" (O. Ivanova 1996, 80)

The Russian woman is "ugly" because she is not a "true woman," one who appreciates a man just because he is a man, whether he is drunk or sober, as the "beautiful" French woman does:

> (3.82) A drunken man is lying on a street. Here is how different women react:
> An English woman: "A man! Drunk? Oh, what an indecency!"
> A Russian woman: "Oh! A man! Drunk? Got himself gorged on vodka. Scum. And his wife and children at home. . . ."

A French woman: "Ah, a man! Drunk. . . . Alone. . . . Alone?!
Taxi! Taxi!" (Anon. 1994, 285)

In recent years, with the advent of the Russian version of wild capitalism, the classic macho image of a Russian man underwent a certain
change. In the Soviet years of "equal poverty for everyone," the male image
retained its traditional shape due to the lack of opportunities for individual effort. Under the new social conditions, traditional masculinity is gradually becoming obsolete; it is gradually being eclipsed by a new ideal of
manhood.

In the folk culture, this new, emerging image is signified by the adjective
"tough" *[krutoi]*, which now means not so much a physically formidable
man as a man of means. "Old yardsticks, such as high alcohol tolerance, are
now being forced off the stage by the pressure to achieve and earn money,"
says Olga Zdravomyslova, a sociologist at the Moscow Center for Gender
Studies (quoted in Allen 1998, 20). The owner of a Moscow "leisure club
for real men" defines his client as "someone who's got money and isn't afraid
to spend it."

This gradual supplanting of the old stereotype of Russian masculinity
based on raw physical power is reflected in the following current joke:

> (3.83) An elephant and a "tough" mouse are strolling in the forest. Sud-
> denly the mouse slips, falls into a swamp, and begins drowning. He
> shouts to the elephant: "Save me!"
>
> The elephant turns around and extends his huge male organ to
> the mouse. The mouse grabs it and climbs out of the swamp.
>
> They keep strolling, and suddenly it is the elephant who slips and
> begins to drown in the swamp. He roars: "Mouse, save me!"
>
> The mouse gets into his Ferrari, drives up to the edge of the
> swamp, hooks to it to the elephant, and drags him out.
>
> Moral: If you have a Ferrari, you don't really need a big dick.
> (JFR 3/28/98)

The point of this joke is driven a bit too hard: the choice of male organ as
the tool of salvation is too obviously deliberate: Logically speaking, the elephant's trunk could do the job with the same, if not more, ease.

A vicious circle is created by the need for distancing from women, both
culturally and biopsychologically, and the behavioral imperative of male
promiscuity dictated by the dominant position of men in the Russian gender hierarchy and exacerbated by traditional misogyny and indulgence in

drinking (and the fear of impotence that it provokes). A Russian man is able to escape these double binds only through the free-wheeling fantasy of jokelore. There females are available and willing and men have great prowess. This nexus also explains why the contemporary Russian male jokelore is populated with stupid, ugly, and treacherous women who are at the same time sexually aggressive and insatiable.

CHAPTER 4

Making War, Not Love: Jokelore on Courtship and Lovemaking

Courtship, Russian Style

Drastic social changes in the post-Soviet years have had a tremendous impact on sexual morality. Erotic and sexually explicit materials strictly forbidden in Communist Russia are conspicuous today. Although the Communist elite had never been puritanical in their private lives, their sexual indiscretion had always been hidden from the public eye. The official morality had remained strictly Victorian.

However, despite the dramatic rise in promiscuity, especially among young people,[1] the stereotype of Russian sexual etiquette, by and large, remains unchanged. (Of course, in such a socially and ethnically diverse society, it is hard to talk about established rules of etiquette. We can only discuss a stereotype as it is played out in jokes, for popular humor represents a playful handling of social stereotypes.)

Notwithstanding the many cases of teenage pregnancy in recent years, Russian love etiquette long ago established high romantic standards. School textbooks traditionally include love poems in which relationships between the sexes are presented exclusively as "soul to soul." In his book *The Twentieth Century and Tendencies of Russian Sexual Relations*, S. I. Golod (1996, 143–145) underscores a peculiarity of Slavic love culture—its emphasis on the sublime character of relationships influenced by Russian Orthodox Christian ascetic tendencies. Invariably romantic, these textbook poems represent the cultural consciousness of a nation that considers the carnal indecent. Tolstoy and Dostoevsky refer to sex either as something highly despicable that evokes revulsion (e.g., in Tolstoy's *Kreutzer's Sonata*) or as a destructive force (e.g., in Dostoevsky's *Idiot*). Stories by Ivan Bunin, although wonderfully capturing the excitement of the physical encounter between man and woman, usually end with the death of one of the lovers. In his stories, physical love is seen as a demonic and destructive force, as the "fatal passion." The prudish and artificial culture created in Stalin's time still has a strong hold on Russians, especially those living in the country's vast provinces.

Despite the rapid changes in the fabric of Russian society as it was known for more than seven Soviet decades, the male jokes collected recently show that the old cultural assumptions are alive and well. According to them, the male has an indisputable prerogative in all stages of the sexual relationship. A woman's role is to be invariably passive, modest, and restrained. She should never initiate sexual contact. A Russian man would not find it inappropriate to approach any woman in a public place and try to strike up a conversation. At the same time, it would never cross a Russian woman's mind to go to a bar in search of male company, as an American woman in a large metropolitan area might do. "A modest woman" has long been a highly popularized image; coyness with men who approach her is highly commended.

Russian women taking the initiative in sexual matters are a product either of folk sexual fantasies, expressed in male jokes, or they are the product of those Sovietologists who gained their knowledge not first hand but through reading Russian classics. Thus, in his book *Sexual Behavior in the Communist World: An Eyewitness Report of Life, Love and the Human Condition Behind the Iron Curtain* (1967, 212), Peter Stafford, when talking about the slow pace of changes away from the puritanical attitude toward sex since Stalin's death, comments: "One [thing] has certainly remained largely unchanged, the fact that in Russia, by and large, sexual initiative is with the women—to a far greater extent than with the men." He cites the heroine of Pushkin's *Eugene Onegin*, Tatiana Larina, as an example. Stafford draws from this example a rather dubious conclusion that "the fact that women take this initiative proves that the Russian conception of love and sex is basically a realistic one" (213).

Surprisingly, Stafford makes no connection between Tatiana's behavior and her reading list, as he does for Onegin: "Dostoevsky was probably right when he said that Onegin would have fallen passionately in love with Tatiana if he had found such an example in Byron's poetry" (213). What Stafford fails to take into consideration is that Tatiana behaved not according to Russian native customs but those of foreign origin. The heroine of Rousseau's *Nouveau Eloise* inspired Tatiana to take an unorthodox step in being the first to express her love.

According to the unspoken rules by which his approach is considered decent and acceptable, a male's interest is in the woman's admirable spiritual qualities *[dushevnye kachestva]* rather then her physical attractiveness.[2] Since the Russian classics offer high romantic patterns of sexual behavior, relationships between a young man and a woman often remain a "friendship" for a long time, because admitting physical attraction and passion often violates implicit cultural standards. As a result, it is considered highly proper during a date to talk about such matters as poetry, art, literature, and theater. If the Russian male adheres to these culturally approved topics in his conversations with the female he is courting, then it is assumed that he is showing respect for her.

Such male behavior implies that he admires her inner virtues and that is what has attracted him to her in the first place. Although a light compliment to the female's pleasant appearance is not considered out of place, it should be clear that physical attributes do not matter much. As a contemporary male proverb has it, "If you've grabbed [her] breasts, tell [her] something" [*Vzialsia za grud'—govori chto-nibud'*; Kozlovsky 1982, 231]. A violation of this tacit assumption is, by and large, considered in "bad taste." The suitor exposes himself as driven by "disrespectful" [read: sexual] desire.

Russian male jokes represent a countercultural resistance to this established stereotype of courting behavior. Like his American counterparts (see Legman 1968, 223), a Russian man considers it annoying and superfluous to feign interest in a woman's spiritual qualities. The jokes propagate a more direct course of action:

(4.1) An Armenian complains to his Russian friend that, for some reason, he is unsuccessful with women.
"The thing is that your approach is too forward, " says the Russian. "You should take your time. First you should talk about poetry. Only after that may you go ahead with the rest of the business."
On the next day, the Armenian approaches a woman: "You know Puskhin, Lermontov? Lie down!" (Private collection)

The reason the Armenian is the main actor in this joke has nothing to do with any specific sexual qualities ascribed to this nationality, as occurs in some other jokes. Here it is an artistic ploy to introduce a character who is hot-tempered, as a stereotypical man from the Caucasus is believed to be, and only vaguely familiar with Russian culture, and whose Russian is stereotypically more abrupt, to make his pitch to the woman even more succinct. Instead of what a Russian character would say in the situation: "*Vy chitali*

Pushkina i Lermontova?" (twelve syllables), the Armenian, with a nonnative speaker's grammatical distortion of Russian, uses seven syllables only: "*Pushkin, Lermontov znaesh'?*" Note also the familiar second-person singular form of the verb "to know" *[ty]* rather than the proper second-person plural *vy,* more appropriate for a first encounter.

Elistratov (1994, 404) gives another example of the same nature. A girl is asked whether she has read anything by the French writer Remont Obuvi. Pronounced with a misplaced accent, these words are actually Russian, meaning "shoe repair," but they give an impression of a French first and last name.

The culturally acceptable "pickup technique" suggests that a man has to approach a woman with an innocent remark and introduce himself. This ritual, as well as other clichés of established romantic standards, is especially ridiculed in a series of jokes about a fictional character, Lieutenant *[poruchik]* Rzhevsky. Most of them are nothing but brushed-up versions of oral jokes that circulated among Russian army officers in the middle of the nineteenth century (Lurie 1992, 139); some may be from earlier. Lieutenant Rzhevsky, the hero of a popular play entitled *A Long Time Ago [Davnym-Davno]* by Alexander Gladkov,[3] is a cynical ladies' man who often makes antiromantic comments in the most romantic situations. He often advises less experienced young officers on love matters. A new series of jokes about him became popular in 1962 when the film *A Hussar's Ballad [Gusarskaia ballada]* based on Gladkov's play was released.

(4.2) Lieutenant Rzhevsky and Natasha Rostova [of Tolstoy's *War and Peace*] are strolling along the Summer Garden in St. Petersburg. Looking at swans swimming in the pond, Natasha asks coyly: "Lieutenant, would you like to be a swan?"

"With my naked ass in cold water? Oh no! Please spare me!" (Private collection)

(4.3) Lieutenant Rzhevsky learns that to get to know a young lady one should approach her, talk casually about the weather, and then introduce oneself. On one of his strolls he meets a young woman walking along the street with her Bolognese lap-dog. He approaches her and kicks the dog, which flies a long way.

"It flies low," he says. "It's a sign that it's probably going to rain. By the way, permit me to introduce myself: Lieutenant Rzhevsky." (Private collection)

Here the act of cruelty toward the animal is an act of transferred aggression toward the woman. The lieutenant's freedom from the constraints of cultured life that the dog represents (it is not just any dog, but a specially bred one) epitomizes his scorn for the obstacles to his sexual advances that decorum commands. The series propagates the straightforward approach deemed most effective for the Russian man. The following joke of the series presents Rzhevsky's ideal courtship tactics.

(4.4) A young officer approaches Rzhevsky and says: "Lieutenant, you have so much success with women. But they pay no attention to me. . . . What's your secret?"

"Very simple, my friend. You come up to a madam (or mademoiselle) and ask her: 'Madam, may I stick it in you?'"

"But, Lieutenant, that way you might get a slap in the face."

"You might. And you might also get a lot of sticking in." (Lurie 1992, 142)

Russian sexual humor is not much different from Western sexual humor in this respect. Rzhevsky's ideas about the most effective approach to a woman are not unlike those recorded by Legman (1968, 223); in fact, there is an American version of joke 4.4.

As for female courtship behavior, many Russian male jokes depict it as marked by hypocritical, culturally prescribed behavior patterns that frustrate the Russian male. Consider the following rather elaborate story, which points to what the Russian male finds irritating in the Russian female's behavior. These courtship jokes often involve French women, whose function is obvious: The French are considered models to follow when it comes to love etiquette. Thus the French woman provides an ideal picture of woman's behavior on a date—a Russian male fantasy par excellence:

(4.5) You make a date with a French woman. If you agreed on seven o'-clock, come at half-past six—you are already expected. You invite her to a restaurant. She accepts with pleasure. In the restaurant, she eats little, drinks little, but smokes a lot. Then you invite her to your home. She readily agrees.

At home you propose a bath, but she answers that she has already taken one, since she knew how things would go. You spend a wonderful night. Upon waking in the morning, you discover by your bed a cup of freshly brewed coffee and a note: "Dear, if you liked me and want to see me again, call this number. . . ."

You make a date with a Russian woman. If you agreed to meet her at seven o'clock, come bravely at eight. She'll appear half an hour later. And she'll come not alone but with a girlfriend. After some time, you manage to talk her girlfriend into leaving, and you invite

the woman to a restaurant. After a long argument, she agrees. In the
restaurant, she smokes little but eats and drinks a lot.
 Then you invite her home. She again gets indignant: "What do
you take me for!" but after long coaxing, she agrees. At home she
asks you to wait five minutes while she takes a shower. She comes
back half an hour later, for she has taken the opportunity of using
the hot water that is in short supply at her house and has washed her
clothes. All night she keeps asking you: "Do you love me?" In the
morning it is you who make the coffee. Upon awakening, she
sweetly stretches herself in the bed and says: "Dear, that's where I'll
put my chest of drawers."[4] (Private collection)

While punctuality is not a forte of Russians in general, the fact that this
woman is usually late is another cultural assumption, a condescending sexual stereotype. For a woman to be late on a date is not only all right but ad-
visable. To be disorganized and nonpunctual is considered feminine; the
tardier, the more feminine. It sends a message to the man that, although she
has accepted his invitation, she has still to be conquered.

 She may come to a date with a girlfriend. This is supposed to signal that
she does not fully accept the sexual character of the meeting; she reserves the
right to behave in a manner that makes the encounter a casual get-together
with a male acquaintance. As for the woman's indulgence in food in the
restaurant, the joke inadvertently shows her low income; Russian women,
especially young ones, are usually grossly underpaid, unable to afford a visit
to a restaurant.[5] Finally, the joke reflects a male fantasy of a noncommittal
and unrestrained sexual relationship. The woman's pragmatic attitude punc-
tures the male's dream world of "sex for the sake of sex." She sees the male
sexual activity as part and parcel of a marriage proposal. (Finding a place for
her chest of drawers is its implicit acceptance.) Thus the tacit meaning of her
own participation in the sexual act is, first and foremost, a down payment
for marriage.

 It is interesting to explore the folk attitude toward sexual relationships
and the corresponding positions of the sexes in it in the context of the most
recognizable literary love story in Russian culture, that of Eugene Onegin
and Tatiana Larina (already mentioned above), in which the initial approach
is Tatiana's. Onegin rejects her; some years later he, upon pursuing her, is re-
jected by her. No physical consummation of the attraction has occurred.

 To the Russian folk mind this pattern of events is incomprehensible.
Such dynamics of a male/female relationship do not square with folk attitudes. The following three jokes in the form of a take-off on the novel aim
to bring the famous characters in line with how the action should have gone

if the lovers had followed the folk script of sexual behavior. The take-offs are in the form of three questions and answers to the fictitious Radio Armenia (Milgram 1985, 56).

In contrast to the original, where no sexual act takes place, the first question implies the traditional male initiative and conquest. It is the male who should approach the female, not vice versa, and he should do it in the most resolute manner. At the same time, the woman's resistance to intercourse is seen as part of the normal ritual of lovemaking:

> (4.6) "What did Tatiana say to Onegin when he dragged her to bed?"
>
> "Onegin! I'm not getting into bed [with you]" [*Onegin, ia v krovat'—ne stanu'*, instead of Pushkin's *skryvat' ne stanu* "I won't hide (my love)."]
>
> The second question: "What did Tatiana tell Onegin after their first intercourse?"
>
> "Onegin! I'm not getting out of bed" [*Onegin, ia s krovat'—ne vstanu"].*[6] (Milgram 1985, 56)

This is supposed to suggest the next stage of the folk lovemaking script: After once experiencing sex, a woman is invariably ecstatic and insists on continuing the act ad infinitum. Her refusal to leave indicates her attempt to pressure the man into a permanent relationship, which, in the Russian folk mind, spells only one thing—marriage.

In the third part of the joke, the folk male resists marriage, making it clear to the woman that as soon as his sexual thirst is satisfied, the relationship has no future:

> (4.7) "How did Onegin respond to Tatiana's love?"
>
> "I've had you. What more do you want!" *[Ia vas imel. Chego zhe bole!]* (Milgram 1985, 56)

Onegin's response is a take-off of Tatiana's line in the original: "I am writing to you. What more do you want!" *[Ia vam pishu. Chego zhe bole!]*. The joke implies that the affair is over. Tatiana should see their sexual intercourse as a more than adequate manifestation of Onegin's attraction to her; she should be grateful to him for the sex alone.

Making War, Not Love

The intrinsic difference in male and female capabilities and functions as sexual beings is a main source of sexual humor. Murphy (1989, 67) points out such psycho-physiological facts as the man's greater need for arousal for the sex act to take place. Women can fake orgasm, but men cannot. Usually a man also cannot match the frequency of sexual contact that a female enjoys. Not only is the woman's sexual capacity greater than a man's, it can also last much later in life. Male sexuality peaks at the age of nineteen, and female, around forty, yet the almost universal tendency is for men to marry younger women, thus setting themselves up for at least the potential tension created by the wife's lack of sexual fulfillment.

Murphy (1989, 67) points out another critical source of conflict between the sexes:

> Men tend generally to become aroused more easily and reach orgasm more quickly than women. It's probably for this reason that there is striking cross-cultural similarity in complaints that men and women make about the other gender's sexual performance: Men chide women for infrequency, and women fault men for brevity. This lack of neat fit between the physiologies of male and female sexual function cannot be deemed an error of either nature or culture, but must be considered as a contributing agent to the undercurrent of tension that characterizes all gender relationships. Because of it, sex is often funny, commonly a problem, and always something of a mystery.

Mystery or not, with the unpredictability of many psycho-physiological conditions, sex can turn only to humor to negotiate between its high desirability and its inherent uncertainties.

Besides biology, culture and societal norms and structures contribute greatly to already existing tensions, chief among which is "the myth of the natural superiority" of men (Murphy 1989, 69) in many societies. It is not by chance that there are no words for sex in Russian apart from vulgar language or scientific terms (Kon 1995, 134–135). Because in the Russian consciousness sex is treated as a contemptible function of the lower bodily stratum—Ronald Hingley (1977, 191) cites the "standard prerevolutionary peasant custom of veiling the holy icon with a curtain, or removing the cross from one's neck, before engaging in sexual intercourse"—Russian language has only foul words to describe this function:

(4.8) "What does it mean 'to make love'"?
"It's what your girlfriend is doing while you're simply fucking her." (Private collection)

In Russian there is not even a euphemism equivalent of "pussy," the American euphemism for a vagina.[7]

The asymmetrical character of gender treatment in Russia, as reflected in sexual humor, is especially clear in the body of jokes devoted to coitus. As sexual deprivation of both males and females is often addressed, it is noteworthy that in many jokes Russian males experience frustration only when deprived of a sexual partner under special circumstances—in faraway places, such as an isolated military outpost somewhere in a desert (4.9), a Far North area (4.10), a geologists' camp, lost in the middle of nowhere (4.11), or, emblematically, on an uninhabited island (4.12), while it is assumed that female sexual frustration is not localized but ever present:

(4.9)   A colonel inspecting a border sees that there are only men around him. He asks the outpost commander: "How do you deal with sexual needs?"
"With the help of female camels."
"Well," said the colonel, "a camel. Then a camel it shall be."
And he did it to one of them.
"What a strong man!" said the commander admiringly. "We do it in another way. We saddle female camels and head for broads in a neighboring village." (Private collection)

(4.10) A newspaper man came to the Far North to study the lives of the Evenks, deer-breeders. He wrote a good story about them. At the end of his trip, he asked: "I understand all about your life. One thing is not clear to me. Everyone is male here. How do you manage without women?"
The Evenks: "With the help of deer. Choose any one of them."
The pressman chose one and made love to her. The Evenks burst into laughter:
"Is something wrong?" the reporter asked.
"You chose such an ugly one." (Private collection)

(4.11) Geologists on fieldwork, far from any human dwellings, noticed that one of their colleagues had gotten dressed up and, looking in a mirror, straightened his tie. They all began laughing and asked:
"Who are you dressing up for? Do you have a date with that goat, or what?"
"Don't laugh. She and I are getting serious about our future together."[8] (Private collection)

(4.12   On a desert island, Robinson Crusoe holds a female goat and strokes her back: "Oh, my dearest, if only you could do laundry as well. . . ."
(Private collection)

Only in jokes set in outposts are men deprived of women, and even there, it is suggested that they "adapt." But women's deprivation is universal, due to the greater number of females than males, the result of tremendous losses in the Russian male population in this century addressed in chapter 3. Thus, a joke about female sexual deprivation seems not so much a joke as a statement of the plight of a single Russian woman:

> (4.13)   "Maria Ivanovna, what do you like more: the New Year's party or sexual intercourse?"
> "The New Year's party. It happens more often." (Private collection)

The same theme is found in a number of chastushkas, a primarily rural genre, which reflect the fact that in the Russian countryside females outnumber males in even greater proportion.

(4.14)	Ty mne ne rodnaia	You're not my dear one,
	Ne rodnaia, net.	Not my dear one—no!
	Mne teper' drugaia	Nowadays another babe
	delaet minet.	sucks me off.
	A eshche drugaia	Yet another babe puts out
	prosto tak daet.	for me for free.
	Kto iz vas rodnee,	Which of you are dearer to me,
	Khui vas razberet.	Nobody can tell. (Kozlovsky 1982, 317)

There are few jokes about male masturbation (unless it is a case of an oversexed man, as in Draitser 1998, 50) but plenty on female masturbation:

> (4.15)   Three women stand in line to buy fresh cucumbers.
> The first said: "Gimme those that are the longest and hardest."
> The second: "Gimme those that are the thickest and hardest."
> The third one is silent.
> "What kind of cucumbers do you want?"
> "It doesn't matter. I need them for salads." (Private collection; for an American joke about old maids and bananas see Fine 1981, 220).

One of the few jokes that refer to a man's masturbation is actually just a misogynist jibe: Women are worse than a man's left hand. In Russian culture, the left can suggest something wrong or inferior (cf. a saying about a bad mood: "he got up on the left foot," *vstal s levoi nogi*):

> (4.16)   The diary of a masturbating man.
> "Today, I tried my right hand. I received a great pleasure."

"Today, I tried my left hand. Not as good as with my right hand, but also okay."

"Today, I fucked a woman. A pitiful resemblance to my left hand." (I. Raskin 1995, 307).

In the folk mind, male masturbation is generally looked upon as a contemptible act, which the word "onanism" [onanism] connotes. To call a man an *onanist* is a strong insult.

Even harsher is the folk attitude toward homosexuals. The very word "pederast" (colloquially most often *pidor;* Elistratov 1994, 329) has been used traditionally as an insult to all males, and it refers to all male homosexuals, not necessarily pedophiles. The following joke, which reflects this usage of the word, is a jocular rendering of a homosexual's wish to take revenge on the insensitive public and come out of the closet:

(4.17)   One pederast was asked about his greatest dream.
"My greatest dream is to take part in the finale of the World Cup in soccer as a member of Russia's team. And at the last minute, I'm assigned to do an eleven-meter penalty kick. And I intentionally miss the goal. And they jump up from the stadium's 100,000 seats and shout: 'Pederast, pederast, pederast!' And I'm bowing, and bowing, and bowing!" (I. Raskin 1995, 314)

Some Russian jokes on homosexuality are surprisingly gentle considering the harsh treatment of homosexuals in Russian law, which only recently dropped the article punishing homosexual acts, and in public opinion:

(4.18)   A homosexual is tried in court. In accordance with Soviet law, he is sentenced to a few years of confinement in prison. He is allowed one last word before he is taken away. He stands up and says, "I like the prosecutor's right-hand man very, very, very much." (Private collection)

Beginning in the late 1970s, an emotionally neuter term "blue one" [goluboi; popularly attributed to the color of infant boys' clothing] began to be used in Russian everyday discourse to denote male homosexuals:

(4.19)   Two "blue ones" are sitting in a trench. One says: "The Whites are coming!"
The other asks:"Are there handsome ones among them?"
"No."
"Well, then—fire!" (Kulikov 1997, 417)[9]

Many jokes on homosexuality, however, show Russian unwillingness to accept the reality of homosexuals existing among them; they shift it outside of the group: to foreigners (usually Frenchmen), minorities (Armenians and Georgians), or socially disparaged members of law enforcement agencies (police). Sometimes the targets are combined, as in 4.21:

(4.20)   A question to Armenian Radio: "Is it true that Tchaikovsky was a homosexual?"
"True. But that's not the only reason we love him." (Private collection)

(4.21)   In a Parisian police precinct, a telephone is ringing: "Police! Come over quickly! There is a fight here between homos and prostitutes."
"And how are ours doing?" (I. Raskin 1995, 314)

Attributing what is perceived as a vice to an outsider group is a known tendency in folk humor. For example, the open-mouth kiss called "French" in contemporary American culture was called "Tartar" in medieval Russia (Eve Levin 1989, 175). By the same token, the Russians call oral sex "French love," as it is clearly identified in the opening chapter of Bulgakov's *The Heart of a Dog.* In the Chukchi jokes, the Chukchi learns about it by marrying a French woman.[10]

While the main concern of Gallic off-color jokes is variety and refinement of sexual technique (Hartogs and Fantel 1967, 157), Russian sexual jokes show little interest in either but simply in the fact that an act takes place. In this respect, they are closer to Anglo-Saxon jokes in their nastiness and (often barely disguised) aggression. Most Russian jokes express the simple truth that in the world of Russian sexual humor, there is no such thing as making love. (See 4.8.) Since in contemporary male folklore, a sexual encounter is filled with misogynist feelings, it reverses the slogan of American youth in the late 1960s—"Make love, not war." In Russian male folklore, hostility and cruelty toward women are rarely hidden. As Mulkay (1988) observes, "men's domination of women can never be entirely divorced from the ways in which women's bodies are used by men, nor from the ways in which this use is given meaning through men's, and women's, use of language. The use of, and attitudes towards, a human being's body by other person can involve a fundamental form of domination. It is this kind of domination which is most clearly evident in the course of humor where, of course, it is not taken seriously" (142).

Thus the language of sex is the language of dominant masculinity. Popovsky (1985, 436–437) notes the cruel, mocking, and contemptuous nature of such expressions, frequently used in Russian man-to-man conversations referring to sexual intercourse, as "to shove it to her" *[zapendriachit' (ei)]*; "to work [her] out" *[otdelat' (ee)]*; "to keep [her] frying" *[nazharivat' (ee)]*. I would add "to bang her" *[trakhnut' (ee)]*; "to flog [her]" *[drat' (ee)]*.[11] (Similar expressions exist in American males' slang: "to bang," "to belt," "to do a grind," and so on; Spears 1982, 18, 291).

"Sexuality as a physical force" is a folk metaphor present in other cultures, even in the language of sexual attraction (e.g., in English "She's devastating," "He bowled me over," "She's a bombshell," "He's strikingly handsome," and so on; Lakoff and Johnson 1987, 74; there are similar Russian ones: "I saw her and got dizzy" *[uvidel ee i zakachalsia]*. The language of violence is also used in a jocular way to describe passionate lovemaking, in which male sexual initiative and his active part in intercourse are presented in an exaggerated manner, as, for instance, in one of Woody Allen's stand-up routines describing "his" sexual escapades with a "tall blonde": "I showed her no mercy." It is with this attitude in mind that sex may symbolize corporal punishment, as in the following item:

(4.22) A wife comes home and sees that her husband is fucking their housemaid. He keeps his cool.

He comes up to the TV set, touches it with his finger: "See dust?"

Then he does the same thing on their bureau, on the windowsill . . .

"So, here it is, for the first offense, I fucked her. Next time I'll fire her." (I. Raskin 1995, 132)

These coital slang expressions also treat women as objects. They may connote a wish to bring bodily harm to a woman's vagina.[12] Beyond these emotionally highly charged verbs one of Russian men's many sadistic notions can be sensed; the more he hurts a woman during intercourse, the more pleasure he derives from the act. In his satirical travelogue *Abroad [Za rubezhom]*, the Russian writer Mikhail Saltykov-Shchedrin gives a description of the sadistic sexual fantasy of an average St. Petersburg official. Looking at a Berlin street, he recalls St. Petersburg "at around five o'clock, before dinner": "Here is that fop, a railroad official, who rushes past as fast as his [horse] can go—why does he look so preoccupied? What high thoughts is he thinking? Alas! he thinks the simplest thought, just this: either how to overeat so much that his pants would split (hitherto he had, for some reason, been unable to achieve this effect), or how to [work over] 'that scamp Alfonsinka'[13] so that afterward she would not be able to sit for a whole month" (quoted in Draitser 1994, 78).

Another frequently used vernacular expression for intercourse is "to throw her a stick" *[kinut' (ei) palku]*, (cf. an American expressions "to throw her a fuck" and "stick it to her"). The very words used here are also used in reference to a dog whose master tests his obedience. The following joke (Genis 1994, 3: 13) reflects this notion. The double meaning of the word "to bang" ("to strike" and "to fuck") is its main comic device:

> (4.23)   A grandfather with his little granddaughter and a doggy are having a walk. The doggy is barking nonstop.
> "Grandpa, is our doggy, Zhuchka, a bitch?"
> "Yes," the grandpa replies.
> "Then bang her, and she will quiet down."
> "What are you saying, little girl! Who gave you this idea?"
> "Well, I heard Daddy say to Mummy: "If I don't bang you in the morning, you bitch, you'll keep barking all day." (Private collection)

The expression "to throw a stick" implies a distance between a man and a woman and underscores the absence of any intimacy. Also, without a modifier, a stick *[palka]* is usually assumed to be wooden. When applied to humans, this serves as a synonym for insensitivity, as in "I became wooden [numb]" *[ia oderevenel]*, or "He is not a human being but a block of wood" *[On ne chelovek, a dereviannaia churka]*. Thus, the phrase "to throw a stick" *[kinut' palku]* becomes an expression of the male's attitude toward intercourse as something that does not get him emotionally involved.

There is no question that Russian behavioral prescriptions in sex matters are used to sustain and reinforce the gender hierarchy. A Russian man sets standards for a woman that are impossible to meet. On one hand, she is supposed to be modest and virtuous; her complete ignorance in sexual matters should serve as the ultimate proof of her purity. A woman who initiates sex is considered "extremely forward" (Visson 1998, 122). Russian writer Vassily Aksyonov (1989) observes that "in English you can say 'She fucked him,' thereby acknowledging the woman's initiative. The equivalent in Russian sounds strange, almost ungrammatical" (137). If the woman shows the slightest acquaintance with lovemaking during the first sexual encounter, she risks being accused of debauchery and scorned as a "slut." As a Russian proverb collected by Dahl (1984) attests, treatment of female sexual ignorance as praiseworthy is part of a peasant tradition: "What a girl doesn't know makes her more beautiful" *[Chto devushka ne znaet, to ee i krasit]* (2: 206). (See also Rubina 1995, 82.)

(4.24) A man finds a friend painting his penis green on the eve of his wedding.
"What are you doing that for?"
"That's for the wedding night. When I undress, if she asks me why it's green, I'll ask her, 'And how do you know what color it's supposed to be?'" (Private collection)

This folkloric concept is echoed in a Russian sex consultant's experience with his patients. He found that a wife would not dare to tell her husband how she wanted to be caressed: "The husband would demand to know where she had gotten the idea . . . and it would come out that the woman had either experienced it with a more imaginative man or that she had discovered it for herself, through masturbation. Husbands detest both" (reported in Kon 1995, 172).

A verb used most often to connote a woman's passive function in sex is *davat'*, literally, "to allow." (In contrast, the American term for a similar female act is active: "to put out.") A bride is often rendered as dough and lovemaking as kneading it, as, for example, in a children's teasing rhyme: "Bridegroom and bride! Do it, do it to the dough" *[Zhenikh i nevesta, tili-tili testo]*. The repeated verb *tili* most likely derives from old Russian *tililis-nut'* or *tilisnut'*, both meaning "to strike, to beat" (Vasmer 1986, IV: 57–58). The woman's passivity (often frigidity) does not bother the Russian man, who is interested mostly in his own sexual gratification:

(4.25) A man and his wife are making love. The husband asks his wife:
"Did I hurt you?"
"No, why do you ask?"
"You moved."[14] (Dolgopolova1982, 99)

In this joke the man's anxiety can be discerned, albeit vaguely, by his all-too-readily suggested reason for his wife's "unusual" behavior—apparently the only explanation he can handle. (Note that this is a married couple.)

On the other hand, while being passive, the woman should not bore the man and should be willing and able to fulfill any of his sexual whims. (See Kon 1995, 174.) However, if she does so, she is, again, rebuked for it. Even a request for a variety in lovemaking could get her in trouble; she might be immediately reminded who is in charge. As in courtship, sexual initiative is always a male prerogative:

(4.26) A man brings a woman to his apartment and begins fucking her. She keeps whispering to him all the time: "My dear, a bit higher. . . . My dear, a bit lower. . . ."

Then again: "My dear, a bit higher. . . . My dear, a bit lower. . . ."
Finally, he can stand it no longer: "Listen, who is fucking whom?
Am I fucking you or you me?" (Private collection)

(4.27)   One friend asks the other, "Listen, why don't you marry?"
"Well, here's the thing. I'm looking for a wife who would be a
boss in the kitchen, a prostitute in bed, and a queen with [our]
guests."
Time passes. The friends meet again.
"They say you finally got married?"
"Well, I just got divorced."
"Why?"
"She got it all mixed up. She turned out to be a queen in the
kitchen, a boss in bed, and a whore with [our] guests." (Genis 1994,
1: 16)

As a Russian man cannot stand a woman who tries to take charge in bed
and Russian sexual education is rudimentary (see Kon 1993, 27–35; Shcheglov 1993, 158), it is no wonder that fellatio (in Russian, *minet*—Flegon
1973, 196, evidently from French *minet*, "pussy"; *sdelat' minet* literally "to
make a pussy") is usually initiated and requested by the man only.

(4.28)   "What is the five-letter word for a female sexual organ?"
"A mouth." [In the original the word has three letters: *rot*.] (Milgram 1985, 9)

As another example of transferring to other cultures sexual practices considered immoral, fellatio in Russia is often considered French. The following
joke hinges on the double meaning of the word *iazyk,* which in Russian denotes both "language" and "tongue."

(4.29)   Two girlfriends meet.
"How is your French *iazyk* (language) progressing? Have you
mastered it?"
"Not yet. But I have mastered my *iazyk* (tongue) in the French
way." (Kulikov 1997, 338)

However, it is the woman submitting to this practice who, in the male folk
mind, comes across as perverted (Popovsky 1985, 411). The act is considered degrading to her, as a Russian male insult directed at a woman (sometimes at a man as well; in that case it carries a homosexual connotation)

reveals: "you, the fucked in the mouth" *[ty, v rot ebanaia]*. See also a nick-name for a girl—"a female sucker" *[sosalka]*—in contemporary Russian slang (Elistratov 1994, 442).

In his book *Sex Talk*, Myron Brenton (1972, 55) shows that the male compulsion to engage a woman in this technique points to misogyny; such a man "views his penis as an instrument of degradation and when it's in the girl's mouth in effect he's saying, 'I'm defiling you.' (All the more so if she allows him to ejaculate in his mouth, or if he does so before she can stop him.)"

On the other hand, a husband's request for fellatio may mean to his wife that he has a dirty mind. Sexual ignorance is a constant feature of many Russian marriages (Popovsky 1985, 411) and it has even broken up some. At the same time, the Russian man seldom expresses a desire to rec-iprocate with cunnilingus, a practice acknowledged in Russian erotic folk-lore of the past (e.g., in a proverb: "The cunt has lots of sweets in it—you can't lick all of it with your tongue" (*Mnogo v pizde sladkogo: vsego iazykom ne vylizhesh'*; Claude Carey 1972, 71); and in an erotic tale collected by Afanasiev (1991, 53) entitled "In a Doggy Style" *[Po-sobach'i]*, and pro-hibited by the Russian medieval religious codes (which banned fellatio as well; Eve Levin 1989, 175).

Brenton (1972, 56) points to the symbolic meanings of men's refusal to perform cunnilingus on their female partners. Noticing that "not infre-quently they're the same men who must have fellatio," he explains such re-fusal as the man's preoccupation with power ("'It would put me in a position of subservience, something I can't abide'") and misogyny: "'I'm basically nauseated by the female sex,'" and "'I don't want to give you all that plea-sure.'" A contemporary Russian proverb states with contempt: "Instead of chewing a salty clitoris, it's better to drink a liter of vodka" *[Chem zhevat' solenyi klitor, luchshe vypit' vodki litr;* Kozlovsky 1982, 230]. In contempo-rary Russian slang, a man who practices cunnilingus has a disparaging nick-name: "one who licks whores" *[bliadoliz;* Iliiasov 1994, 23; on a pattern of *bliudoliz,* "lickspittle"; literally, "one who licks dishes;" "toady").

Legman's (1968, 357) observation about Western erotic folklore—that "not a single joke has been collected" in which a man acknowledges his re-sponsibility for not bringing a woman to orgasm—is not only fully applic-able to Russian male folklore but must be taken one step further. Since female satisfaction is treated as totally irrelevant, Russian male jokes do not address it in any way. Even such a widespread form of male impotence as premature ejaculation, about which there are plenty of jokes in Western folklore,[15] is virtually absent in Russian jokelore for the simple reason that this notion is related to a female's sexual fulfillment. The following rather crude jokes give a quite accurate picture of a typical Russian sex act, which is not unlike the well-known American "bang, bang, thank you, ma'am" (minus "thank you"):

(4.30) Mounting his wife, a husband says: "Klava, I'll buy you a new fur coat. A new fur coat. A new fur coat. A new fur . . . coat." He exhales. "Klava, why do you need a new fur coat?" he says, dismounting. (Private collection)

(4.31) Feeling that she's near her orgasm, a wife whispers to her husband: "Vassya, do something painful."
Her husband responds: "Right now I'll come [have an orgasm] and beat up your ugly mug." (O. Ivanova 1996, 510).

Sometimes absence of one kind of jokes in a culture helps to understand the jokelore of the other. There are no Russian jokes similar to the American "Screwing a woman who doesn't screw back is like talking into a dead telephone" (Fine 1981, 119) because such jokes would not work in Russia. There are very few Russian jokes about female frigidity—from the outset, her participation in sex is not expected.[16]

In fact, the word "orgasm" came into the speech of educated Russians rather recently, with the breakdown of Communist ideology and influx of Western sex manuals on the post-Soviet book market. In Russian jokelore, there are no jokes about the "Big O" similar to those in American popular culture, for the simple reason that a woman is not expected to have one. Russian jokelore of the latest vintage (1998) occasionally treats a woman's orgasm as an act of male benevolence, an extra for which a man expects special gratitude:

(4.32) A husband lies with his wife in bed resting after sex.
The husband: "Have you had your orgasm?"
His wife: "Yes!"
The husband: "What do you say?"
"Thank you!!!" (Kulikov 1997, 289)

The Russian verb "to finish" *[konchit']* indicates the male's ejaculation. While the English equivalent of the state of the highest sexual excitement ("coming") connotes approaching a partner, the Russian counterpart word signals quite the opposite—the end of a sexual act and a parting. A contemporary take-off of a Russian proverb "Once you've finished your business, you're a free bird" *[konchil delo—guliai smelo]* expresses the male attitude rather clearly: "Once you've finished [i.e., ejaculated] into a body, you're a free bird" *[konchil v telo—guliai smelo;* Elistratov 1994, 206]. The following joke shows the male's "concern" for his sexual partner's fulfillment:

(4.33)   The man gets out of bed and says to the woman: "You know what, Masha, you go ahead and finish [have an orgasm] on your own here, and I'm going to have a smoke."[17]

If the word "orgasm" is mentioned in Russian sexual humor, it is, as a rule, the orgasm of the one who is entitled to it, the male. The following joke clearly demonstrates that coitus is solely for a male's enjoyment:

(4.34)   "Listen, does your wife close her eyes when you, Ivan, have an orgasm?"
"Always—she can't stand it when something is good for me."
(Private collection)

It is significant that, despite the similarity of many Western and Russian sex jokes, not a single Russian joke can be found that is analogous to the American item: "Telephone service is getting worse. One fellow put his finger in the operator's hole, and it took her ten minutes to come" (Fine 1981, 219).

Putting aside, for the sake of argument, the demeaning, misogynist nature of the joke and the male's ignorant and egotistical expectation that a woman should reach orgasm instantaneously, a joke of this kind could not even enter the Russian male's mind for at least two reasons: The whole focus on the female orgasm is absolutely non-Russian, and Russian men consider emasculating any substitute for a phallus.

In the post-Soviet period, Russian media have hastily taken up mass sexual education and introduced the notion of orgasm as a novelty, as a new kind of prestige commodity worth having. The newspapers are full of articles with such catchy titles as "Sexuality Businessman Style" or "A Man Always Wants, a Woman Wants Love" written by psychologists and sexologists. Here is one of the jokes about this sudden rush of sexual openness:

(4.35)   An attractive young woman comes to a sexologist's office: "Doctor, my husband and I have everything: money in our bank account, a car, an apartment. The only thing we don't have is an orgasm" (*Moscow Komsomolets,* July 23, 1995: 8).

Other Russian jokes of the post-Soviet period play with this new word in the unfamiliar sexual vocabulary.

(4.36) "We keep making an unforgivable mistake," says an old Odessan to his wife.
"What's that?"
"Today I visited a doctor. It turns out that what we think is orgasm is just an asthmatic episode." (Rastaturina 1995, 204)

The newly discovered idea of a need to vary sexual intercourse is met cautiously by the Russian folk whose crammed living conditions have always hindered normal sexual life; Western sexual norms cannot be considered on Russian soil. Although slowly improving, this situation is still quite dramatic: in 1992, 51 percent of Moscow respondents to a sociological poll lived in the same room with other family members (cited in Pankratova 1997, 23). Predictably, numerous Russian jokes treat the absence of privacy. This one is told by a Russian in Ukrainian, another example of the tendency of folk humor to transfer any awkward or emotionally ambivalent practice to outsiders; Ukrainians are often cast as unsophisticated hicks:

(4.37) "Mikola, did you love you wife at least once in the light of day?"
"No, Mikhailo, never."
"Why don't you try it? It's such a joy!"
In a few days: "Mikhailo, I thank you. We made love in the daylight. It's such a joy, such a joy. Especially for the children: they almost died laughing." (Alaev 1995, 140)

(4.38) What is drama? It's when you have what is needed to do it but don't have one to do it to.
What is tragedy? When you have what is needed to do it and one to do it to—but there is no place to do it. (Private collection)

(4.39) A husband decides to make love to his wife and says to their five-year old son: "Go to the window and watch carefully. As soon as you spot a soldier, I'll give you a ruble."
As the couple begin their love making, their son shouts: "Here comes a soldier!"
"Good fellow!" shouts his father from the back of the room. "You have just earned yourself a ruble. Keep looking for more."
"Daddy, one more soldier is coming!"
"There you go! You've got yourself another ruble."
Some time later, the son says: "Well, Daddy, it looks like you and Mummy are going to go bankrupt with your sexual intercourse. Right there, a whole platoon of soldiers is marching. . . ." (Private collection)

(4.40) A father tells his son to sit on a windowsill and tell him what's going on in the street, while he retreats to the back of the room with his wife.

The son comments: "A cat is crossing the street. . . . A tram is running. . . . The Ivanovs in the opposite flat are also making love. They've put my friend Yury in the window. . . ." (Private collection)

(4.41) After putting his son to bed, a husband suggests making love to his wife. She asks him to wait until their son is asleep.

Some time later, the husband repeats his request, but his wife feels that the child's sleep is not deep enough. The frustrated husband gets up and goes to the kitchen. Not knowing what to do with himself, he sees a bottle of champagne and decides to treat himself to it. He uncorks the bottle with a pop, pours some into a glass, and drinks with pleasure.

On hearing the sound, his little son raises his head from the pillow and says to his mother: "See what your fussiness has led to! Because you were so stubborn, father has shot himself in the kitchen!" (Smetanin and Donskaia 1992, 57)

(4.42) On the first bunk of a double-decker bed, two little children are sleeping, and above them their parents are making love. The younger one wakes up and shakes the older one:

"Hey, what's that? An earthquake?"

"No, it's not an earthquake," is the reply. "It's two idiots who are trying to make a third one and wreck us in the meantime. . . ." (JFR 3/8/98)

Even those lucky enough to have a place of their own have often been embarrassed and intimidated by the poor quality of Soviet-style housing. As in the student dormitory of the 1920s in Ilf and Petrov's famous novel *The Twelve Chairs* (Chapter 16), lovers had to burn Primus stoves to guard themselves from neighbors listening to their "kisses." Such a condition continued throughout Soviet period and is still known today.

(4.43) A man is visiting his friends in a new dwelling. In the middle of conversation, he interrupts himself and asks: "Do you have mice, or what?"

"No, it's our neighbors eating salad." (Nikulin 1997, 366)

Although they hardly could be accepted as true-to-life experiences, a number of Russian jokes tickle the Russian funny bone by having unlikely places as substitutes for the lack of private spaces in the Soviet Union. These are jokes about sexual contacts in transportation, in a doctor's office, in public bathhouses where a married couple could get a family room.

(4.44) A man presses his partner to himself tenderly and whispers in her ear as they dance: "Ah, I feel I'm in paradise!"
"Really? And I feel I'm in a city bus." (JFR 3/19/98)

(4.45) In a packed-to-capacity bus, a woman says in a rough, stern voice: "Citizen, take your hand off my breast!"
In a soft voice: "No, not you, you may leave it there. . . ." (Private collection)

(4.46) During rush hour, in a streetcar, there is a terrible jam. A young woman says to her mother: "You know, mother, it seems I'm going to have a baby."
"From whom, dear?"
"I don't know. I can't turn around to look at him." (JFR 3/7/98)

(4.47) A young couple comes to a sex consultant's office.
"You know, Doctor, we don't enjoy each other at all. We read literature on the topic, we try, but nothing good happens."
"Well," the doctor says. "Do the following. Go behind this folding screen, undress, try another position."
After a while, the doctor asks: "So? Any progress?"
"Nothing. We don't feel a thing."
"Well . . . try to do it in this way. . . . Again nothing? How about this way? . . . No success?"
"No, Doctor."
"What a complicated case!" says the doctor in dismay, and dials his colleague's number to consult with him.
"Chase them the hell out of your office." his colleague shouts. "They've already visited all the doctors ten times. They just don't have a place of their own where they can do it." (Rastaturina 1995, 185–186)

(4.48) A husband says to his wife: "Let's go to the public bath. We'll bathe at the same time." (Private collection)

Kon (1995, 81–82) describes the homelessness of Russian lovers, citing not only lack of living quarters and hotel rooms that could give them refuge, but the puritanical attitude of hotel personnel who would keep a couple from sharing a room if they failed to prove that they were married. (In the Soviet period, those with local addresses on their passports would also be turned away). As a result, many young people's sexual encounters typically take place in a hallway *[paradnaia]*, usually late at night when there is less possibility of interruption. In current youth slang, such love making is nicknamed "biathlon" (McLovsky, Klyne, and Chtchuplov 1997, 41).

(4.49) "I love having sex in the hallway," says one man to another. "If a woman is taller than I, I stand one step above her. If she's much shorter, I step down."

"I also love it, but for a different reason," says another. "You can always tell: 'Oh, somebody's coming!'" (Private collection)

Russians acknowledge the demeaning and degrading character of such encounters. A man may say about a woman whose behavior seems to him sexually loose: "She's the type that you pay 2.50 for in a hallway" *[ona—2.50 v paradnoi]*.

Absence of a suitable place for intimacy is often not the only hindrance to achieving it. As Hingley (1977, 186) notes, " . . . in this land of restricted privacy, the domestic hearth is more vulnerable to the intrusion of licensed or self-appointed snoopers in accordance with the assumption, so characteristic of totalitarian mores, that everybody's affairs except the state's are everybody else's business."

This custom of snooping in a neighbor's affairs is hardly a product of a totalitarian regime alone, although it was definitely encouraged. The old village scene—babushkas sitting in front of a building and making snide remarks about visitors to the building—"sitting on earthworks and warming their little bones in a little sun" *[sidet' na zavalinke i gret' starye kostochki]*—was carried over to the city.

(4.50) "Listen," says one man to his friend, "when I'm away on business, I suspect that my wife cheats on me. What should I do to check up on her? Hire a private shamus?"

"What for?" says his friend. "I have the same suspicions. But there's no need to hire anyone. As soon as I come back from my business trip and come to my building, I say to all those babushkas sitting in front of it: 'Greeting, sluts!' And they shout back right away: 'Do you think that *we* are sluts? You just don't know anything about your wife! As soon as you left, she . . . ' And they tell me everything that happened in my absence." (Private collection)

Coital Positions

Perhaps the most telling in terms of gender hierarchy is the treatment of the choice of coital positions. As in many other cultures, in which the earth is female (mother earth), and the sky is male (the heavenly father) (Vern L. Bullogh, as cited in Highwater 1990, 8), Russians consider normal the "male-on-top" position, known as "missionary " in the West. In medieval Russia, this position was called "on horseback" *[na kone]* and believed to correspond to "the divinely ordained structure of the universe" (Eve Levin 1989, 172–3). The mythology of creation as the root of such practice aside, this position is highly metaphoric as to the overall relationship between the sexes in Russia.[18] As "the submissive female sexual patterns and the dominant male patterns have come to stand for submissiveness and dominance in non-sexual contexts" (Morris 1970, 105), in the Russian male-centered culture, the male-on-top position often epitomizes social domination. The expression "to be on horseback" *[byt' na kone]* in Russian means to be in the saddle, that is, in a commanding position, to succeed, to be the victor. Considering the semiotic significance of such a position, the following peasant joke (Popovsky 1985, 425; for a variant, see Flegon 1973, 322) treats the very act as an expression of domination over the other, a woman being a token object of male social contention:

(4.51)   A husband warns his wife that, if she doesn't do things his way, he'll spend the night with the neighbor's wife Man'ka.
   His wife rebuffs him with: "What if I go to [Man'ka's husband] Pet'ka, would you be pleased with that?"
   "You are a fool, and a fool you are!" says her husband. "Why can't you understand a simple matter! After all, if I fuck Man'ka, that means we fuck them. And if you get involved with somebody else's husband, it would mean they fuck us." (Private collection)

In a more subtle form this semiotic significance of the sexual act (who is doing what to whose wife) and the same cultural concept of men fighting through the sexual conquest of one another's women is at the core of the following post-Soviet joke about the new Russian capitalism. In this item, the absence of modifiers for "wife" give the word a double entendre. (It could mean "my wife" or "your wife," thus allowing an innocent question to be turned into an implication that the responding man has slept with the inquiring man's wife, and then made known that he was aware of similar tactics used against him.)

(4.52) Heads of two competing firms meet at a conference.
"How's the wife?" one says.
"Thank you, well," the other says, "and mine?" (JFR 3/12/98)

The reversed position, a woman on top, was considered "a great sin," severely punishable by the medieval Orthodox church (Eve Levin 1989, 172). In contemporary Russia, such lovemaking is commonly treated as highly objectionable by religious and nonreligious men alike. To permit a woman to take the top position during intercourse (even temporarily) signifies for a Russian his weakness, both physical and sexual; it is perceived as totally unmanly and emasculating. One of my Russian male informants, a secondary-school teacher of physics in his late 40s, was highly irritated and indignant at the very thought that he would allow a woman to position herself on top of him during intercourse. He went on to say that he would never tolerate such humiliation. (See also Kon 1995, 123.) When the perestroika film *Little Vera* was shown to Russian audiences, the viewers accused the filmmakers "of not even understanding the sex act, since in several scenes they placed the women on top" (Attwood 1993b, 112).[19]

Brenton (1972, 53) also suggests that a man's insistence on the missionary position may indicate that he "[doesn't] know any other and would be very unsure of [himself] if [he] tried. But if he show[s] that much reluctance to experiment it amounts to the same thing—[he has] to be in full control of [his] environment." Brenton also gives the following interpretation of the female part in accepting this position as the one and only way to make love, which is a rather common case with Russian women:

And what about the woman whose needs dovetails with [the] man's . . . ? She, too, may be saying she's afraid to try any other position. She may be saying sex isn't nice and she can bring herself to engage in it only in the most conventional, unexceptional way. There are other possibilities: being on the bottom may also give her the feeling that she's being forced to have it, which in a way removes the responsibility from her. All such feelings can dovetail into one major assumption: woman is to be dominated by man. More than likely, she shows her submissive nature in other respects as well—always deferring to a man, maybe, or acting more the servant than the equal. (53)

From the mid-1960s, when translated Western sex manuals began to circulate in underground self-publishing, known as *samizdat*, Russians became aware of the larger sex repertoires of other cultures. The following joke of the time reflects the apprehension of Russian men about this threat to the tradition:

(4.53) At the clinic lab, they mixed up urine specimens. A man comes
home with a note from the lab and shows it to his wife:
"They say my urine shows signs of pregnancy. It's all because of
you!"
"Me?"
"Yes! It's all your stupid insistence: 'Let me try on the top, let me
try on the top!'" (Private collection)

People in Moscow and other big cities are considered more sophisticated and
knowledgeable in sexual matters, as the following post-Soviet joke illustrates:

(4.54) A husband and wife are arguing about painting their bedroom ceiling. The husband wants it painted blue, and his wife—pink. The
husband turns to a family friend for advice.
"I think it's better to make it pink. After all, your wife looks at
the ceiling more often than you."
"What's with you? Are you from the provinces?" (McLovsky,
Klyne, and Chtchouplov 1997, 110)

The only other coital position, besides man on top, that is prominently
featured in Russian sexual jokelore is the so-called crayfish position *[rakom]*
(Stern and Stern 1980, 72; Flegon 1973, 295–296): the rear-entry one,
known as the "doggy style" in American slang. As part of a larger sexual
repertoire, it is used in many cultures. While in medieval Russia, such practice was strictly prohibited by the Orthodox church as being "cattlelike"
(Eve Levin 1989, 173), in contemporary Russia it is often the only position
practiced. It is perceived as characteristically Russian, as the following joke
suggests:

(4.55) A French hotel. After a long day of sightseeing a Russian tourist tries
to get some sleep, but he can't do it because of a persistent voice behind the wall, which repeats the same words in a heavy Russian accent: "La *krevetka* (shrimp), la *krevetka*, la *krevetka* . . ."
Unable to bear it any longer, the tourist finally bangs on the wall
and shouts in Russian: "Stop it. You'll wake everybody up!"
And here a rejoicing voice responds to him in relief: "Listen,
brother, can you speak her language? Well, could you tell her: 'I want
it in a crayfish position, in a crayfish position?'"

The crayfish position is featured so prominently in male jokelore that its
psychological and sociological implications deserve a special discussion. The
proclivity of Russian men to such lovemaking can be explained by the fact

that the crayfish position carries a strong symbolic meaning in terms of "status sex" (Morris 1970, 100). It is another culturally conditioned way to reinforce dominant masculinity and uphold and reconstruct the gender hierarchy. As the approach from behind is used by many quadrupeds and semiquadrupeds, such as the bear, the kangaroo, and the ape, among other animals, this "ancient female pattern of presenting the rump to the male still survives as a gesture of subordination" (Morris 1970, 105). Thus, by insisting on the crayfish position, the Russian male, sometimes consciously, often subconsciously, seeks the female acknowledgment of his dominance and her subordination. While punishment through sex is not unknown in many other cultures (Katchadourian 1972, 45) and Russian men do not resort to the crayfish position exclusively for that reason, nevertheless it is this very position that Russian popular culture considers the most denigrating to a woman, as many men recognize (Popovsky 1985, 184).

The protagonist of Pavel Lungin's film *Taxi-Blues* (1991) does exactly this—to punish his girlfriend for her flirtatious behavior with his friend the saxophone player, he sexually attacks her from behind and, despite her protests, forces her into a crayfish position. A street curse: "I'll fuck you by putting you in a crayfish position" *[Ia tebia vyebu rakom]* always aims to degrade the verbally attacked (be it a woman or a man, in the latter case it is, of course, a homosexual threat). Russian jokes featuring the crayfish position invariably carry a heavily negative connotation:

(4.56) "Why are all women sluts?"
        "Because they are fucked from front and from behind." (Milgram 1985, 101).

The crayfish position is featured prominently in many of Afanasiev's *Secret Tales*. There it usually underscores a man's outsmarting and taking advantage of a woman. The denigrating underpinning of the position is also evident in a number of Russian sayings collected by Dahl: "One must get milk [assumed: for one's children] even if one has to put oneself in a crayfish position" *[Khot' rakom stat', a moloko dostat'*; Claude Carey 1972, 58], that is, no matter how difficult or humiliating it may be. Another old Russian saying seems to justify treatment of children born out of wedlock as inferior on the grounds that they are conceived in a low-grade way, substandard or shameful for the woman: "Out-of-wedlock children are made over the ass" *[Nezakonny deti—cherez zhopu delany;* Claude Carey 1972, 73]. In contemporary colloquial Russian, the everyday expression "to do (or make) something over [one's] ass" *[sdelat' (chto-libo) cherez zhopu]* is widely used in its invariably negative meaning in a great variety of non-sexual contexts:

(4.57)   "Why does AIDS spread so drastically in our country?"
         "Because everything in our country is done over the ass." (I.
         Raskin 1995, 380).

The crayfish position is convenient for the Russian man from another point of view as well. Since Russian males are rarely concerned with the clitoral stimulation necessary for most women to achieve orgasm and are oblivious to (or simply ignorant of) the fact that intercourse from the rear "is often less pleasurable [for a woman] than frontal coition, because clitoral stimulation is lessened" (Eve Levin 1989, 174) and a female is unlikely to have an orgasm that way, the Russian man uses this self-indulgent position for it gives him total control in coitus and helps him to ignore the woman's feelings. Brenton (1972, 54) notes that because in this position "one partner doesn't face the other it can be a way of saying, 'I don't want to look at you,' or 'I don't want to take note of your feelings.'"

(4.58)   "It's already twenty years of the same thing," a man says to his friend.
         "I'm fed up with my family life and this sex with my wife."
         "Try an approach from behind," the friend says.
         "I've already tried, but nothing changes anyway."
         "It doesn't change indeed, but, on the other hand, you don't have
         to make a happy face." (Kulikov 1997, 288)

In the following joke of the Lieutenant Rzhevsky series, the self-indulgence in the male perception of this position is quite clear.

(4.59)   Masha, a gushing female gymnasium student, asks Rzhevsky in a
         languid voice: "Lieutenant, have you loved anyone to the depths of
         [your] soul [do glubiny dushi]?"
         "Do you mean, in a little crayfish position? Oh, it goes without
         saying, I have had it, I have indeed had it." (Private collection)

(This joke's cynical implications, although quite obvious, are somewhat lost in translation. Because of the absence of any article before "soul" [dusha], the word implies the soul of the man questioned. In his response, he substitutes the purely physical for the soulful. Thus his positive answer refers not to the depth of anybody's soul but to the depth of his penetration. This also implies that the women he refers to in his answer have no soul, just sexual organs.

The degrading connotation of such "lovemaking" for Russian women is evidenced in the following chastushka:

(4.60) Nadenu novo pal'tetso,	I'll put on a little coat,
Pokrashu nogti lakom,	I'll lacquer my nails,
Puskai posmotriat na litso,	Let them look at my face,
A to ebut vse rakom.	For all they do is fuck me in a crayfish position. (I. Raskin 1995, 187)

Because to give a woman pleasure is the least of the Russian man's considerations, he rarely cares about such preliminaries as making the atmosphere conducive to lovemaking or foreplay (Kon 1995, 174). Since physiologically a woman is able to satisfy a man while remaining completely passive, he is rarely concerned with her state of mind; ideally, she is expected to please him on demand. His utter disregard of her mood or inclination to have sex at a particular time is justified by stereotyping her as an insatiable being who just needs an excuse to engage in sex, as discussed in chapter 2. Since she always wants sex and just pretends she doesn't, none of her excuses should be taken seriously. As the male jokes instruct, tenacity always pays off—inevitably, the approached woman drops her "pretenses." For example:

(4.61) Riding in a train compartment are an imposing man and an elegant woman in mourning dress. At nightfall the man begins to seduce her. She is indignant at his advances. "Aren't you ashamed of yourself! My husband just died . . . . "
The man is persistent. After his long urging, the woman gives up: "Okay, let's do it. . . . But slowly and sadly. . . ." (Private collection)

A number of jokes reveal the Russian man's lack of consideration for a female's need of emotional comforting. Of the ten varieties of goals of human sexual activity described by Morris (1970, 80–123), most Russian jokes reveal a male interest in exclusively physiological and/or recreational sex devoid of emotional involvement. The following joke seems to reflect many women's complaints about the lack of postcoital tenderness:

(4.62) An artificial insemination of cows is in process. Without rushing, a veterinarian goes around the herd with a special syringe and a glass jar of sperm. Having finished the process, he gets into his Muscovite car but finds himself unable to move. The cows surround him from all sides. He blows the car's horn many times to no effect. Then he brings down the window and shouts: "Hey, you stupid cows, get the hell out of my way!"

One of the cows with big sad eyes gets her head through the window and sadly asks: "And what about a kiss?" (Private collection)

Considering that "a cow of a wife" *[zhena-korova]* is a stock phrase of the Russian male's everyday speech and "a heifer" *[telka]* is a contemporary Russian slang equivalent of "a young woman," this joke metaphorically renders the lamentable relationship between the sexes. The veterinarian in this joke stands for any Russian man who, thanks to his position of power, is able to have as many women as he can handle. The procedure of artificial insemination is a metaphor for a man's emotionless and impersonal sexual act. The plea for a kiss is the plea for at least a token of male affection. A contemporary chastushka sounds almost like a succinct version of the joke: "I'll give her lots of sperm and a tiny bit of attention" *[Podariu ei mnogo spermy i chut'-chut' vnimaniia';* Kozlovsky 1983, 39). The following joke, told from a female point of view, contrasts lovemaking with a tender lover and the usual everyday sex with a boorish husband:

(4.63) Two girlfriends meet. One asks the other:
"Why are you so sad?"
"Well, I visited my lover yesterday. Such a terrific guy! Tender, affectionate, attentive. . . . I spent three hours with him and they passed as one moment. I flew home as if I had wings. And my husband, that rough dirty drunk, took me and refucked me in his own way." (I. Raskin 1995, 186)

These jokes reflect the Russian male's attitude toward a woman as a sexual partner observed by sociologists (Kon 1995, 173): She is treated as an object the sole purpose of which is to satisfy the male. The vernacular describing the male's role in coitus is telling: "to make use of her" *[upotrebit' ee]* or "to utilize her" *[ispol'zovat' ee]*. Since the Russian man expresses no interest whatsoever in returning the pleasure given, the woman's sexual functions are mechanical at best. She is treated, therefore, not as an object of love or even lust but rather as a sexual plaything of sorts, little more than a means of masturbation:

(4.64) "What is the difference between a woman and masturbation?"
"In principle, there is none: only that in the second case there is no one to chat with." (Milgram 1985, 5)

In a rare, frank personal expression of the Russian male's attitude toward a woman, Mikhail Armalinskii (1991, 300), a Russian émigré erotic (perhaps, more properly, "self-erotic") writer, finds that "the woman is indeed a wonderful apparatus for masturbation, a living pancake batter. . . ." It is not surprising, then, to find jokes in Russian males' repertoire about a machine replacing a woman:

(4.65)　A man sees a piece of machinery called "a female substitute," buys it, and takes it home. He plugs it into an electric outlet, puts his organ in a hole, and the machine begins to work. Suddenly, the man feels an acute pain. He pulls his organ out and finds a button sewn at its tip. (Private collection)

In a variant of this joke about a woman's substitute, the result is no less disastrous for a man. The machine turns out to be an automatic milker; it can switch itself off only when a bucket's full (Dolgopolova 1982, 89). Putting aside the strong masochistic nature of these jokes, the moral seems to be quite clear: The only reason a woman cannot be replaced by a machine as a sexual partner is that she is safer.

Recent social developments in Russia have given birth to new trends in sexual behavior that are slowly changing the sexual climate. As Kon (1995, 175) attests, "general shifts in Russian sexual values and behavior seem to be clear and going in the same direction as in the West: liberalization of sexual behavior, weakening of double standards, cultural acceptance and growing consumption of erotica. The leaders and agents of these shifts are also the same people as in the West: young, better educated urban dwellers."

(4.66)　A question for Armenian Radio:
　　　　　"What's the maximum speed in sex?"
　　　　　Answer: "68. Because when at 69 you already capsize." (JFR 3/16/98)

Thus current Russian jokelore acknowledges the existence of this new youth trend; by treating it negatively, however, it shows the uneasiness that it produces.

CHAPTER 5

"What Luck! She Has a Husband and a Lover and What's More They Raped Her": Gender and Violence in Russian Jokelore

It has long been observed that many Russian folk songs, proverbs, and sayings prominently feature unexpected and unmotivated outbursts of violence directed at women. A study of contemporary folk material proves that folklore which refers to the beating and rape of women is by no means confined to the Russia of the past. In fact, the motif of violence against an unmarried girlfriend or a wife of many years permeates the whole body of contemporary Russian folklore, from children's ditties (5.1), to folk rhymes (chastushkas) (5.2), to adult jokes (5.3–5.6):

(5.1) Zhili-byli ded da baba,

Eli kashu s molokom,
Rasserdilsia ded na babu,
Trakh po puzu kulakom.

Once upon a time there was a grandpa and a grandma,
Once they were eating kasha with milk,
And the grandpa got angry at grandma,
And he punched her in the stomach with his fist.

(5.2) Menia milyi provozhal,

Vsiu dorogu tseloval,
A u samykh u dverei
Mne naveshal pizdiulei.

My dear one brought me back to my home,
He kissed me all the way there,
But at my very door
He beat me up. (Kozlovsky 1982, 71)

(5.3)   A wife comes home, and her husband, without saying a word, punches her in the face.

"Why are you beating me up?" she cries.

"If I had a reason, I would kill you, you bitch." (Private collection)

(5.4)   Husband comes home thinking: "If she dares to be absent, I'll kill her."

She was at home.

"If she does not untie my shoes, I'll punch her face."

She untied his shoes.

"If my soup is cold, I'll give her a kick."

His soup was hot.

"If she doesn't give me my newspaper, I'll hit her over her head."

She gave him his paper.

"Well, if she does not pour me a shot of vodka, I'll give her hell."

She poured him vodka.

He finished his dinner and all of a sudden punched her in the face.

"Vassya, what I have done wrong?" she cried.

"Stop fussing around so much!"[1] (Private collection)

(5.5)   A young Indian comes to his chief and says: "I want a wife."

"And do you know how to treat her?"

"How would I know? I never had a wife."

"Okay, go into a forest, find yourself a tree with a small hollow in its trunk, and get yourself trained."

A week later, the young Indian again appears.

"Did you get some experience?" the chief asks.

The young man nods.

"Well, since you know how to treat a wife, take the Little Flower. Hey, Little Flower! This young man knows how to treat a woman. You'll be his wife."

The Little Flower takes her husband by the hand and leads him to her wigwam. Once they are undressed, the husband hits her on her bottom as hard as he can.

"Why did you do that?" she cries. "It hurts!"

"Do you take me for a fool? I've had experience. First you need to chase the bees out from the hollow." (Smetanin and Donskaia 1993, 61).

(5.6)   A wife says to her husband:

"Vanya, please tell me that you love me."

"I love you, you cobra."

"Vanya, please tell me that you want me."
"I want you, you bitch."
"Oh, Vanya, you could even talk a corpse into doing it."
(Smetanin and Donskaia 1993, 4)

That a Russian male may resort to an aggressive act against a female is so deeply ingrained in the folk psyche that a girl expects a boy to behave irrationally and violently. In the game of fortune-telling with daisy petals, an American girl stops after learning that "he loves me" or "he loves me not," but a Russian girl continues with: " . . . he'll kiss me, he'll spit on me; he'll press me to his heart, he'll send me to the devil" [. . . *potseluet—pliunet, k serdtsu prizhmet—k chertu poshlet*].

Although, taken separately, the emotions expressed in the first alternative ("he loves me, he loves me not") are not necessarily opposed to each other (not loving may mean there is liking, or mere indifference), when included in the whole formula of fortune-telling, together with two other pairs of mutually exclusive actions, the expression gets emotionally "loaded" and is perceived as guessing between the male's diametrically opposed feelings, love and hate.[2] To understand such habitual female premonitions, let us look at folklore related to violence against women. Chapter 4 discussed elements of it in Russian folkloric idioms and vocabulary related to coitus. In this chapter, I examine wife-beating and rape.

Wife Beating Folklore

At least twenty proverbs and sayings in the famous Dahl collection approve of wife-beating as benefiting marriage. Here are some justifications given in folk proverbs, generally considered to be "the pearls of folk wisdom:" Beating does not really harm a woman (5.7); on the contrary, it makes her better, more precious (5.8). It even improves her health (5.9) and livens up her mood (5.10). (Cf. a Polish proverb: "If a man does not beat his wife, her liver rots" quoted in Perlez 1998, A1.) In fact, there is no such thing as too much beating (5.11). Moreover, if a wife is not reduced to tears, she can't function properly (5.12). A husband should not be disturbed by her tears, for they mean no more than the tears of a drunkard (5.13). Thus a man is ridiculous if he beats his wife and feels any compassion for her (5.14).

(5.7) "A wife is not a pot—you won't break her [when you hit her]" (Dahl 1879, I: 470).

(5.8) "Hit the *baba* [here: your wife] as hard as if you do it with a hammer. You'll make her as good as gold."

(5.9) "If your darling [a man] hits you, it only does your body good."

(5.10) "If your darling beats you up a bit, it'll only entertain you a bit."

(5.11) "Beat your wife with the back of an ax, kneel down and check it out: If she's still breathing and shows signs of life, that means she wants more."

(5.12) "Without crying a woman can't carry out her duties." (Dahl 1879, I: 439)

(5.13) "The tears of a woman and a drunkard are cheap." (Dahl 1879, I: 439)

(5.14) "What is funny is not that he's beating her, but that he's crying while he beats her." (Dahl 1879, I: 471).

This everyday "wisdom of the people" is reflected in other forms of folklore. Discussing Russian popular street entertainment of the past, Catriona Kelly (1993, 80) concludes that "[the] standard scene of the Petrushka [puppet street] show represented violence and violent licentiousness that were directed against a woman."

Contemporary samples also show that a husband needs no excuse for beating his wife. (See 5.3.) He will always come up with something, no matter how trivial the grounds may be. (See 5.4.) What are the social implications of such folklore?

Many old proverbs and sayings reflect the complete subjugation of a wife by her husband in peasant Russia. They also point to deep religious beliefs as moral justification for violence against women. Thus proverbs 5.15 and 5.16 convey the medieval Orthodox Christian church teachings according to which a woman is intrinsically evil and potentially as dangerous as the devil itself. She is seen as an inexplicable element that has to be restrained for her own good (5.17). Because a woman is treacherous and self-willed, beating her is the way to show her who is boss; hence she is always guilty as charged (5.18):

(5.15) "A woman and a devil are one and the same." [*Baba da bes—odin u nikh ves;* literally: "they have the same weight"]

(5.16)   "From our rib one shouldn't expect anything good." [*Ot nashego rebra ne zhdat' dobra;* Dahl 1879, I: 440]

(5.17)   "If you give freedom to a woman, you won't stop her." [*Babe voliu dat'—ne uniat'*]

(5.18)   "For a husband his wife is always guilty" (Dahl 1879, I: 466).

These proverbs and sayings that treat violence against one's wife as pedagogic and therapeutic echo quite closely the notorious sixteenth-century household manual, *Domostroi*. In this book a husband is instructed to beat his wife not with his fist but with a whip, "beat her carefully, removing her shirt" for such punishment is "sensible, and painful, and frightening, and healthy" (V. V. Kolesov 1991, 66).

Most contemporary jokes about wife-beating reveal the same motivation for the violence. The message of 5.5, which utilizes a folkloric figure of a young Indian who is both a "nincompoop" (a term revived by Legman [1968, 116], connoting a sexually incompetent man) and a savage-savant, is essentially the same as that of old Russian proverbs: A woman is potentially dangerous, and beating her is a way to render her harmless. As bees sting anyone reaching for the honey in their hives, a woman stings a man. Although in another sample (5.6), the abuse of a woman is only verbal, its message is not very different from that of the old proverbs: A man's mistreatment of his wife never destroys her feelings toward him. She will ignore and forgive any abuse because of the existing folkloric postulate of her sexual insatiability, discussed in chapter 2.

The notion that beating *improves* a woman is deeply rooted in the Russian psyche. Real life provides ample evidence for it. In a case recently reported in the American press, a Russian couple was divorced after eight years of physical abuse. The former husband (who got custody of the couple's seven-year-old daughter because of his substantially higher income and living conditions) still keeps phoning his former wife, saying that he only regrets not being man enough, for "if he'd only beaten [her] more, and more often, she would have been a better wife."(Vanora Bennett, December 6, 1997, A9). "In Russia," his former wife tells a reporter, "everyone expects men to beat their wives. It's considered normal."

Jokes often reveal a man's inclination to use force to keep his wife in check. A husband should be able to rule his woman with an iron fist [*derzhat' v ezhovykh rukovitsakh;* literally: to handle with gloves of porcupine quills]. In the following item, in response to his young bride's romantic expectations, the newlywed husband lets her know what kind of treatment is really in store for her. His reference to "Mumu," a famous Turgenev story, is important since it concerns the protagonist's predicament: He is forced to drown a living being (a puppy) to which he had become attached:

(5.19)   Leaving the Marriage Bureau, the young wife says to her husband:
        "Have you read Shakespeare, Vanya? Will you love me as Romeo loved Juliet? And will you be as jealous as Othello was with Desdemona?" she added coyly.
        "I read no Shakespeare," Vanya says and spits on the side walk. "But I read 'Mumu.' And I tell you right now that if you're going to give me much trouble, I'll drown you." (Private collection)

The idea that a woman has to be straightened out and disciplined at least once in a while has deep roots in popular consciousness. Many Russian women accept this notion of the husband's right to correct his wife. One of my Russian female informants, a college-educated woman in her late thirties with a successful career, claims that "we women, often stray [from the right path] *[nas, zhenshchin, chasto zanosit]*; she feels that she should be thrashed by her man at least once a month *[mne nado khotia b raz v mesiats dat' vzbuchku]*. During a scholarly conference at which this material was presented, one of its participants, a young Russian scholar, assured the audience that he had known many women who "wanted this kind of treatment." According to the following popular rhyme, a woman sees rough handling as a kind of foreplay; she doesn't seem to mind it:

(5.20)   A ia udaril tebia lopatoi   And I hit you with a shovel
        Po shirokoi spine.   Over your wide back.
        A ty skazala: And you said:
        "U, chert polosatyi!"   "Oh, you darned devil!"
        I ulybnulas' mne.   And smiled at me. (JFR 2/4/98)

This physical flirting of sorts is a juvenile form of relating to a member of the opposite gender that could be often observed in peasant culture, of which chastushka 5.20 is representative. The source of humor of the following item of the Lieutenant Rzhevsky series is another matter; it lies in the incongruity between the refinement expected of an army officer and his rough way of approaching a society lady—Natasha Rostova, the heroine of Tolstoy's *War and Peace*, with whom he is often paired in this joke series:

(5.21)   Lieutenant Rzhevsky walks along a beach with a paddle on his shoulder. He sees Natasha Rostova sunning herself. He sneaks up on her

from behind and bangs her over her head with the paddle. She cries
out in indignation: "Lieutenant, what are you doing! That hurts!"
"Oh, oh, oh—look how touchy we are!" (JFR 3/9/98)

This punch line echoes the scolding of people "with those outdated manners
of the petty-bourgeois and the gentry" with their "pretense to refinement"—
a disparagement typical of the Soviet propaganda of the 1920s. Such a dismissive attitude toward rules of civilized courtship lasted throughout most
of the Soviet period.

How did this tradition evolve in Russian society? In *The Slave Soul of Russia: Moral Masochism and the Cult of Suffering*, Daniel Rancour-Laferriere
(1995, 153–158) analyzes various reasons for peasant wife-beating. First of
all, a husband could beat her to fight off his feeling of being trapped in an
undesirable marriage. Many vows were taken not only without a bride's con-
sent but without the groom's. Under the prevailing patriarchy of a peasant
family, a son would be married to a girl from a rich family for economic reasons; it was the father's duty to marry him off. At least one old proverb addresses beating one's wife on the grounds of age difference: "An old husband
and a young wife—one should expect children; a young husband and an old
wife—one should expect flogging."

Wife-beating could also occur as a way of shifting a serf's anger at humiliation outside his household. And the situation did not improve. What
Iakob Ludimer, a liberal justice of the peace at the turn of the century, observed about the society of his time continued to be true for the rest of the
century under the Soviet regime: " . . . the state, in resorting to institutionalized violence and failing to respect the personal dignity of its subjects, created conditions that reinforced the worst aspects of traditional culture"
(quoted in Engelstein 1992, 126).[3]

In the late Soviet and post-Soviet years the problem of wife-beating became even worse because of the increased stress of male life. Natalia
Gavrilenko, deputy director of a shelter for battered women in St. Petersburg, attributes the increase in domestic violence to the fact that "[m]en
suddenly threatened with unemployment, instability, unbelievably high
prices and crime on all sides [are] more likely than before to take out their
resentment on the women at home" (quoted in Vanora Bennett, December
6, 1997, A10). The following current item addresses this issue:

(5.22) "What does a man need a wife for?"
        "Only so that he would have somebody with whom he could get
    even for the multiple wrongs that our government has committed."
    (Kulikov 1997, 382)

According to government estimates, violence occurs in one out of four Russian families (Vanora Bennett, December 6, 1997, A10). The problem is aggravated by the fact that many cases of wife-beating go unreported. With official statistics—70 percent of the unemployed are women—imprisoning a husband, the breadwinner, endangers the whole family. The following joke catches this irony of women forced to care about the well-being of their abusers.

(5. 23) Two girlfriends meet: "Manya, how's your husband?"
"He keeps drinking just as he did before. He keeps beating me just as he did before." [In Russian the line sounds like a proverb with an amplifying effect of rhyming, *kak pil, tak i p'et; kak bil, tak i b'et.*]
"Well, pray to God he doesn't get sick. . . ." (Kulikov 1997, 283)

A Russian man would also resort to beating when he feels that his wife behaves too independently. This is the most primitive way of reinforcing gender hierarchy. "Violence is . . . wrapped up, simply, with status," American writer Tom Wolfe (1989, 149) writes. "Violence is the simple, ultimate solution for problems of status competition, just as gambling is the simple, ultimate solution for economic competition." The Russian man's inclination to take out on women their unresolved anger and their proneness to violence against them has ontological roots. His deep-seated fear that a woman's independence is emasculating can be explained by peculiarities of his upbringing, as discussed in chapter 3. As in other matrifocal cultures (Rancour-Lafferriere 1985, 229) where this phenomenon also takes place, the Russian male, due to his excessive closeness to his mother and other women in his formative years, demonstrates hypermasculine behavior, part of which is a tendency to make evident his aggressiveness and physical strength. A man may beat his wife to get even for the deprivation of freedom in early childhood; his wife becomes a psychological icon of his mother.

However, what seems especially puzzling is the number of Russian proverbs insisting that wife-beating is not only a way of keeping a woman in check but an expression of true love, part and parcel of happy married life. One proverb (5.24) expresses a strong folk conviction that if a man does not beat his woman, it is a sure sign that he really does not care for her. Other proverbs claim that a woman will not care for a nonviolent husband either (5.25), for love and beating go hand by hand (5.26).

(5.24) "If a muzhik does not beat up his *baba,* it means he does not love her."

(5.25) "When you beat up a fur coat, it gets warmer. When you beat up your wife, she gets more loving toward you." (Dahl 1879, I: 470)

(5.26) "Love [her] like [your own] soul, shake [her] up like a pear tree." [Liubi kak dushu, triasi kak grushu] (Dahl 1879, II: 305).

"Tanya's Happiness" [Tanino schastie], a short story by Evgeny Chirikov (1864–1932), illustrates this notion. Tania, a young prostitute, is courted by a young servant, Nikifor. The romance advances fairly smoothly until one day, in a fit of jealousy, Nikifor severely beats her. As she weeps from pain and humiliation and curses her abuser, her girlfriend, Arisha, comforts her:

"You don't understand anything, girlie. . . ."
And Arisha began . . . telling her that if Nikifor loved her the same way her other clients loved her he wouldn't soil his hands on her; he would just spit and leave. It means that Nikifor loves her in a completely different way, truly, as a wife or a dear lover. His jealousy tortures him, and he does not have the strength to keep his heart in check.
"You, girlie, should rejoice—not cry! . . . If he weren't in love with you, he wouldn't behave like a beast. All this comes from true love, great love."
. . . And Arisha began telling her about village customs and omens and about many instances in life when a husband who loved his wife would beat her, and as soon as his love cooled, would stop beating her.

While recuperating from the ordeal, Tania looks into the mirror and says:

"He disfigured me, this madman! What a jealous character he has—I can't take it."
And at the same time she laughed, because, really, she felt that all these [beatings]—[came] from great love.
"This is all trifling, it'll pass!" Arisha soothed her. "There is a proverb 'When dear ones battle, they are only amusing themselves'" [Milye braniatsia—tol'ko teshatsia]. (Chirikov 1993, 180–181).

Why would a man be driven to beat a woman he loves? In this respect, why would he not do it to a woman he stopped loving or did not love to begin with?
In my view, there are two reasons for this behavior—one psychological and the other cultural. Putting aside for the sake of argument the possibility of a sadomasochistic relationship (after all, while not all men and women are

sadistic or masochistic, wife-beating in Russia has been an ordinary phenomenon), let us look in other directions.[4] The answer may be found in the peculiarity of male and female perception of sexuality as it has taken shape in Russia. Substantial psychoanalytical studies reveal the infantile nature of the association of sex with violence in the Russian psyche.

Rancour-Lafferiere (1995, 155–156) cites the famous case of Freud's Russian patient, Pankeev. As an infant he had inadvertently witnessed what is known as "the primal scene" (parents' coitus), which had a profound affect on his psyche and created a strong connection between violence and sex. Rancour-Lafferiere argues that, due to the crammed living conditions of the typical peasant quarters and the communal apartments of the Soviet period, the Russian child has had plenty of opportunities of exposure to "the primal scene." In the 1998 film *The Thief* set in the post–World War II period when housing shortages were especially acute, an eight-year-old boy exposed to this scene rushes to save his mother from her lover who, in the boy's mind, is trying "to strangle" her.

The association of sex with violence is corroborated by folkloric evidence and everyday speech. Nearly three dozen Russian word combinations describing physical violence—pelting, pounding, thrashing—are based on roots that denote both male and female sexual organs, as well as coitus [see, e.g., *otpizdiachit', otkhuiarit', v"ebat*].[5] And the verbs for a sex act generally denote inflicting pain on a female. Besides the verb *trakhnut'* ("to bang");[6] we may add such folk terms as "to flog her" *[drat']* and "to whip her" *[porot']*, already cited in chapter 4. Although it is not exclusively Russian (e.g., the English word "prick" comes from a meaning: "anything that pierces"), there are more nicknames for the male organ in contemporary Russian street language connoting wounding objects; for example, "a stick" *[palka]*, "a bayonet" (Elistratov 1994, 580; a sexual act is called correspondingly "a bayonet attack," "a nail," "a thorn" *[ship]*, "a broad's splinter" *[bab'ia zanoza]*, "a white fang," and so on. In fact, according to Russian linguist Nikolai Trubetskoi, the basic Russian name for a male organ *khui* comes from "pine needles" *[khvoia]*.[7] Thus one of the meanings of contemporary slang words for a male organ *shihska* (a pinecone) is quite close to the word's origin.

Russian folk association not only of genitalia with violence (Rancour-Lafferriere 1989, 228), but, by way of suggestion, of the very act of coitus with violence is seen in the erotic saying referring to abandoned lovemaking collected by Dahl: "Either the dick [is broken] in two or the vagina [is smashed] into small pieces" [*"Libo khui popolam, libo pizda vdrebesgi;* Claude Carey 1972, 51]. A recently collected item, a pun on the proverb "You can't force anyone to love you" *[nasil'no mil ne budesh']* expresses the male perception that only aggressive lovemaking is welcomed by a woman: "You can't [make a woman] love you if you don't do it with force" [*nesil'no mil ne budesh*; JFR 5/15/98].

Referring to works of various sexologists and anthropologists as well as folkloric sources, Rancour-Lafferriere (1995, 152) also discusses the psychological reasons for a peasant woman's acceptance of her husband's beating as a sign of love—her traditional upbringing in obedience and subservience to her husband, her need for love and, therefore, her "moral masochism," that is, an inclination to feel morally good as a suffering person.[8]

Since excessive consumption of alcohol was an integral part of peasant life (Semyonova Tian-Shanskaia 1993, 109), a Russian man, often drunk, would beat his wife when experiencing temporary impotence due to alcohol intake (Rancour-Laferierre 1995, 158). Some samples of Russian folklore directly associate habitual drinking with outbursts of wife-beating, unmotivated and seemingly inexplicable: "He who does not drink wine is not a drunk [implied: as any man should be]; he who does not beat his wife is not dear to her" [*Kto vina ne p'et, p'ian ne zhivet, kto zheny ne b'et—mil ne zhivet;* Dahl I: 470]. Instead of having sex (which he is, at least temporarily, incapable of) the man beats his wife, substituting one action for another that is closely associated with it in the Russian consciousness.

However, substituting one action for another can hardly be a mere reflex or evidence that the couple knowingly practices sadomasochism. Of course, beating a woman may give a sense of sadistic satisfaction similar to the one that rapists seek (Morris 1970, 17). The psychological underpinnings of beating may be more complex.

Since the ability to perform sexually is of utmost importance to the male ego, a man's sexual malfunction caused by intoxication evokes a deep feeling of humiliation, guilt, and shame, all of which he conventionally denies. Hence, he may attack his wife to fight off his feeling of "not being a man." In her book *Violent Emotions: Shame and Rage in Marital Quarrels,* Suzanne Retzinger (1991, 190) concludes: "If shame is denied, the other can be perceived as the source of hostility; [and] anger almost inevitably follows. Anger can be seen as a protective measure and represents an attempt to repair the bond. One function of conflict is to reinstate the bond."

Thus, no matter how clumsy his attempt may be, a man's violence may signify his willingness to keep this particular mate. The manifestation of his physical strength can be seen as his attempt to prove to his mate, in a way other than sexual (in which he has already failed or, based on his experience, in which he anticipates failure) that he is virile after all. In the Russian (though not only Russian) folk consciousness, strong physicality is associated with strong sexuality. (The reverse notion is also widely accepted: intellect connotes impotence; see chapter 7.) Demonstration of a man's physical power is an attempt to show that his sexual failure is of a temporary nature. By beating his wife, he sends her a message that he wants to keep her as his mate, and will regain his potency; she should not regard him as a sexual weakling.

Hence, if tradition and experience suggest strongly that wife-beating is part of normal family life, then at least some Russian proverbs may be read differently—not just as instructions for punishing one's wife. Such proverbs as "If a muzhik does not beat up his woman, it means he does not love her" or "The one I love, the one I beat" may really mean what they say. Beating, then, may be a Russian man's clumsy manifestation of his emotional attachment to the attacked woman.

Rape Jokes

While contemporary wife-beating jokes are centered on males, those about rape deal with aggressive females and are of a different psychological nature. Sexual humor may perform various functions. Told in mixed company, it may be used as a hidden invitation, what Freud calls a "proposition in earnest"[9] or, when told within the same gender group, it "may express and foster the particular values of the group" (Wilson 1979, 188). Sociologists R. Ransohoff and J. Emerson suggest that sex jokes may reflect anxiety and serve as "a request for reassurance and support"; they may be an attempt by adolescents to introduce "difficult" topics (cited in Wilson 1979, 188). And sex jokes may be used as entertainment, as temporary relief from societal inhibitions through the playful handling of tabooed topics. They are also used by adolescents to process and "evaluate sexual information, attitudes and emotions which have restricted passage within serious modes" (Mulkay 1988, 122).

However, a number of sex jokes are, and fully function as, pornography. Since what constitutes pornography is open to a wide range of interpretations, I have based my definition on the law written by the feminists Catharine MacKinnon and Andrea Dworkin at the request of the city of Minneapolis in 1983, paraphrased here by MacKinnon: "Our law defined pornography as the sexually explicit subordination of women through pictures or words that also includes women presented dehumanized as sexual objects who enjoy pain, humiliation, or rape; women bound, mutilated, dismembered, or tortured; women in postures of servility or submission or display; women being penetrated by objects or animals" (quoted by Alexandra Bennett 1997, 216).

While there is no shortage of jokes that fit all of these categories in today's Russian lore (especially those of the Lieutenant Rzhevsky series),[10] I concentrate here on rape jokes. Although similar male humor exists in Western popular culture,[11] the pervasiveness of rape jokes in Russian everyday discourse is striking. Every collection of sex jokes published since the beginning of perestroika includes a great number of them, and they are frequent on the websites that post current Russian jokes. (Jokes from Russia cited here is one of several similar sites).

What makes these jokes pornographic is that they invariably portray women as enjoying rape[12]:

(5.27) In a church: "Father, what should I do? Those bastards raped me. . . ."
    "Grate six lemons and eat them without sugar, my daughter!"
    "And what, will I be a virgin again?"
    "No, you won't. But you will be able to wipe the bliss off your face." (JFR 3/7/98)[13]

(5.28) "That he caught you was by chance, that he undressed you was also by chance, that he had you was also by chance. But that you moved your ass when you were under him, that's your sluttish behavior [bliadstvo]." (Private collection)

In the following item the fact that the female does not accept rape seems to surprise the attacker.

(5.29) An old man attacks a young woman and starts to rape her.
    "Help, help!" she shouts.
    "Why are you screaming?" the old man asks. "Do you think I can't manage it myself?" (Private collection)

To cast an old man as the attacker is an artistic ploy: His advanced age is the only reason why the girl would call for help, that is, to assist *him*.

The fact that some Russian rape jokes are set in court is not an admission of the criminal nature of the act but rather the teller's strategy to defy the notion that the law is violated.[14] The victim in these jokes expresses nothing but delight regarding the crime:

(5.30) A woman has been raped. They ask her at the police precinct:
    "How did it happen?"
    "He approached me from behind and raped me."

"Why didn't you call for help?"

"He blackmailed me all the time, he threatened me all the time: 'If you call for help, I'll leave right away.'" (Nikulin 1997, 155)

(5.31)   A woman is asked to identify the rapist in a lineup. "I think he's the one who raped me." She points to one of the men. "But for me to be absolutely sure, make him do it one more time." (I. Raskin 1995, 225)

In the following item, the very thought that rape cases should be tried is rendered laughable:

(5.32)   An old woman comes to the police precinct and says: "I was raped thirty years ago."

The policeman on duty: "We can't help you. The case is too old, it would be hard to find the criminal."

"Oh, don't tell me that, dear officer! It's so pleasant to recall, but there's no one to share it with." (Anon. 1994, 45)

This male conceptualization of rape as an enjoyable and enviable sexual escapade accounts for the narrator's indignant tone in Yury Miloslavsky's (1994) short story "Lyudmila Ivanovna's Son;" he comments on a gang-rape trial: "[T]he government, *whose resolutions reflected a keen and understandable envy-hatred for anyone who succeeded in transgressing and taking a bite at a forbidden fruit,* consistently applied the severest punitive measures, as if the rapists were traitors to Motherland or speculator-black-marketeers on an especially grand scale" (84; emphasis added). In a number of jokes, rape is not only decriminalized, it is treated as consensual intercourse, as in the following take-off of a fairy tale.

(5.33)   Gray Wolf meets Little Red Riding Hood in the forest and says to her: "Little Red Riding Hood, let me rape you?!"

"It can't be done, Gray Wolf. . . ."

"Why is that?"

"First, I'm still a virgin. And secondly, after that kind of business I get a headache." (JFR 3/31/98)

In the next item, this equating of rape with ordinary sex is achieved by featuring innocent children who do not know what they are talking about but ostensibly play the game that adults play:

(5.34)   Little Vanya and little Manya are playing hide-and-seek.
"If I find you," says little Vanya, "then I'll rape you."
"All right, and if you don't find me, I'll be behind the door." (Private collection)

However, in many other rape jokes, the same message is rendered explicitly.

(5.35)   Someone has raped Maria Ivanovna. Her girlfriends discuss this:
"What a lucky broad: She has a husband and a lover and, what's more, she's been raped." (Private collection)

(5.36)   A mother and daughter are going through a dense forest. Nobody is around. It's scary. "Mom," the daughter says, "they say you can be raped here. . . ."
"Little daughter! Not with our luck!" (Anon. 1994, 37)

(5.37)   A wife returns from a group tour of Paris.
"How did you girls spend your time there?" her husband asks.
"First they took us to the Champs-Élysee. We walked around there, and then they raped every one of us, except Maria Ivanovna. The next day, they took us up the Eiffel Tower, and when we came down, they raped every one of us, except Maria Ivanovna. The next morning, we went to the Bois de Boulogne, and then they raped every one of us, except Maria Ivanovna."
"Why didn't they touch Maria Ivanovna?"
"Well, she didn't want to. . . ." (Private collection)

These and other jokes equate raping a woman with having rough sex for the purpose of fulfilling the female's wild sexual dreams. American researches Susan Bond and Donald Mosher (1986, 163) show that, although some women may have erotic fantasies that take the form of "rape," this experience is very different from realistic rape:

When a woman selects the theme of "rape" for erotic purposes, she imagines a sexually desirable man, motivated by passion that is aroused by her sexual attractiveness, who uses just enough force to overcome her resistance and to promote her pleasure. . . . Rape is a crime in which a sexually and violently callous man, motivated by power, anger, or sadism, selects a victim of opportunity, uses force, often excessive force, to overcome resistance and to degrade the victim.

A number of assumptions about female behavior underlie actual rape worldwide. These assumptions are deeply seated in the male popular mind and surface in numerous jokes, rhymes, proverbs, and sayings. As sex jokes make "most clearly visible . . . men's most basic, serious assumptions regarding women and sexuality" (Mulkay 1988, 142), this jokelore carries one potentially dangerous message: "A true man should not listen to a woman's objections to his sexual advances." According to Russian male jokelore, "if a girl says 'no' it means 'maybe'; if she says 'maybe' it really means 'yes;' if she says 'yes', she's not a girl anymore" (implied: "not a virgin").

(5.38) "Serdtse devushki—zagadka,"   "A girl's heart is a mystery,"
        Tak skazal odin poet.   As the poet said.
        Esli dazhe liubit sladko,   Even if she loves you tenderly,
        Vse ravno otvetit—Net!   She will still answer: "No." (JFR
                                         3/18/98)

Numerous jokes dwell on the same point: Women lie when they talk about love just to cover up what they truly long for:

(5.39) A question to Armenian Radio: "Why do women love to talk about love so much, and men talk just about sex?"
        Answer: "Women always say what they're not thinking. . . ." (Private collection)

As in the West,[15] a male folk belief that every woman is full of unbearable desire, that normal intercourse does not satisfy her, that she is nonselective, that is, that she secretly welcomes *any* man lies behind rape jokes. The notion is expressed by a young man in the opening lines of Todorvsky's film *Love*. If she is unresponsive to male advances, she is just pretending to be modest and cold. She declines a male's approach only because of a cultural convention according to which a "decent" woman, who "does not want to lose a man's respect," should not reveal her sexual urges. It is this kind of assumption of female "undue modesty" and "pretending" that is behind the rampant sexual harassment that takes place on the street and at work in contemporary Russia (Powell and Palchikoff 1997, 52; Riordan 1993, 6). In the following item, the message is that even the most innocent female, a nun, not only wants to be raped but prefers it to normal intercourse for in that way she may still pretend to be innocent:

(5.40) A few soldiers catch a nun in the forest and rape her. She walks on and crosses herself: "Glory to you, O Lord! I've got it without committing sin and to my full satisfaction." (I. Raskin 1995, 224)

A woman's cry about rape is heard as evidence of excessive touchiness and immaturity, as indicated by the age of the characters in the following joke:

(5.41) Two babies are lying in a stroller, a boy and a girl. Suddenly, the girl begins to scream: "They are raping me! Help!"

The baby boy looks at her and says: "What's all that noise about? Shut up! Nobody's raping you. You're just lying down on your pacifier." (JFR 3/8/97)

As the male folk logic goes, when resisting his advances a woman implicitly invites a man to be more aggressive in order to provide herself with an excuse for engaging in sex. She is just looking for a reason to pretend that she cannot resist the man's pressure, because she is "only a weak woman," after all. A number of Russian jokes play with the notion "they ask for it."

(5.42) "I'm being raped!" a woman shouts from the second story of an apartment house.

On the first floor, a man hears the shouts and asks: "Who is raping you?"

The woman says: "You."

"How can I rape you if you're on the second floor and I'm on the first?"

"I'll come down right away." (Private collection)

(5.43) Two female cats, neighbors, meet.

"Can you imagine," one complains to another, "it's utterly impossible to walk on the next street nowadays. The day before yesterday they raped me there, and yesterday too. Today I'll go there to stroll again."[16](Private collection)

In this joke, female cats are cast because of their promiscuous image in popular culture. In male everyday discourse about women, there is an expression: "[she is] as fuck-hungry as a female cat" *[ebuchaia, kak koshka]*. Male cats are portrayed similarly (cf. Russian sayings "as lustful as a tomcat," *[pokhotlivyi, kak kot]*, and "It's not spring rites time for a cat," *[ne vse kotu Maslenitsa]*, a reference to the sexual license of the spring festival; Farrel 1991, 552).

In other jokes, immediately after the rape a victim insists on a repetition (sometimes even coercing the rapist through blackmail) usually beyond his capacity to deliver:

(5.44) A robber rapes a princess. He asks her whether she will tell her father about it.
"I'll tell him you raped me four times."
"How come—four? It was only once."
"Are you in a hurry, little robber?" (Private collection)

Of course, such a distorted male vision of female sexuality is self-serving. Telling rape jokes serves primarily as a way of keeping alive the myth of the oversexed female. Such a myth fulfills an important psychological function: By attacking women on the grounds of their alleged sexual insatiability, rape jokes help fight the Russian male's fear of sexual inadequacy—that is, in its ultimate meaning, impotence. Although such fear is familiar to males in many cultures, it is especially keen for Russians, many of whom suffer from alcoholism and, in a drunken state, experience sexual failure, at least temporarily. These jokes may proliferate because this act is "so exclusively an act of a male; [it] expresses aggressive masculinity better than other types of sadistic activity" (Morris 1970, 117).

It is noteworthy that in rape jokes little time is given to the act:

(5.45) A schoolgirl stays out all night. She shows up in the morning. Her father meets her at the door: "What were you doing all night?"
"Da-daddy, they . . . they raped me . . ."
"For this one needs ten minutes, and I am asking you what you were doing all night!" (Private collection)

In many versions of this joke,[17] the time spent on rape is even shorter—only a minute. This is not by chance. We have already noted that the folk male view of a sexual encounter as invariably quick and to the point reflects self-centeredness and widespread ignorance of the woman's needs[18] and is reinforced by the living conditions of most of the population. The vast majority of Russian émigré writer Mark Popovsky's (1985) respondents in his sampling of former Soviet citizens (immigrants in the United States) reported the absence of a separate apartment or even a separate bedroom along with "the excessive attention of their neighbors" in communal apartments as major obstacles to a normal sex life. For many urban dwellers, under circumstances that afford limited opportunities for privacy, "quick sex" is often the only option.

Jokes treating rape not as a display of power and hatred toward women but as a sign of male passion through violence welcomed by women may have other cultural roots. Russians see passionate love as necessarily spontaneous, mysterious, awesome (Gray 1990, 115), and barely manageable (Visson 1998, 121). This concept may be traced to the deep pagan traditions that pervade everyday culture.[19] What Denis de Rougemont says about this concept—that it spread in medieval Europe "as a reaction to Christianity (and in particular to its doctrine of marriage) by people whose spirit, whether naturally or by inheritance, was still pagan" (quoted in Highwater 1990, 141)—can be said about today's Russia.

Whatever the reason, the more passionately a Russian man claims to be in love, the more forgivable he assumes his lack of self-control. Under such cultural expectations, a tender and gentle sexual encounter is considered not only counterproductive but almost a contradiction in terms.[20] This assumption serves as grounds for a Russian man's complete projection of his feelings onto a woman, whom he may well respect, desire, and even love. He assumes that she derives the same pleasure as he does (or even more) from the sheer act of penetration, no matter how short it may be (Stern and Stern 1980, 72).

This, in part, explains why Russian men adopt a quick and forceful style of lovemaking; the word "rape" seems no more than an idiomatic term for sex. Russian men often act under the assumption that the more force they show, the more romantic the image they project. It is not accidental that treatment of rape as an expression of uncontrollable passion is reflected in such Russian films as *The Hostage* and *The Assassin,* in which female characters fall in love with their recent rapists (Attwood 1993b, 85). Commenting on a recent film, Professor Alexandra Heidi Karriker of the University of Oklahoma notes:

> Why does Tanya in *Time of the Dancer* fend off the rapist before melting in enjoyment? Does her depiction just reinforce the maxim that "women want it" when "it" refers to forcible violation of the body, and certainly not love, or even sex? Why the pleasurable response toward defilement? Besides the enigma surrounding the character of Tanya, her response to rape is typical of a whole slew of scenes from contemporary Russian films, so in this sense, *Time of the Dancer* repeats what has become a traditional portrayal of the sex act in Russian film: brutal, unsolicited, without foreplay, speedy, usually in the standing, face-to-face position, and with the woman changing from initial horror and fear to acceptance and pleasure.[21]

In the following Russian joke, a man clearly treats fierceness in lovemaking as more than adequate compensation for his lack of physical attraction:

(5.46) A woman placed a personal ad: "Looking for a man with the face of Marcello Mastroianni and the figure of Rock Hudson."

The next day somebody knocked on the door. On the threshold stood a cross-eyed, shabby little man. "I've come in response to your ad," he said. "I know that I have neither the face of Marcello Mastroianni nor the figure of Rock Hudson. But I'm as passionate as the Hound of the Baskervilles." (Draitser 1980, 73)

Jokes not only reflect prevailing attitudes and mores but also help to reaffirm and sustain them. In *Russian Talk,* Nancy Ries (1997) discusses the effect of everyday discourse, whether it "mourns or mocks" a certain pattern, on "its reproduction over time." Although in today's Russia there is no longer the total approval of violence against women, the circulation of jokes about wife-beating and rape—their light tone notwithstanding—sustains a permissive atmosphere toward misogynist practices and validates such acts in the consciousness of listeners. While adult listeners of rape jokes who know that in real life women are not that "easy" and eager to be violated may see these jokes as no more than entertainment—male fantasy about the availability of females—it is different for younger listeners.

Since rapists are frequently very young—most of them are sixteen to seventeen, and "the number of fourteen- and fifteen-year-old and even younger rapists is growing" (Kon 1995, 212)—rape jokes have a special impact on them. Usually the secondary function of sex jokes is to provide information to inexperienced adolescents. From jokes of this kind, young males often shape their perception of the opposite gender.[22] As pornography in general provides, in Catharine A. MacKinnon's words, a code of looking at women, "so you know what you can do with one when you see one" (quoted in Alexandra Bennett 1997, 216), these pervasive jokes about female sexual appetite contribute indirectly to the continued physical abuse of women.

Sex Jokes as a Vehicle of Social Satire

The vernacular often uses rape as a metaphor for social, nonsexual, domination. As a Russian saying in the Soviet period states, "If you're raped and help doesn't come, relax and try to enjoy it" *[Esli vas nasiluiut i pomoshchi zhdat' neotkuda, rasslab'tes' i postaraites' poluchit' udovol'stvie].* Reliance on sexual images to express outrage is hardly exclusively Russian. Hartogs and Fantel (1967, 175) observe: "The same kind of joke—if unfunny crudity can be so called—is also frequently heard among economically exploited groups, to whom oppression is a fact of life as primary and pervasive as sex. To them, the sexual crudity becomes a form of quasi-political protest, a generalized outcry of hate."

Because for most of this century, Russians lived in a totalitarian state with its huge apparatus of persecution for those who dared to deviate from a prescribed behavior, traditional Russian misogyny associated the hated regime with the feminine gender. The properties of the Russian language helped to reroute resentment in the Soviet period. Both words denoting the keepers of the tight grip on the Russians—"[Communist] party" *[partiia]* and "[Soviet] power" *[vlast']*—are feminine. It was, then, not a coincidence that a nickname for Soviet power used by dissidents took the form of a woman's given name and patronymic—"Sofia Vlasievna" (sometimes "Vladimirovna"). The dissident literature of the Brezhnev period used the same device. In Vasily Aksyonov's short story "Randevu" *[Randes-vous]*, the party is symbolically rendered as a treacherous and debauched woman who seduces the artist.

Fear of violence for which there is no recourse or protection was such a part of Russian life for such a long time that, in the post-Stalin period, when there was no longer mass terror, the country was ruled by virtue of popular memory of this violence, by fear that lingered in people's minds for a long time. The following joke collected in the early 1970s is highly symbolic of that state of affairs:

(5.47) During a circus performance, an elephant appears in the arena. The master of ceremonies announces a competition. Anyone who makes the elephant nod and then shake his head and kneel will get 10,000 rubles.

Many in the audience try to get the elephant to do what was asked—to no avail.

Finally, an undistinguished man in work clothes comes down to the arena, approaches the elephant, and whispers something into its ear. The elephant nods in response. Then the man whispers in the other ear. And the elephant shakes its head and kneels.

A standing ovation. After handing him the prize, the master of ceremonies asks the winner: "Congratulations! It's amazing! Tell us, how did you do it? What did you tell the elephant?"

"Oh, it's simple," says the man. "First I asked him: 'Do you remember this morning when I was unloading you from the railroad platform and to make you move, I smacked you in the balls with a stick?' The elephant nodded. Then I asked him: 'Do you want me to do it again?' And he shook his head 'No.' Then I said: "If so, don't fuck with me. Kneel.'" (Private collection; for another version of this joke, see Nikulin 1997, 379.)

Many elements of this joke make it a parable of the mechanism of controlling, first through violence and then just through fear of it. It is easy to see that an elephant, a huge, strong but good-natured and patient animal, able to carry a heavy load on its back, stands for the Soviet people, who endured decades of extreme political domination. And the man in work clothes who uses his stick to make the elephant move stands for the ominous Soviet state apparatus that used oppression as its main governing tool.

Because power in the sexual act can easily be used as a metaphor for social domination, many anti-Soviet jokes used sexual innuendo as a means of satirizing the regime. For example:

> (5.48) A man and his wife brought urine specimens to the clinic. In the analyses of the specimens the bottles somehow got mixed up. When the husband came in for results, the doctor said to him: "Listen, Ivanov, it's strange, but signs of pregnancy showed in your urine!"
>
> "I'm not surprised," sighed Ivanov. "At work, my boss fucks me just about every day. At party meetings I get fucked. . . . Why would I not get pregnant?" (Draitser 1980, 61)

In the following item, the Russian popular perception of fellatio as degrading for a woman is used in a social context:

> (5.49) A young factory worker is called into the manager's office.
>
> "Tell me, Tatyana, people have noticed that you're wearing new and fancy dresses lately. Yesterday you came in wearing imported shoes, which you can hardly afford on your salary. Rumor has it that you're getting a lot of money for performing oral sex. Is it true?"
>
> "True."
>
> "So, it means they fuck you in the mouth, don't they?"
>
> "Ivan Ivanovich, may I ask you, what do you earn per month?"
>
> "Two hundred rubles plus another fifty every quarter," the manager says proudly.
>
> "Well, then it is you they fuck in the mouth. And I'm engaged in the oral sex business." (Private collection)

Sexual situations in underground jokes were also used to put down a Soviet leader:

> (5.50) Brezhnev dies and winds up in hell. The devil comes up to him and says:
>
> "You, Leonid, are a prominent Communist, a man of great importance. Therefore, you may choose your own torture."

Walking around, Brezhnev sees Adolf Hitler bathing in a tub of boiling oil and Joseph Stalin stretched out on the rack. Suddenly he spots Nikita Khrushchev with Brigette Bardot sitting on his lap. "Well, well," exclaims Brezhnev. "That's the one. I want the same torture as Khruschev."

"No, no, that can't be," says the devil. "It's not Khruschev who's being tortured; it's Bardot." (Draitser 1980, 73)

In his article "On the Intelligentsia's Contempt for TV Ads," Alexei Levinson (1998) notes that the old perception of the state as a repressive force remains strong in the Russian mind even today. The Russian perception of sex as an act of subjugation (see Chapter 4) keeps cropping up in folk political humor, referring not only to the Communist era but to the current governmental mismanagement of the economy. The first of the following items refers to the endlessly repeated phrase in Soviet newspapers claiming that the Soviet people met any new decision of the Communist party and the Soviet government "with a feeling of deep satisfaction" [s chuvstvom glubokogo udovletvoreniia]:

(5.51)   It's interesting: what had the Soviet government done to the people that they had been experiencing a feeling of deep satisfaction for such a long time? (JFR 12/19/98)

(5.52)   After what [Yeltsin's] government has done to the people, it has to marry them. (JFR 12/18/98)

Hence, in its both nonmetaphoric and metaphoric forms, violence against women is prominently featured in Russian humor, which reflects both the country's turbulent history and its traditional misogyny.

CHAPTER 6

"Walking Next to Your Mother at Your Funeral Will Spoil the Whole Pleasure of the Day:" Russian Marriage and Mother-in-Law Jokes

Marriage Jokes

Married life is funny; both strange and amusing. In his book, *Cultural and Social Anthropology: An Overture*, Robert F. Murphy (1989, 73) sees marriage as

a truly peculiar institution. Although it is widely regarded as a natural state, or at least one ordained by deity, it is actually one of the more ingenious traps set for us by society. Consider its dubious benefits. A woman (or women in plural unions) agrees to place herself in lifelong thralldom to a man (or men) for whom she will cook and clean, giving herself sexually to him on demand and bearing and raising his children. His side of the bargain requires that he restrict his sex urges to his wife (or wives), or at least to keep his liaisons secret from her, live with her, and support her children under compulsion of custom or law. Both sides experience a drastic reduction in independence and autonomy and both have had a lien placed against their labors.

Two polar motivations are considered crucial for Western marriages— love (Gray 1990, 54) and "crude self-interest" (Legman 1968, 700). According to Gershon Legman, in "Anglo-Saxon" countries most marriages are not undertaken entirely due to love. He cites a woman's need to obtain her own social position, free herself of her family's control, and, if lucky enough to marry an affluent man, stop working, and have children who will be adequately provided for. As for the Western man, often he sees marriage as a means of acquiring a lifetime home-bound cook and housekeeper, someone to show off to other men, and a permanent sex partner.

For Russians, these reasons for seeking marriage are not only valid but greatly reinforced by the atmosphere of much keener urgency and, often, desperation. The absence of decent public eating places, the miserable state of domestic services and facilities, crammed apartments where sometimes all three generations of the family are forced to live together, make Russians eager to marry, skipping such a luxury as love.[1] Ronald Hingley's (1977, 186) Soviet-period observation that while "in the West, an individual may be suspected of marrying for money, in Russia he or she may more probably be suspected of embracing wedlock for the sake of a half share in a room or small flat" holds true for the post-Soviet period as well. And "the coveted and elusive Moscow residence permit" (186) is still required. These incentives may explain why Russian females in jokelore talk about a marriage proposal as the first thing they expect to hear after the very first sexual encounter:

> (6.1)　How lovers of different countries part:
> In America: "Good-bye, baby, twenty bucks are on the table. . . ."
> In France: "What's your name?"
> In Russia: "Vanya, oh, Vanya, will you marry me? . . ." (Private collection)

Although official Soviet studies in the 1960s and 1970s found love "the chief motivating force in the vast majority of marriages" (e.g., Anatoly Kharchev's research, reported by Shcheglov 1993, 158), the sincerity of the respondents can be seriously questioned. Indeed, while love has been accorded great prestige in Russian culture (see Shlapentokh 1984, 39–66), for all practical purposes it has been paid lip service. The tremendous pressures of Russian life often force people to act against their own values. Having lived in Russia most of my life, I find Francine du Plessix Gray's observations of Russian marriages much closer to the truth.

Talking to Soviet women in the late 1980s, Gray (1990, 54) concludes that love in the Soviet Union is "an accessory, but hardly a prerequisite for marriage . . . tend[ing] to recede in importance before the far deeper bonds of blood kinship, filial responsibility, matriarchal ties." The following items agree with her finding that Russian marriage is "a coolly pragmatic commodity reserved for a variety of utilitarian reasons":

(6.2)   A miner finds a gold nugget, receives a reward of 50,000 rubles, and, crazy with happiness, runs home: "Wife, I found a gold nugget and got 50,000. Gather up your things!"

His wife rushes about the apartment, wondering where their travels will take them: "Kolya, dear Kolya, what kind of clothes should I take? Summer things or winter?"

"Take both and—get the hell out!" (Private collection; there is an American version of this joke.)

The following post-Soviet joke shows the same attitude toward marriage as a mere convenience; the teller uses the New Russian to establish the idea that it is plausible for an individual to buy his way out of a marriage:

(6.3)   A New Russian in a restaurant orders the most expensive dishes. Suddenly he see a homeless man sitting next to him and ordering about the same.

"Where do you get your money?" he asks.

"You see, I have a beaver that gives an excellent blow job. I rent it out for big bucks."

"Don't pull my leg. It can't be."

"Well, give me a thousand bucks and check it out yourself."

The New Russian gives the man a grand, takes the beaver, and goes to the men's room. In an hour, he comes back and begins to talk the homeless man into selling him the beaver, but the owner doesn't want to do it.

Finally, the New Russian talks him into selling it for 100 grand. He puts it under his coat and goes home.

There he throws the beaver into his wife's lap and says: "Listen, teach it to cook and then get the hell out of the apartment!" (JFR 2/2/98)

Citing findings of leading Soviet sociologists, Shlapentokh (1989, 177–178) concludes that "newlyweds rank love only as fifth among eighteen motives for marriage, and no more than one-quarter of married people regard mutual love as an important condition for family happiness."

Male jokelore supports this pessimistic view of this human institution:

(6.4)   Marriage is not a lottery. In a lottery you have a chance. (JFR 1/11/97)

(6.5)   Luck in choosing a spouse consists of an ability to put your hand in a barrel of snakes and pull out a garter snake [in Russian: *uzh*]. (JFR 2/15/98)

An analysis of American marriage humor (Perlis 1954, 49–50) shows that it works as "a conflict tool that functions largely for the husband's purpose." It has been demonstrated that marital humor supports traditional values, that is, "the man should be the head of the house, should be in charge of the money and parcel out money to his wife, should not do household chores, and should accept marriage as a necessary evil; while the wife should be submissive, a good cook, and should consider marriage her only means of financial security" (Duvall 1964, 35).

Although since the time of Duvall's observations (in the late 1960s) not only the Russian but the average American household can no longer be supported by a husband's earnings alone, male jokes persist in trying to hold on to outdated expectations. Many Russian marriage jokes are almost identical with Western jokes dealing with the hardship of marital life (6.6), weariness with the other (6.7–6.10), boredom with conjugal sex (6.11–6.14), warfare between spouses (6.15–6.16):

(6.6)   "What is the difference between a married man and a bachelor?"
"A married man lives all his life as a dog but dies as a man. A bachelor lives all his life as a man and dies as a dog." (Milgram 1985, 20)

(6.7)   A schoolboy doing his homework asks his father: "Dad, what's the word when a man has several wives?"
"Polygamy."
"And when he has just one?"
"Monotony. . . ." (Private collection)

(6.8)   A wife returns from a vacation at the seashore and asks her husband: "Dear, didn't you miss me while I was away?"
The husband lowers his newspaper: "Were you really away, dear?" (Kulikov 1997, 310)

(6.9)   A husband paid no attention to his wife. To make him notice her, she put a gas mask on her face.
The husband came home, sat down with his wife at the dinner table, ate, and went to sleep, still paying no attention to her. Then the wife said: "Why don't you look at me?
"I do look."
"Why then don't you see any change in my face?"
The husband glanced at her and said: "You have plucked out your brows, is that it?" (Private collection)

(6.10)   Two friends meet. One says: "I'm still a bachelor. I live as I please. I'm my own master. I cook dinner for myself, do laundry."

"And I'm married. You won't believe it. I come home, and my wife greets me, kisses me, seats me at the table, serves my dinner. I sit and eat, and she chirps, chirps, and chirps, and chirps . . . she just won't shut up, that bitch!" (Barsky 1994, 246).

(6.11)   In a sex therapist's office: "Help me, Doctor. I can't make love in the way everybody else does."

"And how can you make love?"

"Lying on my side."

"Why?"

"Otherwise I can't watch TV." (Private collection)

(6.12)   A husband comes home from work late at night. There is a note in the kitchen: "Soup's on the stove, meat casseroles are in the fridge. If you fuck me, don't wake me up." (I. Raskin 1995, 368)

(6.13)   A husband returns from a business trip. He enters his apartment and finds his wife in bed with another man. They both look very frightened. The husband says to the lover with sympathy:

"Well, I do this because I'm her husband. But what's in it for *you*." (I. Raskin 1995, 269)

(6.14)   A husband and wife are going along a narrow path in a forest. Suddenly, a huge orangutan jumps out of the woods, grabs the wife and drags her up a tree. The husband shouts up to his wife:

"Go ahead and tell him that you are not in the mood today, that you're tired, that you have a headache and feel like sleeping!" (Private collection)

(6.15)   A conversation in a train.

"You know, my wife is an angel."

"Lucky you! Mine is still alive." (Barsky 1994, 245)

(6.16)   "Excellent little mushrooms!" a husband praises his wife while putting some of them in his mouth. "Where did you get the marinade recipe?"

"From a detective novel." (Private collection)

A projection into the future of spousal relationships in general is not hopeful either:

(6.17)   A dialogue from the twenty-first century:
"Tell me, don't your gas masks interfere with your sex life?"
"What are you saying! Just the opposite! First, my wife can't talk with it on. Secondly, I don't see her face. Thirdly, when I close the incoming air valve, she begins to move at least a bit." (Private collection)

In these jokes, marriage is portrayed as advantageous for women only. Men are always the victims:

(6.18)   It's widely known that, according to statistical data, married men live longer than bachelors. And what is not made widely known is that, according to the same data, married men are much more willing than bachelors to meet death. (JFR 2/16/98)

(6.19)   A father gives his daughter a lesson: "You have to drive your boyfriend crazy. Only in that condition is a man capable of marriage." (Private collection)

(6.20)   "Why do women live longer than men?"
"They don't have wives." (JFR 1/19/97)

(6.21)   A man without a wife is like a fish without a bicycle. (JFR 10/18/97)

(6.22)   Unfortunately, it's not true that married men live longer than bachelors. It only seems that way to them. (JFR 10/18/97)

A man is a prisoner of marriage who constantly dreams of escape:

(6.23)   Nighttime. Falling asleep, a wife is smiling: "Does my dear husband remember that tomorrow is the fifteenth anniversary of our marriage? Of course he remembers, and he's prepared a present for me. . . ."
Falling asleep, her husband is thinking sadly: "If I had strangled her fifteen years ago, tomorrow I would be a free man." (Anon. 1994, 14)

(6.24)   A judge to an inmate: "What do you plan to do after your term's over?"
"I plan to get married."
"You have a rather strange notion of freedom. . . ."[2] (Private collection)

(6.25)   Two neighbors talk:
"Have you heard? Petrova's wife has left him."
"Are you kidding? And how has he survived it?"
"He's calmed down now. But in the beginning I thought he'd lose his mind from happiness." (Ivanova 1996, 486)

Many of the preceding jokes are generic and could be found in the repertoire of Americans and other Westerners. (It is enough to recall such witticisms as Oscar Wilde's "One should always be in love. That is the reason one should never marry," or Mae West's "Marriage is a great institution, but I'm not ready for an institution yet"; both quoted in Tom Carey 1987, 41, 99.) Many others, told by Russians, reflect Russian conditions more specifically. These are jokes that address the distribution of gender power in contemporary Russian life. As in some other cultures,[3] Russian women, while often deprived of power in the society at large, exercise it in informal areas of life. Gray (1990, 89), Tolstaya (1990, 3–5), and Kon (1995, 146–147) have shown that despite the country's patriarchal tendencies, Russian women of today wield significant power in the framework of marriage. In the realm of family life, the situation is often reversed: It is not the woman who feels oppressed but the man under the matriarchal rule of his wife, who often reduces his role to that of a commodity to be disposed of, if necessary. In the vast majority of cases, it is women who initiate divorce (according to Larisa Kuznetsova, up to 70 to 80 percent of applications are from wives; cited in Rancour-Laferrierre 1995, 177; see also Shlapentokh 1984, 208–209). As a reflection of the growing awareness of Russian women that a husband may not be one's life-time partner, a first husband is nicknamed "a little rough draft" in contemporary female slang [chernovichok; Elistratov 1994, 546]. The same perspective is addressed in the following item:

(6.26)   "How should a girl introduce her fiancé to her parents?"
"Mom, Dad: here's my future first husband." (Kulikov 1997, 398)

Talking about a young Russian family, Kon (1995, 151) observes that a young husband "is seldom a decision maker." Following her mother's steps, his wife "is often very domineering," and the husband's role is often reduced to just following her instructions. In many respects, among contemporary Russian women, there is not even a myth of male supremacy in the realm of family life. Says Tatyana Tolstaya (1990, 4): "A Russian woman is entirely a mistress of her household, the children belong to her and to her alone, the family often doesn't even ask for male advice."

(6.27)   A wife, talking to a friend about her marriage, says, "I make all the
trivial, unimportant decisions—where we will vacation, if we will
move to a new apartment, if we will buy a car.... My husband
makes the really important decisions in the family, you know: Can
we build communism in one country? Should the two Germanys reunite? (Ries 1997, 73)

Although other people's humor also questions the notion of a man being the
boss in his home,[4] Russian jokes on the subject seem to be much more numerous and bitter. Consider the following take-off on astrological forecasts,
currently gaining popularity in the Russian press:

(6.28)   For Sagittarius: "This week your wife will help you to find your place
in life. You'll understand that your place is in the hallway, beyond a
coffee table, under a coat rack."
   For Aquarius: "On the whole, this week is favorable, but on
Wednesday conversations with your superiors are not recom-
mended. Therefore, postpone talking things over with your wife
until Thursday."[5]

Shlapenotkh (1984, 209) talks about a new type of family that emerged
in the last few decades of the Soviet period, "a family with authoritarian rule
by the wife." Many Russian male jokes portray a wife, women in general, as
the dominant force:

(6.29)   After thirty years, a man meets an old friend and is amazed on
counting sixteen children in his house.
   "It seems you and your wife get along very well."
   "What are you talking about!" says the host, a meek little man.
"She is constantly grouchy and nagging. To tell you the truth, she
scares the hell out of me."
   "Why then did you have so many children with her?"
   "It's much easier to get lost in a crowd!" (JFR 3/16/98)

Many jokes associate wives with overpowering military and law enforcement authorities, with threatening and menacing forces of all sorts:

(6.30)   "The time will come when only women will serve in the army."
   "It will never happen. No army can consist only of generals."

(6.31)   "Hello! Is this the police?"
   "No, it's a private apartment. But I can call my wife to the telephone." (Genis 1994, 3: 54)

(6.32)   One lieutenant says to another: "I don't know what to do. My life
has become unbearable. Everything is strictly regimented. Every
minute's under control. Orders come one after another. . . ."
"Do you have a new platoon commander?"
"No, I have a new wife." (Anon. 1994, 335)

(6.33)   "How is a wife different from a terrorist?"
"You can negotiate with a terrorist." (JFR 12/25/96)

This distribution of power in everyday affairs is, by and large, the result of
changes in Russian society during the Soviet period. First of all, with the
emerging mass involvement of women in the workforce and the low wages
that prevented men from exercising the traditional role as breadwinner, so important for the male ego, male power was significantly diminished. Second, as
a reaction to the rigid Soviet system, with its emphasis on the collective and
the disparagement of the individual and the loss of the traditional male functions of responsibility for self and family in a larger world, the Russian man
often resorted to "social passivity and learned helplessness," fleeing from

> personal responsibility for oneself and one's actions into the careless, childish
> world of eternal boyhood. Not having learned in time to manage themselves
> and to overcome difficulties, many Soviet men fully renounced personal in-
> dependence, compensating for it by a pervasive irresponsibility. Social re-
> sponsibility was entrusted to the boss, family responsibilities to the wife. Such
> behavior would seem to contradict the traditional canon of strong masculin-
> ity, but in the circumstances of social and economic captivity, this strategy
> seemed psychologically sensible and justified. Why worry, why suffer humili-
> ating disillusionment and frustration, if you can get someone else—women,
> in this instance—to do so instead? (Kon 1995, 152)

A husband unable to take care of his own child is a staple of Russian jokes:

(6.34)   In a city park, a young daddy pushes a crying baby in a carriage. He
repeats quietly: "Be calm, Vassya. . . . Calm down, Vassya. . . ."
An old lady says: "The baby doesn't understand you anyway.
You'd better take him in your arms and pat him a bit."
"You see," says the daddy, "*I'm* Vassya." (Nikulin 1997, 178)

(6.35)   A wife says to her husband: "While I'm in the kitchen doing the
dishes, you go and bathe our little daughter."
"All right."
After a while, the wife hears wild screams coming from the bathroom. She rushes there and sees the following picture: her husband

holds their daughter by her hair and rinses her in the bathtub, while she screams wildly.

"What are you doing, you monster? Why do you wash her by grabbing her hair?"

"Oh yeah? Why don't you try doing it yourself in such hot water!" (JFR 2/25/98)

In other jokes, however, a man resorts to his physical power to drive home the point—domestic work is a wife's job:

(6.36)   Three women—an American, English, and Russian—talk about family life.

        The English woman: "Right after our wedding, I said to my husband: 'I won't cook.' He disappeared. I didn't see him for three days, and on the fourth day he dragged a huge food processor into our kitchen. Now he cooks everything himself."

        The American says: "And I said to my husband that I won't do laundry. I didn't see him for three days and on the fourth one he brought in a washing machine. Now he does all our laundry himself."

        The Russian says: "And I said to my husband that I would neither cook nor do laundry. I didn't see him one day, another day, but on the fourth one . . . my right eye was able to open up a bit." (JFR 2/2/98)

The next, no less sad, joke of the Soviet years portrays accurately the burdens of everyday family life that rested (and still rests) solely on a woman's shoulders. The inhuman conditions gave rise to the zoological terms used in this joke:

(6.37)   A woman addresses her doctor: "Tell me what animal species do I belong to?"

        "Woman, what are you taking about, you're a human being!"

        "What kind of a human being am I? In the morning I get up as untidy as a sheep, run to work as hungry as a wolf, jump on a streetcar like a monkey, ride on it like a rabbit, then push my way through the crowd like a bear. Until I reach my job, I manage to bark like a dog at everybody around me.

        "I get out of the streetcar plucked all over like a chicken ready-for-soup. I work all day like a bull, and then run around the grocery stores like a bloodhound. I load myself up like a camel and drag myself home like a winded donkey.

"At home while I'm preparing dinner, I growl at my children like a tigress and hiss at my neighbors like a snake. My husband comes home and says 'Pussycat, is dinner ready?'"

"I feed everybody, wash the dishes, put the children to bed, and lie down myself. Lying down next to me, my husband says: 'Move over, you cow, you're hogging the bed!' What kind of human being am I, Doctor?" (Efimov 1994, 131)

Even if a man yields to his wife's pressure and does some of the domestic work, his resentment of it is widespread:

(6.38) Coming home, a woman finds her husband washing floors.
"You know," she says, "my boss's hinted that he would abandon his family for me. Perhaps he's just joking?"
"But maybe he isn't . . ." says the husband hopefully. (Nikulin 1997, 377)

In the following joke, a wife is solely preoccupied with her husband's usefulness.

(6.39) "Doctor, please don't hide anything from me. . . . After breaking his hand so horribly, will my husband ever be able to wash dishes? (JFR 3/7/98)

The choice of a Ukrainian in the following joke is another instance of shifting unflattering qualities of the teller's group onto outsiders:

(6.40) A Ukrainian strolling along a village street sees his son's godfather behind a fence lying in a hammock dressed in a bathrobe, wearing slippers. With a cup of coffee in his hand he is smoking a cigarette while his wife is repairing the roof of their house.
"Godfather, why are you resting and you wife is working?"
Comes the reply: "And what if a war starts, and I'm tired?" (JFR 3/12/98)

According to the latest inquiries of the Russian Institute of Sociology, the distribution of family duties remains the most troublesome aspect of family relations; 26 percent of respondents reported frequent conflicts on this basis (Pankratova 1997, 24). Russian men greet the growing tendency toward sharing household responsibilities with resentment believing it to be emasculating.

(6.41) A man gave birth to a baby. Correspondents rushed to the clinic and asked him how this had come about.

"It all began the day I got married," he said, "and started doing laundry. . . ." (Private collection)

(6.42) A man comes to a doctor: "Doc, I haven't been able to urinate for three days now."
"Please undress."
The man undresses himself.
"But your male organ is tied into a knot!"
"Damn it! Again I've forgotten to buy bread at the store." (JFR 2/22/98)

Male conceptualization of domestic chores as emasculating is observed in many cultures (Murphy 1989, 72). In the tale "A Man Does Woman's Work" collected by Afanasiev in the nineteenth century, a man who takes upon himself his wife's housework is eventually castrated. The tale comes across as precautionary, justifying Russian men's abhorrence of domestic chores (Rancour-Laferrière 1995, 172). As a Russian proverb collected by Dahl goes: "He who gets mixed up with a woman will be a woman himself" [*Kto s baboi sviazhetsia—sam baba budet*]. Ries (1997) concludes that stories told during perestroika "reflected and reproduced a structure of relations between spouses defined less by patriarchal principles than by maternalism. . . . These stories turned patriarchy upside down via mini-exposés of intrafamilal relations: in them the patriarch was merely a spoiled little boy (albeit one who could make life miserable) in domestic orbit around the all-controlling, all-managing, all-giving mother" (75).

In an interview with *Newsweek,* a Russian businesswoman, Natalya Diakonova, says: "A lot of Russian men are lazy and [need to be] treated like children. I treated my first husband like a child. I really thought that if I didn't take care of him, he wouldn't be able to survive on his own" (quoted in Powell and Palchikoff 1997, 52). Her former husband's behavior is quite telling with respect to treatment of a wife as fulfilling his mother's functions: "He got tired of coming home and there'd be no food on the table. So he [left] to go live with his mother."

In the following item, going to mother in time of trouble is another take on the immaturity of Russian men:

(6.43) A son says to his mother: "I won't go to school anymore."
"Why is that? Tell me."
"Well, to hell with it. . . . Again Petrov will shoot at me with his slingshot. Sinitsyn will hit me over the head with a textbook. Vasiliev will trip me up. . . . No, I won't go!"

"No, little Vova, you must go. First, you're already forty. And, secondly, you're the school's principal." (Nikulin 1997, 162)[6]

Thus the notion of the "infantile husband" (Kon 1995, 152; Rancour-Laferriere 1995, 177–178), from whom no help is expected and who, at the same time, has to be taken care of as if he were a child, has evolved in Russian society:

(6.44)   The first woman: "The whole day I'm on the job. Then I bustle around with house chores. I'm totally exhausted. Today, I'll come home and do laundry, wash dishes. Tomorrow I'll have to wash the floors in the kitchen and the windows. . . ."
    The second woman: "What about your husband?"
    The first woman: "What about him? No way! He can wash himself by himself." (Repina and Rostovtsev 1995, 22: 37–38)

The burden of going to stores, standing in line, and taking care of numerous domestic chores on a daily basis almost solely rests on women. According to Larisa Kuznetsova, the only line in which men outnumber women is the line for vodka (cited in Rancour-Laferriere 1995, 164). The following joke addresses the woman's predicament.

(6.45)   Why is it that the heels of French woman's shoes don't wear out, and a Russian woman's do?
    When a French woman walks, her lover supports her on one side, her husband on the other.
    When a Russian woman walks, she has a shopping bag [setka] in one hand, a little Sveta [Svetka] in the other, a five-year plan ahead of her, and a drunk [husband] Ivan behind her. (Smetanin and Donskaia 1992, 55).[7]

Another joke, also touching on acute and unrestrained alcoholism, makes graphic the man-as-helpless-child motif:

(6.46).   A drunk pushes his way to a subway seat reserved for children and the handicapped. Other passengers block his way. His wife interferes on his behalf. They try to reason with her:
    "But these seats are for children and the handicapped!"
    "But to me he is both. He can't stand up and he can't say a word."
    (Repina and Rostovtsev 1995, 22: 121–122)

To entrust a Russian man with family money is often dangerous. Because of rampant alcoholism, in jokes, as in real life, this money is often spent on hard liquor.

(6.47) "Dad, Mom said that vodka's expensive now, and you'll drink less."
"She's wrong, sonny, it's you who's going to eat less now."
(Kharkover 1993, 1: 17)

(6.48) "Little husband, go and buy a half a liter of cooking oil," a wife says. The husband leaves. After a while, he returns.
"Well, did you buy it?"
"Yes, I bought a half liter, but there wasn't enough money for oil." (O. Ivanova 1996, 62)

The irresponsible behavior of drinking men is not merely a humorous exaggeration but often a matter-of-fact statement: A man may squander his monthly salary in one evening of merrymaking with boon companions:

(6.49) A husband says to his wife: "Well, finally I got my monthly salary."
"So, where is it?"
"Well, on the way home I drank a mug of beer." (O. Ivanova 1996, 86)

(6.50) A man returns from a hunting trip and says to his wife: "That's it, wife, you may skip buying meat for the next month."
"What, did you kill an elk?"
"No. I drank up my monthly pay with my friends." (Anon. 1994, 31)

The next joke reverses a typical wife's charge that her husband is drinking up money supposed to support the family:

(6.51) "Well, just imagine my wife," says one man to another. "There's not a drop of liquor in the house, and she's spent the last money on food." (Ivanova 1996, 79)

Many Russian women are forced to take charge of family finances due to their husbands' alcoholism. The husband then is given a minimum allowance for transportation and lunch. The following joke reflects his resentment of this arrangement:

(6.52)   Three men compare the daily allowances their wives have given them.
"Mine gave me five rubles," says one man.
"And mine three rubles," says another.
"And my little Zoya gave me fifty kopecks."
"She gave you just fifty lousy kopecks, and you still call her 'little Zoya'? Are you sick?"
"Well, Zoya is not her real name, but a nickname I gave her. It stands for 'Specially poisonous snake.'" [in Russian, *Zoya—zmeia osobo iadovitaia*]. (Private collection)

To keep strict control over a husband's wages, a Russian wife is often forced to confiscate his money. Thus, hiding at least a small amount of it for drinks with buddies has become an everyday practice for Russian husbands. In contemporary slang, a wife is nicknamed "the customs" (*tamozhnia,* as in "They took away half of my salary at the customs. You won't fool my customs"; Elistratov 1994, 463). A Russian slang verb *zanachivat'* (imperfective aspect) and *zanachit'* (perfective aspect) means "to hide, stash away" money from one's wife (Shlyakhov and Adler 1995, 76). There is also a noun "a cache" [*zanachka*]:

(6.53)   A tailor asks a customer: "Are you married or not?"
"I'm married."
"Then we should add a secret pocket in your jacket's lining." (O. Ivanova 1996, 485)

(6.54)   A man was two hours late to work. His coworkers asked what happened.
"My wife lost a ten and was searching for it for two hours."
"Well, so what held *you* up?"
"I was the one who stepped on it in the first place." (Nikulin 1997, 152)

(6.55)   In the middle of the night, a husband screams and wakes up in horror. His wife asks him:
"What's the matter with you, Vania?"
"You know, I dreamed that instead of my salary I gave you my cache." (Efimov 1994, 80–81)

The stereotype of a husband whose drinking habits are totally controlled by his wife lies behind the satirical barb, in a form of a parody of a newspaper crime report, that appeared in the *Literary Gazette's* famous "Club of 12 Chairs":

(6.56)   *A Robbery*
Yesterday, a masked man charged into one of the city shops. Threatening the female cashier with a toy gun, he counted out two rubles and 87 kopecks and disappeared in an unknown direction. Soon they arrested him [near a liquor store]. He explained that this was the only possible way to take back from his wife a part of his salary that she systematically took away from him. (Sabashnikova 1973, 122)

Considering that 2 rubles and 87 kopecks was the standard price of bottle of vodka in Brezhnev's time, the parody is rather telling of the predicament of a Russian drinking husband.

In many instances, an alcoholic husband becomes such a trial for his wife that the only way to ensure survival for herself and her children is divorce. The view of a husband as "disposable commodity," discussed earlier, is particularly appropriate when he is a drunk. In the following joke, this view is treated literally:

(6.57)   "Mom! Mom! Daddy's turned up!"
          "How many times have I told you not to rake up the garbage!"
          (Ivanova 1996, 64)

Recently more and more jokes, now published in collections, have a women-strike-back motif. Many have a clearly female point of view and often are reworked variants of antifemale jokes. Thus a classic male joke, "My wife's an angel" "Lucky you, mine's still alive" (6.15), has appeared not only in the reversed form, "My husband's an angel" "Lucky you, mine's still alive" (Genis 1994, 1: 22), but—much more degrading for the male ego— hints at his impotence: "My husband's an angel!" "Mine's not a man either." More and more items turn the tables on men with respect to such traditional motifs of male humor as:

Ugly Women
(6.58)   A wife asks her husband: "Why are you going out when it's already dark?"
          "I'm going to visit my relatives."
          "What, is the monkey's house open around the clock these days?"
          (Private collection)

(6.59)   Two crocodiles swim along and see a monkey sitting on the shore. One of them says to another: "Let's swim up to her and ask if she's married. If she says 'no,' we will say: 'Of course, who's going to marry such a monkey!' If she says 'yes,' we'll say: 'Who in the world could marry such a monkey!'"

They swim up to her: "Monkey, are you married?"

"How could I get married when there's nothing around but crocodiles?" (Genis 1994, 1: 190–191)

Wife-Beating

(6.60)   A woman visits a local police station and reports that her husband has not come home for four days.

"Does your husband have any special marks?"

"No. But as soon as he comes home, he will." (Genis 1994, 1: 218)

(6.61)   In a surgeon's office: "Nurse, what do we have for today?"

"Two light cases: an automobile crash and a workplace trauma. And one heavy one: a husband who refused to do the dishes." (Genis 1994, 1: 40)

Frigid Women

(6.62)   A man picks up a woman and takes her home. . . .

When they wake in the morning, the woman says: "Dear, do you want me to guess your profession?"

"Well, go ahead, try. . . ."

"You're a physician."

"You've got it! How did you guess?"

"And do you want me to say what kind of a physician you are?"

"Well? . . ."

"You're an anesthesiologist!"

"Right! How did you guess?"

"Last night I didn't feel *anything*." (2/12/98 JFR)

Mother-in-Law Jokes

The mother-in-law is a butt of numerous Russian jokes and witticisms, and the male derision of her is quite clear. In everyday male conversation, the very word "mother-in-law" [*teshcha;* wife's mother] often provokes a sardonic smile of recognition. Jokes about mothers-in-law have been such a pervasive part of Russian everyday discourse, that, in the short period of political chaos in the early 1990s that was marked by a noticeable falling off of all jokes, a Russian journalist of the popular *Kuranty* newspaper wrote: "Have you noticed? Jokes about mother-in-laws have stopped. . . . The end of the world is coming!" (quoted in Alaev 1995, 151):

(6.63) At a manager's meeting: "I can't fire Tuchkova. She's my mother-in-law, and people will think that I'm trying to get even with her." (Repina and Rostovtsev 1995, 22: 91)

(6.64) Two men are sitting opposite each other in a street car. One sighs heavily. The other: "And do you think I don't have a mother-in-law?" (Nikulin 1997, 199)

(6.65) "Little Anya, why are you yelling at little Vova?"
"We are playing mother-in-law." (Nikulin 1997, 155)

American scholar Joyce Hertzler (1970, 137) hears in mother-in-law jokes the laughter that deals with "delicate or ambiguous relationships"; these jokes "serve almost classically to vent feelings of antagonism in sons-in-law." Although mothers-in-law are featured in Western jokes as well and some on this topic are quite similar,[8] Russian humor is much more hostile. The figure of "the evil mother-in-law" [zlaia teshcha] in contemporary Russian jokelore is so widespread that it easily compares with the ominous figure of "the evil stepmother" [zlaia machekha] in Russian fairy tales.

Hertzler's characterization of the relationship between a son-in-law and mother-in-law as "delicate or ambiguous" is to the point. In psychoanalytical terms, Freud sees this relationship as based on suppressed mutual attraction. For a son-in-law, she is both a mother figure and a somewhat older variant of the woman he loves. Thus his hostility serves as a way to suppress culturally tabooed, incestuous feelings (Legman 1968, 438). For a mother-in-law, he is a man her daughter loves, and her strong tendency to identify with her daughter may make her feel amorous with him as well. Her animosity may be her means of dealing with confusing and potentially destructive feelings.

This sexual identification of the mother-in-law with her daughter is clear in the following item.

(6.66) Divorce procedures are in progress. A wife is suing her husband.
The judge: "Citizen Ivanova, why do you want a divorce?"
"What's the point of living with him, comrade judge? Anyway, there's nothing to the marriage. He doesn't even have a dick. . . ."
A young man stands up: "Comrade judge! I even have a certificate from a doctor that I have one. . . ."
The voice of his mother-in-law comes from the back of the court: "What we need is a dick, not a certificate. . . ." (Private collection)

The taboo sexual attraction surfaces in some samples of chastushkas:

(6.67) Kak ziat' teshchu	A son-in-law lures
Zatashchil v roshchu.	His mother-in-law in a grove.
Treshchit roshcha—	The grove crackles and rustles—
Ne daet teshcha.	The mother-in-law does not put out for him. (Private collection)

And in jokes:

(6.68) After the wedding, a son-in-law explains to his wife and her mother: "There should be order in the house! In the morning I want my coffee served in bed. For dinner, meat, veggies, and fruits. In the evening, a light supper with wine."

His wife and mother-in-law are indignant.

"Shut up!" the man says. "Furthermore—on odd days my wife sleeps with me, on even ones—my mother-in-law."

His wife shouts at him: "What an insolent man!"

The mother-in-law: "A man is master of his house. Whatever he decides, that's the way it's going to be." (Smetanin and Donskaia 1992, 44)

(6.69) A personal ad: "A beautiful cultured woman, blond, into music and sports, is looking for a groom for her daughter." (JFR 12/5/96)

However, most of the current folk humor shows utter disdain and hatred toward mothers-in-law. That the latter feelings are superimposed over the former can be seen in the following item:

(6.70) Two boon companions meet.

"Listen, why do I always wind up in the drunk tank, and you get home safely?"

"I know my limit."

"Teach me."

"It's very simple. I come to a restaurant and put a picture of my mother-in-law on the table right away. As soon as I begin to like her—that's it. It's the limit!" (Private collection)

There are other reasons for tension between mother-in-law and son-in-law, those that have to do with the former's nurturing functions, which continue after her daughter's marriage (Rancour-Laferriere 1985, 171). A mother-in-law is diligent about whether her daughter's husband is an adequate replacement for her as a protector of her offspring. She tends to supervise him continually, most often inconspicuously, to be sure (and reassured) that he is as caring toward her daughter as she has been. In spousal conflicts, it is not hard to guess which side she usually takes. Thus, a husband she perceives as weak-willed or otherwise inadequate—a poor breadwinner, uncaring, and so on—perceives her as a dominant and domineering figure.[9]

Strange as it may seem, neither Vladimir Shlapentokh in his sociological study *Love, Marriage, and Friendship in the Soviet Union: Ideals and Practices* nor Mikhail Stern *(Sex in the USSR)* pays much attention to the relationship between the mother-in-law and son-in-law. In his study of the Soviet family, Kharchev (1964) claims that the presence of a mother-in-law in a young family creates no significant problem; he cites a sample of families of blue-collar workers in Leningrad that showed only fifteen cases out of 100 in which her presence caused family spats. Such a rosy picture, however, contradicts his own admission elsewhere that the tension of such situations is a "psychologically natural phenomenon" and it may lead to "mutual frictions, embarrassment, and even quarrels" (233).

Glimpses of the true state of the relationship within a young family with a live-in mother-in-law can be found in some works of Western writers traveling to Russia. Thus, in *Soviet Women: Walking the Tightrope*, Gray (1990, 50–62) finds that the very existence of the mother-in-law is threatening to a son-in-law's married life, especially after the birth of a child. She cites several cases of families without men, often as a result of the conscious choice of young women who count on the assistance of their mothers in raising children. In the words of one of those interviewed, a university student: "Here's the way our order of priorities go: One—career. Two—child. As for a man, that's irrelevant. He can go on his way as soon as the child is conceived" (51). While there exists, in Gray's words (53), a "man-as-disposable-commodity" attitude among many contemporary Russian women, in the context of Russian life with its scarcity of accommodations, mothers are indispensable. Often a young woman's mother is a baby-sitter while the couple is at work. The following jokes are based on this rather common arrangement:

(6.71)   A hunter comes into a bear's lair. He sees only a little baby bear sitting on a potty.
　　　　The hunter approaches the baby bear: "Is your mummy home?"
　　　　"No-o-o. . . ."
　　　　"Is your daddy home?"
　　　　"No-o-o. . . ."
　　　　The hunter pushes him off the potty: "Get lost!"
　　　　The baby bear cries: "Granny! . . ." (I. Raskin 1995, 308)

(6.72) "Why are children so nervous nowadays?"

"Because they worry too much. During the first three months as fetuses, they ask themselves: 'Am I going to be or not?' The next three months: 'Will my father marry my mother or not?' And the last there months: 'Will my grandma babysit me or not?'" (Private collection)

Since a working wife simply cannot make it without her mother's help, a Russian husband inevitably loses in competition for his wife's devotion. Mother-daughter ties become genuinely "indissoluble" (Gray 1990, 53). Facing a choice between her husband and her mother, "mother always comes first." Although, according to Shlapentokh (1984, 193–195), such a custom has waned somewhat in recent years, it has still not changed enough to break the stereotype on which mother-in-law jokes are based.

Animosity between the son-in-law and mother-in-law has long been reflected in Russian folklore. In a folk song recorded in the last century by the Russian ethnographer P. V. Shein (1889, 252), a son-in-law beats up his mother-in-law when she visits. In another song (253), it is she who acts: After welcoming two sons-in-law in her home, she takes advantage of them by extorting money for the drinks she serves and then chases them away.

In contemporary male jokelore, the warfare is much more bitter, even savage. In the vast majority of jokes, disapproval of the mother-in-law is total; by definition she is not a person to be liked:

(6.73) "Why does a cockerel sing all his life?"

"Because he has many wives and not a single mother-in-law." (Barsky 1994, 187).

(6.74) A man runs into a veterinarian's office and asks him to cut off the tail of his dog.

"What happened?" the doctor asks. "Why so urgent?"

"Tomorrow my mother-in-law's coming, and I don't want any signs of friendliness." (Kharkover 1993, 3: 45)

A mother-in-law is usually not ridiculed for any specific misdeeds. It is assumed that the teller's loathing is shared with his listener(s). In many jokes the point of derision seems to be the mother-in-law's moral support of her daughter. Several jokes cite her proverbial nagging, her "poisonous" tongue—that is, her interference in family matters. It is not by chance that a long footbridge in the city of Odessa is nicknamed "a mother-in-law's tongue" [teshchin iazyk]:

(6.75)   A man comes home from a doctor's visit and says to his mother-in-law: "Spit on my back!"
"Oh, little son-in-law, why should I do that? What are you saying?"
"I'm telling you, spit!"
The mother-in-law sees that by refusing she will anger her son-in-law. She spits on his back.
Then she asks: "Why did you need that, little son-in-law?"
"That was my doctor's prescription—to have my back rubbed with snake venom." (Private collection)

(6.76)   Two friends are talking about life.
"My home's a genuine paradise."
"In what sense?"
"I'm Adam, my wife's Eve, and my mother-in-law's the Snake."
(Nikulin 1997, 197)

(6.77)   "A dog bit my mother-in-law yesterday."
"And how does she feel today?"
"She's feeling well, but the dog croaked." (Kharkover 1993, 3: 45)

In contemporary Russian male folklore, hatred of the mother-in-law is often expressed in its most extreme form: Nothing less than her death seems to satisfy the protagonists in these jokes:

(6.78)   They asked Armenian Radio: "What's better, a mother-in-law or a beer?"
"Both are good—on a table and cold." (I. Raskin 1995, 413)

Her absence from the surface of the earth is the son-in-law's dream, a fairy tale:

(6.79)   A woman says to her son-in-law: "Every evening you tell my grandson a fairy tale. Would you please explain why every one of them ends with 'They got married and lived happily ever after, for the bride was an orphan?'" (Barsky 1994, 252)

(6.80)   A lawyer sends a telegram to his client: "Last night, your mother-in-law passed away. Should I order her buried, cremated, or embalmed?"
"Order all of them. I don't want to take any risks." (JFR 3/16/98)

In fact, many Russian jokes focus on capital punishment of mothers-in-law; such punishment is contemplated, attempted, and often actually inflicted:

(6.81)   A young man comes to an electrical appliance store. "I want to buy a present for my mother-in-law."

"Oh, we have plenty of things for her. An electric iron, an electric pot, an electric coffee-maker. . . ."

"Tell me, do you have an electric chair?" (Kharkover 1993, 3: 45)

(6.82)   In a pharmacy: "We can't sell arsenic to you. To buy it, you need a doctor's prescription with a seal. Just show the doctor a photo of your mother-in-law. That would do it." (Nikulin 1997, 184)

(6.83)   A little boy asks his father: "Why is Grandma running around the house?"

His father brandishes his hunting rifle and says: "For you she's grandma, for me she's a mother-in-law. Gimme another cartridge, sonny." (Private collection)

(6.84)   A crowd of passersby noticed that on the sixth story a young man was trying to throw an elderly woman off the balcony. The people were shouting: "You scoundrel! Leave the lady alone! Where are the police when you need them?"

From the doorway a neighbor explained: "That's his mother-in-law."

"The old battle-ax!" cried the crowd. "Look how she's trying to resist!" (Draitser 1980, 31)

(6.85)   A son-in-law dangles his mother-in-law over the railing of his fifth-floor apartment's balcony.

"Do you know what our second-floor neighbor did to his mother-in-law?"

"Yes," mutters the woman, "he sawed her in half with his hand-saw."

"And what did the ninth-floor neighbor do with his mother-in-law?"

"He quartered her with an ax."

"See, and I am letting you go." (Private collection)

(6.86)   What is superhypocracy? It is when a son-in-law throws his mother-in-law from his balcony and asks her while she's falling: "Where are you going, little mama?" (Private collection)

(6.87)   "What can you tell us about dogs?"

"One young man threw his mother-in-law into the stair-well of his building. And she didn't even bark." (Milgram 1985, 105)

(6.88) "Listen, what did your mother-in-law die from?"
"She ate some poisonous little mushrooms."
"Then why does she have all those blue spots on her neck?"
"She did not want to eat them. . . ." (Private collection)

Sons-in-law who are lucky enough that their wife's mother dies naturally, are upset if something delays the process.

(6.89) A mother-in-law is dying. She looks out the window and says: "What a sunset! Isn't it beautiful?"
Her son-in-law cuts her off right away: "Little mother, little mother, don't get distracted. Do what you're doing. . . ." (Kharkover 1993, 3: 44)

There is no obstacle that the son-in-law would not overcome if only he could get rid of her once and for all:

(6.90) A mother-in-law comes up to her son-in-law: "Here's what I want to say, sonny: Do whatever you want, do whatever it takes, but I see the Kremlin wall as a burial place of eternal rest."
The next morning the son-in-law comes home in a great hurry: "Here's what I want to say, Mummy: Do whatever you want, do whatever it takes, but funerals are today at noon. . . ."
(Private collection)

In similar American jokelore there are no jokes against the son-in-law (Duvall 1964, 35), but many Russian jokes attest to full-fledged warfare during which neither side shows any mercy:

(6.91) "Mama!" a daughter shouts into the phone. "It's already two A.M., and my husband isn't home. He may have got himself a girl on the side."
"Dear daughter, why suspect the worst right away? Maybe, he was run over by a car and lies now in an intensive care unit or in a morgue." (Smetanin and Donskaia 1992, 44)

The motif of the mother-in-law's death surfaces in some American male jokes as well (Duvall 1964, 22–36; Fine 1981, 230). But the emotional climate is quite different. The American son-in-law usually treats her departure as a stroke not of ill fate but of luck. Upon hearing the news about his mother-in-law's death, he responds causally. For example:

"Your mother-in-law fell in the well, and we haven't been able to fish
out the body."
"It doesn't matter. We drink bottled water." (Fine 1091, 236)

No such "gentleness" is present in Russian jokelore. To demonstrate the
difference between American and Russian treatment of mothers-in-law, consider the following American joke:

> 1st cannibal: "I don't care much for my mother-in-law."
> 2nd cannibal: "Well, just eat the beans." (Fine 1981, 230)

To make this joke fit Russian sensibilities, it would go something like this:

> 1st cannibal: "I don't care much for my mother-in-law."
> 2nd cannibal: "I know how you feel. I can't stomach mine either. But
> all the same, go ahead and do it. You don't have to swallow her, just
> chew her bones well, and spit her out."

In jokelore the Russian son-in-law is usually the murderer. The violent
death of the hated woman takes many forms. The classic joke of this kind is
the one that warms the heart of a son-in-law with the implication that
putting an end to his mother-in-law may not be complicated; the weapon is
always available to him. In fact, it is a domestic appliance of a peaceful nature that is often right there, under the hated woman's hand:

> (6.92) "Can you kill your mother-in-law with a sheet?"
> "Yes, you can. If you wrap an iron in it." (Private collection)

If murdering a mother-in-law is not satisfying enough by itself, in many
jokes the son-in-law has his last heart-to-heart conversation with his victim,
the sole purpose of which is to reassure her sadistically that she is given the
gentlest kind of death, a fact that she must appreciate (as in 6.85, about
being dropped from a balcony).

The primary cause of the tension is crammed living conditions. Because
of lack of housing, a mother-in-law often lives in an adjacent room or, not
infrequently, in the same room with the young couple. This often results in
the lack of privacy and opportunity for sexual intimacy addressed in chapter
4. In this situation, the wife is also a deprived party, but she usually adjusts
better than her husband, accepting it as the price she pays for her mother's
help.

It is noteworthy that attacks on mothers-in-law in chastushkas, primarily the rural folk genre, are less widespread; when they occur, they are less vicious than those in the urban jokelore. That may be because in the countryside mothers-in-law usually live separately from a daughter's family. The tension between mother-in-law and son-in-law has increased with the general shift from traditional Russian rural living arrangements to urban ones (virilocal vs. uxorilocal; Rancour-Laferriere, personal correspondence). An ancient folk custom according to which a mother-in-law invited her son-in-law for pancakes *[bliny]*—in some villages on Wednesday, in some on Friday of Shrovetide week—demonstrates the important role of living arrangements in their relationships. As Russian ethnographer Polina Rozhnova (1992, 51) notes, the ritual was quite telling: A son-in-law was given a lavish feast if he was liked (on Friday, called "Mother-in-Law's Evening," he would reciprocate); in most cases this meant that he lived separately from his mother-in-law. (He was given a less than friendly treatment when living under the same roof.) As the current saying goes, "Love for a man's mother-in-law is measured in kilometers" (JFR 3/26/98). Traces of this custom are to be found in a contemporary Russian saying. Referring to something unpleasant, by way of contrast, a Russian may say: "That's not quite like going to your mother-in-law to be treated with pancakes" *[Eto tebe ne k teshche na bliny]*.

It is not surprising, therefore, that the setting for the son-in-law's murder of his mother-in-law is a balcony of a high-rise building, as in jokes 6.84–6.86. The balcony scenes are also telling as to the would-be-murderer's sense of righteousness. He has nothing to hide and feels completely guilt-free about what he is about to do, for anyone [read: any man] would understand his motive and be on his side. This is seen especially clearly in joke 6.84; the crowd's sympathies instantaneously shift to the attacker's side once it learns that the woman is his mother-in-law. When it comes to mothers-in-law, male solidarity is taken for granted.

(6.93) A man sees a huge, mostly male, funeral procession. Next to the coffin, a little doggy trots along.
"Who has died?" the man asks.
"Well, my mother-in-law," one of the men answers.
"What did she die from?"
"That little doggy bit her."
"Listen, buddy, can I borrow your doggy for a day?"
"All right, take your place in line," says the man, and points to the end of the procession. (Genis 1994, 1: 165)

(6.94)   A court hearing of Ivanov I., who killed his mother-in-law by hitting
          her head with a hammer, is in progress.
              They ask a friend who is present at the hearing: "What do you
          think about Ivanov's act?"
              "Well, in my view, every man is a blacksmith of his own happi-
          ness." (JFR 2/24/98)

The humor of the following joke is based on the son-in-law's perception that
it is taken for granted that killing his mother-in-law is the right thing for any
man to do. Therefore, he interprets the question addressed to him not as
about his motive but about his timing.

(6.95)   A court hearing is in session. The prosecutor says to the accused:
          "Would you explain to us why you killed your mother-in-law?"
              The accused: "See, I stopped in our kitchen, and my mother-in-
          law was standing with her back to me washing dishes. And next to
          her was that frying pan. And I thought to myself: 'You might never
          have a better chance!'" (JFR 2/25/98)

A mother-in-law is dreaded so much that even her death does not put her
son-in-law at ease:

(6.96)   A son-in-law buried his mother in-law. He's returning home. From
          above, from a roof a [big] icicle drops on his head. He raises his eyes:
          "O Lord! That bitch's already in heaven." (Nikulin 1997, 190)

Humiliating her after her death seems to bring him a morbid satisfaction:

(6.97)   Shortly before her death, a mother-in-law calls her son-in-law and
          says: "Here, little son-in-law, a thousand rubles. You'll bury me and
          put up a monument."
              He takes the money, goes to the street, meets his friend, and tells
          him about his mother-in-law's request.
              "Last year," says the friend, "I buried my mother-in-law and it
          cost me just fifteen rubles."
              "How did you manage that?"
              "I buried her up to her waist and painted the rest of her the color
          of stone." (Repina and Rostovtsev 1995, 16: 24)[10]

Russians voted the following joke as the best of the top 100 jokes for 1997
on the JFR website:

(6.98) A man returning with his daughter from a crematorium carries an urn with the ashes of his deceased mother-in-law.

The daughter says: "Daddy, let's put this urn on my piano, and when I play it, it would please Grandma. When she was alive, she liked to listen to my playing. . . ."

Her father: "Oh, no. No way, daughter. We'll pour her into an hourglass. Let the bitch keep on working!"

The son-in-law would even prefer to go to hell after his own death, just to avoid her:

(6.99) "You're clairvoyant. Can you help me?"

"Absolutely. What do you need to know?"

"Tell me where my mother-in-law went after death—to heaven or hell. I wouldn't want to run into her." (Repina and Rostovtsev 1995, 22: 216)

In a number of Russian jokes, both the mother-in-law and her daughter are equally dreaded:

(6.100) A wife asks her husband: "It's my last wish—when I die, please do me this last favor. Walk next to my mother at the funeral."

"Okay, okay," said the husband. "I'll do it if you ask me. But I have to warn you that it'll spoil the whole pleasure of the day for me." (For an American variant, see Fine 1981, 221).

(6.101) Two men meet in a cemetery.

"Who are you burying?"

"My wife. And you?"

"My mother-in-law."

"Also not bad."

(6.102) A New Russian returns from Hawaii and shares his memories with his friends:

"A wonderful place! Where I spent my vacation there was everything that one can desire: luxurious restaurants for me, beautiful coral beaches for my kids, scorching sun for my wife, and giant blood-thirsty sharks for my mother-in-law." (Kulikov 1997, 121)

(6.103) Sidorov has severely beaten up his wife and mother-in-law. After hearing the case, the judge announces: "The accused is to pay a fine in the amount of 100,050 rubles."

Sidorov is puzzled: "Why 100,050 and not just 100,000?"
"50 rubles is our local entertainment tax." [*Argumenty i fakty,* 51 (896), December 1997: 1].

Legman (1968, 439–440) argues that such double-targeted jokes in Western folklore are projections of general misogynist attitudes toward one's wife and mother-in-law. In the context of Russian everyday living arrangements, the attacks targeting both women seem to express male frustration with married life as well. In fact, different versions of jokes 6.84 and 6.97 are also circulating that feature a wife instead of mother-in-law (e.g., in Nikulin 1997, 146–148). This is not a strictly Russian phenomenon. Anthropologist Walter Ong (1981, 84) notes that the worldwide stock of mother-in-law jokes accounts for the fact that "mother and daughter tend to merge symbolically and socially."

The fact that crowded living conditions, the necessity to live under one roof with a mother-in-law, is the main source of Russian men's fierce hatred of her is clearly seen in a change of tone of jokes of the post-Soviet period, when newly rich Russians could afford separate housing for a mother-in-law. In fact, the following joke is an exact copy of an American joke in a work by psychoanalyst Samuel Janus (1981, 165):

(6.104)   "When does a New Russian have ambivalent feelings?"
"When his brand-new Mercedes with his mother-in-law in it is sitting on the edge of a cliff." (Private collection).

Thus, while Russian jokelore expresses hostilities similar to those found in other cultures toward women in the framework of marriage, many Russian jokes reflect a more complex dynamic of the power struggle within the family, exacerbated by low standards of living in general and crammed housing in particular.

CHAPTER 7

Splitting the Bottle Three Ways: Jokelore of Impotence and Adultery

Impotence Jokes

"People do not joke about what makes them happy or what is sacred to them. They joke only about what frightens or disturbs them, or about the pinnacles of happiness they would like to have scaled but have failed at." Legman's (1968, 664) observation applies with particular force to jokes about impotence and adultery.

Impotence is a strictly male problem. "The mature woman," writes Martin Grotjahn (1957, 59–60) in his *Beyond Laughter,* "pretends to accept the male's false claim to superiority over her . . . because every time the man approaches her sexually she can show her superiority. She is always ready; he must get ready. . . . The woman is always potentially potent, the man is always potentially impotent." For a man to be virile and sexually active is not so much a physiological and biological necessity as it is a cultural imperative. His fear of being unable to carry out this imperative represents the main source of his anxiety. To fit the cultural standard, if he does not have great sexual drive, he has to at least to pretend that he does:

(7.1)   Two girlfriends go to the horse races, and don't know which horse to bet on. One asks another: "What size is your bra?"

"Size two."

"Mine too. Let's put it on horse number four."

Horse number 4 comes in first. With the money they've won, the girls rush to share their winnings with their husbands. The next day the men meet at the betting box office.

"How many times you make love to your wife at night?" one of them says.

"Three."
"And me four. Let's put it on number seven."
Horse number 2 came in first.
Moral: Don't bullshit. . . . (JFR 3/4/98) (See also 3.68)

Hartogs and Fantel (1967, 42) talk about fear of impotence as "one of the most fundamental and pervasive of all [men's] fears—the fear of losing one's manhood, which carries with it the corollary fear of never fully attaining it." Men's ability to attain an erection at will is a crucial signifier of male identity, and impotence is a male identity crisis par excellence, often no less frightful for the male ego than death itself. "[M]ales emerge from the Oedipal period with orientation toward future heterosexuality, a male identity, and a good deal of insecurity about the strength of their hold on this status" (Murphy 1989, 66). What Freud termed "castration anxiety" refers to this uncertainty. Robert Murphy (1989, 66) concludes: "The masculine career is a treacherous venture, fraught with the apprehension that one can lose his autonomy, slip back into passivity, and be swallowed in the ambivalent fantasies that spring from mother love"

In a culture where male dominance is sustained and promoted on all social levels, a male's inability to perform undermines not only his self-image but the whole gender hierarchy to which he feels he belongs. Cross-cultural studies have shown that fear of impotence is the crucial male issue. Observing Japanese men in a hostess club, anthropologist Anne Allison (1994, 196) notes: "Men want to appear 'functional'; the failed penis, the penis that doesn't stand up and therefore cannot stand for a man who has power is the fate men fear. It goes even further—the impotent [man] may dread his condition as something equal to [the] dread of death while having no sexual desire as such or the need either to procreate or have a sexual partner. In psychological terms, an impotent [man] does not see how he is now different from a woman. . . ."

This explains why male humor as a strategy to express hidden anxieties in many cultures often deals with impotence. Grotjahn (1957, 103) notes that "the clown or other comic figure often directly suggests in behavior or accouterments the limp phallus, total ineffectiveness. The phallus can be mocked, as the womb cannot be." Russian male jokelore is no exception:

(7.2)   "What's the lightest thing in the world?"
        "The male organ. It can get up with the least impulse."
        "What's the heaviest thing in the world?"
        "The same. If it drops, no force in the world can get it up."
        (Barsky 1994, 278)

(7.3)   "What is called 'semiautomatic equipment'?"
        "A male organ that you lift by hand, and it falls down by itself"
        (Milgram 1985, 13)

(7.4)   "My husband lives on a day-to-day basis."
        "Mine too. At night he's no good for anything" (I. Raskin 1995, 292)

The theme is found in chastushkas:

(7.5)   Zhizn' proshla, kak sabantui,   Life passed by like a wild party,
        Kak odno mgnovenie.   In a twinkling.
        Ran'she podymalsia khui,   It used to be my dick that would go up.
        A teper' davlenie.   Nowadays it's my [blood] pressure.
                                              (Private collection)

As in other cultures, the Russian folk assumption is that men who do
manual labor, those who are physically strong, are good lovers. The hero of
the following joke is a janitor, not the zoo director:

(7.6)   A city zoo acquired a rare specimen of female gorilla. In a few weeks,
        the veterinarian found that she was in heat. To preserve this breed,
        the zoo needed a male gorilla.
            The search was unsuccessful. Then somebody noticed Vassya
        who cleaned the cages and had a reputation as a big-time stud.
        Would he fuck the gorilla for 100 bucks?
            Vassya asked for time to think about the offer. The next day he
        accepted it but set three conditions: first, no kisses; second, no rela-
        tionship with the possible consequences of the intercourse.
            The zoo director quickly agreed. "What was the third condi-
        tion?" he asked.
            Vassya's reply: "I need another week to find 100 bucks some-
        where. . . ." (Private collection)

In many Russian jokes, high intelligence is a hindrance to sexual performance and an intellectual is a sexual weakling:

(7.7)   A job ad at a harem: "Eunuchs and Ph.D.s are accepted with no ref-
        erences." (Private collection)

(7.8)   Two young women return from vacationing in the South and tell
        each other how they spent their time. One says:

"I met a metallurgist on the first day. He gave me quite a hot workout. In twenty four days he and I had an uninterrupted welding job."

"Well, I met a scientist," says another woman. "He got right down to business. He spent twenty-three days setting up an experiment which failed on the twenty-fourth day for technical reasons." (Private collection)

In the following joke, the same message is delivered in a more subtle way. It plays on the linguistic distinction between words denoting the male organ: "penis," used by educated people, and "dick" *[khui]*, used by common people.

(7.9)   Two girlfriends, whores, meet.
"How are you doing?"
"Badly. I'm wasting my time near the hotels and I'm earning peanuts. Men often abuse me. I see no future in the profession. What about you?"
"I, my dear, live a wonderful life. Every night I'm on call at the Actors' Club, the Architects' Club, the Journalists' Club. My clientele belongs to the intelligentsia. You go to a man's home. All the shish-kebab you can eat, all the cognac and champagne you can drink. Then you lie in bed with him, he puts his penis into your hand and sleeps all night."
Her girlfriend says with envy: "Gosh, you've got it made! Listen, sweetie, explain please, what is this—penis?"
"Well, how to explain it to you, dear? You know, it's like a dick, but it's limp." (I. Raskin 1995, 315)

The same idea is expressed in the form of a chastushka.

(7.10)	Ia eblas' s intelligentom	I fucked an intellectual
	Noch'iu na zavalinke.	Last night on the earthworks beyond the hut.
	Devki, penis—eto khui!	Gals, a penis is a dick,
	Tol'ko ochen' malen'kii.	Only a tiny one. (JFR 2/4/98)

The treatment of intellectuals as utterly impotent is accounted for in part by the fact that, due to the rigidity of a Soviet system that was notoriously slow in promoting talented people, most of these men achieved prominence at an advanced age, as this real-life story illustrates. At the banquet in his honor, a well-known scientist played on the double entendre of his new title *deistvitel'nyi chlen,* which, besides meaning full member [of the Academy of

Science], may also mean "a functioning member": "Of course I'm very pleased that those close to me—relatives, friends, and colleagues—have come to congratulate me on my election as a Full Member of the Academy of Science. But the tragedy of our lives lies in the very fact that we become Full Members at the time when our members have already stopped functioning" (quoted in I. Raskin 1995, 22).

In Russian jokelore, the virility of military officers is assumed to be in inverse proportion to their rank: As a rule, colonels are rendered as sexual weaklings and generals as the ultimate impotents. Sexually endowed privates usually put their superiors to shame and often appear as the adored lovers of their officers' wives. Sometimes an orderly may even pity his impotent commanding officer and take over his conjugal role out of kindness.

This folk notion of academicians, scientists, generals, and other prominent figures, while relating in part to their advanced age, may be seen as verbal revenge to compensate for social inequality. This is especially clear in a proverb collected by Dahl about the sexual problems facing the poor and the rich: "The rich one cries because his dick does not serve him, and the poor one because he can't hide it" *[Bogatyi tuzhit, chto khui ne sluzhit, a bednyi plachet, chto khui ne spriachet]* (Claude Carey 1972, 44).

Many collections contain a number of impotence jokes in which sexual failures are Jews. This is another case of the transfer of an unwanted condition onto another group, as discussed in previous chapters. There is more than one reason for this shift. On one hand, such a portrayal of Jewish men comes from the assumption that they are all circumcised and thus sexually inadequate, according to the folk belief that the one and only sign of male sexual prowess is the size of the male organ:

(7.11)   A recent bride tells her girlfriend: "Of course, I knew that the Jews get circumcised. But not to such a degree!" (Private collection)

Of course, circumcision does not affect the measurement that really counts. Such jokes are so prevalent simply because it is much easier to relieve one's own performance anxiety by ascribing it to men of the disfavored group.[1]

On the other hand, some Russian men still share an ancient belief, one supported by doctors in medieval times (Bakhtin 1986, 97) and alive and well today in other cultures (Simons 1973, 166), according to which the length of a man's nose signifies the length of his phallus and therefore his reproductive ability. One Russian saying has it, "What's in a shop window is in the shop" *[Chto na vitrine, to i v magazine]* (Loginov 1996, 451); another,

"An aquiline nose means a dick like a club" *[nos s gorbinkoi, khui dubinkoi].* Russians see the Jews as hook-nosed and so endowed with great sexual prowess. Russian doctor Mikhail Stern's observation that Russians portray stereotypical Jews as "tireless sexual performers" may well be based on this popular belief (Stern and Stern 1980, 240). Unconscious phallus envy may well be the source of scornful jokes about the Jews as lovers.

Russian tellers benefit in other respects by down playing Jewish sexuality. Some Russians stereotype Jews as formidable sexual competitors, thanks to a belief that Jewish husbands are better breadwinners (Gray 1990, 56). Some mothers encourage Jews to court their daughters for want of a better choice. It is considered everyday wisdom that a Jewish husband, unlike a Russian one, would not indulge in alcoholism and wife-beating. The Russians' awareness of this as potential threat to their sexual territory is seen in the following jokes:

(7.12)   An old Jew is sitting on a beach with his young grandson.
"Listen, Moishe. Do you like that blonde in the red bathing suit?"
"I like her, Grandpa."
"And that brunette with the puffy little tushi?"
"I like her," says the grandson shyly.
"And that redhead with her high bust?"
"Yes, Grandpa. . . ."
"Then remember, Moishe, in order to have them, you have to study hard." (Soloviev 1992, 2: 28)

(7.13)   In a train, a young man and a girl strike up a conversation. The young man asks, "What kind of people do you like most of all?"
"Well, maybe the American Indians because they are strong and brave and the Jews because they can adjust to any living conditions."
"Then let me introduce myself: Chingachook Aron Moiseevich (Soloviev 1992, 2: 42)

True to sexologists' observations, lack of physical potency is often linked to the loss of social potency, a man's ability to be a breadwinner. The following item was collected in the post-Soviet period when there has been a marked decrease in the average Russian man's ability to support his family:

(7.14)   After the liberation of Kuwait from Saddam Hussein's invasion during the Gulf War, a Muskovite comes home and begins to pack his suitcase.

"Where are you heading?" his wife asks.

"I'm leaving for Kuwait. They killed all the men there and any woman will pay 20 bucks to sleep with a man once."

His wife doesn't say anything and just begins to pack her suitcase as well. The husband looks at her with surprise: "And where are you going?"

"I'll come along. I want to see you survive on forty bucks per month." (JFR 2/25/98)

Since according to Russian machismo, "A true man can always do it" (I. Raskin 1995, 228), jokelore related to the male-ego disaster, sexual inadequacy, plays down the real importance of the failure, treats it as no more than a cause for mild confusion. As a contemporary Russian saying has it, "A man [read: a true man] blushes [only] twice in his life: for the first time, when he can't do it for the second time, and the second time, when he can't do it the first time."

By the same token, some impotence jokes do not address the painful problem directly but allude to it by depicting the male's lack of sexual interest, a tendency to treat intercourse as a chore to be avoided at all costs:

(7.15) A woman complains about today's men: "You put him on top of you—he falls asleep. You put him under you—he loses his wind. You put him beside you—he watches TV. You put him on the floor—he's gone." (Private collection)

(7.16) A wife wakes her husband up at night.

"I'm cold," she says.

Her husband gets up reluctantly and closes the window. After a short while, the wife again says: "Make me warm, I'm cold."

The husband grudgingly brings her another comforter. After a while, she says: "I want a man."

"Well, dear," the husband answers, turning away from her, "you are unreasonable. Where will I find a man for you at two in the morning?" (Smetanin and Donskaia 1992, 3)

(7.17) Question: "What kind of sex do you prefer?"

"Group sex."

"Why?"

"You can always fake it." (Smetanin and Donskaia 1992, 14)

In the following joke, the wife knows her husband's true interests:

(7.18)   A man spends the night out and tries to persuade his wife that the reason was sexual abandon.

"You know, my dear," the husband says, "I was going home after work, and met such a beautiful girl that I could not resist the temptation. I talked her into it and spent the night with her."

"Liar!" says his wife, "You played cards all night with your good-for-nothing friends again!" (Private collection)

The following is another instance of the transfer of an unwanted condition or shortcoming to an outsider:

(7.19)   A *khokhol* [Russian nickname for a Ukrainian] is hiding in a hayloft. His wife comes out on the steps of their house and shouts:
"Mikola!"
Silence.
"Mikola!"
Silence.
"Mikola, damn you!"
"What, you want to fuck again?"
"Come eat. You're some fucker." (JFR 3/31/98)

Because household chores are still considered solely a female's duty (see chapter 6), in the following joke, impotence accounts implicitly for the man's abandonment of his long-held convictions.[2]

(7.20)   A husband comes home. His wife asks him: "Have you bought bread?"
"That's not a man's business."
"Well, then do the man's business."
"What's the matter with you, don't you get a joke? Give me the shopping bag." (Smetanin and Donskaia 1992, 4)

The following jokes cleverly turn a man's sexual failure into a weapon in the marital battle of the sexes:

(7.21)   A man brings his wife to a doctor. Upon examining her, the doctor asks to talk to the husband in private.
"If you don't make love to your wife at least once a month," he tells him, "she will die."
Later, the wife asks her husband: "What did the doctor say to you?"
"What, what? . . . He said you'll die soon." (JFR 3/21/98)

(7.22) Newlyweds are making love on their first night.

"Dear," say the young man. "You know, I can't do it for some reason. Can you help me by your hands?"

Three hours pass, and no results.

"Listen, dear, my hands hurt."

"Why the hell are you getting married if your hands function poorly?" (JFR 3/7/98)

While a woman could be responsible for a man's psychologically based impotence under certain conditions (see Goldberg 1987, 24–29), the following item holds that all women are inherently emasculating:

(7.23) The latest scientific findings have established that when God created woman he took from Adam not his rib but a bone from his male organ. (JFR 2/25/98)

A few jokes suggest that a man's obesity is the result of his impotence, his replacement of women with food. In contemporary Russian slang, the expression "a mirror disease" signifies that a man has grown such a big stomach that he cannot see his organ without the help of a mirror. What is implied here is that because of his impotence, he has no other chance to see it. The loss of potency is metaphorically rendered in the contemporary saying: "A [fat] man's stomach is like a watermelon: it grows and his tail is getting dry." The following joke elaborates on the same comic theme:

(7.24) On the street, a little boy approaches a man with a big stomach: "Little uncle, your fly is open and your pee pee is showing."

"Say hello to it, little boy. I haven't seen it in seven years." (I. Raskin 1995, 323)

Other impotence jokes show concern about the low nutritional quality of the average Russian's diet:

(7.25) "Doctor, my husband is so weak in bed. . . ."

"What do you feed him?"

"Potatoes. . . ."

"My dear, it's shirts collars that starch stiffens." (McLovsky, Klyne, and Chtchuplov 1997, 150)

(7.26) A wife sues for divorce on the grounds of her husband's refusal to fulfill his spousal duties.

"What do you say in your defense?" the judge asks. "Why don't you do what a man should do to his wife?"

"Comrade judge," says the man. "Give me a little bowl of soup, and I'll fuck all present in this court house." (Private collection)

(7.27) In a store: "Do you have meat?"

"No. But we have fish. It's also very good for you. It has lots of phosphorus."

"I need something to get it up, not give a fluorescent effect." (Barsky 1994, 279)

Another much more frequent cause of impotence in Russian men comes as no surprise. Legman's (1968, 684) observation that the drunk as "a sexual failure par excellence" rarely surfaces in folk humor is not true of Russian jokelore. In the following joke, a Russian woman's choice of men begins and ends with an alcoholic:

(7.28) "If he's not an alcoholic, he's a fool; if he's not a fool, he's impotent; if he isn't impotent, he's gay; if he isn't gay, he's an alcoholic." (Kulikov 1997, 428–429)

(7.29) For the man of 1993, one bottle [of vodka] is too little, one broad is too much (I. Raskin 1995, 291).

(7.30) A drunken husband comes home. His wife attacks him: "You're loaded again! Day after day it's all you do—get loaded! I wish you'd fucked me at least once a month!"

"Are you out of your mind? Once a month! What, have you turned nympho?" (I. Raskin 1995, 84)

(7. 31) A drunk comes home late.

"Again you got loaded!" his wife says. "After all, you told me that today you'd come home sober and make love to me."

"I'll do it for sure. Just give me another drink."

The wife brings him his drink. He drinks it and thinks for a while.

"You know, my dear, to make our lovemaking really hot, I need another drink."

In despair his wife runs out on their balcony and cries: "O Lord! Are there any true men in this house!"

A voice from the first floor: "What, do you have something to drink?" (Nikulin 1997, 87–88)

A correlation between sexual prowess and drink is seen in a chastushka referring to Gorbachev's campaign against alcoholism:

(7.32) Spasibo partii rodnoi   Thanks to our dear party
       I Gorbachevu lichno: And personally to Gorbachev:
       Trezvyi muzh prishel domoi   A sober husband has come home
       I vyebal otlichno.   And has fucked me excellently.
                                       (I. Raskin 1995, 44)

Alcohol is an inseparable part of a Russian sexual encounter, an aphrodisiac par excellence. (See chapter 3): "Nothing makes a woman more beautiful than two glasses of vodka in a man's stomach."[3] The following joke, told during Gorbachev's anti-alcohol campaign, during which it was suggested that sobriety be observed even at wedding parties, is a case in point. Since alcohol makes a man more of a man, it is suggested that if he doesn't drink, he can't father a child: "Let's respond to the nonalcoholic wedding with immaculate conception!" The alcoholic cannot get out of a vicious circle of his own making:

(7.33) In a sex therapist's office: "Doctor, I have a problem with women. When I have a drink, I can't come" [in Russian "finish," *konchit*].
       "So, don't drink."
       "And if I don't have a drink, I can't begin [can't get it up]."
       (Kharkover 1993, 1: 18).

The following joke implies sexual failure on alcoholic grounds. A plumber is a contemporary folk stereotype of a drinking man, as he is often paid for his services in vodka. He does not respond even to a world-famous movie star who is the epitome of sex appeal:

(7.34) Sofia Loren arrives at the Metropol Hotel in Moscow. She takes a bath. And the faucets don't work. She calls the front desk and asks for a plumber. He works on the faucets for some time. Loren decides to have some fun with him, to play a practical joke. She opens up her bathrobe.
       The plumber pays no attention to her.
       She does it again.
       The same result.

Then she takes off her robe and stands stark naked in front of him.

The plumber turns to her and says: "Why are you staring at me? Haven't you ever seen a plumber or what?" (Private collection)

Some jokes find miraculous cures for impotence.

(7.35) After starting a recovery program, a man who had been kicked out by his wife knocks on the door of his former apartment.

"Go away, you drunken impotent!" his wife shouts.

"Masha, if you only knew what I'm knocking with right now!"

"Come in, you barbarian. . . ." (Smetanin and Donskaia 1992, 6)

Another strategy for dealing with fear of impotence is to redelegate this malfunction to some distant future, to make it a problem reserved for old age.

(7.36) Two aging men talk: "You know, before, when I was young, it was enough for me to think about a woman, and I would get aroused right away. And now—I think about her, and think—and nothing happens. Maybe something's wrong with my head?" (Private collection)

(7.37) A group of dilapidated retirees decide to have a drink. They collect money and send the youngest for wine. One of the men realizes: "We've sent for wine but we didn't think about snacks."

They send someone to buy food.

"Well, well," says another. "There'll be wine and snacks. Why not invite the ladies?"

They send one of the able-bodied grandpas to ask the ladies.

"Here's what I'm going to say, comrades," says the most decrepit senior. "As we have wine and snacks and even ladies, we should have sent somebody for men!" (Nikulin 1997, 395)

(7.38) "What's a demagogue?"

"It's an old man who tries to convince a woman that a soft dick is better than a hard one." (McLovsky, Klyne, and Chtchuplov 1997, 150)

The following joke assumes that any man over fifty is impotent, another manifestation of the rampant ageism in Russian popular culture:

(7.39) A plane crashes in the ocean. Survivors land on two desert islands: men on one, women on another.

On the "men's" island, they are deciding what to do.

A twenty-year old: "Hey, fellows, why are you standing around? Let's swim over to the women!"

A thirty-year old: "Calm down! We'll make a raft and we'll all get there together."

A forty-year old: "Listen, guys, why bother? They'll swim over to us by themselves."

A fifty-year old: "You with your evil prophecies! . . . They're already swimming toward us." (JFR 2/12/98)

Other jokes that defer impotence to old age are fantasies of the opposite:

(7.40)   "For a man of your age you look great."
           "I look normal. I'm 83."
           "I suppose your father lived a long life?"
           "What makes you think he's dead? He's 104."
           "God! And how long did your grandpa live?"
           "And who said he died? He's 124, and he's going to get married next week."
           "Lord! How can a man of 124 want to marry?"
           "Who told you he wants to? He has to marry out of decency."
(Repina and Rostovtsev 1995, 22: 106)

The importance of sexual prowess for male ego is emphasized by a man's readiness to admit other effects of aging, but not losing the faculty that really counts:

(7.41)   A seventy-year old man marries an eighteen-year-old girl. On their wedding night, he knocks on the door of his bride's bedroom: "Dear, I came to fulfill my spousal duty."

           After doing so, he wishes his young wife good night and leaves. In an hour, he knocks again: "Dear, I came to fulfill my spousal duty."

           An hour later: "Dear, I came to fulfill my spousal duty."

           "But, my dear, you've already done it twice tonight!"

           "Oh, forgive me, dear. It's my memory playing tricks on me."[4]
(Private collection)

(7.42)   A grandpa comes to a doctor and says: "Something is wrong with my potency, Doc!"

           "What's the matter?"

           "Well, my wife is a charmer, my female neighbor is a sweetie pie, my mistress is a miracle, my female dog is a beauty, my cow is

a little sun, and my female goat is wonderful. . . . Here it is. Lately
I don't have enough strength for my goat. . . ."
  "How old are you, after all?"
  "I just hit my seventy-third year. . . ."
  "Well! This is because you're getting old!"
  "Thank God, Doc! Well, you've really put me at ease! And I,
blockhead that I am, thought that it's because of masturbation!"
(JFR 3/2/98)

(7.43) Old man Mitrich walks along the village street carrying a bucket of
water on his member.
  Old lady Lukinichna is walking by. "What's the matter with you,
Mitrich? Have you gone mad? What do you think you're doing?"
  "Well, I am aging, Lukinichna, my hands aren't strong enough
anymore. . . ." (JFR 2/11/98)

In fact, the one faculty that truly counts for the male ego may even magi-
cally increase in a dramatic way.

(7.44) In the circus, an old man breaks walnuts with his pecker.
  Twenty years pass. He begins to break coconuts.
  "What's happened? Has something gone wrong with you?"
  "I've developed a problem seeing the walnuts." (I. Raskin 1995,
129)

  Since for heavy drinkers an alcoholic stupor is the most desirable state in
which to find themselves (i.e., a bottle is his dearest lover), given a choice between a woman and booze, the drunkard invariably chooses the latter.
Sinyavsky (Tertz 1980, 41) considers such a preference intrinsically Russian:
"Vodka is the white magic of a Russian man; he decidedly prefers it to the
black magic—the female sex. A ladies' man, a lover, takes over the traits of a
foreigner—a German (the devil in Gogol), a Frenchman, a Jew. But we, the
Russians, will give away any beautiful woman for a bottle of pure vodka."

(7.45) A young woman invites Ivan to her apartment for dinner. She puts
a bottle of vodka on the table. Ivan drinks shot after shot without the
slightest attention to his hostess.
  "What's the matter, Ivan? Don't you like me at all?"
  "Oh, no, no! Please forgive me, dear! You're lovely. But you've
mixed things up. I'm not a womanizer. I'm a boozer." (There is a
rhyme in Russian: *Ia ne babnik, ia alkogolik;* private collection)

(7.46) A Hare drives a Bear along a forest road. They see a Vixen waving
her tail.

"Stop, squinty," says the Bear.

They stop.

"Hi, boys," says the Vixen. "Gimme a lift. You won't regret it."

"Get in," says the Bear.

They ride together.

"Stop here," says the Vixen after a while. "Now tell me, guys, what do you prefer: Should I take off my panties or should I rush over and get you a bottle of vodka from the store?"

The Bear looks at the Hare.

"Get it," the Hare shouts. "Get us the bottle."

Then the Bear and the Hare get drunk. The Bear hugs the Hare: "You are such a smart son of a bitch! It's just dawned on me. Really, why the hell do we need her panties! For you, they're too big; for me, too small." (Private collection)

What makes this joke genuinely Russian is not only the fairy-tale format, which is still part of the popular culture, but the Bear's sense of what constitutes adequate payment for a ride. The Bear must be truly Russian to think, at least for a moment, about the Vixen's panties as having some value: Shortages of the most essential goods were a constant feature of Russian life for decades. Also, the folklore nickname for a hare in Russian folklore—"squinty" *[kosoi]*—is also a slang name for a drunk, as in: "I drank a glass of vodka and got squinty [pie-eyed]" *[Ia vypil stakan vodki i okosel]*.

It comes as no surprise that, in a lot of Russian jokes, all pretenses and camouflages are removed, and impotence humor is bitter and hopeless, recalling the typical gallows humor of those who have nothing to lose:

(7.47)   Nobody has died from impotence so far. It's true that nobody has been born from it either. (JFR 3/6/98)

(7.48)   A question to Armenian Radio: "Can a carrot increase potency?"
         "In principle, it can. But it's mighty difficult to tie it to it." (Private collection)

It is noteworthy that, despite the proliferation of jokes connecting impotence with alcohol, when it comes to Russians as a group, should a Russian cross the national border or confront a foreigner, miraculously his masculinity becomes not only strong but legendary, something out of a fairy tale.

(7.49)   One Russian decides to escape to Alaska and become a citizen of that state.

"You see," they tell him, "to become a citizen of Alaska, you should fulfill three conditions: eat a pot of raw fish, give a handshake to a female polar bear, and spend a night with an Eskimo woman."

The Russian agrees and leaves. In a while he appears again: "I ate the pot of raw fish, I spent a night with the female polar bear, but where is that Eskimo woman whose hand I have to shake?" (Draitser 1998, 182. See also 183; V. Raskin 1985, 202–203)

While in jokes that deal with international competition they are portrayed as world drinking champions (see chapter 3), in others Russians are invariably champions of lovemaking. As a group Russians seem to feel that failing as a sex partner in an international competition is much more than a lapse. It's a national disgrace.

(7.50)   A Frenchman, an Italian, and a Russian talk about sex.

"Last night I made it four times with my wife," the Frenchman boasts. "And in the morning she made an excellent breakfast for me and told me again and again how much she loved me."

"And I managed to do it six times last night," says the Italian. "In the morning my wife was more caring than ever, and she told me that she'd never be attracted to another man."

The Russian is silent till his curious neighbors ask him how many times he had made love to his wife last night. Finally he answers "Once."

"Once only? And what did she say to you in the morning?"

"'Don't you stop.'" (Private collection)

(7.51)   Clinton calls Yeltsin on the hot line.

"Boris! Trouble! Yesterday terrorists blew up all of the condom factories in America. This is a true disaster for the American people!"

"Bill," Yeltsin answers, "you know the Russian people are always ready to help. We'll do whatever we can."

"All that I ask you is to send us one million condoms. As soon as possible."

"We'll do it in no time," Yeltsin calms him down.

"Splendid!" Clinton says. "Well, Boris, can you do me a favor?"

"What kind?"

"Could you make condoms having a blue stripe, ten inches long, and two inches in diameter."

"Those little Americans have some dicks!" Yeltsin thinks but he says out loud: "No problem, Bill. We'll do it."

Right after this conversation, Yeltsin calls a man responsible for condom production in Russia: "Listen, here's an emergency order.

You should make one million condoms and send them to Washington, D.C."

"Consider it done," the man says.

"Yes, there is one specification," Yeltsin adds, "they should be blue-striped, ten inches long, and two inches in diameter."

"That's easy to do," says the man. "Anything else?"

"Yes," says Yeltsin, "On every condom print clearly: 'Made in Russia. Size Medium.'" (JFR 2/16/98)[5]

There is other, less obvious, evidence of the pervasiveness of the theme of impotence in Russian male consciousness—the ever-present use of *mat*. Hartogs and Fantel (1967, 43) believe that the basic mechanism of verbal obscenity is one of masking. Besides dealing with many frustrations of ordinary life, the penetration of *mat* into Russian everyday discourse may have deeper significance, masking men's fear that they lose their manhood when the system deprives them of decision making about many aspects of human life.

"Trust but Verify": Jokes on Adultery

It is to be expected that marital fidelity is not greatly valued in today's Russia; after all, few marriages have been based on devotion and love. Infidelity has become so widespread in Russian society since the 1960s that humorous terms for illicit lovers were coined: "first-cousin wife" and "first-cousin husband" (or: "wife [or husband] once removed"; in Russian: *dvoiurodnaia zhena, dvoiurodnyi muzh;* Corten 1992, 44–45).[6] Many marriages fall apart when an alternative partner is encountered. Predictably the jokes often point directly to alcoholism as the cause of marital discord:

(7.52)   Late at night a wife opens the door to confront her drunken husband and explodes: "That's it! Enough is enough! Make your decision right now: wine or me."

"Oh?" the husband raises his head. "And how much wine?" (Private collection)

In some "drinking" jokes, even a wife's infidelity, so painful to the male ego, is taken lightly or even dismissed altogether because of the primacy of alcohol in the guzzler's life:

(7.53)   A man, quite drunk, bought another bottle of vodka and took a friend home with him to go on partying.

"Listen," said the host, feeling around in the refrigerator for some appetizers, "go into the other room and get some glasses."

His friend soon returned, surprised and confused: "There's . . . your wife is sleeping in there with some guy. . . ."

"Shh!" exclaimed the host, "you'll wake him up . . . and he'll ask to split the bottle three ways." (Private collection)

At the same time, a wife's possible infidelity presents a formidable source of male anxiety which has deep biological roots. "The precariousness of the male's claim to his own children can establish a permanent, if not always conscious, stress situation for the human male by contrast with the female," Ong (1981, 74–75) notes: "[H]ow can the man prove that his sperm was the only sperm she received? Her chastity is his only assurance."

Lubki, the (often) erotic prints circulated in Russia until the end of the nineteenth century, provided "a way of purging men's fear of being betrayed by their wives and laughed at by their fellows" (Farrel 1991, 560). Contemporary Russian cuckoldry jokes serve the same psychological function. To tell a joke in which somebody else's wife commits adultery and to make fun of the situation helps the teller avoid the thought that a similar misfortune might befall him.

In many other male-dominated cultures around the world, "playing around," "having fun," "having an adventure" do not trespass on any moral boundaries, and a wife is foolish to take infidelity seriously. Murphy (1989, 74) observes that "in most societies, the injunction to be faithful rests most heavily on the wife, leaving the husband relatively free to philander. Nonetheless, fidelity is the ideal, and extramarital sex is defined as adultery."

The vast majority of Russian adultery jokes are also about a wife's infidelity, not a husband's, as if what a man does outside of the conjugal bed is not violating marriage vows; his infidelity is insignificant:

(7.54) A man comes home late, exhausted. His wife rushes to him and shouts: "Where have you been??"

"You're such a smart gal," says the husband. "Come up with something yourself." (Private collection)

If spouses are separated by job requirements, it is the wife who is suspected of infidelity.

(7.55) "Comrade students! Don't worry about working with sources of radiation. This is quite safe. For example, some navy officers spent from three to four years on the nuclear submarines without vacations, and at the same time their wives gave birth to completely healthy children!" (JFR 2/20/98)

Emblematic of the asymmetrical male attitude toward spousal fidelity are a number of jokes that make the point that, given the opportunity, a wife would commit adultery on much greater scale.

(7.56) A young couple spent their vacation separately. They agreed to cheat on each other only twice. When they returned home, they compared notes. He cheated on her twice, as agreed: once with a female athlete, then with an actress. The wife cheated on him twice also: once with a soccer team, and again with a variety show orchestra. (Private collection)

During the Soviet period, when hotel rooms and other facilities were scarce, passes to sanatoriums and "rest homes" where sexual transgressions could take place were in great demand:

(7.57) An elephant comes to the resort with a young gazelle. A tomcat comes there alone. A sheep comes with his own wife, and a jackass sends his wife over there. (Private collection)

The female is inherently treacherous.

(7.58) "Did Eve cheat on Adam?"
"We can't know for sure. But scientists claim that human beings descend from apes." (Private collection)

A Russian proverb, "Trust but verify!" is widely used in nonsexual contexts. (It was used in a televised speech by President Reagan to stress the need to check Soviet assurances of arms reductions.) However, it is of sexual origin, expressing a Russian husband's lasting apprehension about his wife's fidelity.

(7.59) A young family in a one-room apartment was having a guest over from out of town. Night was falling. What to do? They had only one bed, so the host put the guest in bed between himself and his wife.
In the morning, the host asks: "So, did you sleep well?"
"It was okay. I have to tell you this as one friend to another. I know you trust your wife, but she was acting rather strange. She kept holding my private part with her hand all night long."
"No, my friend, it wasn't my wife who was holding you, it was me. Trust but verify." (*doveriai, no proveriai;* in Russian the rhyme gives the phrase additional impact; private collection)

In the old *lubki* prints husbands accosted wives (who managed to out-maneuver them through their shrewdness—Farrell 1991, 559). In contemporary Russian jokes the confrontation is usually between the husband and the lover. Although it is quite clear that the lover would hardly find himself in the wife's arms without her cooperation or encouragement, the premise of such a shift is that the adulterer alone is the true perpetrator of the abominable act, not the cuckold's wife. The wife's immoral behavior, then, is taken for granted, suggesting that it is the man who should know better than pursue someone else's wife; as for her . . . well, what else can one expect from a woman but betrayal!

Although the confrontation between a cuckold and the adulterer, which represents "a displaced attention from the central immorality of the situation to a man and lover relationship" (Legman 1968, 737), is present in many Western jokes as well, in Russian jokes it is resolved differently. While punishing the adulterer seems to be a response to the situation in jokes in English (Legman 1968, 720–7), Russian jokes, at least those collected in the past decade or so, have the action reversed. It is the husband who is punished by the adulterer. In many jokes the Russian lover, caught in the act, does not even bother to hide or seek ways to escape. Instead, he humiliates the husband as if his docility were common knowledge:

(7.60) Sidorov catches his wife with her lover and says to him: "If I had a knife, I would slaughter you. If I had a gun, I would shoot you. But I don't have either of these. What should I do with you?"
"Why don't you go ahead and butt me to death?" (Private collection)

A variety of reasons for the husband's docility are either explicit or implicit. Although other grounds besides sexual dissatisfaction may be the cause of infidelity, in Russian jokes of the classical triangle type (a husband, a wife, a lover), the cuckold is usually impotent:

(7.61) A husband catches his wife in bed with her lover and promptly hits him. The wife tells him: "Right on! He doesn't live here and yet keeps visiting."
The lover picks himself up and punches the husband in return.
Wife: "Right on! Can't do it himself and doesn't let others."
(Smetanin and Donskaia 1992, 21)

True to life, the jokes often cite alcohol as the reason for a husband's sexual malfunction and, as a result, his wife's infidelity. Here the drunken husband's sexual inadequacy is metaphorically alluded to in the model of the plane he flies, which is inferior to the one his wife's lover pilots:

(7.62) A pilot returns home drunk and rings the doorbell. His wife asks: "Who's there?"
>   "TU-134 asks permission to land," answers her husband.
>   "Permission denied."
>   "Then I'm going to circle over the airfield again."
>   He walks around the building, goes up stairs to his apartment, and rings his doorbell again.
>   "Who's there?"
>   "TU-134 asks permission to land."
>   "You're drunk, permission denied."
>   "Okay, then I'm going to the auxiliary landing field."
>   He goes to a neighbor. Next morning he rings the doorbell again.
>   "Who's there?" asks his wife yawning.
>   "TU-134 asks permission to land."
>   "You'll have to wait, TU-134. IL-62 hasn't taken off yet."
> (Smetanin and Donskaia 1992, 24)

More often than not, however, the husband is depicted as inadequate in a wider sense than purely sexual. Thus his sexual deficiency may be suggested through his stupidity. (These jokes concern husbands—poor providers—who differ from the men in items 7.7–7.10 who are sexually inadequate because they are mentally superior.)

(7.63) An angry husband discovers a man in his spousal bed.
>   "What are you doing here?" he yells.
>   "You see," says his wife to the man. "Didn't I tell you that he's an idiot?" (Smetanin and Donskaia 1992, 16)

In the following jokes, as in many similar ones, the husband demonstrates an odd docility when confronted with the fact of his wife's infidelity:

(7.64) "Can you imagine? I come home from work in the evening, and I catch my wife in bed with some Swede."
>   "And what do you tell him?"
>   "What can I tell him? After all, I don't know any Swedish."
> (Nikulin 1997, 47)

(7.65) A jealous husband says to his friend: "No matter what I do, I can't find out what my wife's up to. For instance, yesterday she goes with her coworker to our house. Without being noticed, I follow them. They get to our apartment. I climb the tree opposite our house and see that everything is decent: They sit and have supper. And then the lights go off, and I can see nothing. Again this damned mystery!" (Smetanin and Donskaia 1992, 16)

Often the state of intoxication softens the blow to a husband's ego:

(7.66)   A drunk brings his friend home one night. Everyone's asleep. He shows his guest around:
"This is our living room, this is our bedroom, and this is our bed. Here my wife sleeps, and I'm next to her. . . ." (Private collection)

In the following item, drunkenness is replaced by a surrealistic vision.

(7.67)   Because of bad weather, a husband cancels his business trip and returns home. His wife hides her lover behind a curtain next to the TV.
The husband sits in his armchair to watch a hockey game on the TV. To distract him and to give her lover an opportunity to escape, the wife drops a crystal vase in the kitchen, but it does not break.
"Vassya," the wife shouts. "Come here quickly. It's just a miracle. A vase fell out of my hand and didn't break."
"That's nothing!" says the husband. "They just removed a Swedish player from the field for two minutes, and he just strolled by me." (Private collection)

In other jokes, the husband completely accepts the fact of his wife's infidelity and manages to remain numb by displacing the obvious object of his concern.

(7.68)   A man goes to a doctor: "Doctor, you know, every time I catch my wife with a lover, I drink a cup of espresso."
"So, what is your question for me?"
"I'm worried that I'm getting too much caffeine." (Private collection)

(7.69)   A man goes to a doctor: "Tell me what's wrong, Doctor: My wife cheats on me, but my horns do not grow!"
"What nonsense! After all, that's just an expression, a joke. . . ."
"Ah-ah-ah! And I thought my body lacked calcium. . . ." (Genis 1994, 2: 54)

In Western adultery jokes collected by Legman (1968), a man's mild behavior when he meets his wife's lover face to face is explained either by his total economic dependency on the adulterer (who is his boss) or by the threat of a deadly weapon; otherwise, only too much drink would prevent a fight between the men (737, 728). No such excuse is given in the Russian jokes. As a rule, instead of fighting, the husband engages the adulterer in meaningless and senseless dialogue (7.70 and in preceding jokes as well) or delights in his luck at being absent from the scene, thus avoiding a confrontation with his wife's lover that he knows would hold nothing for him but physical abuse and additional humiliation (7.71).

(7.70)   A husband just back from a business trip is awakened by a suspicious noise and sees a naked man crawling out of the closet, wrapped up in his wife's fur coat.
"Who are you?"
"Don't you see? I'm a moth."
"And where are you taking the fur coat?"
"I'll finish with it at home." (Private collection)

(7.71)   A wife and her lover lie in bed. The wife asks him: "You're so strong, dear! What you would do to my husband if he showed up right now?"
"Oh, I'd bend him like a sheep's horn! I'd tear off his legs! He'd wash his face with his own blood! . . ."
From the entrance hall of the apartment, a thin shy voice is heard: "Up yours! I'm still away for two days on a business trip." (Private collection)

One possible explanation of such incongruous behavior lies in the husband's feeling of total inability to change the situation. His impotence is rendered as physical weakness; he has little hope of prevailing over the trespasser of his sexual grounds. To emphasize this, in several jokes collected in the late 1980s and early 1990s the lover is not just well built but of awesome proportions. In some jokes he is called Arnold. Although this name in the Russian mind usually connotes a Jew (the name is used by Russian Jews), it is clear who is meant here: not a Jewish character (as noted, the stereotypical Jew is a weakling) but the American actor Arnold Schwarzenegger, whose movies were very popular.

Such a formidable opponent openly laughs in a husband's face, as if saying that he knows that in his little miserable heart the husband would rather pretend that nothing has happened than confront the adulterer:

(7.72) Arnold is with a married woman. Suddenly, the bell rings.
"Hide!" says the frightened woman.
Arnold goes into the bathroom and calmly lights a cigarette.
The husband comes in, spots somebody's shoes, and throws him-self into a search for their owner. He stops by the bathroom and sees Arnold.
"So, have you found whoever it is you're looking for?" Arnold asks.
"No," says the husband. "But I'm going to take some more time looking for him in the kitchen." (Private collection)

In the following item, instead of attacking his wife's lover, the husband tries to save face through senseless defiance:

(7.73) A husband comes home. A huge fellow answers the door and asks him: "Who are you?"
"Hu-husband . . ."
"Uh, come in then."
Then the fellow draws a circle with chalk on the hall's floor.
"Listen you, husband. I'll go back to the bedroom to make love to your wife. Step into this circle and don't you dare step out with-out my permission. Comprehend?"
"Y-yes . . ."
The fellow goes to the bedroom. After a few hours he leaves. Upon his departure, the wife appears shining with pleasure and ex-claiming: "What a man, what a man!!"
"What a man, what a man!" the husband says mockingly. "Big deal! I've stepped out of the circle twice!" (Private collection)

The husband's meek behavior when confronting his wife's lover may be explained not so much by his assumed low sexual potency but by his low earning power. Virility is often identified with money (Legman 1968, 735), and many cuckoldry jokes, both Russian and Western, portray the symbolic "disgracing of a husband as less than a 'good provider.'"

It is also noteworthy that while in Western cuckoldry jokes the husband's occupation is often given (e.g., in Legman 1968, 735), in Russian jokes it is usually omitted—the Russian is a generic husband for the simple reason that the line between those who have money and those who do not is much more clearly defined. Although similar jokes have circulated for a long time, they became more pervasive as living standards deteriorated in the late 1980s and early 1990s. The Russian man's ability to provide for his family had never been great under the Soviets, but it has been weakened disastrously in the economic decline of the post-perestroika and post-Communist periods. The adultery jokes seem to reflect this. In the following item, a Russian husband cannot even provide adequately for himself. Thus he loses his sexual territory to a more successful provider who completely takes charge of the classic husband vs. lover situation:

(7.74)   A man comes home very hungry. He rings the doorbell. A stranger opens the door.
"Who are you?" asks the stranger.
"Well . . . I'm the husband."
"What do you want?"
"I want to eat."
"Will you eat yesterday's borscht?"
"I will."
"Then come tomorrow." (Barsky 1994, 250)

The husband's dependence on a lover to support his family is explicit in this joke:

(7.75)   A husband comes home after a business trip, finds a naked man in his bathroom, and begins to fume. His wife interrupts him:
"Well, don't make too much of it! Do you remember when new furniture appeared in our house last year? Wasn't that something we needed!"
"But . . ."
"Don't make too much fuss! And do you remember that we got a new car half a year ago?"
"But . . ."
"Not so loud! And do you recall, I got a new fur coat recently?" his wife continues.
Finally the husband completes his sentence: "But . . . may I ask you how come you keep our benefactor standing barefoot on the cold floor? God forbid, he might catch cold!" (Genis 1994, 2: 134)[7]

In the following item, the situation is taken one step further—the lover becomes a part of the permanent arrangement, *menage-à-trois* Russian style. It is noteworthy that this joke has the lover not a well-heeled member of the Soviet elite or an underground wheeler-dealer, but a blue-collar worker (the one usually associated with night-shift work):

(7.76) A man comes home and finds a note on a table: "Meat dumplings are in a freezer, soup's on the stove. Don't wake up Gennady in the wardrobe, he got the night shift." (JFR 1/14/98)

In this and preceding chapters we have been focusing on Russian jokes, *anekdoty*, the traditional urban genre. Chastushkas, another no less popular genre, mostly of the countryside, are set in a somewhat different sexual world.

CHAPTER 8

"We've Been Doing It to Everything in the World But an Awl and a Nail": The Erotic World of Russian Chastushkas

Chastushkas are short, mostly four-line folk rhymes (usually ABCB) that are sung in Russian villages and small towns. Although fully formed as a separate genre in the 1870s, they derive from several sources, including the couplets of medieval street performers, *skomorokhi* (Keldysh 1991, 621).[1] They are accompanied by a small accordion, called *garmon'*, or by a balalaika.

While many chastushkas express loneliness, sadness, and longing, a great many of them are humorous. Although in his well-known study of Russian national character Sovietologist Geoffrey Gorer (1962, 182) concludes that obscenity does not play a part in Russian humor and that none of the chastushkas are obscene, quite the opposite is true.[2] Chastushka language is close to street vernacular; it too uses *mat*, "the salty little word" *[solenoe slovtso]*, as it has euphemistically been called. Thus not only is a considerable part of rural humor risqué; the chastushka often provides an excuse or an opportunity to use foul language in a recognized artistic form.

Although many chastushkas were collected and published before and during the Soviet period and have enjoyed a considerable amount of attention from scholars, the bawdy ones—the Russians often call them "mischievous" *[ozornye]* or "indecent" *[pokhabnye]*—have not been so studied. An inalienable part of Russian rural life for at least a century, ribald chastushkas were nevertheless routinely excluded from publication and ignored as a material worthy of scholarly study. In the beginning of this century, a few Russian folklorists (P. A. Florensky, V. I. Simakov, V. V. Kniazev, Yury Sokolov) had noted their existence, but the first collection of obscene chastushkas appeared only in 1978 published by a Russian émigré press in New York: V. Karbonsky's *Nepodtsenzurnaia russkaia chastushka* (Uncensored Russian chastushka). It was followed in 1982 by an expanded edition, Vladimir Kozlovsky's *Novaia nepodtsenzurnaia chastushka* (The new uncensored chastushka).

The earlier silence and the scholar's neglect of this rich and flamboyant folkloric subgenre were caused not only by the prudishness of the Soviet regime[3] but by what had been part of Russian literary tradition. After all, neither Dahl nor Afanasiev could publish their collections of erotic folklore in their homeland. The expression "unprintable (uncensored) words" *[nepechatnye (netsenzurnye) slova]* is the Russian euphemism for obscenity; bawdy chastushkas, of course, were in this category, utterly unacceptable for publication.[4]

Only in recent times have such omissions been partly corrected. Although no quantitative data exists as to the ratio of bawdy chastushkas to those perfectly decent in content,[5] a few collections published abroad and in the post-Communist censorship-free Russia show that the number of recorded chastushkas with ribald content is considerable enough to warrant scholarly inquiry.[6] Now they can be discussed as a subgenre with a distinct poetics, the poetics of folk humor.

In the 1920s some Russian linguists offered several scattered remarks on the poetics of erotic chastushkas.[7] Victor Raskin (1981) analyzed their semantics of abuse and undertook a study of the subgenre from the point of view of his theory of humor (1985, 170–177). Vladimir Kozlovsky (1982) provides some cultural footnotes and chastushka variants. Recently, with the prohibition on their study lifted from Russian scholarship, a few short articles on bawdy chastushkas have appeared in the academic press.[8]

What happens when texts of bawdy chastushkas are analyzed outside their "natural habitat," out of the context of an "on-the-site" performance, can be demonstrated by Tatyana Mamonova's (1989, 127–129) feminist attack on the text of the folk rhymes published in V. Karbonsky's (1978) volume. Although for a moment she allows us to see outrageously offensive chastushkas for what, in fact, they really are—that is, "capricious whimsical sexual fantasies" (128)—Mamonova then rejects such a reading, citing an appalling real-life story from *Sex in the USSR* by Mikhail Stern with August Stern. (This is a story of a teenager who, as a member of a gang, gang-raped a woman who, he later discovered, was his mother.) Such an argument does not really indict bawdy chastushkas but rather represents another case of the question of whether art imitates life or vice versa.

Judging bawdy chastushkas, rural folk rhymes, many of which have ancient cultural roots by present-day urban sensibilities, as Mamonova does, may lead to denouncing the necrophilic element in some of them (e.g., in K-63, items 215–217). Russian scholar Andrey Toporkov (1995, 10) writes that a person reared in today's urban culture finds sex and the lower bodily parts "surrounded by prohibitions and omissions . . . , tabooed, sinful, dirty and shameful. In the popular tradition, however, sexual life is perceived much more casually. They talk about it quite freely, naming a spade a spade, and with this there is no feeling that anything sinful or dirty is talked about."

The medieval tradition of Russian Christmas plays that Uspensky (1993, 123) finds in *Secret Tales,* a fertility tradition that often took the form of erotic adventures with the deceased, may be found in chastushkas as well. (Although Mamonova's examples were not quite appropriate, she is right in her account of misogynist tendencies widespread in Russian culture in general.)

Another problem to be solved before an in-depth analysis of bawdy chastushkas can be undertaken consists of the fact that many items in Kozlovsky's collection were recorded, on the editor's own admission (1982, 5) haphazardly—items given in sequence were recorded at different times (sometimes decades apart, from the Civil War period up to Gorbachev's time), in different settings, outside the cycles in which they were usually delivered. Some chastushkas are of obvious opening stanza *[zachin]* type; others are of parting stanza *[kontsovka]* type; that is, with a typical line "We have sung chastushkas for you" *[My chastushki vam propeli].*

To a greater extent than their "decent" counterparts, bawdy chastushkas may be much more clearly seen in their dynamic development as a chain of them unfolds, a mode found in Nikolai Starshinov's collections: A string of 80 chastushkas (1992a, I: 37–52) entitled "I am going out to dance in the circle" *[Vykhozu pliasat' na krug]* presents an opportunity to better understand the dynamics of chastushkas and the interaction between the singers and dancers (often the same people) and other participants who may join the performance on the spur of the moment.

Kozlovsky's collection is a "mixed bag"; it contains a number of urban items. Although seemingly composed in the spirit of rural chastushkas, they are, however, different in text and context from their village counterparts. Beginning in the early 1960s (V. Raskin 1985, 171), these city-spun imitations of chastushkas have circulated among Russian intellectuals and white-collar workers. They have a larger (and more sophisticated) vocabulary and tend to reflect not local events but those of a larger world. And they reveal the mentality not of the village and the small town but of the city. As a rule, they are not sung (or danced to) but are recited in mostly male company. Often these city products are nothing but verse variants of the joke *[anek-dot]*, a mostly urban genre.

Chastushka vs. *Anekdot*

As Russian folklorists O.V. Vasilieva and S. B. Gliukhina (1989, 95–99) show, chastushkas and *anekdoty* share many qualities. Both carnivalian, they surface during informal, more or less socially homogeneous, gatherings whose main purpose is recreational: eating, drinking, dancing, and, generally speaking, merrymaking. Both genres are relatively short in form and tend to be linked in cycles. Both can be topical and satirical and may render a penetrating social observation. The following chastushka is a mocking folk response to the failed promise of the Gorbachev government that perestroika will bring prosperity.

(8.1) Mne ne nado shokolada,   I don't need chocolate,
       Mne ne nado kolbasy.   I don't need sausage.
       Daite mne kusochek myla—   Give me a little piece of soap—
       postirat' svoi trusy.   To wash my underpants. (Private
                                      collection)

As in jokes, chastushkas use world political events for artistic purposes:

(8.2) Ne nalila mne zhena   My wife has poured me
       Ni stakana, ni vina.   Neither vodka, nor wine.
       Zaebu, zamuchaiu,   I'll fuck her to death, I'll torture her,
       Kak Pol Pot Kampuchiiu.   As Pol Pot did to Kampuchea. (Illiasov
                                      1994, 177)

Chastushkas and *anekdoty* are both able to sustain contact within a group and diffuse a tense situation by placing the conflict on a playful, joking plane. They may express aggression, sublimated in laughter, when it is forbidden by social norms. Thus they serve similar social functions. That is, by attributing to fictional characters their own anxieties and emotional problems, they vent personal frustrations in public without losing face.

Yet chastushkas and *anekdoty* differ in several ways. The darling of villages, small towns, and settlements, bawdy chastushkas, predictably, are less literary than *anekdoty* (with their frequent dependence on plot) but make a wide use of folk imagery and folk poetics, not unlike those of folk songs, riddles, and fairy tales. While *anekdoty*'s success heavily relies on a punch line that must be economical, exact, and killing, bawdy chastushkas, although at times witty, often rely on the spirit of playfulness, on sexual suggestiveness, and on verbal mischief.

An important feature of many chastushkas is their marked improvisational character. Although *anekdoty* are also rarely passed on verbatim, their tellers are much more constrained by the need to retain all the important details of the plot or characterization in a story; special care must be taken in delivering the punch line. Much less wit is expected from chastushkas. While *anekdoty* tellers may fail because no one laughs, the chastushka performers are free of such pressure; as long as it sustains the festive mood of the party, it is perfectly acceptable.[9]

Thus another distinction between the two genres of popular humor lies in the quality of laughter. *Anekdot* is a genre especially popular with middle-age people; it reflects their sensibilities and psychological preoccupations, such as anxieties about aging and increasing difficulties in coping with life. Many times marked by a certain cynicism and disillusionment, *anekdoty* often lack the sense of vitality and vigor that is characteristic of chastushkas. This fact is especially clear if one compares sexual chastushkas with sexual jokes. In the former, marriage is either planned or in its beginning stages; many marriage jokes focus on boredom and on what a chore marriage is. A vehicle of expression of mostly young people, rural chastushkas may not always be hilariously funny, but they are invariably jolly; the joy of living spills over in many of them.

Although both genres have been used as vehicles of folk political satire, it may be argued that they have been subversive in a wider sense. Anthropologist Mary Douglas's (1975, 98) qualification of a joke as that of "the triumph of intimacy over formality, of unofficial values over official ones" can be fully applied to chastushkas. Their informality is underscored by the casual character of their performance, usually informal gatherings [*gulianki*, from *guliat'*," to have a good time,"] or parties, traditionally called *posidelki* (from the verb *sidet'*, "to seat"), by their mostly personal content, and by their colloquial, substandard language.

Paradoxically, joking may be a way of conforming with the system; as Douglas (1975, 106) shows, "the joke works only when it mirrors social form; it exists by virtue of its congruence with social structure. But the obscenity is identified by its opposition to the social structure, hence its offense." Russian *anekdoty* of the Soviet period, "while making fun of the absurdism of Soviet power stances, legitimized them" (Ries 1991, 46–7). No such conformity is conveyed by the ribald content of chastushkas.

It should also not be forgotten that, for most of this century, chastushkas of this kind flourished against the background of the very formal and rigid linguistic phenomenon known as "Sovietese." Through truly ubiquitous government and party mass media, this artificial language penetrated every area of Soviet society. Obscenities in chastushkas can be seen, therefore, as a reaction to the deadening effect of the daily barrage of propaganda, as defiance of the language devoid of human feeling that had been force-fed to the Russian people for decades. Douglas's (1975, 106) treatment of dirt-throwing rituals in primitive societies as "an apt enough expression of undifferentiated, unorganized uncontrolled relations" can be applied to a great extent to the exchange of smut in modern chastushkas.

The very mode of chastushkas' performance signifies informality. Although some are sung in a relatively relaxed and even slow manner, the bawdy ones are invariably delivered in a way that corresponds to the name of the genre, that is, quickly. The name "chastushka" may be derived not only from the word *chastyi* (Vasmer 1986, IV: 318), meaning "frequent," but also from the verb *chastit'*, "to do something rapidly, hurriedly." In the case of "chastushka," the verb applies to the fast pace of dancing and singing. Listening to somebody's fervent, half-understood speech, a Russian might interrupt: "Don't jabber, speak more distinctly" [*ne chasti, govori iasnee;* Smirnitsky 1992, 697]. Since, in Douglas's (1975, 105) terms, "articulateness in speech" symbolizes "structured relationships," the rapid delivery of chastushkas, discernible only to an experienced ear, constitutes the inarticulateness symbolic of "the personal, undifferentiated network."

Chastushkas, thus, may be seen as a link between the very private and the public. As a vehicle of popular sentiments free of external control for decades, many chastushkas (sung under the sky, far from official Soviet overseers of culture) have presented an uncontrolled sphere of expression in the Russian countryside. Thus their performance can be well defined in the anthropologist Victor Turner's terms, that is, it is "a dionysian ritual . . . expressing the value of 'community' as against 'structure'" (cited in Douglas 1975, 104). The communal versus structural orientation of this folkloric material has a long history.

The Ancient Roots of Bawdy Chastushkas

As part of Russian merrymaking (*balagurstvo, shutovstvo,* as Likhachev [1976, 31] calls them) from time immemorial, the tavern songs [*kabatskie pesni]*, usually accompanied by heavy drinking, quite often resorted to a substandard language and spoke of sexual matters. Russian scholar Dmitry Likhachev (1976, 31–32) sees making fun of one's own wife in such songs as an ancient Russian carnivalian tradition.

Ribald songs were also the core of the medieval street entertainers', *skomorokhi*'s, repertoire—performances taking place during such festivities as Christmas, St. John's Eve, and Shrovetide *[Maslenitsa]* (Rancour-Laferriere 1985, 122; Sinyavsky 1991, 108). The latter, a traditional weeklong (in the Orthodox church calendar) fertility rite celebrating the end of winter and the beginning of spring, was a time of "gluttony, drunkenness, revelry, sexual jesting, and ribaldry" (Bobroff 1983, 213).[10] Russian folklorist Jury Sokolov notes the proliferation during *Maslenitsa* of "bawdy songs, sayings, and jokes whose eroticism amounted at times to a license which cannot be reproduced in print" (cited in Bobroff 1983, 213).

Along with erotic riddles and salacious tales, ribald chastushkas have been sung on many other occasions, such as seasonal peasant celebrations and weddings. Some contemporary chastushkas, like this one in Starshinov's (1992a, II: 68) collection, clearly belong to this tradition of ancient fertility rites:

(8.3)	Pliashi, veselis',		Dance, and be merry,
	Chtoby kurocki velis',		So that chickens will breed,
	Petushki rodilisia,		So that cockerels will be born
	Na kurochek sadilisia.		And make it with the chickens.

The connection between chastushkas and other, more ancient folkloric genres is marked. I have already noted a kinship between many bawdy chastushkas and the *Secret Tales* collected by Afanasiev. Not only are playful folk rhymes *[pribautki]* incorporated in the texts of a number of these tales (Uspensky 1993, 128), but both genres treat sexual relationships in a matter-of-fact manner. Moreover, in both of them the indiscriminate and abandoned sexuality of clergymen is exposed and viciously attacked (in chastushkas, e.g., in K-178; S. I: 118–9; II: 176–7). Although some bawdy chastushkas may seem to echo Soviet antireligious propaganda of the 1920s, it is hard to see them as being part of the pseudofolklore fabricated by the regime, for these chastushkas are utterly indecent and could never be officially blessed for public performances. The presence of such anticlerical chastushkas in the body of contemporary rural folklore can be explained in the terms employed by Uspensky (1993, 120–124) in interpreting a similar phenomenon in Afanasiev's *Secret Tales*. Both folkloric genres, although operating in different time frames, are verbal forms of archaic "reverse behavior" *[anti-povedenie]* with strong pagan overtones. It seems that the contemporary chastushka corresponds to old erotic folk tales depicting the kind of conduct that took place in old Russia around certain religious holidays—that is, premeditated blasphemous and sacrilegious acts committed for the sole purpose of repenting them later. As Uspensky shows, such behavior was intended to reinforce religious doctrine in a paradoxical way.

Chastushkas, like erotic tales, use the erotic imagery of riddles. In one of them, a vulva is rendered as a ram (S. I: 98) in another, as a nightingale (124); a male organ is depicted as a pestle (134). Male-female genitalia appear in a form of a padlock with a key (148) and, in modern rendering, as an electrical switch and socket (S. II: 100).

The Primacy of Coitus

Even without big holidays and such special occasions as weddings, the presence of sexual matters in chastushkas can be explained by the very nature of this rural genre. Performed during informal family or community gatherings at small *[vecherinka]* or large parties *[gulianiia],* intended for close friends and fellow villagers only, chastushkas tend to talk about things that are otherwise excluded from official interactions. Whether in language or subject matter, most often both, many chastushkas address sexuality in a straightforward manner. As sowing of grain is of prime interest in a peasant's life, so is human coitus. Its primacy is established and reaffirmed as praiseworthy human activity in numerous chastushkas. People are sometimes injured— some even die—driven by an uncontrollable carnal urge. As an abundance of grain thrown in the plowed earth ensures a good harvest in real life, in chastushkas a larger-than-life sexuality ensures procreation.

(8.4) Otchego galosh ne stalo   Why have galoshes disappeared
       V nashykh severnykh kraiakh?   From our northern regions?
       Potomy chto vsia rezina   Because all the rubber got worn out
       Poisterlas' na khuiakh.   On [our] dicks. (K-123)

Since for a peasant, humans are an inalienable part of nature to a much greater degree than for city folks, in the folkloric world of the chastushka not only people but everything is first and foremost sexual. People have sex not only with each other but with animals (e.g., in S. I: 108, 111), and animals do it with people (e.g., in K-81). In fact, in many chastushkas all the mammals, birds, and insects joyfully engage in coitus. As in Afanasiev's *Secret Tales,* they often do it in a cross-species manner. A hare does it with a wolf (K-155), a sparrow with a dove (K-38),[11] a mosquito with a fly (K-101), and ants manage to do it with a camel (K-184). The folkloric tendency to see the whole world as sexual is also evident in some of the proverbs and sayings collected by Dahl: "Anything that breathes loves pushing [sexual thrusting]" [*Vsiakoe dykhanie lubit pikhanie;* Claude Carey 1972, 44); "A little worm gnaws away wood, but even it wants to fuck" [*Cherviachok derevo tochit, a i tot et' khochet;* Claude Carey 1972, 61]; "In the spring, even a wooden chip crawls over another chip (one chip rubs itself against another)" [*Vesnoi i shchepka na shchepku lezet (shchepka o shchepku tretsia);* Claude Carey 1972, 64].

With the primacy of coitus axiomatically accepted, inanimate objects also behave as if they were possessed by carnal urges. Here a festive and joyful regression to magical thought endows with a living soul not only people, animals, and plants (e.g., mushrooms in S. I: 104) but objects as well.[12] In one chastushka (K-23), a poker does it with a shovel, in another (S. I: 119), a cart does it with a shaft-bow and a horse collar with a cart seat. As if to emphasize that who (or what) does it to whom (or to what) makes no difference, as long as sex is involved, the female narrator of one chastushka (S. II: 134–5), strolling through a forest, meets something that is not described, only named "a miracle" [*chudo,* neuter in Russian], and in no time it has sex with her.

In contrast to such oral folkloric genres as love songs, ballads, and fairy tales (but again very much like the *Secret Tales*), when it comes to coitus, nothing is sacred in ribald chastushkas. No moral or physical boundaries are set in their unbridled erotic world. As in many jokes, age barriers are easily overcome. In one chastushka (S. I: 109), 90-year old women make out with young boys. In another (113), a 300-year old man covets a 200-year-old woman; the chastushka calls for help to get him closer to her. Bawdy chastushkas are free of any moral considerations. Incest of all kinds is widely represented. A sexual bond may be described between either of a young husband or a young wife with an in-law (K-47).[13] In one chastushka a son copulates with his own father (K-99); in another a father does it with his daughter while her mother (his wife) looks on approvingly (K-130). In yet another the protagonist boasts that he did it to the whole extended family, sparing only his grandmother because she took care of him in his tender years:

(8.5) Pereeb ia vsiu rodniu,   I've fucked every one of my kin,
       Ostavil babushku odnu.   I spared Grandma only.
       Ostavaiasia, khui s toboi,   Be spared, what the hell,
       Ved' ty zhe nianchilas' so   After all, you were my nanny. (K-128)
       mnoi.

The highly hyperbolic manner of perceiving an all-embracing sexuality of nature makes lewd claims in chastushkas primarily figures of speech. Although the Russian countryside has not been spared instances of incest, it would be wrong to read these rhymes as true-to-life statements about village sexuality. It is rather the Dionysian element, characteristic of this essentially carnivalian phenomenon, that is at play. Performed during village gatherings in spare time, usually on holidays or weekends, and often accompanied by feasting (drinking, eating, singing, and dancing), like the songs of the Rabelaisian carnival world, chastushkas glorify all earthly cravings of the human body, of which the act of procreation is one of the most important. As Russian riddles and other folkloric material of ancient roots address sexuality as a symbol of the earth's fertility, so do many chastushkas. As Uspensky (1988, 202) notes, swearing by using sexually explicit language was often included in various Russian fertility rites of pagan origin, forerunners of today's weddings and agricultural holidays during which bawdy chastushkas are sung.

What American Slavist James Rice (1976, 367) says about a Russian bawdy song of the eighteenth century is true for contemporary risqué chastushkas. First and foremost, they are " . . . ribald entertainment, revealing desires of the unobtainable, giving expression of what is more or less unthinkable, doing in words what is, generally, not done." As the nineteenth-century humorous prints *[lubki]*, in their time "provided relief from rigid hierarchical structure, constricted lives, and economic scarcity" (Farrel 1991, 553), so do chastushkas. Sex in them is often pronounced a solace in hard times (K-179, S. 1992: I: 115) and a source of optimism. As one of them says: "We have been fucking and haven't perished; [so, as long as] we keep fucking, we won't perish" [*my ebali, ne propali, a ebem—ne propadem;* K-87].

Phallic Boasts

Quite in the carnivalesque tradition, sexual boasts, of which the most frequent are phallic,[14] are widely present in Russian folklore. While one finds phallic boasts in the *anekdot*,[15] a mostly urban genre, they are far more frequent in chastushkas. Russian folklorist P. A. Florensky compares these rhymes with phallic songs of Greek Dionysian festivities (cited in Kulagina 1995b, 433). Clearly, such boasts are remnants of primordial fertility rites. One chastushka (S. II: 136), for example, renders coitus as cultivation of soil, while others treat the male organ as an object typical of a rural household: an ax (S. II: 109), an ax-handle (K-110), a rake handle, a log (K-20, 82).

As in other cultures, according to Russian folklore, the sure sign of masculinity is the size (most often the length) of a male organ. In chastushkas, as in Western folklore (Legman 1968, 268), it is treated as a signifier not only of sexual potency but of physical might: Often it is rendered as a weapon of destruction. One quatrain claims that a penis is strong enough to smash three boards (K-77); in another, it can destroy a peasant stove (S. I: 128). Sometimes it becomes a weapon of mayhem and even murder (e.g., in S. I: 104). In the anonymous nineteenth-century erotic tale about Luka Mudishchev, his encounter with a merchant's widow ends in her death. The intensity of intercourse can kill, as in the Russian male curse: "I'll fuck [her] to death" *[Zaebu do smerti]*. As an ultimate proof of the ability to prevail under any circumstances, the following chastushka boasts of the singer's larger-than-life sexual prowess:

(8.6)	My ebali vse na svete	We've fucked everything in the world
	Krome shila i gvosdia.	But an awl and a nail.
	Shilo—ostroe, krivoe,	For an awl is sharp and crooked,
	A gvosdia ebat' nel'zia.	And you can't really fuck a nail.
		(S. I: 146)

In complete disregard of the physiology of sex (Katchadourian 1972, 13), the bawdy chastushka assumes as an indisputable truth that the presence of a big penis alone is full assurance of male sexuality. It is considered a man's only attraction; not pleasant appearance, not intellect, not good behavior—nothing compensates for an inadequate organ. One chastushka (K-110), addressed to a young man, says that girls love him neither for his curly hair nor for his "white" [read: refined] face but for the fact that his genitals are of a formidable size. In another chastushka, a parody of the genre, a woman's sexual preference is bluntly expressed:

(8.7)	Na okne stoit gorshok,	A pot is sitting on a windowsill,
	V nem tsvetochek alen'kii.	With a little red flower in it.
	Ni za chto ne promeniaiu	For nothing in the world would I trade
	Khui bol'shoi na malen'kii.	A big dick for a little one.[16] (Private collection)

Since according to the male folk belief, to have a big phallus is good, and a small one is bad, those unfortunate enough to possess the latter are mocked and pitied. "Don't go to the bath house, girls," one chastushka advises (K-113), "They're dipping Vanya in vitriol, so that his dick will grow a bit." A small male organ (violation of a sexual code, presumed universal) and a worn-out jacket (violation of a dress code) are two reasons why, in one chastushka (K-31), a young man does not go to meet girls at a dance.

An archaic fertility rites' association of a phallus with a treasure, characteristic of *Secret Tales* (Uspensky 1989, 124), surfaces in chastushkas as well. Because the value of a penis is "that of silver" (K-44), then the bigger it is the better. Like Ivan the Fool of Russian fairy tales, Luka Mudishchev is of modest mental abilities, but he is enormously proud of being endowed by nature with an outstanding male organ. In one chastushka, a soldier has a penis long enough to undergo five axe marks (K-32). In another, the male organ is big enough to transport 48 communists (K-150), and in yet another it is so enormous that it has a fantastic ability to influence the weather:

(8.8)	My ne seem i ne pahsem,	We are not sowing and plowing,
	My valiaem duraka.	We're fooling around.
	S kolokol'ni khuem mashem,	We're waving our dicks from a bell-tower,
	Razgoniaem oblaka.	Chasing clouds away.[17] (K-88)

As in jokes, in chastushkas men of lower social strata (most often peasants and soldiers) are much more virile than those of higher social standing. Soldiers are usually better lovers than their officers. In fact, one is not quite fit to be a soldier if his organ is "somewhat short" (K-68), that is, if, from the folk point of view, he is a sexual failure.

At the same time, however, as in the folklore of other cultures, Russian chastushka also treats the phallus as a symbol of social power among members of the hierarchy. Morris (1970, 106) holds that phallic boasts in humans may have the same behavioral roots as those of their biological antecedents, monkeys and apes, for whom "the erection of the penis is used as a threatening display of male dominance, . . . the greater the erection, the greater the threat."[18] In chastushkas, the higher a man's social standing, the bigger his organ. Hence, a major's penis is longer than a lieutenant's (K-138). Quite expectedly, the mighty man, Stalin, is endowed with an outstanding male organ, bigger than that of his one-time rival, Rykov,[19] and even bigger than that of the great Russian tsar:

(8.09)	Kalina-malina,	Snowberry, raspberry,
	Khui bol'shoi u Stalina,	Stalin has a big dick,
	Bol'she chem u Rykova	Greater than Rykov's
	I Petra Velikogo.	And greater than that of Peter the Great. (K-59)

Along the same line of folk reasoning, it is not surprising that another leader, Lenin, rather feeble (especially in his later years), is said to have a penis long enough to make him able, while lying in his coffin in the Mausoleum, to blow kisses with it to passersby (K-186).

In chastushkas, a long penis is a privilege of not only powerful, but otherwise famous people, like popular actors and cosmonauts (Titov in K-192, and Gagarin in K-208). Sexual relations with the powerful and famous are described as highly desirable, although sometimes, they carry mocking overtones.

Perhaps the most famous of such chastushkas is the one in which a man boasts that he is going to marry the Minister of Culture, Ekaterina Furtseva, at one time the only highly visible woman on the Soviet political arena. Therefore he prides himself on the prospect of having access to the most Marxist female breasts:

(8.10) Nichego ia ne boius',   I'm afraid of nothing,
        Ia na Furtsevoi zhenus'.   I'm going to marry Furtseva.
        Budu shchupat' sis'ki ia   I'll be feeling her tits
        Samye marksistskie.   The most Marxist ones, you bet.
                                       (K-115)

To denigrate a male leader means to deprive him of his sexual organ (i.e., castrate him in psychological terms). Thus one chastushka claims that Khrushchev has, instead of a penis, a substitute in the form of a corncob (K-27), an allusion to his obsessive plan to plant corn all over the country, no matter what the cost or what the local conditions. Another way of disapproving of a leader is to portray him as a man who is unable to prove his sexuality in "normal," from the folk point of view, coitus. In K-108, "a secretary general" (implicitly Gorbachev) is mockingly called sexy because a famous pop singer, Edita Piekha, performs fellatio on him (K-108). In the Russian folk view, sexual practices that are not strictly genital invariably connote male impotence.

Those chastushkas that sexually denigrate any non-Russian males frequently reflect a degree of animalistic territoriality. It seems that their aim, jocular tone notwithstanding, is to keep away any intruder on the Russian male territory by means of sexual slander. These "nonlocals" *[nezdeshnie]* in general terms are described as having organs that folk belief finds either too small (K-111) or too large, presenting a threat to local women's health and even their lives (K-113). Thus in K-114 girls are warned against "malicious" Kyrgyzians who can "tear up their cunts." It is noteworthy that no such concern about females is expressed when, in other chastushkas, it is a Russian man who is a proud possessor of a formidable, often superhuman, sexual organ.

Some chastushkas reveal strong nationalistic tendencies. In one of them (K-46), it is said with pride that a woman did not "put out" either for a German,[20] or for a Jew but saved her "narrow" (i.e., in the male folk view, sexually most desirable) vagina for one of her own, for a Russian man. In another (K-57), Chuvashians get settled in a Russian woman's vagina, and the chastushka calls for guarding the place and deporting the intruders.

Chastushkas display a number of denigrating sexual beliefs in regard to ethnic minorities, most frequently Jews, Georgians, and Armenians. Some chastushkas are bluntly anti-Semitic (K-136, 189) and a suitor's Jewishness seems sufficient ground for a girl's rejection (K-194). As in jokes (see Chapter 7; also Draitser 1998, 33), other chastushkas portray Jews as sexually inadequate because they are all assumed to be circumcised. At the same time, the folk awareness of the Jews as potential threats to Russian sexual territory explains the existence of some chastushkas evidently intended for those Russian girls who are not deterred by a suitor's religion. For instance, to discourage sexual contacts with Jews, one chastushka (K-197) suggests that they carry disgusting sexual diseases, an echo of an old anti-Semitic association of Jews with venereal diseases. (See, for example, Engelstein 1992, 306.)

(8.11)   Ia k professoru idu—   I'm on my way to see a professor—
         Stradaiu gonoreeiu.   I suffer from gonorrhea.
         On evrei i ia evrei,   He's a Jew and I'm a Jew,
         Oba my evrei.   Both of us are Jewish.[21]

The two other most frequent butts of Russian popular laughter are nationalities, such as Georgians and Armenians, also disapproved of as sexual partners of Russian women. As in jokes (Draitser 1998, 49–54), Georgians are usually stereotyped as oversexed and philandering. (See also Gray 1990, 56). Armenians are invariably presented as sexual weaklings at best and frequently as homosexuals, sometimes implicitly (K-191), most often explicitly.

The only other group that is featured is gypsies. However, their treatment varies in several instances. In some chastushkas, they embody a traditional image of fated lovers. In others, they are rendered as cheats and thieves (e.g., in S-II: 158–161).

Women in Bawdy Chastushkas

Central to bawdy chastushkas, however, is the relationship not between nationalities or classes but between the sexes. Considering that most often chastushka performers are women, the effect of alcohol notwithstanding (village festivities without drinking are almost unthinkable), it is puzzling that they would sing so many chastushkas that are not only degrading to them but often express typically male phobias, for instance, fear of female genitalia (e.g., K-203): The fear can take the form of a vision of the vagina as a complex mechanism of an intricate, incomprehensible, and dangerous nature.

(8.12)	Poezd edet, rel'sy gnutsia.	A train is moving, rails are bending.
	Otkazali tormosa.	The brakes refuse to work.
	V pizde lopnula pruzhina,	A spring gets busted in a cunt,
	Van'ke vybilo glaza.	And Van'ka's eyes got knocked out.

The mechanism is able to give birth to other mechanisms or, thanks to its cutting capabilities, is clear evidence of the vagina dentata.[22] Upon swallowing three boards out of longing for a beloved, a woman produces boxes, which begin to fly from her vagina (K-85).

Most often, however, fear of the vagina is expressed through an image of a beast. Thus a series of chastushkas addressed to a woman has the same first line ("I won't make love to you") with the ending that explains that the reason for rejection is the bear in the addressee's vagina. The threatening nature of the animal is reinforced with another image: The bear has a weapon aimed at the man. These weapons range from a relatively innocuous slingshot (K-194), to a rifle (201), to a machine gun (202), to a cannon:

(8.13)	Ia tebia ne budu et'	I won't fuck you
	Okolo opushki.	On the edge of the forest.
	U tebia v pizde medved'	In your vagina, a bear
	Tselitsia is pushki.	Is aiming a cannon. (K-208)

Why a bear? A staple of Russian folklore, it is considered to be of a borderline nature, that is, it is able to turn easily into a human (even, as one fairy tale has it, able to marry a woman and conceive a son, a human being; Sinyavsky 1991, 106–7). While epitomizing both sexuality and violence in Russian folklore (Rancour-Laferriere 1989, 227–228), this animal is the strongest creature found in the Russian countryside, thus representing the supermale being, the only one who is able to fulfill the inhuman task of satisfying insatiable females.

(8.14) Otvedu tebia ia k dubu,   I'll take you to an oak,
        Ia tebia ebat' ne budu.   And I won't fuck you.
        Ia tebia ne budu et',   I won't fuck you,
        Pust' tebia ebet medved'.   Let a bear fuck you. (K-122)

Thus these chastushkas seem to address the same need served by many male jokes, discussed in chapter 3: By gross exaggeration of female sexual needs, they act as a psychological maneuver for dealing with the fear of impotence.[23]

A bear may also be chosen because of its considerable size—to manifest male's dissatisfaction with, by implication, too large a vagina that cannot, because of its excessive roominess, bring pleasure to the penis. As Legman (1968, 377–378) and others show, such claims have no physiological basis and represent another excuse for antifemale sentiments. Because it is important to establish the vagina as incredibly large, sometimes many baby bears are used.

(8.15) Ia tebia ne budu et'   I won't fuck you,
        U tebia v pizde medved'.   You have a bear in your vagina.
        Sorok vosem' medvezhat   Forty-eight baby bears
        Poperek pizdy lezhat.   Are lying across it. (K-202)

But perhaps the main reason the bear occupies a vagina in chastushkas is its conspicuous hairiness. In his paper on fetishism, cited by Legman (1968, 370), Freud indicates that, among other things, fur serves as a token reproduction of female pubic hair (the one thing that a man sees at the last moment before exposure of female genitals); thus the sight of fur triggers his unconscious fear of a woman as a nonphallic being and, by inference, his fear of castration.

There are several ways to look at the underlying causes of women singing chastushkas with strong misogynist overtones. It can be argued, for instance, that such behavior represents another case of women acting within a male-induced system of values. Sociologists Timothy Moore and Karen Griffiths (1987, 184) cite Paul McGhee's theory based on North American socialization patterns according to which women tend to "internalize a subordinate social role—relative to men." In this theory, because both the male and female may each implicitly take such a position, they both may accept, and even prefer, humor humiliating women. Moore and Griffiths's own findings lead them to conclude that "attitudinal dispositions [serve as] a more crucial influencer of mirth than nominal group membership" (185).[24]

Some of Catriona Kelly's (1993, 82) hypotheses with respect to the laughter of female spectators at Petrushka performances that degrade them may be helpful in understanding why women would sing misogynist chastushkas. Kelly explains such women's conduct in terms of "compensatory" behavior, that is, of "a process by which women might feel their status to be enhanced by adopting a position that an external observer would regard as degrading" (86).

Another, not altogether contradictory, possibility is that, like the Petrushka spectators, women may find men's vision of their bodies not so much appalling as bizarre, puzzling, and ridiculous. They may also unconsciously sense men's anxiety and fear of their sexuality, which, in fact, reinforces their sexual power over males. Having such an edge over men may make them feel comforted by the thought that, in a male-dominant culture, their sexuality presents a formidable force, compensating for their lack of social power.

Nor should the sadistic element in many bawdy chastushkas—harm inflicted on female organs—be taken at face value. As violence and genitalia are often connected in Russian folklore (Rancour-Laferriere 1989, 228), such sadistic pronouncements in the jolly atmosphere of a party might be read by women as a sign of males' desperate need of them, as an expression of overwhelming unfulfilled male desire and, thus, an admission of total dependence on females in sexual matters. In view of the subjugated social position of women, such male pronouncements may give women, although perhaps for the moment only, a sense of empowerment.

Another reason for Russian women's interest in bawdy chastushkas may well be their sexual deprivation. As Mark Popovsky (1985, 184) suggests, with females overwhelmingly outnumbering males in many Russian rural regions, "for sexually unsatisfied women, utterance and repetition of words of crude sexual nature, to some extent, [may] serve as a psychological release." (Hartogs and Fantel [1967, 179] also point out the sublimation function of foul language.)

All these suggestions do not exclude, however, a masochistic side to the phenomenon of women singing misogynist chastushkas. As Rancour-Laferriere (1995, 279) shows, "A woman who thinks a man must have a low opinion of her in order to have an erection has a low opinion of herself without realizing it. Without knowing, however, how she feels about herself, she will inevitably act out her feelings instead, that is, she will behave in a self-destructive or masochistic fashion."

At the same time, we should not forget that the whole atmosphere in which chastushkas are performed is one of merrymaking, fun, and festivity with its traditional sexual license. The more bizarre the sexual pronouncements are, the *less* likely they are to be taken seriously. Performance context is essential to the right reading of them; an outsider's disregard of it may lead to a lapse of judgment. Thus American scholar Geoffrey Gorer (1962, 182) finds that, while in Russian literature and poetry,[25] love is seen according to a strong romantic tradition ("It is likely to be tragic and disastrous"), it is not the case, he laments, with many chastushkas. He finds it incomprehensible that many of them contain verbal attacks on a beloved; this leads him to conclude that the behavior of the Russians is strangely contradictory (181).

Missing the specific carnival nature of the phenomenon, Gorer cannot see that finding something wrong with the beloved in chastushkas is not a strange contradiction of love but a confirmation of it, an expression of affection in a playfully hostile way. (A similar phenomenon takes place in American culture: Verbal insults between close friends may display not animosity but fondness and may function as "terms of endearment" [Jay 1992, 177]).[26] From the very outset of an outdoor festivity, a "public merrymaking" *[gulianie]*, the emotionally uplifting atmosphere of the performance establishes a special "joking relationship" between the sexes, the one that anthropologist A. R. Radcliffe-Brown (1961, 90–91) characterizes as "a relation between two persons in which one is by custom permitted . . . to tease or make fun of the other who in turn is required to take no offense"; such a relationship is one of "permitted disrespect." Because of the close acquaintance of many members of a party (where chastushkas are sung), the popular rhymes may be seen as a form of dyadic communication in which insults are often perceived and intended as an expression of intimacy and affection (Oring 1992, 142).

In the case of bawdy chastushkas, a verbal attack on a woman may also be not an act of hostility but a signifier of sexual attention, which, in the carnivalistic atmosphere of the party, is, after all, what is sought. It is a flirting game in which no party wants openly to admit sexual dependency on the other. As in *lubki* in their time (Farrel 1991, 559), the popular comic tradition of contemporary chastushkas suggests a playful male-female relationship, replete with salacious teasing, erotic suggestiveness, and sexual advance and retreat. These sometimes flirting, sometimes outright erotic chastushkas, not unlike the obscene riddles that Andalusian women tell during harvesting (Brandes 1980, 135–136), are also part of a traditional seduction game. Their sexual content, ranging from mildly risqué to explicitly lewd, serves the purpose of arousal; the Freudian (1960, 97) concept of the intentional use of "smut" for seduction purposes is quite relevant here. As if to exemplify Freud's idea that "exposure jokes" aim to visualize sexual situations, the Russians call these chastushkas "rhymes with little pictures" [chastushki s kartinkami], a clear indication of their intentionally erotic design.

Chastushkas and Dancing

Rancour-Laferriere (1982, 346) notes that "unleashed sexuality and a general emphasis on the lower parts of the body are characteristic of Slavic festivities in general." That which accompanies the performance of Russian chastushkas is definitely a case in point. Here the poetic rhythm of chastushkas, the singing and dancing, possess teleological qualities[27] that, while reinforcing each other, are used for the purpose of engaging a partner in a love game.

Most of the female roles in the chastushka cycle "I am joining a dancing circle" in Starshinov's collection are performed by women. Although we do not know whether all stanzas were written by the same person, nevertheless we can follow the logic of the performer's behavior. "The opening stanza" [zachin] of this cycle is one that, by alluding to sexual attraction between a godfather and a godmother, also a typical motif in Russian proverbs and sayings, sets an amorous mood for the whole cycle. The zachin is followed by a stanza in which the female performer flirts rather innocently with the most important merrymaker (Sokolov 1971, 538), an "accordion player" [garmonist], who usually serves as a stand-in for the other men present; he is a generic man as far as sexuality is concerned. The female singer directs the sexual teasing at him. In one stanza it is stated that he's not popular with the girls because something is wrong with his organ: It is of strange color, as in K-28, or it's too small, or its possessor is too choosy.

The character of the arousing chastushkas and their sequence follow along the line of seductive behavior. The erotic ones, however, do not follow one another but are staggered; they are interlaced with those whose aim is simply to sustain the festive mood and the fast pace of the dance. From being first just sexually suggestive, as the dance progresses the female dancer(s) and chastushka performer(s) (usually the same people) become more and more openly seductive. For example, in the following item the female singer brings into play her sexual attraction, while being forthright about why she does it:

(8.16) Pered mal'chikami   In front of little boys
        Khozhu pal'chikami.   I walk [move] my fingers.
        Pered zrelymi liud'mi   In front of grown-ups [read: men]
        Khozhu belymi grud'mi.   I walk [move] my white breasts. (S. I: 44)

In this context, the female expression "I walk" *[khozhu]* usually means, while dancing, shaking the breasts alluringly.

The singer closes her titillating cycle with a chastushka that puts aside all the metaphoric implications and daringly admits that now, with the game of seduction over, the results will soon be known: "Tonight we'll know which one the accordion player chooses." A traditional praise for the musician concludes the cycle, and the prize offered him is in the spirit of the whole game—he should be rewarded with abandoned lovemaking:

(8.17) Garmonistu za igru—   [One should give] the accordion player
        Polosaten'kii matrats,   A striped mattress,
        Odealo, pokryvalo   A comforter, and a cover
        I zhenit'sia sorok raz.   And forty chances to make love.
                                              (S. I: 51)

In this context, the verb *zhenit'sia* ("to marry someone") is a euphemism for coitus.

Bawdy Chastushkas and Verbal Pranks

It would be wrong to assume that all bawdy chastushkas have a sexual or political agenda. Quite often they are primarily a means of entertainment, which has always been scarce in rural Russia. (The notorious "village boredom" is a traditional motif of Russian literature.) As fairy-tale introductions *[priskazki]* are "pronounced in a jolly and glib manner, as non-serious folklore preliminary, not necessarily related, to the tale" (Sinyavsky 1991, 78), so are many bawdy chastushkas. This penchant of Russian folklore to use linguistically playful words is characteristic of the ancient tradition of *balagurstvo*, "a national form of Russian laughter in which a significant part belongs to its linguistic side" (Likhachev 1976, 21). A Russian saying calls such verbal flippancy "for the sake of a beautiful word," *radi krasnogo slovtsa*.

In the case of bawdy chastushkas, the word or an expression may be not as beautiful as it is deft or witty. In the spirit of *balagurstvo,* in bawdy chastushkas, as in *priskazki* (Sinyavsky 1991, 80), the words are played with, transposed (e.g., in one chastushka, a woman milks a cow, and a cow milks a woman), and are often absurd. Most words played with in bawdy chastushkas are foul ones, however. In that respect, we should distinguish between a salacious chastushka with sexually explicit language and one that uses foul language extensively for the sake of using it. As Russian literary scholar Alexander Iliushin (1992, 18) remarks regarding the Barkovian type of poetry (to which many bawdy chastushkas are close in spirit), obscenities by themselves are less erotic than a milder, sexually suggestive vocabulary.

In chastushkas with profanities, the titillating content gets obscured and subsides under the shocking effect of uncouth words. This linguistic crassness often anesthetizes the aphrodisiac aspect of chastushkas, desemanticizes them. Singing such chastushkas primarily means playing a verbal prank, committing a mischievous act. The tendency of Russians to use foul language at each step of everyday life lets linguists F. Dreizin and T. Priestly (1982, 233) consider this *mat* "a special genre of folk-art, . . . a kind of parody of non-obscene language and of non-obscene folklore." The chastushka, as an expression and reflection of the Russian soul, not only does not avoid *mat* but uses it for artistic purposes.

For example, the content of the following chastushka is not even remotely sexual; it is rather mundane. It tells of an unhappy accident in the narrator's life: When he and his friend worked on a diesel engine, it was stolen because of their negligence. Apparently, the only reason for singing the chastushka is to introduce obscenities by rhyming the word "diesel" *[dizel']* with a colloquial vulgar synonym for "to steal"—*spizdit'* (with *pizda,* "cunt," as its root) and to use the smutty colloquial synonym for a "fool"— *mudak* (from *mude,* "testicles"):

(8.18) My s priatelem vdvoem   My friend and I
        Rabotali na dizele.   Worked together on a diesel.
        On—mudak i ia—mudak,   Both of us, pricks that we are,
        U nas dizel' spizdili.   They stole the diesel from us.
                               (S. I: 105)

For the sole sake of linguistic mischief, in a series of chastushkas and short songs collected by Vladimir Kozlovsky (1982, 283–293) and entitled "Substitutions," endings, beginnings, or fused pronunciation of several perfectly innocent words assume an indecent meaning.[28] These shame-on-you, you-have-a-dirty-mind verbal pranks constitute an entertainment act, a sort of "juggling with heavy [read: indecent] objects," which, as Victor Shklovsky (1922, 67) suggests, is in the nature of much folk humor.

Behind a slew of chastushkas lies the native Russian fascination with the linguistic richness of the core foul words, the ability of these words to substitute for virtually any part of speech (as demonstrated by Dreizin and Priestly 1982, 238–241). The following item is the most successful of this type. In this quatrain, the performer plays with several sexual and non-sexual meanings of the foul word for a male organ. Besides its basic connotation, in this chastushka the word is used six times on three distinct semantic planes: (1) as a derogatory metonym, *pars pro toto,* for "a male"; (2) in the interrogatory mode, with the preposition *na,* as part of the rhetorical colloquial expression of total disregard or dismissal of something (as in: "what do I need it for?" *na khui mne eto nuzhno?*); and (3) with the preposition *do,* as a part of the street expression that connotes abundance:

(8.19)	Poluibila ia khuia	I fell in love with a prick
	Okazalsia bez khuia,	He turned out to be without one.
	A na khuia mne bez khuia,	Why do I need [a man] without a prick,
	Kogda s khuem do khuia.	When there are plenty of them who have one.[29] (K-141)

To the same category belong chastushkas that represent nothing but the native speakers' reaction to new and unusual ("funny" in the sense of "strange") lexical items that from time to time enter the public domain.[30] For instance, a term characteristic of the post-Soviet period—a "sponsor," a business or a businessman who, for the sake of publicity or charity, subsidizes a cultural event—is played with in the following chastushka, collected recently.

(8.20)	Ty zachem, milenok moi,	"Why did you, my honey,
	Do utra gulial s drugoi?	Wander all night with another girl?"
	"Ne revnui, kakaia chush'!	"Don't be jealous, what nonsense!
	Ia ei sponsor, a ne muzh!"	I'm her sponsor, not her husband."
		(Private collection)

The linguistic reason for the chastushka's birth is evidenced by the fact that in this chastushka, evidently produced impromptu, as many of them are, the word "husband" *[muzh]* is not a good choice, for it violates the stereotypical folk script of male sexual behavior; according to this script, a husband is not supposed to wander all night with his own wife. It is clear that the adherence to stereotypes, generally important to humor, in this case is secondary to the temptation to introduce the new word of Russian-reborn capitalism in the context of the traditional folk genre. He could have said "I'm her sponsor, not her lover," but the word "husband" *[muzh]* was needed to rhyme with *chush'* (nonsense).

Some chastushkas are created for the sole purpose of self-parody of the genre, a sign of its wide popularity. In such items, the conventional content of lyrical chastushkas is replaced with the one in which obscenities are used.

The following chastushka parodies the device of psychological parallelism characteristic of folk poetry in general and of chastushkas in particular: A metaphoric description of nature in the first two lines is juxtaposed with the mood of a lover (or lovers) in the next two.

(8.21)	Na gore stoit bereza,	A birch stands on a hill,
	Vetka k vetke klonitsia.	Its branches lean on one another.
	Paren' devushky ebet—	A lad's fucking a girl—
	Khochet poznakomit'sia.	He wants to introduce himself to her.
		(K-94)

(Also note the inverted sequence of actions, a parody of the traditional courting script).[31]

An ultimate parody of the genre are those quatrains that intentionally violate both the chastushka's meter and rhyme pattern. (In fact, avoiding rhyming altogether.) Kozlovsky (1992, 211–214) calls them "the awkward ones" [neskaldushki]. For example:

(8.22)	Ot liubvi ot bol'shoi	I'll go and drown myself in the sea
	Poidu v more utopluis.'	Out of great love.
	I komu kakoe delo	And it's nobody's business
	Kuda brysgi poletiat.	Where the splashes fly. (K-212)

For the sake of a verbal prank, the chastushka, a genuine carnival genre, makes use not only of sexual matters but also of scatological elements. This presence of unpleasant images, at times overwhelming, may seem tasteless at best and may produce a sensation of discomfort, even disgust. Yet the crowd attending a chastushka performance invariably cheers and laughs.

Why does this happen? Besides substituting the functions of the lower stratum for those of the upper ones as a means of satirical denigration in chastushkas that address political issues,[32] obscenities also serve as entertainment, as a means of evoking laughter through a shock effect. A similar strategy is used by some stand-up comedians of the American nightclub scene who intentionally include vulgarities in their routines. Such routines liberate the audience (alcoholic drinks facilitate the process) from repressive social taboos on the use of foul language in public.

The same effect is not that easily achieved in chastushkas. Unlike stand-up comic routines, chastushkas are meant not for strangers' ears, but for those of fellow villagers whose everyday speech incorporates *mat* rather freely. Thus the gap between the language of the Russian countryside and that of chastushkas is not as wide as it is in the case of American comedians; obscenities in chastushkas, therefore, are relatively much less shocking. However, what could not be achieved through the use of coarse vocabulary alone is made up for by a heavy saturation of offensive words. In fact, many chastushkas are so rich in scatological elements that they seem to be no more than opportunities to give the obscenity a recognized artistic form. Some chastushkas seem nothing more than an attempt to squeeze as many profanities as possible into the traditional format; as a result, a chastushka may be read as an extended curse.[33]

I have addressed only a few aspects of the phenomenon of bawdy chastushkas. More in-depth studies should be conducted by trained ethnographers or folklorists in on-site situations, with all the contextual considerations reported. Only then may the Russian bawdy chastushka be fully assessed. As an important product of Russian folklore, it may serve as a rich source of study of the Russian ethos.

Conclusions

That the Russian standards of well-being, health, and beauty in jokes and everyday expressions still reflect peasant life may be accounted for in part by the tardiness of the industrial revolution and the subsequent belated urbanization of the country. Physical endowment as a peasant measure of abundance in the poverty-stricken country is alive and well in today's Russia. The society's gradual evolution into an urbanized industrial nation, in which Western beauty standards have begun to signify progress, has created a cultural conflict, a collision of new and traditional values. Many contemporary Russian jokes not only deal with this conflict in one way or another, but often the tension between two disparate cultural standards constitutes their only raison d'être.

Russian male jokelore is heavily permeated with items that reflect a long tradition of neglectful, condescending, and denigrating attitudes toward women. Catriona Kelly's (1993, 91) rejection of Bakhtin's notion that "the popular culture is in no way hostile to a woman and does not approach her negatively" can be supported by my observation of Russian oral humor. Bakhtin exonerates popular culture of misogyny by pointing out its roots in fertility rites. If, as Kelly reasons, the misogynist Petrushka shows of the cities (known from the first half of the seventeenth century; Prokhorov 1991, 2: 141) were remote from these rites, contemporary male jokes are even less involved with them.

As in many other cultures, many Russian male jokes are built on a woman-as-object principle. Especially vicious are attacks on females' intelligence as a way of stressing their inferiority. And as in many other cultures, Russian jokes of this kind are often combined with another striking feature—they depict women as perennially promiscuous and sexually insatiable. The Russian sexist vocabulary is vast. Besides a slew of denigrating nicknames, the very word for a woman [baba] of pre-Revolutionary Russia is still used today primarily as a disparaging nickname. Russian foul language, *mat,* is invariably offensive to women.

Male jokes often portray women as having a strictly mercenary interest in men; that is, they are just eager to sell their bodies, whether in exchange for marriage or mere valuables. Higher cultural standards, education, and superior social status do not exempt a woman from being rendered as a prostitute. A number of contemporary Russian jokes reflect a true-to-life situation in which a female office worker is habitually coerced into providing sexual services for her male boss(es).

This overall assessment of Russian male humor is supported by observation of jokelore devoted to various aspects of a male/female relationship. While mocking Russian cultural expectations, courtship jokes portray women as immature, penniless, totally dependent on men, and overly demanding at the same time. As they reflect a dating culture with fluctuating rules and unclear behavioral expectations, these jokes also function as a means of keeping women in their place.

Nastiness toward women is especially pronounced in jokes that deal with the most intimate aspect of the male/female relationship. As most Russian male jokes reflect the low level of sex education, they scold women for engaging in the very same practices on which men insist (most often fellatio). Russian men use those coital positions that convey dominance ("on horseback," *na kone*) and serve as a means of denigration and emotional alienation of women ("in the crayfish position," *rakom*).

As in other cultures, misogyny takes its ugliest form in the physical abuse of women. While most current jokes dealing with wife-beating are directed at the male's lame excuses, stressing its irrationality, numerous rape jokes are much more forgiving. In many such jokes, rape is decriminalized. It is treated as a case of female insincerity, implying that women secretly welcome sexual violence. The word "rape" is often semantically equated with a passionate sexual encounter. At least in part such treatment of the word may be attributed to the behavioral assumption characteristic of a culture with lingering pagan traditions, according to which unrestrained passion is semiotically indicative of true and deep feelings.

Although many Russian marriage jokes are similar to those of other cultures, with such constant motifs as spousal weariness and warfare, they show an especially pronounced hostility toward wives, a result of the emergence of a new type of family in the last few decades, one ruled by the domineering wife. This concentration of power in female hands occurred during the Soviet period as a result of the mass involvement of women in the workforce and the rigidity of the system that, by curtailing independence and initiative, conditioned men's passivity. Another reason for women's authority in these matters is rampant male alcoholism that has laid waste to family funds.

While reflecting rather universal tensions between the parties involved, Russian mother-in-law humor is much more hostile in urban settings than in rural areas. Due to the shortage of living quarters and the lack of social services available to an average young family, a wife's mother often has to share the same household in order to care for the children, thus tipping the balance of power in a family toward the women. Often the absence of privacy for sexual intimacy further exacerbates the situation. Russian mother-in-law jokes express intense hatred for the unwilling intruder. Murdering a mother-in-law in a self-righteous manner is a constant motif in these jokes.

The Personal Functions of Sex Jokes

Renatus Hartogs and Hans Fantel (1967, 169–170) observe that sex jokes "regardless of geography, cultural history, national character have . . . multiple goals: seduction, aggression, or release from sexual anxiety, depending on the story and the teller." Such a sweeping assessment of bawdy jokes as serving both seductive and aggressive purposes has only limited application to Russian popular culture. Unlike rural rhymes—chastushkas—most Russian sex jokes are not erotic. While eroticism aims at pleasure, these jokes are aggressively defensive. The vast majority of collected material is male-to-male jokelore aimed at relieving tension caused by either unfulfilled sexual desire or failed sexual relationships.

Since a "dirty joke lets a person deal vicariously (i.e., on the symbolic level) with psycho-sexual problems which he cannot readily express in any other way" (Hartogs and Fantel 1967, 172), humor serves as a sugar-coating of many painful issues. Most of these jokes are self-reflective discourses, meant primarily to relieve male sexual dissatisfaction or performance anxieties. Because they arise from suppressed frustration, many of them are very crude and verge on obscenity, a quality of Russian sex humor that has stunned foreign observers exposed to them—from German diplomat Adam Olearius in the seventeenth century (quoted in Kon 1995, 11) to American scholar Ronald Hingley (quoted in Visson 1998, 118) in the twentieth.

Jokelore that treats women as unstoppable voracious nymphomaniacs responds to a male unconscious need to cope with fear of sexual inadequacy. In view of the dramatic rise in the divorce rate, prompted by widespread male impotence caused by alcoholism, such jokes shift the blame to women, whose excessive sexuality is considered specifically Russian (as evidenced in jokes involving women of other countries). Another strategy to the same end is portraying women as "ugly," that is, undesirable. Such humor on avoiding women echoes an old belief that women present a danger to men's health and even lives, a notion not unknown in other cultures—for example, the Irish.[1]

The function of erotic jokes as "a kind of universal safety valve" (Hoffmann 1973, 93) for suppressed fears and anxieties is especially clear in humor that directly addresses male impotence and female infidelity. In Russian male jokes, high potency is usually ascribed to manual laborers; intellectuals and people of high social status are often treated as impotent. As a way of both denigrating outsiders and shifting dysfunction onto them, many Russian jokes cast Jews as sexual weaklings. In part, Jews are assigned this role because they are stereotypically assumed to be financially successful, thus presenting a threat to Russian males' sexual territory. In many Russian jokes, any man over fifty is assumed to be totally impotent. However, sometimes the age script is also used as a way of fantasizing never-ending sexual prowess.

As in other cultures—for example, the Andalusian (Brandes 1980, 110–114)—Russian cuckoldry jokes serve as a relief valve for men's fear of their wives' sexual betrayal. They differ from Western jokes on the same subject by putting the husband, not the lover, on the defensive. The husband's docility can be explained by his weak earning power. The drastic decrease in a man's ability to provide for his family, especially marked in the late Soviet and post-Soviet periods, accounts for such a view of male behavior.

Unlike jokes concerned primarily with middle-age men's sexual anxieties, chastushkas, the main humorous genre of rural Russians, are intentionally erotic; they often serve as a vehicle of seduction or, at very least, as an invitation to flirt. That bawdy chastushkas function as a conduit of sexual liaisons during rural festivities is well established by the ritualization of theme sequences, musical accompaniment, boisterous singing, and dancing. This genre is a clear instance of the survival of the carnival tradition in Russian popular culture. Its ribald content and performance style link private and public. In spirit, these popular rhymes can be traced to Dionysian rituals celebrating the values of the community over those of the society at large.

The fact that many chastushkas are also misogynist, despite being sung by women, can be explained by women's complacency about existing male/female relationships and by the fact that this singing is not a performance in earnest but a seductive act in which women signal their submissiveness as a way of encouraging sexual pursuit.

An analysis of a typical chastushka sequence in a real setting shows that it is carefully ordered so as to sustain the festive mood and the seductive atmosphere. Chastushkas are also used as verbal pranks in the ancient tradition of folk merrymaking *[balagurstvo]* that goes back to the tavern songs, medieval street performers' *[skomorokhi]* repertoire, and peasant festivities. Close in spirit to Russian *Secret Tales,* chastushkas have deep ancient roots in pagan rites and agrarian rituals, to which they can be easily linked through analysis of word play and scatological references.

The Social Functions of Sex Jokes

As sex jokes serve as psychological crutches for men's sexual phobias and dissatisfaction, they often perform other, group-related, functions. Cultural behaviorists see male joke-telling as an instrument that serves the intragroup needs, one of the most important of which is related to the male's own questioned sense of psychological belonging to his own gender. Walter Ong (1982, 81–82) maintains that "male bonding is often effected by shared hardships. And in male clubrooms and bars around the world the most casual companions can often establish immediate bonding by recalling the hardships that all men share, namely, the threats that woman poses to man—one of the constant themes of 'bull sessions.' . . . A man who knows and by telling tops another man's antifemale joke . . . is implicitly showing that he is even more distanced from a woman, that is, that he is 'more of a man.'"

The traditional male image, which male jokes promote in Russian popular culture, is that of a physically strong man who smokes, chases women, and, most important, drinks a lot without showing any signs of intoxication. A signifier of true masculinity, alcohol consumption has deep cultural roots, with religious undertones traceable to the most ancient Russian sources. In the Soviet period, drinking in the company of other men served as an important outlet for frustrations caused by the rigidity of the system and the total dependency on the state. Because spiritual intimacy with a woman is culturally suspect as emasculating men, male friendships and loyalties often prevail over those between a man and a woman.

Male jokes clearly show the double standard applied to male and female sexual behavior. While scolding women for their excessive sexuality, they celebrate male promiscuity. The Russian popular attitude toward womanizing is much more tolerant than it is in English-speaking countries. Sexual indiscretion is often treated as an ultimate sign of masculinity. This proliferation of folklore promoting male licentiousness may signify interrelated underlying motives that may go back to primordial times. Robert Murphy

(1989, 67) suggests that "the double standard that censures female promiscuity but encourages it among men" is related to the "workings of genitalia," that is, to the fact that "men have to be psycho-physiologically aroused for sex, but women do not."

In the Russian cultural context, there is an additional impetus for males' need at least to demonstrate, if not to act on, their interest in the relentless pursuit of women. Because of matrifocal tendencies in Russian life, excessive closeness to the mother in childhood results in a boy's strong psychological identification with the feminine gender, as many cross-cultural anthropological studies have shown. The constant sexual pursuit of women serves as a means of proving masculinity. Desmond Morris (1970, 116) observes: "If the modern Status Sex practitioner is unable to achieve real conquests, there are still a number of alternatives available to him. A mildly insecure male can express himself by telling dirty jokes. These carry the implication that he is aggressively sexual. . . ."[2] Jokes about impotence told by men help to make light of a disturbing factor in their lives and lessen the threat to their sense of male identity.

Because homosexuality deeply disturbs men's fragile sense of belonging to their gender, many Russian jokes, as in other cultures, are homophobic, often treating homosexuality as a shameful vice and transferring it onto outsiders, either ethnic minorities (most frequently, on Armenians, Georgians, and, in recent years, Jews) or socially scorned members of law enforcement agencies (police). Jokes dealing with sexual practices other than strictly genital are also often attributed to outsiders—the Chukchis and the French.

Let us return to the question raised in chapter 2: Why is there such a contrast between the elevated image of women in many Russian classics and the callous denigration of them in jokes, sayings, and everyday language?

The answer to this question is neither obvious nor simple. First of all, as "romantic poetry of the period clearly did not reflect the unsavory state of affairs in regard to the sexual behavior of the knights of the Middle Ages nor the position they allotted to women in the feudal world of Europe" (Highwater 1990, 144), the usually reverent portrayal of women in nineteenth-century Russian literature did not reflect the subordinated place of women in the society.

A product of high culture, Russian literature since the Middle Ages promoted female images related not to unrequited love and passion but to ideals of statehood. As Francine du Plessix Gray (1990, 114–131) shows, the society built on the moral strength of the mother figure has portrayed her as a spiritual icon, an example to follow, attributing to her such qualities as moral strength, faithfulness, dutifulness, and even sainthood. American Slavist Barbara Heldt (1987, 13) observes that a Russian female literary character, while being "more nearly perfect than the male," is a "mere foil for the male and his larger preoccupations."

At the same time, Russia has long been a country of profound sexism,[3] especially conspicuous in the realm of popular culture. True, Russian folklore has treated women ambivalently. Affected by the strong female pagan cult that lingered longer in Russia than in the West (Hubbs 1988), ancient, pre-Christian products of folk creativity such as *byliny* and fairy tales by and large extol women's virtue. Consider, for example, such fairy-tales characters as the kind-hearted Vassilisa the Beautiful and Little Sister Alyonushka, the selfless protector of her younger brother Ivanushka. Even the proverbial witch Baba Yaga shows mercy and kindness from time to time.

However, many folkloric genres that appeared later—everyday tales *[bytovye skazki]*, street puppet performances (Petrushka's adventures among them; Kelly 1993, 73), and especially a considerable body of proverbs and sayings, old and newly coined—often denigrate women. Like Russian peasant woodcut prints *[lubki]* of the nineteenth century, current Russian male jokes "show women as negative only: wayward, false, acquisitive, and insatiably lustful" (Farrel 1991, 560).

Besides age-old antagonism between the sexes, the unabashed negativism and downright callousness toward the female in popular culture undoubtedly reflects the misogynist treatment of women by the medieval Russian Orthodox Church. In its need to exist in the privacy of all-male company, this jokelore differs from fairy tales and lullabies. Like most humor, it is impelled by a combination of apprehension and aggression that attempts to overcome it.

Hatred of women is deeply rooted in Russian peasant society, in which they were treated as lowest of the low. Russian ethnographer Olga Semyonova Tian-Shanskaia (1993, 103) reports that misogyny would manifest itself every time a man's inhibition succumbed to alcohol. The great availability of peasant women in tsarist Russia made men take female compliance and subordination for granted.

With industrialization, the mass migration of peasants to the cities added another psychological dimension to traditional misogyny. What American psychologist Vamik Volkan (1994, 90) has to say about ethnic relations is quite applicable to gender ones: "Group members may turn to shared targets not only to patch up a disturbed sense of self, but also to establish grounds on which to reunite for mutual support and strength." In the cities working unskilled blue-collar workers, disoriented male peasants, often exploited and mistreated by capitalists even more than they had been by landowners, found relief in traditional misogyny. Their "disturbed sense of self" in an unfamiliar environment made them look for an enemy—somebody who was "different." It was not by chance that the widely popular street puppet Petrushka picked a Gypsy, a Jew, and a woman (Petrushka's bride or wife) as targets for his physical attacks. Kelly's observation is on point: "The misogyny of the Petrushka puppet plays intensified [before and after reforms of 1860s] during and perhaps because of this period's urbanization" (cited in Costlow, Sandler, and Vowles 1993, 12).

The current upsurge of violence against women and the marked increase of misogynist attitudes in the jokelore is the result of the newly developed "disturbed sense of self" of Russian men in the post-Soviet economic and cultural disarray. The stick that Petrushka customarily used to beat up his "ugly and stupid" bride or wife in the puppet shows has become in today's male vernacular a metaphor for a sexual encounter with a woman, a symbol of punishing her and distancing from her, expressed in the often used expression for coitus "to throw [her] a stick" *[kinut' [ei] palku].*

As in other male-dominant cultures, such as the American (Dundes 1980, 160), the birth of a Russian boy is still cheered much more than that of a girl. In the contemporary vernacular the nickname "bungler" *[brakodel]* applies to a man who has fathered a daughter (Elistratov 1994, 50). Consider the following Soviet-period joke targeted at the party elite, at its self-appointed entitlement to privilege:

(9.1)   A young father comes to the hospital: "Tell me, what did my wife give birth to?"
"It's a girl."
"How come? Didn't they call you from the regional party committee *[obkom]?*"
"Oh, excuse me, please. Then it's a boy." (I. Raskin 1995, 355)

Deeply imbedded in Russian consciousness, this gender bias has not changed in the post-Soviet period. Current jokelore about the New Russians reveals the same gender preference. In the following item, the obstetrician gives to the young father numbers that denote the weight of a newly born baby in kilograms and grams. But since bribing for getting anything really good is a way of life for the New Russian, the father happily parts with his money for the same reason—"it's a boy":

(9.2)   A New Russian comes to a hospital. The obstetrician tells him: "It's a boy. Three and eight hundred."

"Listen, no problem." The happy father pulls out his wallet and counts: "One, two, three thousand. . . . And here's more! One, two, three . . . eight hundred dollars!" (Erokaev 1997, 120)

In his article "Notes on the Tenth Muse," the well-known writer Igor Guberman (1993, 110), while exalting the freedom and playfulness the Russian foul language unwittingly exposes a raison d'être of national misogyny: "the age-old slavishness (on all levels of the society) and the age-old hypocritical atmosphere of Russian life would be fatally-suffocating for almost any living soul, if in the language itself [there wasn't] a blissfully life-giving spot, a lacuna, a space of freedom, of open abandon. Because *mat* is also a play and carnival of the living spirit; it is a gulp of fresh air and quick freedom."[4]

What seems important for this relieving mechanism to function is that the target of the verbal attack, of these "soul-liberating" curses, is not just anyone. To discover this target, let us take a closer look at the sample provided by Guberman, which he believes the Russian audience finds hilarious:

(9.3)   Govorit starukha dedu: Grandma says to Grandpa:
        "Ia v Ameriku poedu."   "I'll take a ride to America."
        "Chto ty, staraia pizda,   "Are you out of your wits, old cunt,
        Tuda ne khodiat poezda."   Trains don't go there."[5] (Guberman
                                          1993, 111).

Guberman (1993, 111) cites another example of male humor that he considers incomprehensible to foreigners ("the happiness experienced by those who heard this chastushka is inaccessible to anyone in the [outside] world"):

(9.4)   Nashu oblast' nagradili,   Our region was honored,
        Dali orden Lenina;   It was given Lenin's order.
        Do chego zhe moia milka   How I'm fucking fed up with
        Mne ostoebenela.[6]   My girlfriend.

On citing the first chastushka, Guberman (1993, 111) exclaims: "Tell me who else in the whole wide world would laugh at it besides us?" The answer to this rhetorical question is that an outsider may not join the Russians in their merriment, not because the chastushka, in Guberman's words, is "utterly incomprehensible to an American specialist in Russian folklore," but because, although the outsider understands the teller's tacit cultural assumptions, he or she may not share them.

The target of laughter here is clearly the old woman, the old man's wife, and her ignorance of geography, although, from a strictly grammatical point of view, nothing is wrong with her statement. The verb *poekhat'* (to go by a means of transportation) is used in Russian with and without specifying the means, and there are no other indications in the text that she plans on going overland from Russia to America. Apparently, in this case the cultural expectation behind the stereotype—a backward old village woman—takes over.

However, the old woman's presumed benightedness is a rather mild cause of laughter and functions primarily as an excuse for insulting her by using foul language, at the very core of which lies an utterly denigrating attitude toward women. The true source of delight for the teller, therefore, is nothing more than the old man's obscenity directed at his wife.[7] It is clear that the satisfying feeling—shared, Guberman assures us, by tellers and listeners—comes from nothing else but debasement of a woman through the use of the tabooed language of the curse. In the context of the village, the word "grandpa" *[ded]* evokes the stereotype of an old backwoods man. As "a man using four-letter words to a woman symbolically asserts his power over her" (Hartogs and Fantel 1967, 84), by attacking his wife (the curse is, in fact, a reduction of her whole being to genitalia), he takes the opportunity to put down someone whom he considers worse than he is. While he is just a *ded*, she is a dilapidated old woman (*starukha;* note the ageistic suffix *-ukh*, as in *razrukha*, "the state of ruin"). That alone makes her inferior. The source of laughter, thus, is a happy realization of teller and listener that even for the worst of men—no matter how backward and old they may be—there is still someone more deserving of contempt.

And the true source of delight in Guberman's second sample is not in its mild satirical reference to the Soviet propaganda practice of rewarding regions for production but in its putdown of a woman, no longer loved, through the use of tabooed language. If in the first sample there is at least a semblance of pretext, however slight, for the putdown, in the second chastushka there is none. A typical device of artistic parallelism in this genre is used mockingly—the first two lines seem to have no connection to the second two (except in suggesting annoyance with Soviet propaganda practices).

Guberman's samples are emblematic for much of oral male humor, in which misogyny serves as the last resort of the utterly powerless. If a man has nothing to be proud of, he can always resort to the ultimate consolation: that at least he is not a woman. Bringing sexual terms into his swearing is an unconscious reminder to himself that, at least in the physical act of sex, a man is an order-giver, not an order-taker.

Consider two items, a chastushka and a proverb:

(9.5)	Lezu, lezu na berezu,	I'm climbing, climbing a birch
	Na bereze chainichek,	There's a little teapot on it,
	Khot' i malen'kii khuek,	Though a dick is small,
	A nad pizdoi nachal'nichek.	It's still a little boss over a vagina.
		(Kozlovsky 1982, 64)

(9.6) "A little dick is a little king [when it's] in a vagina" (Kozlovsky 1982, 229).

These items can be interpreted in both sexual and nonsexual terms. In the first reading the male has an active role in intercourse and the female a passive one. Since the length of the penis is important to the folk male's self-esteem, the message may be seen as solace for a man who feels himself sexually substandard. Even if his manhood, defined by folk belief as proportional to the size of his organ, is deficient, he is still not the lowest in the human tribe; there is a woman submitting to him, at least in the sexual act. In a nonsexual context, to be the active participant in any active/passive relationship often gives the impression of being in command. Translated *pars pro toto,* the gist of both folkloric items comes to: "No matter how little [read: of low social standing, insignificant] a man is, he is still a boss over a woman."

Thus one of the main functions of obscenity in Russia is to relieve the intolerable tension between the opposing cultural polarities of being a strong male whose personal power over his actions has long been taken over by the state. Because for a Russian man a woman equates with a mother and a mother with Russia—and such equation is reinforced both psychologically and culturally—rage toward women may be seen as displaced hatred toward Mother Russia, an emotion culturally tabooed and therefore sublimated in jokes.

Hence, from a sociological vantage point, the central theme of Russian male humor is preoccupation with the issue of power in male/female relationship. As in Andalusian jokes, which show the heavy impact of forty years of General Francisco Franco's dictatorship, Russian jokes show the vulnerability of men to the issue of dominance and submission. What Stanley Brandes (1980, 207) has to say about Andalusian male jokelore is applicable to Russian male jokelore to an to an even greater degree: "There is no doubt, too, that the folklore perpetuates existing power relationships by providing a temporary sense of domination and control to men who normally lack it."

Russian misogynist jokes serve as a safety valve on an internalized rage caused by social humiliation, on the deep feeling of powerlessness that Russian men experienced through centuries of serfdom and autocratic rule, only to be replaced by several decades of an even more oppressive, totalitarian regime. As many chronic frustrations do, this rage surfaces in an oblique way: in the form of women-hating laughter.

In order to reproduce gender hierarchy and ensure masculine dominance, in Russian everyday culture a boy's maturing, his acquiring of a male identity, is signified by his ability to disparage women. Most Russian sex jokes serve this end for young males. These jokes do not so much express male sexuality as they reproduce the culture of gender hierarchy, helping to reinforce and sustain it.

While many jokes reflect male power in the public world, others remind us of the existence of a binary opposition between it and the private world. As the position of a woman within a family structure does not always epitomize her place in the society at large, in many societies there is a trade-off of spheres of influence—men's external and women's domestic. In the Soviet period that trade-off reached the point of clearly expressed female domestic tyranny.

There is also evidence of male resistance to the new stand that Russian women have begun to take. It is clear that the following joke is a male attack on women's insistence that they be treated as persons, not as auxiliaries to men's needs. A Russian nationalist writer, Valentin Rasputin (quoted in Voronina 1993, 98), described the emancipation of women as "a moral mutation, the moral degradation of the weaker sex." In this item, this is rendered as interspecies mutation:

(9.7)   A frog was sitting on the shore of a pond, flipping her legs in the water.
    A camel passed by, saw the frog, and asked her, "Hey, froggy, is the water cold or warm?"
    "I'm sitting here as a woman," the frog replied with a sneer, "not as a thermometer." (Private collection)

Here a frog [in Russian *liagushka* is of feminine gender] is a caricature that fits the misogynist stereotype of a feminist: She is ugly, big-mouthed [gossipy], cold-blooded [read: sexually frigid]. Writing in the *Literaturnaia gazeta,* Russian publicist Svetlana Bestuzheva-Lada (1995, 15) concludes that the women in contemporary, post-Soviet Russia are "formally prohibited from taking part in corporate structures and in religious activities" for "'the upper tier' [men] is panic-stricken by fear of 'the lower tier' [women], because it does not understand it. As a result it prefers to keep it far from power."

Thus the function of many contemporary Russian male jokes may well be to provide an outlet for the frustrations of those who are losing ground. On one hand, the tradition of dominating women in social life and using them as scapegoats for oppression continues. On the other hand, more and more men have begun to feel the pinch of female power within the framework of the family. What was formerly a kind of power trade-off has begun to tip in women's favor. In this last respect, males telling these jokes can be seen as engaging in a compensatory activity, a verbal, behind-the-back "voodoo" practice of sorts, not unlike political joke-telling during the Soviet period, which Russians used to call "giving the finger in one's pocket" *[pokazat' kukish v karmane]*. This phrase meant attacking those in power by telling jokes that had a limited circulation only.[8] Similarly, the misogynist jokes may be seen as war waged against women without giving them a chance at reprisal. Male jokes reassure the tellers that the battle of the sexes is not completely lost.

Noting that Western sexual humor is primarily male, Michael Mulkay (1988, 141) concludes that, in constructing it, "men take over from the serious realm the assumption that women are subordinate to men, that women exist for men, and that this is the natural relationship between men and women which women, on the whole, recognize and accept." The same observation can be made about Russian sexual humor.

As the Russians "often take gender inequality for granted, and either do not see inequality or interpret it as a natural and unavoidable difference" (Kon 1995, 176), through numerous jokes, proverbs, sayings, catch phrases, and chastushkas, this message is passed to the next generation, and there is evidence that it is absorbed and learned fairly early. Phallic boasts, bragging that one is a male, not a despised female, can be found in the coming-of-age humor of Russian boys, as seen in the following parody of a Mayakovsky's famous poem "Verses about the Soviet Passport" written by a Russian secondary school student (collected by M. L. Lurie 1992, 156):

(9.8) Ia khui dostaiu iz shirokikh shtanin — From my wide pants, I take my dick,

Tverdyi, kak konservnaia banka. — Hard, like a tin can.

Smotrite, zaviduite: ia— grazhdanin, — Look and envy: I am a male citizen,

A ne kakaia-nibud' grazhdanka. — Not some kind of a female one.[9]

Jocular misogynist discourse sustains mistrust of women and animosity toward them. By presenting a woman as "independent and self-reliant. Especially if there's a man nearby" (JFR 3/5/98), these jokes justify and approve male dominance.

Notes

Introduction

1. The Russian word *anekdot* should not be confused with the English "anecdote." In contemporary Russian, it is used in a wider sense, meaning any joke, whether the story is true or fictitious; most often, however, it is the latter.

   On the origins of the genre, the history of its adaptation on Russian soil, its structure and comic effects, see Dolgopolova 1983; Draitser 1982. On the *anekdot*'s function in Soviet society, see Abdulaeva 1996; Draitser 1980, 1989.

2. This series appeared in the 1960s, its protagonist a boy called endearingly (with a mocking overtone) "Vovochka." According to Enrid Alaev (1995, 161), the character derives from a vaudeville act by E. A. Mirovich entitled *Vova Got Adjusted [Vova prisposobilsia]*, first staged in 1916. The character in this play is a spoiled brat, the son of a baroness; it became popular and entered the realm of city jokelore. In the 1920s it appeared in some of Mayakovsky's poems. For a discussion of this series, see Belousov 1996.

3. Quoted in Brown 1988, 134. Cf. Jerome Clark's comment (1976, 31) on the popularity of ethnic jokes in America:

   > ... they [ethnic jokes] are occasionally hilarious, and therein lies the sad truth: Whether because they unleash the dark, secret hatreds, or appeal to the weaker sides of our natures, or play on some archetypal human delight in formulaic characters (the tricksters, the Polack), these jokes are immensely popular, even among those who most disapprove of them. This is a paradox that will not be resolved, I fear, for a long time to come.

4. Elucidation of the national stereotype of sexual behavior in a culture can be useful for scholars and students of many other realms of this culture. Thus, observing the post-Soviet scene, Costlow, Sandler, and Vowles (1993, 27) note that "criticism of culture and politics increasingly includes analysis of sexual behavior and relies on sexual metaphor." Current jokelore parallels this phenomenon. For example:

   > "Dad, I have to do a special report for school. Can I ask you a question?"

"Sure, son. What's the question?"

"What is politics?"

"Well, let's take our home, for example. I am the wage earner, so let's call me Capitalism. Your mother is the administrator of money, so we'll call her Government. We take care of your needs, so let's call you The People. We'll call the maid The Working Class and your baby brother we can call the Future. Do you understand now, son?"

"I'm not really sure, Dad. I'll have to think about it."

That night, awakened by his brother's crying, the boy went to see what was wrong. Discovering that the baby had seriously soiled his diaper, the boy went to his parents and found his mother sound asleep.

He went to the maid's room, where, peeking through the keyhole, he saw his father in bed with the maid. The boy's knocking went totally unheeded by his father and the maid. So the boy returned to his room and went back to sleep.

The next morning he reported to his father: "Dad, now I think I understand politics."

"Good, son. Can you explain it to me in your own words?"

"Well, Dad, while Capitalism is screwing the Working Class, Government is asleep, the People are being completely ignored, and the Future is full of shit." (JFR 4/17/1996)

5. On the growing tendency among educated women to quietly advance their positions in today's Russia, see Powell and Palchikoff (1997, 50). As for the absence of female jokelore in public, the anonymous reviewer of this book in its manuscript form notes that

> women's general discourse constantly stresses the same male attributes/gender dynamics, and women often "joke" with each other about men though not always in the structured genre of anecdotes; furthermore . . . at the female gatherings/drinking parties (which definitely take place and are very bawdy and raunchy) women do tell these kinds of anecdotes about men, although the social/gender position from which they experience their humor is somewhat different. There are also plenty of singular [sic!] women who tell bawdy jokes in mixed company; older women especially have often astonished me in this way.

On female bawdy, see also Emily Toth (1985).

6. For a thorough discussion of this phenomenon, see Draitser 1998, chapter 1.

7. "The identity of the narrator is just as crucial as the identity of the audience. Specifically, just as the gender makeup of the audience can influence text and texture, so can the sexual identity of the raconteur be a critical factor" (Dun-

des 1980, 28). Both Toporkov (1995, 9) and Kulagina (1995, 434) acknowledge the lack of proper scholarly attention to these details in published collections.

Chapter 1

1. For an in-depth treatment of the historical development of Russian Eros in gender-related literature and art, see Igor Kon 1995, 23–38.
2. It would be wrong, however, to attribute the return to puritanical sexual mores strictly to the Stalinist regime. As in many other spheres of life, Stalin benefited from and exploited for his political ends the attitude prevailing in the masses. On the current tendency of Russian nationalists to blame Westerners for eroticizing Russian culture, see ibid., 11.
3. Purity of ideology was reflected not only in demands for purity of the physical body but that of the social body, that is, of language as well. As foreigners ceased to be welcomed and cosmopolitans were witch-hunted, the language was also considered contaminated by foreign words, to be purged and replaced by true Russian.
4. On the traditional diet of a Russian peasant in the late tsarist period, see Olga Semyonova Tian-Shanskaia (1993, 112). Stephen and Ethel Dunn's (1967, 120–123) study of the 1960s shows the same predisposition for starch, with the tendency to overeat.
5. In the original, the capitalized expression stylistically belongs to foul language, which amplifies the denigration; Vladimir Shlyakhov and Eve Adler (1995, 31) erroneously omit this meaning of the word *vyebyvat'sia.*
6. From an open letter of Anatoly Adamishin, a former Russian ambassador to England, published in the May issue of the *Sunday Times* of London (quoted in *Harper's Magazine,* October 1997: 24): "England is a caring country, in which public conveniences (as lavatories are called here) are reasonable distances from one another. . . . When I return to Russia and run around in search of a badly needed convenience, I truly appreciate the civilized life of the British Isles. I believe that the people here may have left the rest of mankind in the dust."
7. On the peasant tradition of drinking hard liquor in late tsarist Russia and for glimpses of peasant grooming and washing habits, see Semyonova Tian-Shanskaia (1993, 110–2, 115).
8. On the impact of folklore on everyday behavior, see Dean Farrer 1973.
9. Here are some of these expressions:

"If there is a neck, a horse-collar won't be hard to find" *[Byla by sheia, a khomut naidetsia]*

"Reins got under his/her tail"—about an unruly person *[emy/ei vozhzha pod khvost popala]*

"Once you've grabbed the tug, you shouldn't say that you're too weak [to do it]." (you can't back out once you've begun) *[Vziavshis' za guzh—ne govori, chto ne diuzh]*

"To bend into a shaft-bow"—"compel somebody to submit" [*Sognut' v dugu*, Smirnitsky 1992, 165]

"Law's like a horse pole—it goes wherever you turn it" *[Zakon kak dyshlo—kuda povernesh', tuda i poidet]*

"Eyes in blinders" *[Shory na glazakh]*

10. Shlyakhov and Adler (1995, 74) erroneously give the passive form: "to be overfed."

11. In contrast, women of nomadic peoples like the Tartars and Mongols in the Middle Ages were, as a rule, on the thinner side due to the impracticality of transporting heavy loads on horseback (as noted by a Russian anthropologist, Professor Natasha Sadomskaya, formerly of Columbia University, in conversation).

12. Pointed out to me by Professor Rancour-Laferriere of the University of California at Davis.

13. The Russian word contains an additional humorous connotation when read literally—"an immobile thing."

14. There is another, figurative meaning of this jocular toast: an acknowledgment of a woman's protective role. On the notion of the "infantile husband" in contemporary Russian culture, see chapter 6.

15. From a psychoanalytical perspective, "female fatness and big breasts refer to the pre-Oedipal, 'oral' phase, when the child is concerned primarily with putting something in the mouth. Male interest in 'edible' women reflects that stage of human development when the genital gets confused with the oral" (Rancour-Laferriere, personal correspondence, 1995).

Chapter 2

1. Exceptions are few. The archetypal concept of the "evil wife" *[zlaia zhena]* appears in medieval church literature, derived from Greek church literature of the fourth to sixth centuries. In excerpts from the dark ascetic poems of Efrem Sirin that were part of the Byzantine collection *Parenesis* (Kuskov 1977, 28), a woman is seen as the source of evil; especially venomous are the attacks on her "evil tongue" and spitefulness. Echoes of these are heard in modern Russian mother-in-law jokes. (See chapter 6.) In the sixteenth-century work *Domostroi*, which prescribed the proper family order, a husband is considered the unquestionable head of the family and urged to rule it with an iron hand. Corporal punishment was considered the most reliable and appropriate means to teach a wife sense. She was considered completely subjugated to her husband and had no right to act on her own in even the most insignificant matters. Her

will and wishes were placed in the full authority of the husband to such an extent that certain kinds of conversations were proscribed.

2. For example, as depicted in the classic Soviet socialist realist film *Chapaev.*
3. Cf. George Fine's (1981, 215) list of men's grievances about women in American jokelore: "driving, cooking, spending, blabbing, fatness, skinniness, vanity, self-beautifying, greed, prudishness, cowardice, and a barrel of other faults."
4. Most of the time, however, the word *baba* is much milder than the American "broad," which connotes "a promiscuous woman; a prostitute; a woman whom the speaker does not respect" (Wenthworth and Flexner 1968, 41).
5. On the word used as an insult to a man, see also Ostrovsky's play *The Dowerless Bride,* cited in Barbara Heldt (1987, 28). A. Flegon (1973, 25) gives some other meanings of the word *baba.* All of them convey the same primitive image. His reading of the expression "a ballsy woman" *[baba s iaitsami]* as an "energetic and able woman," is not quite correct; it usually means a rather aggressive and pushy woman. There is also a variant of this expression: "not a *baba* (woman), but a stallion with balls" *[ne baba, a kon' s iaitsami].*
6. Although this word may seem an echo of a bride's being metaphorically (and poetically) called "a little heifer" *[telochka]* during old Russian marriage rituals (a groom correspondingly was called "a little bull" *[bychok;* Kulagina 1995a, 174), contemporary usage of the word for a young female is invariably denigrating.
7. The ubiquitous and widespread phenomenon of foul language with its multiplicity of meaning serves as an instrument of humor in several jokes where the profane language is paraphrased in a more conventional form. The source of delight for Russians is exactly that the hearer of the joke knows very well the profanity concealed by the normative language. The discrepancy between an emotionally highly charged situation in which foul language would be used and a calm and polite response creates the comic effect in the following joke:

> There is high excitement in the kindergarten: The children have begun to swear, to use foul language. The manager goes to the neighboring military unit, which had sent two privates to fix the wiring in the kindergarten. The lieutenant asks them:
> "Did you let yourself use foul language in the presence of children?"
> "No, Comrade Lieutenant, nothing like that happened. Private Sidorov was soldering wires, and I stood underneath holding the ladder. Then boiling metal began dripping on my forehead."
> "And what did you do?"
> "I said: 'Private Sidorov, don't you know that you are pouring hot metal on your comrade's forehead?'"

(On detailed functions of Russian obscene expressions, see Iu. Levin 1996, 108–120).

8. At least half the samples of erotic sayings from collector M. Zimin's sampling, quoted by T. Ivanova (1995, 535), consist of jocular homosexual threats by these young men to one another. These verbal threats may be symbolic substitutes for fistfights, in many cultures a traditional way to establish male domination. Jocular homosexual threats serve as signifiers of the boys' confidence in their virility as they mature.

9. Afro-American people, among whose lower-class families the mother also plays a domineering role, use the insult involving the "mother-mounting complex." (On the similarity of families ruled by strong women in Russian and Afro-American cultures, see Francine du Plessix Gray 1990, 84.) These insults are absent in male-dominant cultures, such as the Anglo-Saxon. It is not clear yet whether other examples of matrifocal cultures, like that of the East European Jewish culture of the *schtetl*, would support this observation.

10. For more detailed discussion of the linguistic confusion in Russian, see Daniel Rancour-Laferriere 1985, 226.

11. This index was twelve times more than the highest comparable index of this kind among European countries (Austria) and twenty-two times more than that of West Germany (Timroth 1986, 97). The process of contamination of everyday speech started much earlier. In his 1995 interview with a Russian newspaper, Dmitry Likhachev notes that in 1932, upon his return from prison, where he spent five years, he was astonished that "many camp expressions began to be used in everyday situations" (quoted in Bychkov 1995, 3).

12. On the proliferation of *mat* in public statements and press, see, for instance: V. Linetsky 1993, 122; V. Gershuni 1994, 281–282; Alexander Podrabinek 1991, 5. On breaking the taboo of using foul words in fiction, see V. Linetsky (1993, 121–129) and Vladimir Kolesov (1991, 76, 78). On the current phenomenon of the infiltration of obscene language into works of arts, see A. Zorin 1996, 121–142.

13. Dostoevsky points out that the Russian man resorts to "unnatural" swearing when he runs out of arguments (cited in Vladimir Kolesov 1991, 76).

14. Cited in Tatyana Mamonova 1989, 45, 59.

15. In contemporary slang, a woman is also called "a chink" (*shchelka;* Elistratov 1994, 583; not to be confused with a similar U.S. and British slang term for a Chinese).

16. On linguistic asymmetrical treatment of the traditional male and female roles in English, see Dale Spender (1980).

17. Cf. "to snatch" in English; Rancour-Lafferiere 1982, 199.

18. With the suffix *-ets,* the noun *pizdets* means the unfortunate end of a hope of getting something good and worthwhile; it also means "somebody's death," as in "that was the end of him" *[emu prishel pizdets]*.

19. For more examples of semantic associations with the word *pizda,* see F. N. Iliiasov 1994, 25–29.

20. On Russian understanding of sexual conquest as a way of subjugation, see Barbara Heldt (1987, 29) regarding Pechorin [of Lermontov's *A Hero of Our Time*], his "squarely Russian imagination that sees . . . conquest of women as a corollary of the Russian imperialistic conquest and 'civilizing' of the people of the Caucasus."

21. Cf. comparable Irish proverbs in John McCarthy 1968, 337–229: "Better a fistful of a man, than a basketful of a woman"; "Three without a rule—a wife, a pig, and a mule"; "Where there's women there's talk, and where there's geese there's cackling."

22. This is an obscene contemporary variant of a proverb collected by Vladimir Dahl (1979, I: 469): "If you allow a woman to get away with something, you'll become a woman yourself" *[Babe spustish'—sam baba budesh']*.

23. Cf. American jokes in which a woman is also treated as an inanimate object:

> A college professor is reading in bed and every now and then touches his wife's honey pot. Pretty soon he turns off the lights to go to sleep.
>
> "Hey, sadist," says his wife, "how come you get me all hot and then you go to sleep?"
>
> "I wasn't trying to get you hot," says the professor. "I was just wetting my finger to turn the page." (Fine 1981, 85)

> "WANTED: Girl to work as night-deposit box for sperm bank." (Fine 1981, 91)

24. In 1958, 52 percent of all Russians with higher education were women (Utechin 1961, 604). Later data allowed Vladimir Shlapentokh (1984, 210) to come to the unequivocal conclusion that "Soviet women even surpass[ed] men in their level of education and in the intensity of general cultural aspirations."

25. This word has an interesting history. Until the fifteenth century, it belonged to high-style Church Slavonic and meant: (1) a lie, nonsense, error; (2) a liar *[lzhets, obmanshchik]*, a word of masculine gender (being of the same root as *zabluzhdenie* "fallacy"). The *Dictionary of the Russian Language of the XI-XVII Centuries* gives an additional meaning: a licentious woman. By the 1730s, all other meanings of the word were obliterated, and since then it has been used in this meaning only (Kokhtev 1992, 84).

26. For example, see the observation by Mikhail Stern (Stern and Stern 1980, 97): in the Soviet Union about 45 percent of women suffered from frigidity. Recently, up to 70 percent of surveyed women reported that they have never experienced orgasm (cited in Visson 1998, 119).

27. Some "prostitution" jokes are really not sexual but political. That is, a whorehouse (often called by its colloquial name *bardak,* "brothel") serves as a metaphor for the general lack of order and gross mismanagement of state affairs. Generally speaking, most Russian jokes about prostitution are not as misogynist as other sex jokes for they are really about money, or rather, the lack

of it. That is why many of such jokes take place abroad, mostly in the folk capital of love, Paris. In them, the conflict arises at the moment of paying for the services rendered. For example:

> A Soviet tourist in Paris visiting a whorehouse takes one of the girls and goes into a room with her. Soon the girl runs out screaming: "No, anything but that! Never!"
> The madam asks what has happened, why she, such an experienced girl, all of a sudden refuses to serve a client.
> "No way!" says the girl. "He wants to pay me in Soviet rubles!"
> (Private collection)

The Soviets imposed a strictly observed public taboo on the subject. Since collapse of the regime (and even under Gorbachev), there have been public debates in the press, and the oldest profession has been portrayed in Russian cinema. (See Attwood 1993a, 71–75). Those jokes that reflect a real-life increase in the number of women involved in prostitution pushed into it by the collapse of the economic system, belong to the same category.

Chapter 3

1. See a pamphlet on whiskey written by an Anglo-Irish writer of the sixteenth century, Richard Stanihurst (1992, 388).
2. Cf. proverbs collected by Dahl (1984, 2: 242): "Drink till [the bottle] is dry, so that your stomach won't ache." *[Pei do sukha, chtob ne bolelo briukho]*; "Bread keeps a man alive, and wine makes him stronger" *[Cheloveka khleb zhivit, a vino krepit]*.
3. For a detailed description of a Russian drinking ritual observed in Siberia, see Dale Pesmen 1995, 65–67.
4. In the film *Taxi-Blues,* the Russian taxicab driver asks his alcoholic saxophone player friend-to-be:

> "Are you a Jew?"
> "What, don't I look like one?"
> "I thought your people don't drink."
> "You have driven us to it!" *[Doveli]*

5. For interpretation of the institution of the holiday (festivities in general) as a temporary reversal of social power, see A. Akhiezer 1991, 252–253.
6. For a portrayal of some of these drinking rituals, see Georgy Danelia's 1979 film *Autumn Marathon.*
7. In the original, the passage ends with the famous last line of the monologue of the disenchanted hero of Griboedov's comedy in verse, *Woe from Wit (Gore ot*

uma): "Where's my carriage, my carriage!" (*Karetu mne, karetu!*) See also Vladimir Nabokov 1994.

8. This joke can be traced back to Eastern medieval tales about Khodzha Nasreddin.

9. Cf. Mayakovsky's pronouncement in 1920s: "Better to die of vodka than of boredom (quoted in White 1996, 3)

10. On the difference of meaning(s) between the English word "soul" and Russian *dusha,* see Anna Wierzbicka 1989.

11. A drunk as a "holy fool" often appears in anti-Soviet jokes. In them, this character's state of intoxication serves as an artistic justification for his daring behavior; he thus acquires the license to tell the truth and attack the powerful. For instance:

> On a street corner, a drunk is waving a newspaper: "Long live Comrade Khruschev! Long live Comrade Khruschev!"
> Passersby: "Here he comes again with the cult of personality."
> The drunk: "Long live Comrade Khruschev on my pension!" (Private collection)

> A drunk walks along the park road and sees [the Minister of Culture under Khruschev] Furtseva walking a dog on a leash.
> "Taking the bitch for a walk?" the drunkard says.
> "It's not a bitch, " says Furtseva. "It's a male dog."
> "Shut up," says the drunkard. "I'm talking not to you." (Private collection)

On the use of this artistic convention in Russian theater, see Pesmen 1995, 73.

12. For example:

> ### Making a New Profession Popular
> "Our sociologist!" they say with pride about Nikolai Gul'ba [Reveler], a habitué of a beer bar "Have It with a Shrimp." There is no patron of the bar whom Nikolai wouldn't approach with his questionnaire. It contains the one and only question: "Do you respect me?" (Abramov 1973, 4)

13. See, for instance, Epshtein 1991, 20; Shlapentokh 1984, 218–223; Stern with Stern 1980, 82.

14. In contrast to this behavior, as reported by Rapoport in his *Stalin's War Against the Jews* (cited by Friedberg 1991, 20–21), when Stalin announced to the Politburo his plan for the mass exile of Jews to Siberia, Marshal Klement Voroshilov, who had a Jewish wife, threw his party membership card on the table, thus challenging the dictator. This was an exception to the rule. Also

exceptional was the behavior of a man who married the widow of "an enemy of the people," as reported by Mark Popovsky (1985, 421).

15. For more on the role of nannies in Russian culture and its impact on children, see Alexander Etkind 1993, 112–114.

16. For a Western version of this joke, see Jack Delf 1992, 59.

17. It would be wrong to assume that a man's propensity to promiscuity is strictly psychological, due to declining sexual prowess. David Buss (1994, 80) shows that such behavior is "a widespread mammalian trait, known as the 'Coolidge effect,'" a term that reportedly originates in the following true story:

> President Calvin Coolidge and the first lady were given separate tours of newly formed government farms. Upon passing the chicken coops and noticing a rooster vigorously copulating with a hen, Mrs. Coolidge inquired about how often the rooster performed this duty. "Dozens of times each day," replied the guide. Mrs. Coolidge asked the guide to "please mention this fact to the President." When the President passed by later and was informed of the sexual vigor of the rooster, he asked, "Always with the same hen?" "Oh, no," the guide replied, "a different one each time." "Please tell that to Mrs. Coolidge," said the President.

As a Kinsey study concludes, "There seems to be no question that the human male would be promiscuous in his choice of sexual partners throughout the whole of his life if there were no social restrictions. . . . The human female is much less interested in a variety of partners" (quoted in Buss 1994, 81).

18. Delivered at the Mid-Atlantic AAASS conference in New York, March 20, 1999.

19. On street stalking of women in contemporary Russia, see James Riordan 1993, 6.

20. The real-life boasts and self-glorification of a confirmed Russian womanizer is recorded in Ries 1997, 67.

21. Some studies show that up to 30 million Russians suffer from this disease (Stanley 1996, 5). Other sources list the number of alcoholics in Russia as high as 100 million (cited in Polowy 1992, 461). Vladimir Treml (1987, 153) concludes in his studies: "With respect to per capita consumption of alcohol in the form of strong alcoholic beverages, the Soviet Union ranks first in the world." Treml also shows that "excessive drinking and alcoholism with all their adverse effects on health and productivity are concentrated among the Slavic and Baltic nationalities."

22. Consider the following joke about the tendency to treat women as physically repulsive:

> A newlywed tells his friends about his wife: "She's just adorable. When you see her, you'll be convinced."

At that moment his wife appears. Her ears stick out, her teeth are crooked, her eyes crossed.

The friends look at each other in disbelief. The husband notices it and says: "Of course, if you don't like Picasso. . . ." (Genis 1994, 3: 4)

Chapter 4

1. See, for example, James Riordan 1993, 5.
2. Note, however, the order in which, in a man-to-man conversation, Pushkin's Lensky in *Eugene Onegin* speaks of the attractive qualities of his fiancée, Olga Larina: "Oh, my dear friend, how splendid have Olga's shoulders grown, her bust! Ah, and her soul!" (Pushkin 1981, 109).
3. First staged in 1941 (Lurie 1989, 138).
4. A variant of this joke was voted as one of 100 best for the year 1997 by Russian visitors of the JFR website.
5. According to the World Bank's estimate, the average working woman in Russia earns 71 percent of a man's hourly wages (reported in Vanora Bennett, December 6, 1997, A10).
6. Instead of the grammatically correct "*Ia s krovati ne vstanu.*" In order to make the parody fit the rhythm of the original, the lines of Tatiana's letter to Onegin are rendered with a stereotypical Jewish distortion of the Russian grammatical norm.
7. Not to be confused with a French word *minet,* used to denote fellatio in Russian.
8. The anthropomorphic animal in Russia is a female goat *[koza],* not a sheep (as in Woody Allen's film *Everything You Wanted to Know about Sex*).
9. In the Soviet period, homosexual images were sometimes used in Russian jokelore as a metaphor for political subjugation, signifying the rape of the nation:

   "Is the [Russian] proletariat masculine or feminine?"
   "Generally speaking, it's masculine, but it plays a feminine role. Since it came to power, it puts out, and Stalin fucks it." (Dubovsky 1992, 40).

10. For full discussion of the sexual script in Russian ethnic humor, see Emil Draitser 1998, 33, 49–54, 86–87, 157–158.
11. As discussed in chapter 2, in post-Communist Russia such vulgar vocabulary has ceased to be considered improper for *belles lettres.* Thus in the work of one of the finest of contemporary Russian prose writers, Yury Nagibin (1995, 23) one can read: "You can take turns banging *[trakhat']* a woman, but you should not consider it fighting for her." On the penis as a weapon in contemporary Russian cinema and popular press, see Attwood 1993a, 76.

12. On the sadistic punishment of a girl (whose only fault is her sexual attractiveness) by her own father, see one of the Russian *Secret Tales* recorded by Afanasiev (1991, 30), entitled "A Hot Plug" *[Goriachii kliap]*. A father hears from his daughter that a boy had propositioned her. "Why give out to strangers?" he says. "Let's keep it in the family." Then he heats a nail over an open fire and inserts it in his daughter's vagina. As a result, "for three months she can't urinate."

13. It would be clear to a Russian of that time that this name, both French (Alfonsine) and Russified (the diminutive suffix -*ink*), was a prostitute's.

14. This joke has a cross-cultural quality; it illustrates the stereotypical coldness of English women. (See Dundes 1987, 121).

15. For example, an American one:

> "Did you hear about the marriage between the 78 rpm record and the 33 rpm record?
> It didn't work out because she was long-playing and he always finished in three minutes." (Fine 1981, 23)

Or:

> "I want a divorce, Your Honor. My husband beats me."
> "Very badly?"
> "By about ten minutes." (Fine 1981, 95)

16. I found only one joke, which is of recent vintage and obvious Western origin considering that it mentions cocktails on ice, a markedly non-Russian drink; in fact, D. Soloviev (1992, 1: 22) quite appropriately lists this joke as one about Englishmen:

> Two men are sitting in a bar with their drinks in hand. One of them pokes his drink with a straw and says:
> "What a funny thing—a piece of ice with a hole."
> Says the other: "Big deal! I've been married to one like that for twenty years."

17. Contributed by Professor Zhanna Dolgopolova. On this subject, see also Lynn Visson 1998, 124.

18. On a similar phenomenon in contemporary American culture, see Alan Dundes's article, "The Crowing Hen and the Easter Bunny" (1980, 160–175): a witch riding on a broomstick is "riding on top of and controlling the movements of a symbolic male phallus" (171).

19. For a semiotic analysis of the importance of position on top in a sexual act in Gogol's *Sorochinsky Fair* (*Sorochinskaia iarmarka),* see Daniel Rancour-Laferriere 1982, 357.

Chapter 5

1. Cf. a caption on a Polish poster of a battered wife and child: "Because the soup was too salty"; reported in Perlez 1998, A8. It would be wrong to assume that such attitudes are characteristic of the lower social stratum only. A conviction that violence against a woman is justifiable under certain circumstances is deeply embedded in consciousness of even Russian intellectuals. Here is, for example, an excerpt from a diary of widely known playwright and prose writer Mikhail Roshchin (1995, 9): "With years, a feeling of guilt toward a woman has grown strikingly, as well as a critical view of her which has never been in my youth. All [women] had been charming, all beautiful. And if I had struck them over [their] mug[s] [in street Russian: *morda*], it was in the heat of the moment and for a good reason. There was a joke some time ago: 'One can close a woman's mouth and a door of a Soviet-made automobile with a strong blow only.'" By citing the joke, the writer makes it clear that a woman deserves physical abuse if she is too talkative.

2. The love/hate ambivalence of the Russians was long noted by Sigmund Freud (cited in Etkind 1993, 114–115, 117). D. M. Likhachev (1990, 7), citing Russian philosopher Nikolai Berdyaev as his primary source, lists "kindness and cruelty, delicacy and rudeness, free-thinking and despotism, self-abasement and arrogance or chauvinism" among Russian traits. See also Zara Abdulaeva 1996, 209.

3. On "humility and complaisance in public life" prompted by the emasculating role of the Communist party, which was "combined with tyranny in the home and family with regard to the wife and children" under the Soviets, see Igor Kon 1995, 152.

4. There is factual evidence that at least some Russians read their proverbs on violence against women as having an algolagnic (sadomasochistic) character. According to L. M. Kleinbort, when he met Russian writer Fedor Sologub and his wife upon their return from abroad in 1909, upon asking them "Have you been flourishing? *[Kak tsvetete?]*, Sologub's wife answered "laughingly" with an old Russian proverb: "A wife is not a pot—you won't break her [when you hit her]" (Dahl 1876, I: 470). Kleinbort then said: "So, then you're still in one piece?" to which the woman answered with another proverb: "Beat your wife with the back of an ax, kneel down and check it out: If she's still breathing and shows signs of life, that means she wants more." Sologub then quoted an old Russian love poem:

> Take my right hand
> And lead me to the guestroom.
> Remove my colored dress
> And beat me over my white body awhile,
> Every spot of it ten times.
> After beating, my dear one, spare me.

Put me on the little wooden bed,
Press me to your ardent little heart. (quoted in Pavlova 1996,
344–345)

5. For a full compilation of such verbs, see F. N. Iliiasov 1994, 17–18, 30–32, 43–45.
6. There is also a reflexive form of the verb used by both sexes to designate the act—*trakhat'sia.*
7. Cited by Dr. Robert Orr of University of Ottawa, personal e-mail correspondence.
8. On Russian film representations of women accepting rough treatment as normal, see Attwood 1993a, 75–78.
9. Sigmund Freud (1960, 98) long ago observed the social and psychological functions of erotic humor: "Smut is like an exposure of the sexually different person to whom it is directed. By the utterance of obscene words, it compels the person who is assailed to imagine the part of the body or the procedure in question and shows her that the assailant is himself imagining it. It cannot be doubted that the desire to see what is sexually exposed is the original motive of smut."

    Gershon Legman (1968, 12) adds: "That the 'attacked' and 'denuded' person is generally a woman, when the joke-teller is a man, shows clearly that the telling of jokes in this way is actually intended as a modified form of rape; verbal rape rather than physical—a sort of seduction or preparation of the woman for the man's actual physical approach."
10. For example,

    An officers' club. On a pool table, [the heroine of Tolstoy's *War and Peace*] Natasha Rostova lies naked. The officers push a cucumber in her vagina and then punch her in the stomach. The one hit by the cucumber must kiss Natasha's lips.

    Lieutenant Rzhevsky approaches the table and says with disdain: "Gentlemen, isn't it better simply to give her a big fuck?"

    One of the officers says indignantly: "Ah, Rzhevsky, you're always horning in with your vulgar suggestions." (JFR 2/2/98)

11. See, for instance, George Fine 1981, 21, 138; Legman 1968, 256–265.
12. There are great many Russian jokes of an even more sinister variety of pornography. In them, a woman is not only humiliated and compromised sexually; her reaction to the abuse is simply not addressed. Whether she enjoyed it or not is irrelevant. She is treated as a sexual object not only without dignity but even without a normal sexual desire—an object in a full sense of the word. The following item illustrates the use of the classical "mistaken identity" comedic

plot for the sole purpose of putting a woman in a humiliating and compromising position:

> A young woman comes to a gynecologist, undresses, sits down on a chair and spreads her legs.
> "Higher!" she is told.
> The young woman raises her legs higher.
> "Higher!!"
> The young woman raises her legs higher yet.
> "Higher!!!"
> The woman: "How high can it be? I can't make it any higher."
> Answer: "The gynecologist's office is one floor higher. And this is a hairdressing salon." (Private collection)

13. In a variant, a husband gives the advice to his wife.
14. Cf. Barbara Heldt's (1987, 29) conclusion about Mikhail Lermontov's early "Hussar" poems that "lightheartedly described gang-rape and mistaken identity rape with no consequences of any sort for the hero." On the attitude toward rape in contemporary Russian cinema similar to that found in jokes—as a male prank, at worst as a minor misdemeanor—see Lynn Attwood 1993a, 77.
15. See, for example, Gershon Legman 1968, 256.
16. A variant of this joke features a vixen *[lisa]*, in Russian folklore a sly and lusty animal, here a metaphor for a woman (JFR 2/20/98).
17. For example, see V. Smetanin and K. Donskaia 1992, 17.
18. See Francine du Plessix Gray 1990, 72; Igor Kon 1993, 27–35; Mikhail Stern with August Stern 1980, 204; Lynn Visson 1998, 118. An American joke runs:

> "Y'know, Wanda, a rape is committed here in New York every sixty seconds."
> "So what?"
> "Gotta minute?" (Fine 1981, 21)

19. Andrey Sinyavsky (1991, 109) actually discusses the dual faith *[dvoeverie]* of the Russians, "an inclination to mix and combine pagan traditions with Christian religion."
20. On Russian women's complaints on the lack of courtship manners in Russian men, see Mark Popovsky 1985, 429.
21. From Professor Karriker's comments made during a roundtable discussion of the recent Russian cinema at the Thirtieth National Convention of the American Association for the Advanced Slavic Studies, Boca Raton, September 25, 1998.

22. On the impact of folk conceptions of sexual attraction on real-life rape cases, see George Lakoff and Mark Johnson 1987.

Chapter 6

1. See Ekaterina Aleksandrova 1984.
2. A popular aphorism by Emil Krotky, a satirist of the 1960s, has entered the realm of contemporary urban folklore. Alas, its humor does not translate well into English, for the joke is based on the double meaning of the Russian word *brak,* which stands for both "marriage" and "a defect": "They don't call something good 'a defect'" *[Khoroshee ne nazyvaiut brakom].*
3. See, for example, Susan Rogers's (1975, 727–56) study of French village life in the 1970s.
4. Cf., for instance, the following two jokes, one American, the other French:

> "Don't trust a man who says he's boss in his own home. He might lie about other things too." (Fine 1981, 216)

> On a visit to a doctor: "Tell me, Mme Duvall, do you have any cases of delusions of grandeur in your family?"
> "Yes, I have. From time to time, my husband claims that he's the head of our family." (JFR 3/18/98)

5. Quoted by an anonymous author in an article entitled "KVN," *Moscow Pravda,* 15, 1997: 3. On real-life stories about Russian men avoiding domestic chores, see Nancy Ries 1997, 73–74, Lynn Visson 1998, 116.
6. There is an American version of this joke.
7. In the original, rhyming emphasizes the joke: *setka-Svetka* and *plan-Ivan.*
8. Cf. for example, the following joke, found in an American collection (Fine 1981, 218) and in a Russian one (Kharkover 1993, 46):

> "You have a black smudge on your mouth."
> "I just kissed my mother-in-law good-bye at the railroad station. She has finally left our house."
> "But why the black smudge?"
> "Well, I kissed the engine, too."

9. Such dynamics of the relationship may be found in Western culture, but some other cultures introduce a variation. Thus A. R. Radcliffe-Brown (1961, 92) discovered joking relationships ("permitted disrespect") with mothers-in-law in some primitive societies.
10. Here is an example of how a borrowed joke can be refocused in another culture. In its original form, this joke is about "stingy" Scots.

Chapter 7

1. Some of these jokes are borrowed from the Jewish repertoire, where they perform a different function. On the mechanics of a majority's borrowing of minority jokelore, see Emil Draitser 1998, 21–27.
2. For a full discussion of the Russian man's cultural avoidance of domestic chores as emasculating, see Daniel Rancour-Laferriere 1995, 271–273, 275. It would be wrong to assume that tendency to see sex as a man's chore, to be avoided given the opportunity, is a recent development. A delightful sample of a pre-revolutionary joke was contributed by Professor Natasha Sadomskaya, formerly of Columbia University:

> Upon returning from his trip to St. Petersburg, a *muzhik* [peasant] was surrounded by his fellow villagers, eager to hear about his impressions of the capital.
> "Did you see the tsar and tsarina?"
> "Oh, yes."
> "Tell us about the tsarina. How is she?"
> "Oh, she is splendid! Pale and big, and in such a gorgeous fur coat!"
> "Oh," said one *muzhik* dreamily. "I'm sure the tsar fucks her every night."
> "Why would he be bothered?" asked another. "He'll just say the word, and they'll fuck her [for him]." (in Russian: "*Nuzhno emy! Prikazhet—i vyebut*)

3. Cf. an Armenian Radio joke (Milgram 1985, 98):

> "What's the correlation between wine and crayfish?"
> "After several glasses of wine, a woman assumes a crayfish position."

(In the original, the joke makes use of a double entendre: the word *stanovit'sia* means both "to become [a crayfish]" and "to assume a [crayfish] position.")
4. The separate bedroom for a bride is a sheer invention, impossible under the living conditions of the vast majority of Russians, but necessary for the joke to work.
5. On sexual jokelore of the Russians as an ethnic group, see Draitser 1998, 182.
6. On close ties between illicit lovers in Soviet time and social implications of this phenomenon, see Vladimir Shlapentokh 1989, 178.
7. For an American version of this joke, see George Fine 1981, 151. Predictably, while in the American variant the lover pays for luxuries—the couple's beach cottage, a Corvette, and a mink coat—his Russian counterpart provides essentials.

Chapter 8

1. Some researchers point to foreign sources of the genre, namely Polish and Ukrainian folk quatrains (Alex Alexander 1976, 337–338).

2. Perhaps Gorer based his findings on the Potemkin-village–style performance, especially when foreign guests were present, that was characteristic of the Soviet period.

3. In his work on Russian folklore published in the Soviet period, Yury Sokolov (1971, 533), while acknowledging the presence of bawdy chastushkas, places them safely in pre-Revolutionary times.

4. On the mythological and religious roots of such cultural taboos, see Boris Uspensky 1993.

5. Victor Raskin (1985, 171) believes that most recorded chastushkas are "obscene or bawdy."

6. The main body of chastushkas discussed in this chapter is taken from two collections, which, for the sake of space, are abbreviated K (Kozlovsky 1982) and S (Starshinov 1992a, in two volumes). References to these volumes are shown in Roman numbers followed by the page number in Arabic.

7. For example, Victor Shklovsky (1929, 150) mentions false rhyming with a pause to suggest an erotic image. Roman Jakobson (1981, 331) cites erotic chastushka when he discusses such poetic devices as playing with suffixes.

8. See A. V. Kulagina 1995b; O. V. Smolitskaia 1990; L. D. Zakharova 1994a.

9. Victor Raskin (1985, 177) also believes that "[t]he prescribed format of the genre . . . attunes the hearer to the joke automatically, and lets the authors of the chastushkas get away with much less carefully worded texts than in regular jokes."

10. A hint at holiday sexual license is contained in a Russian proverb "For a cat, not every day is a 'have-it-all' day" [Ne vse kotu Maslenitsa]; in Russian vernacular, kot (tomcat) suggests a philandering male.

11. Typically, it is a sparrow [read: a simple man, a commoner] that does it to (dominates) a dove, a cultivated bird [read: a well-bred person], not vice versa; this is another case of folkloric compensation for social inequality.

12. Discussing similar motifs in Afanasiev's Secret Tales, F. S. Kapitsa (1991, 151) points out ancient mythological roots of sexual relationships between objects (believed to have their own soul and often a gender) and people. Clearly, it would be a mistake to view such relationships from the point of view of late-twentieth-century sensibilities.

13. Such chastushkas may also provide an outlet for the repressed mutual attractions discussed in chapter 6. On a father living with his daughter-in-law [snokhachestvo], see Laura Engelstein 1992, 46–47, 126.

14. Legman (292) calls them "phallic brags."

15. For example, in an Armenian Radio joke:

> Question: "Between which fingers should a man hold his member over the urinal?"

"A real man should hold it with both hands." (Kharkover 1993, 2: 21).

16. Some proverbs collected by Dahl express the same male judgment: "A fool with a dick as long as a horse-shaft is a Godsend for the local women" [*Durak da khui v oglobliu—posadskim babam nakhodka;* Claude Carey 1972, 66); "Don't tell your wife which one has a big dick" (51).

17. Cf. a similar hyperbolization of the phallus in Russian erotic tales (Uspensky 1993, 125).

18. See also Russian-American dominance rivalry in item 7.51. On penile display signs in different cultures, see Daniel Rancour-Laferriere 1979, 49–56.

19. This chastushka evidently dates to the mid-1920s, before Stalin's full consolidation of his personal power.

20. NB: In old Russian, *nemets* meant "mute one"; that is, the word connoted *any* foreigner.

21. It may seem that, since both persons in this chastushka are males (a Jewish woman is not *evrei* but *evreika*), Jewish homosexuality is suggested here. However, in folk humor grammatical rules can sometimes be neglected for metrical reasons.

22. The vagina dentata is expressed more explicitly in an Armenian Radio joke:

"Is it true that women are as kind and good as they seem?"
"Only when they sleep with their teeth toward the wall" (Milgram 1985, 41)

And in a riddle:

"What has never been and never will be, and if it would be, would makes us all perish?" "A cunt with teeth." *[Chego nikogda ne bylo i ne budet, a esli budet, vsekh nas pogubit? Pizda s zubami]* (Iliiasov 1994, 240).

23. The same phenomenon takes place in Western male jokelore analyzed by Gershon Legman 1968, 356–363.

24. This also explains the phenomenon of Jews telling seemingly anti-Semitic jokes—sometimes in mixed Jewish-Gentile, sometimes in exclusively Jewish, company. For a detailed discussion of ethnic in-group/outgroup joke telling, see Emil Draitser 1998, chapter 1.

25. Gorer probably had in mind nineteenth-century literature. However, Russian folk songs also traditionally display a rather romantic vision of love.

26. Of course, Jay talks about male friends, not a cross-gender communication. The male-female relationship is more complex and may be marked by a degree of ambivalence; feelings of hostility and affection may mix.

27. On the teleology of Russian verses, see Daniel Rancour-Laferriere 1980.

28. Shklovsky (1929, 150) cites such a technique used in nightclub comics' singing in the New Economic Policy (NEP) era in the 1920s.

29. For more on the usage of *mat* in chastushkas, see O. V. Smolitskaia 1990.

30. Shklovsky (1922, 66) observed a similar phenomenon talking in jokes of the early years of the Soviet regime.

31. This jocular inversion of the traditional courting script entered the realm of everyday language a long time ago; see, for example, in Yury Nagibin (1994, 14): A young man, a friend of the narrator, tells him about an attractive young girl. "You won't need an introduction," he says: "You'll get acquainted with her when you bang her. It makes [the two of you] closer" *[eto sblizhaet]*.

32. For instance, as in English, the Russian verb for coitus, *ebat'*, is used in two different ways—one as erotic and the other as an expression of hostility in a nonsexual context. See A. Flegon's dictionary (1973) for the full spectrum of the meaning.

33. For example,

Ne pizdi, pizdiulia, gadina,	Don't bullshit, you cunt-like creature, you reptile,
Ebanyt', bliad', gavno.	You fucked one, you whore and you shit. (K-87)

Conclusions

1. Cf. an Irish joke:

   "And how's yer wife, Pat?"
   "Sure, she do be awful sick."
   "Is ut dangerous she is?"
   "No, she's too weak t'be dangerous anymore!" (McCarthy 1968, 49)

2. Desmond Morris (1970, 116) notes that the "obsessive, persistent dirty-joketeller begins to arouse suspicions in his companions. They detect a compensation mechanism."

3. In the post-Soviet period, there is little evidence that this sexism is declining. Thus, on a cover of a pilot issue (March 1995) of a slick Russian magazine, *Elita* (The Elite), a feature article is announced in this way: "A woman, like spring, makes the nights shorter." An advertisement placed on the title page of the same issue reads: "After male hands, the best decoration for a woman's shoulders is a fur coat."

4. This notion of the liberating quality of profane language is hardly valid. As liberating as its usage may be for a slave, obscenity can be used as a means of subjugation as well. Morris (1970, 111) observes: "Almost all the really vicious

swearwords we can use to hurl abuse at someone are sexual words. Their literal meanings relate to copulation . . . , but they are used predominantly in moments of extreme aggression. This again is typical of Status Sex and demonstrates very clearly the way in which sex is borrowed for use in a dominance context." Leo Trotsky sees profanity as "a relic of slavery, the sense of constant humiliation, and lack of respect for human dignity, one's own as well as others. And this particularly applies to Russian profanity. In Russian profanity used by the masses there is desperation, bitterness, and most of all, slavery without hope, without escape. But the very same swear words used in the upper echelons were an expression of class superiority, slave-owners' honor, and the unshakeability of its foundations . . ." (quoted in Mamonova 1989, 126). See also the reference to the use of foul language to break the accused during interrogation sessions in Solzhenitsyn's *Gulag Archipelago* (cited in Rancour-Laferriere 1985, 220).

5. The comic effect of a take-off of this widely known chastushka is based on the incongruity between the original's crudity and foul language and the civilized and cultured manner in which its content is retold for a Western audience. A mockery of Western failure to understand the "mysterious Russian soul" is quite pronounced here; it is not by chance that the action takes place in England, whose prime minister had coined the now-proverbial phrase: "Russia is an enigma wrapped in mystery":

> Before Russian chastushkas are about to be performed in Covent Garden, the master of ceremonies announces:
> "And now, ladies and gentlemen, you'll hear a well-known Russian chastushka in which it is said that an old lady informs her husband that she plans to travel to America. To this, the old gentlemen remarks that, alas, trains run as far as Le Mans only." (Soloviev 1992, 1: 36)

6. On a pattern of "*(ona mne) ostochertela,* "I'm awfully fed up with her."
7. There is also the amplifying comic effect of rhyming *pizda/poezda.*
8. The term also referred to well-hidden messages in literary works, as described in Lev Losev 1984.
9. A variant of this parody can be found in V. S. Elistratov's (1994, 552) dictionary of contemporary Moscow argot. In Mayakovsky's (1963, 350) original text:

Ia dostaiu iz shirokikh shtanin	I take it [my passport] out from my wide pants
Duplikatom bestsennogo gruza.	As a document of invaluable weight.
Chitaite, zaviduite,	Read it, envy—
Ia grazhdanin Sovetskogo Soiuza	I am a citizen of the Soviet Union

Works Cited

Abdulaeva, Zara. "Popular Culture." In *Russian Culture at the Crossroads* edited by Dmitri Shalin, 209–238. Boulder, Colo.: Westview, 1996.

Abramov, E. "Making a New Profession Popular" *[Professiiu—v massy]. Trud* (Labor), April 1, 1973: 7.

Afanasiev, A. N. *Russkie zavetnye skazki* (Russian secret tales). Moscow: Mif, 1991.

Akhiezer, A. *Rossiia: kritika sotsiologicheskogo opyta (sostiokul'turnyi slovar')* (Russia: criticism of [its] historical experience (sociocultural dictionary). Moscow: N. P., 1991.

Aksyonov, Vassily. *In Search of Melancholy Baby.* New York: Vintage, 1989.

Alaev, Enrid. *Mir Anekdota* (The world of the joke). Moscow: Anons, 1995. (as issue 8 of the journal *Anekdoty nashikh chitatelei,*)

Aleksandrova, Ekaterina. "Why Soviet Women Want to Get Married." In *Women and Russia* edited by Tatiana Mamonova with Sarah Matilsky, 31–50. Boston: Beacon Press, 1984.

Alexander, Alex. "The Russian Chastushka Abroad." *Journal of American Folklore,* Fall 1976: 335–341.

Allen, Nick. "Classic Macho Image Takes Beating." *Moscow Times,* February 24, 1998: 20.

Allison, Anne. *Nightwork: Sexuality, Pleasure and Corporate Masculinity in a Tokyo Hostess Club.* Chicago: University of Chicago Press, 1994.

Anon., ed. and compl. *Vam i ne snilos'* (You haven't even dreamed of it). Moscow: IKHS, 1990.

Anon., ed. and compl. *Seks-anekdoty* (Sex jokes). Riga: Delo, 1991.

Anon., ed. and compl. *Anekdoty* [Jokes]. Moscow: Express-kniga "Oniks," 1994.

Armalinskii, Mikhail. *Dobrovol'nye priznaniia—vynuzhdennaia perepiska* (Voluntary confessions—a forced correspondence). Minneapolis: M.I.P, 1991.

———., ed. and compl. *Russkie besstyzhie poslovitsy i pogovorki* (Russian shameless proverbs and sayings). Minneapolis: M.I.P.,1992.

Attwood, Lynne. 1990. *The New Soviet Man and Woman: Sex-Role Socialization in the USSR.* Bloomington: Indiana University Press.

———. 1993a. "Sex and the Cinema." In *Sex and Russian Society* edited by Igor Kon and James Riordan, 64–88. Bloomington: Indiana University Press.

————. 1993b. "Women, Cinema, and Society." In *Red Women on the Silver Screen: Soviet Women and Cinema from the Beginning to the End of the Communist Era* edited by Lynne Attwood, 19–130. London: Pandora.

Bakhtin, Mikhail. *Tvorchestvo Fransua Rable i narodnaia kul'tura srednevekov'ia i renessansa.* [Works of Francois Rabelais and the popular culture of the Middle Ages and the Renaissance]. Orange, Conn.: Antiquary, 1986.

Barret, Richard A. *Culture and Conduct: An Excursion in Anthropology.* Belmont, Calif.: Wadsworth, 1984.

Barsky, L. A., ed. and compl. *Eto prosto smeshno ili zerkalo krivogo korolevstva/Anekdoty: analiz, sintez i klassifikatsiia* (This is just funny, or the mirror of the crooked kingdom/ jokes: an analysis, synthesis, and classification). Moscow: Kh.G. S., 1994.

Belousov, A. "Vovochka" (Little Vova). In *Antimir russkoi kul'tury* edited by N. Bogomolov, 165–186. Moscow: Ladomir, 1996.

Bennett, Alexandra G. "From Theory to Practice: Catharine MacKinnon, Pornography, and Canadian Law." *Modern Language Studies* 27, nos. 3 and 4 (Fall and Winter 1997): 213–230.

Bennett, Vanora. "From Russia—with a Bit Too Much Love." *Los Angeles Times,* October 10, 1997: 5–6.

————. "Russia's Ugly Little Secret: Misogyny." *Los Angeles Times,* December 6, 1997, A1: 9, 10.

Berezin, Anton. "Natsional'nye bliuda v assortimente" (National dishes in assortment). *Magazin: Ironicheskii zhurnal* [A shop: An ironic journal], 6 (1990): 17.

Bestuzheva-Lada, Svetlana. "Zabud', chto ty zhenshchina . . ." [Forget that you're a woman . . .], *Literaturnaia gazeta,* July 19, 1995: 15.

Bobroff, Anne. "Russian Working Women: Sexuality in Bonding Patterns and the Politics of Daily Life." In *Power of Desire: Politics of Sexuality* edited by A. Snitow, 206–227. New York: Monthly Review Press, 1983.

Bogomolov, Nikolai, ed. *Antimir russkoi kul'tury* (The anti-world of Russian culture). Moscow: Ladomir, 1996.

Bond, Susan B. and Donald L. Mosher, "Guided Imagery of Rape: Fantasy, Reality, and the Willing Victim Myth." *Journal of Sex Research* 22, No. 2 (May 1986): 162–183.

Brandes, Stanley. *Metaphors of Masculinity. Sex and Status in Andalusian Folklore.* Philadelphia: University of Pennsylvania Press, 1980.

Brenton, Myron. *Sex Talk.* New York: Stein and Day, 1972.

Brown, Judy. "Women-Bashing Comics: The Joke's on Us." *Mademoiselle* (April 1988): 134.

Buss, David M. *The Evolution of Desire: Strategies of Human Mating.* New York: Basic Books, 1994.

Bychkov, Sergey. "V nadezhde slavy i dobra" (Interview with Dmitry Likhachev). *Moskovskii komsomolets,* July 23, 1995: 3.

Carey, Claude. *Les proverbes erotiques russes* (Russian erotic proverbs). The Hague: Mouton, 1972.

Carey, Tom. *The Modern Guide to Sexual Etiquette for Proper Gentlemen and Ladies.* Chicago: Turnbull & Willoughby, 1987.

Chang, Pang-Mei Natasha. *Bound Feet and Western Dress.* New York: Doubleday, 1996.

Cherednichenko, Tatyana. *Mezhdy "Brezhnevym" i "Pugachevoi." Tipologiia sovetskoi massovoi kul'tury.* (Between "Brezhnev" and "Pugacheva": A typology of Soviet mass culture). Moscow: RIK "Kul'tura," 1994.

Chirikov, Evgeny. "Tanino schastie" [Tania's happiness]. In *Tsaritsa Potseluev: Eroticheskie novelly i skazki russkikh pisatelei.* [The tsarina of kisses: Erotic novellas and fairy tales of Russian writers] edited by N. Popov, 158–188. Moscow: Vneshsigma, 1993.

Clark, Jerome. "All Joking Aside." *The New Leader,* December 6, 1976: 31.

Corten, Irina H. *Vocabulary of Soviet Society and Culture: A Selected Guide to Russian Words, Idioms, and Expressions of the Post-Stalin Era, 1953–1991.* Durham, N.C.: Duke University Press, 1992.

Costlow, Jane T., Stephanie Sandler, and Judith Vowles. "Introduction." In *Sexuality and the Body in Russian Culture* edited by Jane T. Costlow, Stephanie Sandler, and Judith Vowles, 1–40. Stanford, Calif.: Stanford University Press, 1993.

Dahl, Vladimir. *Poslovitsy russkogo naroda* [Proverbs of the Russian people]. Vols. 1–2. St. Petersburg: NP, 1879.

———. *Poslovitsy russkogo naroda* [Proverbs of the Russian people]. Vols. 1–2. Moscow: Khudozhestvennaia literatura, 1984.

Davies, Christie. "Ethnic Jokes, Moral Values and Social Boundaries." *British Journal of Sociology* 33, no. 3 (September 1982): 383–403.

Delf, Jack P., ed. and compl. *Come Laugh with Me.* B. C. Richmond, Canada: J. P. Delf, 1992.

Dezhnov, Iu. B., ed. and compl *Anekdoty . . . Anekdoty? Anekdoty!* (Jokes . . . Jokes? Jokes!). 4 vols. Moscow: DataStrom, 1993.

Dolgopolova, Zhanna. *The Anecdote: Its Genesis, Structure and Comic Effects.* Unpublished Ph.D. diss. in Russian. Melbourne: University of Melbourne, 1983.

Dolgopolova, Zhanna, ed. and compl. *Russia Dies Laughing: Jokes from Soviet Russia.* London: Andre Deutsch, 1982.

Douglas, Mary. *Implicit Meanings: Essays in Anthropology.* London: Routledge & Kegan Paul, 1975.

Draitser, Emil. "The Art of Storytelling in Contemporary Russian Satirical Folklore." *Slavic and East European Journal* 26, No. 2 (1982): 233–238.

———. "Soviet Underground Jokes as a Means of Popular Entertainment." *Journal of Popular Culture* 23, no.1 (Summer 1989): 117–125.

———. *Techniques of Satire: The Case of Saltykov-Shchedrin.* Berlin: Mouton de Gruyter, 1994.

————. *Taking Penguins to the Movies: Ethnic Humor in Russia.* Detroit: Wayne State University Press, 1998.

————., ed. and compl. *Forbidden Laughter: Soviet Underground Jokes.* Los Angeles: Almanac, 1980.

Dreizin, F., and T. Priestly. "A Systematic Approach to Russian Obscene Language." *Russian Linguistics,* 6 (1982): 232–249.

Dubovsky, Mark, ed. and compl. *Istoriia SSSR v anekdotax (1917–1992)* (History of the USSR in jokes). Smolensk: Smiadyn', 1992.

Dundes, Alan. *Interpreting Folklore.* Bloomington: Indiana University Press, 1980.

————. *Cracking Jokes: Studies of Sick Humor Cycles and Stereotypes.* Berkeley: Ten Speed Press, 1987.

Dunn, Stephen P., and Ethel Dunn. *The Peasants of Central Russia.* New York: Holt, Rinehart and Winston, 1967.

Duvall, Evelyn Millis. *In-Laws: Pro & Con: An Original Study of Inter-Personal Relations.* New York: Association Press, 1964.

Eco, Umberto. "Umet' smeiat'sia nad soboi" (To be able to laugh at oneself). *Novoe Russkoe Slovo,* September 8, 1989: 9. [In Russian.]

Efimov, A. N., ed. and compl. *Vot my—tak my!* (Here we are!) Kiev: Dovira, 1994.

Epshtein, Mikhail. "Sem'ia i druzhba" (Family and friendship). *Nezavisimaia gazeta* [The independent gazette], 2, no. 12–13 (December 1991): 20.

Elistratov, V. S. *Slovar' moskovskogo argo (materialy 1980–1994 gg.)* (A dictionary of the Moscow argot [materials of 1980–1994]). Moscow: Russkie slovari, 1994.

Engelstein, Laura. *The Keys to Happiness: Sex and Search of Modernity in Fin-de- Siècle Russia.* Ithaca, N.Y.: Cornell University Press, 1992.

Erikson, Erik. *Childhood and Society.* New York: Norton, 1950.

Erofeev, Venedikt. "Moskva-Petushki" (Moscow stations). In *Ostav'te moiu dushu v pokoe* (Leave my soul in peace) edited by Alexey Kostanian, 35–136. Moscow: Kh. G. S., 1997.

Erokaev, S., ed. and compl. *Zhizn' udalas': Anekdoty o novykh russkikh* (Life has been a success: Jokes about the new Russians). St. Petersburg: DiK, 1997.

Eroshkin, S., et al., eds. and compls. *Malinovye parusa: Anekdoty pro novykh russkikh* (The crimson sails: Jokes about the new Russians). St. Petersburg: DiK, 1997.

Etkind, Alexander. *Eros nevozmozhnogo: Istoriia psikhoanaliza v Rossii.* [Eros of the impossible: A history of psychoanalysis in Russia]. St. Petersburg: Meduza, 1993.

Farrel, Dianne Ecklund. "Medieval Popular Humor in Russian Eighteenth Century *Lubki.*" *Slavic Review* 50 (1991): 551–565.

Farrer, Dean Grimes. "The Soviet Folktale as an Ideological Strategy of Survival in International Business Relations." *Studies in Soviet Thought* 13 (1973): 55–75.

Feifer, George. *Moscow Farewell.* New York: Viking, 1976.

Fine, George, ed. and compl. *Sex Jokes and Male Chauvinism.* Secaucus, NJ: Citadel Press, 1981.

Flegon, A. *Za predelami russkikh slovarei* (Beyond Russian dictionaries). Russian edition. Troitsk, Moscow Region: Rike, 1993.

Freud, Sigmund. *Jokes and Their Relation to the Unconscious*. New York: Norton, 1960.

Friedberg, Maurice. "The Price of an Obsession," *The New Leader*, February 11–25, 1991: 20–21.

Genis, M. V., ed. and compl. *Zabavnye anekdoty* (Amusing jokes). 3 vols. St. Petersburg: Dilia, 1994.

Gershuni, V. "Na putiakh opal'noi slovesnosti" (On the roads of disgraced literature and folklore). In *Russkii mat: Antologiia dlia spetsialistov-filologov* (Russian foul language: Anthology for professional philologists) edited by F. N. Iliiasov, 269–284. Moscow: Lada, 1994.

Goldberg, Herb. *The Hazards of Being Male: Surviving the Myth of Masculine Privilege*. New York: Signet, 1987.

Golod, S. I. *XX vek i tendentsii seksual'nykh otnoshenii v Rossii* (The Twentieth Century and tendencies of sexual relations in Russia). St. Petersburg: Aleteia, 1996.

Goncharov, Ivan. *Oblomov*. New York: New American Library, 1963.

Gorer, Geoffrey. "The Psychology of Great Russians." In *The People of Great Russia* edited by Geoffrey Gorer and John Rickman, 93–196. New York: Norton, 1962.

Gorky, Maxim. "Lev Tolstoy." In Leo Tolstoy, *Povesti/ Vospominaniia sovremennikov* [Tales/memoirs of his contemporaries], 357–402. Moscow: Pravda, 1990.

Goscilo, Helena. *Desexing Sex: Russian Womanhood During and After Perestroika*. Ann Arbor: University of Michigan Press, 1996.

Gray, Francine du Plessix. *Soviet Women: Walking the Tightrope*. New York: Doubleday, 1990.

Grotjahn, Martin. *Beyond Laughter*. New York: McGraw Hill, 1957.

Guberman, Igor (under pen name Igor Garik). *Evreiskie datszybao* (Jewish Chinese wall inscriptions). Jerusalem: Moskva-Ierusalim, 1978.

———. "Zametki o desiatoi muze" (Notes on the tenth muse). In *Dom* (The house) edited by Alexander Polovets, 108–120. Los Angeles: Almanac, 1993.

Hall, Edward T. *The Silent Language*. New York: Anchor Books, 1973.

Hartogs, Renatus, with Hans Fantel. *Four-Letter Word Games: The Psychology of Obscenity*. New York: Evans, 1967.

Heldt, Barbara. *Terrible Perfection: Women and Russian Literature*. Bloomington: Indiana University Press, 1987.

Hertzler, Joyce O. *Laughter: A Socio-Scientific Analysis*. New Exposition, 1970.

Highwater, Jamake. *Myth and Sexuality*. New York: New American Library, 1990.

Hingley, Ronald. *The Russian Mind*. New York: Charles Scribner's Sons, 1977.

Hoffmann, Frank. *Analytical Survey of Anglo-American Traditional Erotica*. Bowling Green, KY.: Bowling Green University Popular Press, 1973.

Hubbs, Joanna. *Mother Russia*. Bloomington: Indiana University Press, 1988.

Hunt, Mort. *The Natural History of Love*. New York: Anchor Books, 1994.

Iliiasov, F. N. *Russkii mat: Antologia dlia spetsialistov-filologov*. [Russian foul language: An anthology for specialists-philologists]. Moscow: Lada, 1994.

Iliushin, Alexander. "Barkov i drugie" (Barkov and others). In *Tri veka poezii russkogo erosa* (Three centuries of Russian erotic poetry) edited by A. Shchuplov and A. Iliushin, 4–22. Moscow: Piat' vecherov, 1992.

Ivanov, Evgeny. *Metkoe moskovskoe slovo: Byt i rech' staroi Moskvy"* [A sharp Muscovite's word: Everyday life and speech of Old Moscow]. Moscow: Moskovskii rabochii, 1986.

Ivanova, O. Iu, ed. and compl. *Anekdoty i tosty* (Jokes and toasts). Moscow: Aurika, 1994.

———. *Anekdoty i tosty* (Jokes and toasts). Smolensk: Rusich, 1996.

Ivanova, T. G. "Skvernoslovie v muzhskikh sobraniakh v russkoi derevne" (Foul language in male gatherings in the Russian village). In *Russkii eroticheskii fol'klor* (Russian erotic folklore) edited by A. Toporkov, 534–536. Moscow: Ladomir, 1995.

Jakobson, Roman. *Selected Writings,* vol. 3. The Hague: Mouton:,1981.

Janus, Samuel S. "Humor, Sex, and Power in American Society." *American Journal of Psychoanalysis,* 41, no. 2 (1981): 161–168.

Jaworski, Adam. "A Note on Sexism and Insulting with Examples from Polish." *Maledicta* 8 (1984–1985): 91–94.

Jay, Timothy. *Cursing in America.* Philadelphia: John Benjamins, 1992.

Karbonsky, V., ed. and compl. *Nepodtsenzurnaia russkaia chastushka* (Uncensored Russian chastushka). New York: Russica, 1978.

Kapitsa, F. S. "Zapozdaloe vozvrashchenie" (A belated return). In A. N. Afanasiev, *Russkie zavetnye skazki* (Russian sacred tales), 149–155. Moscow: Mif, 1991.

Katchadourian, Herant. *Human Sexuality: Sense and Nonsense.* San Francisco: Freeman, 1972.

Keldysh, G. V. *Muzykal'nyi entsiklopedicheskii slovar'* (Encyclopedic dictionary of music). Moscow: Sovetskaia entsiklopediia, 1991.

Kelly, Aileen. "The Russian Sphinx." *New York Review of Books* 46, no. 9 (May 20, 1999): 7–10.

Kelly, Catriona. "'Better Halves'? Representations of Women in Russian Urban Popular Entertainments, 1870–1910." In *Women and Society in Russia and the Soviet Union* edited by Linda Edmondson, 5–31. Cambridge: Cambridge University Press, 1992.

———. "A Stick with Two Ends, or, Misogyny in Popular Culture: A Case Study of the Puppet Text 'Petrushka.'" In *Sexuality and the Body in Russian Culture* edited by Jane T. Costlow, Stephanie Sandler, and Judith Vowles, 73–96. Stanford: Stanford University Press, 1993.

Kerman, Judith B. " Excerpts" In *Sh'ma (A journal of Jewish responsibility)* vol. 28, no. 549 (March 5, 1998): 8.

Kharchev, A. G. *Brak i sem'ia v SSSR: Opyt sotsiologicheskogo issledovaniia* [Marriage and family in the USSR: An experiment of a sociological study]. Moscow: Mysl', 1964.

Kharkover, V. I., ed. and compl. *Anekdoty* (Jokes). vols. 1–3. Moscow: Vikhr', 1993.

Klimkovich, M., ed. and compl. *Anekdoty dlia plei-boia* [Jokes for a playboy]. Minsk: Assotsiatsia detektivnogo i politicheskogo romana, 1990.

Kokhtev, N. N. "Krainie vul'garizmy: sotsial'no-kul'turnaia otsenka" (Extreme vulgarisms: Sociocultural appraisal). In *Mezhdunarodnyi slovar' nepristoinostei: Putevoditel' po skabreznym slovam i neprilichnym vyrazheniiam v russkom, ital'ianskom, frantsuzskom, nemetskom, angliiskom iazykakh* (International dictionary of ribaldry: A guide to scabrous words and indecent expressions in Russian, Italian, French, German, Spanish, English languages) edited by Alexander Kokhtev, 83–88. Moscow: Avis, 1992.

Kolesov, Vladimir. *Iazyk goroda* (Urban language). Moscow: Vysshaia shkola, 1991.

Kolesov, V. V., compl. *Domostroi*. Moscow: Khudozhestvennaia literatura, 1991.

Kon, Igor. "Sexuality and Culture." In *Sex and Russian Society* edited by Igor Kon, and James Riordan, 15–44. Bloomington: Indiana University Press, 1993.

———. *The Sexual Revolution in Russia*. New York: Free Press, 1995.

———. *Seksual'naia kul'tura v Rossii: Klubnichka na bereze*. (Sexual culture in Russia: A little strawberry on a birch). Moscow: O.G.I., 1997.

Kozlovsky, Vladimir, ed. and compl. *Novaia nepodtsenzurnaia chastushka* (The new uncensored chastushka). New York: Russica, 1982.

Krylov, S., ed. *Russian-English Dictionary of Russian Sayings and Proverbs*. New York: NP, 1973.

Kulagina, A. V. "Epizody chukhlomskoi svad'by" (Episodes of Chukhlom wedding). In *Russkii eroticheskii fol'klor* (Russian erotic folklore) edited by A. Toporkov, 173–174. Moscow: Ladomir, 1995.

———. "Erotika v russkoi chastushke" (Eroticism in Russian chastushka). In *Russkii eroticheskii fol'klor* (Russian erotic folklore) edited by A. Toporkov, 432–439. Moscow: Ladomir, 1995.

Kulikov, Victor, ed. and compl. *Anekdoty pro novykh russkikh i drugikh zhitelei zemli* (Jokes about the New Russians and other inhabitants of the Earth). St. Petersburg: Kristall, 1997.

Kuskov, V. V. *Istoriia drevnerusskoi literatury* (History of ancient Russian literature). Moscow: Vysshaia shkola, 1977.

Lakoff, George, and Mark Johnson. "The Metaphorical Logic of Rape." *Metaphor and Symbolic Activity* 2, no.1 (1987): 73–79.

Legman, Gershon. *Rationale of the Dirty Joke: An Analysis of Sexual Humor* (first series). New York: Castle Books, 1968.

———. *Rationale of the Dirty Joke: An Analysis of Sexual Humor* (second series). New York: Breaking Point, 1975.

Levin, Eve. *Sex and Society in the World of the Orthodox Slavs, 900–1700*. Ithaca, N.Y.: Cornell University Press, 1989.

———. "Sexual Vocabulary in Medieval Russia." In *Sexuality and the Body in Russian Culture* edited by Jane T. Costlow, Stephanie Sandler, and Judith Vowles, 41–52. Stanford, Calif.: Stanford University Press, 1993.

Levin, Iu. "Ob obstsennykh vyrazheniakh russkogo iazyka" (About obscene expressions in Russian). In *Antimir russkoi kul'tury* (Anti-world of Russian culture) edited by N. Bogomolov, 108–120. St. Petersburg: Ladomir, 1996.

Levinson, Alexei. "O plokhom otnoshenii intelligentsii k rekalme" (On the intelligentsia's contempt for TV ads)," *Neprikosnovennyi zapas* (Emergency supply) 1 (1998): 36–38.

Levinton, G. "Dostoevskii i "nizkie zhanry fol'klora." In *Antimir russkoi kul'tury* (Anti-world of Russian culture) edited by N. Bogomolov, 267–296. St. Petersburg: Ladomir, 1996.

Likhachev, D. M. "Smekh kak 'mirovozzrenie'" in D. M. Likhachev and A. M. Panchenko. *"Smexovoi mir" drevnei Rusi* (The world of laughter in ancient Rus'), 7–90. Leningrad: Nauka, 1976.

———. *The National Nature of Russian History.* New York: Columbia University Press, 1990.

Linetsky, V. "Nuzhen li mat russkoi proze" (Does Russian prose need foul language?). In *Dom* (The house) edited by Alexander Polovets, 121–129. Los Angeles: Almanac, 1993.

Losev, Lev. *On the Beneficence of Censorship: Aesopian Language in Modern Russian Literature.* Munich: Otto Sagner, 1984.

Lurie, M. L. "O shkol'noi skabreznoi poezii" (About scabrous school poetry). In *Shkol'nyi byt i fol'klor: Uchebnyi material po russkomu fol'kloru* (Everyday school life and folklore), part I, edited by A. F. Belousov, 151–161. Tallinn: Tallin Pedagogical Institute, 1992.

Lurie, V. F. "Materialy po sovremennomu leningradskomu fol'kloru" (Materials on Contemporary Leningrad Folklore). In *Uchebnyi material po teorii literatury. Zhanry slovesnogo teksta: Anekdot* (Study material on theory of literature. The genres of a word text: An anecdote), edited by A. F. Belousov, 118–51. Tallinn: Tallin Pedagogical Institute, 1989.

Maksimov, Vladimir. 1991. "Est' takaia partiia" (There is such a party!). *Novoe Russkoe Slovo* [The new Russian word], July 23, 1991: 5.

Mamonova, Tatyana. *Russian Women's Studies: Essays on Sexism in Soviet Culture.* Oxford: Pergamon, 1989.

Margolis, Richard J. "Pride and Prejudice." *The New Leader,* November 8, 1976: 13–15.

Marshall, Bonnie. "Images of Women in Soviet Jokes and Anecdotes," *Journal of Popular Culture,* 26, no. 2 (1992): 117–125.

McCarthy, John, ed. *The Home Book of Irish Humor.* New York: Dodd, Mead, 1968.

McLovsky, Thomas, Mary Klyne, and Lexandre Chtchouplov. *Zhargon-Entsiklopediia moskovskoi tusovki* [Slang encyclopedia of Moscow Tusovka]. Moscow: Izdatel'skii tsentr, 1997.

Meiers, Mildred, and Jack Knapp, eds. and compls. *5,600 Jokes for All Occasions.* New York: Avenel, 1980.

Meshkova, E. G. "Izmenenie sotsial'nogo statusa zhenshchin v transformiruemom obshchestve" (Changes in social status of women in a transforming society). In *Problemy zhenshchin i sem'i glazami sotsiologov (Doklady na XIII-om vsemirnom sociologicheskom kongresse, Beilefeld, 1994)* (Sociologists on the problems of women and family [Reports at the XIII World Congress of Sociology] edited by A. F. Achilidieva and E. G. Meshkova, 79–87. Moscow: Institute of Sociology of Russian Academy of Science, 1997.

Milgram, Isaac, ed. and compl. *Armianskoe radio v interpretatsii Khaima Chapaeva* [Armenian radio in interpretation of Khaim Chapaev]. Canada: NP, 1985.

Miloslavsky, Yury. *Urban Romances and Other Stories.* Ann Arbor, Mich.: Ardis, 1994.

Mitchell, Carol A. "The Sexual Perspective in the Appreciation and Interpretation of Jokes." *Western Folklore* 36 (1977): 303–329.

Moore, Timothy and Karen Griffiths. "Sex, Attitudes Toward Women, and the Appreciation of Sexist Humor." In *American Humor: Proceedings of the 1986 WHIMSY Conference* edited by Don Nilsen and Alleen Pace Nilsen, 183–185. Tempe: Arizona State University, 1987.

Morris, Desmond. *The Human Zoo.* New York: Dell, 1970.

Mulkay, Michael. *On Humor: Its Nature and Its Place in Modern Society.* New York: Basil Blackwell, 1988.

Murphy, Robert F. *Cultural and Social Anthropology: An Overture.* Englewood Cliffs, NJ: 1989.

Nabokov, Vladimir. "Kembridzh" [Cambridge]. In *Kak ia liubliu tebia* (How I Love You), 130–134. Moscow: Tsentr–100, 1994.

Nagibin, Jury. "Dafnis i Khloia epokhi kul'ta lichnosti, voliuntarizma i zastoia." (Daphne and Chloe of the epoch of the cult of personality, voluntarism, and stagnation). *Oktiabr'* [October] 9 (1994): 3–80.

Nikulin, Yury, ed. *Anekdoty ot Nikulina* (Jokes from Nikulin). Moscow: BINOM and ZAO Godvin–3, 1997.

Nilsen, Don, and Alleen Pace Nilsen. "Humor, Language, and Sex Roles." *International Journal of the Sociology of Language* 65 (187) (1987): 67–78.

Ong, Walter. *Fighting for Life: Contest, Sexuality, and Consciousness.* Ithaca, N.Y., Cornell University Press, 1981.

Oring, Elliot. *Jokes and Their Relations.* Lexington: University of Kentucky Press, 1992.

Ozhegov, S. I. *Slovar' russkogo iazyka* (Dictionary of the Russian language). Moscow: Sovetskaia entsiklopediia, 1964.

Pankratova, M. G. "Sem'ia v Rossii posle raspada Sovetskogo Soiuza: preemtvennost' i izmeneniia" (Russian family after the collapse of the Soviet Union: Continuity and change). In *Problemy zhenshchin i sem'i glazami sotsiologov (Doklady na XIII-om vsemirnom sociologicheskom kongresse, Beilefeld, 1994)* (Sociologists on the problems of women and family [Reports at the XIII World Congress of

Sociology]) edited by A. F. Achilidieva and E. G. Meshkova, 17–24. Moscow: Institute of Sociology of Russian Academy of Science, 1997.

Pavlova, M. "Iz tvorcheskoi predistorii' Melkogo besa.' Algolagonicheskii roman Fedora Sologuba" (From the creative origins of *A Petty Demon*. The algolagonic novel of Fedor Sologub). In *Antimir russkoi kul'tury* (Anti-world of Russian culture) edited by N. Bogomolov, 328–354. St. Petersburg: Ladomir, 1996.

Perlez, Jane. "Dark Underside of Polish Family Life: Violence." *New York Times,* May 8, 1998: A1, A8.

Perlis, Mildred. "The Social Functions of Marriage Wit." *Marriage and Family Living* (February 1954): 49–50.

Pesmen, Dale. "Standing Bottles, Washing Deals, and Drinking 'For the Soul' in a Siberian City." *Anthropology of East Europe* Review 13, no. 2 (1995): 65–75.

Petrosian, Evgeny. *Evgeny Petrosian v strane anekdotov* (Eugene Petrosian in the country of jokes). Moscow: Tsentr estradnoi iumoristiki, 1994.

Podrabinek, Alexander. "Zabavy sovetskoi pressy" (Amusement of the Soviet press). *Novoe russkoe slovo* [The new Russian word], November 5, 1991: 5.

Polowy, Teresa. "Embattled Silence: The Alcoholic Marriage in Galina Shcherbakova's 'The Wall.'" *Slavic and East European Journal* 36, no. 4 (Winter 1992): 452–462.

Popovsky, Mark. *Tretii lishnii: on, ona i sovetskii rezhim* (The superfluous third: he, she, and the Soviet regime). London: Overseas Interchange, 1985.

Powell, Bill, and Kim Palchikoff. "Sober, Rested and Ready." *Newsweek,* December 8, 1997: 50–52.

Pushkin, Alexander. *Eugene Onegin.* New York: Dutton, 1981.

Pyliaev, M. "Kak eli v starinu" (How they ate in ancient times). *Arzamas* (New York) 2 (December 1992): 38–45.

Radcliffe-Brown, A. R. *Structure and Function in Primitive Society: Essays and Addresses.* Glencoe, Ill.: Free Press, 1961.

Rancour-Laferriere, Daniel. "Some Semiotic Aspects of the Human Penis." *Versus: quaderni di studi semiotici* 24 (1979): 37–82.

———. "The Teleology of Rhythm in Poetry: With Examples Primarily from the Russian Syllabotonic Meters" *PTL : A Journal of Descriptive Poetics and Theory of Literature* 4 (1980), 411–450.

———. *Out from Under Gogol's Overcoat: A Psychoanalytic Study.* Ann Arbor, Mich.: Ardis, 1982a.

———. "All the World's a *Vertep:* The Personification/ Depersonification Complex in Gogol's *Sorochinskaia iarmarka.*" *Harvard Ukrainian Studies* 6, no. 3 (Spring 1982b): 339–371.

———. "The Boys of Ibansk: A Freudian Look at Some Recent Russian Satire." *Psychoanalitic Review* 2, no. 4 (1985a): 639–656.

———. *Signs of the Flesh: An Essay on the Evolution of Hominid Sexuality.* Berlin: Mouton de Gruyter, 1985b.

———. "Pushkin's Still Unravished Bride: A Psychoanalytic Study of Tatiana's Dream," *Russian Literature* 25 (1989): 215–258.

————. *The Slave Soul of Russia: Moral Masochism and the Cult of Suffering.* New York: New York University Press, 1995.

Raskin, Iosif. *Entsiklopediia khuliganstvuiushchego ortodoksa* (Encyclopedia of a rowdy orthodox man). St. Petersburg: L.Y.S., 1995.

Raskin, Victor. "The Semantics of Abuse in the Chastushka: Women's Bawdy." *Maledicta* 5 (1981): 301–317.

————. *Semantic Mechanisms of Humor.* Dordrecht: Reidel, 1985.

Rastaturina, E., ed. and compl. *Anekdot, anekdot, anekdot* (A joke, a joke, a joke). Petrozavodsk: AO Amit'e, 1995.

Repina, Irina, and Yury Rostovtsev, eds. *Anekdoty nashikh chitatelei* (Jokes of our readers). Multivols. Moscow: Anons, 1995.

Retzinger, Suzanne M. *Violent Emotions: Shame and Rage in Marital Quarrels.* Newbury Park, Calif.: Sage, 1991.

Rice, James. "A Russian Bawdy Song of the 18th Century." *Slavic and East European Journal* 20 (1976): 353–370.

Ries, Nancy. "The Power of Negative Thinking: Russian Talk and the Reproduction of Mindset, World View, and Society." *Anthropology of East Europe Review* 10, no. 2 (Autumn 1991): 38–53.

————. *Russian Talk: Culture and Conversation during Perestroika.* Ithaca, N.Y.: Cornell University Press, 1997.

Riordan, James. "Introduction." In *Sex and Russian Society* edited by Igor Kon and James Riordan, 1–14. Bloomington: Indiana University Press, 1993.

Rogers, Susan. "Female Forms of Power and the Myth of Male Dominance: A Model of Female/Male Interaction in Peasant Society." *American Ethnologist* 2 (1975): 727–756.

Roshchin, Mikhail. "*Blok 1993–1994*" (Block 1993–1994). *Oktiabr'* (October) 6, (1995): 3–40.

Rozhnova, Polina. *A Russian Folk Calendar: Rites, Customs, and Popular Beliefs.* Moscow: Novosti, 1992.

Rubina, Dina. "Na paneli: Zametki 'literaturnogo metra'" (On the streets: Notes of a "literary maestro"). *Marina* (Russian-American Journal) (April-May 1995): 82–84.

Sabashnikova, E. G., ed. *Klub 12 Stul'ev* (Club of 12 Chairs). Moscow: Iskusstvo, 1973.

Sadovnikov, D. *Riddles of the Russian People: A Collection of Riddles, Parables and Puzzles collected by D. Sadovnikov,* translated by Ann C. Bigelow. Ann Arbor, Mich.: Ardis, 1986.

Sekridova, Tatiana. "Evgenii Men'shov: 'Vse dlia zhenshchiny'." (Everything for a Woman). *Kur'er* (Courier) (Los Angeles) 4, no. 15 (May 29–June 4, 1998): 49.

Semyonova Tian-Shanskaia, Olga. *Village Life in Late Tsarist Russia,* edited by David L. Ransel, translated by David L. Ransel with Michael Levine. Bloomington: Indiana University Press, 1993.

Shcheglov, Lev. "Medical Sexology." In *Sex and Russian Society* edited by Igor Kon and James Riordan, 152–164. Bloomington: Indiana University Press, 1993.

Shein, P. V. *Velokoruss v svoikh pesniakh, obriadakh, obychaiakh* (The great Russian in his songs, rituals, and customs]. St. Petersburg: NP, 1889.

Shklovsky, Victor. "K teorii komicheskogo" (Toward the theory of the comic). *Epopeia* (Epic), 32 (1922): 57–67.

———. *O teorii prozy* (About the theory of prose). Moscow: Federatsiia, 1929.

Shlapentokh, Vladimir. *Love, Marriage, and Friendship in the Soviet Union.* New York: Praeger, 1984.

———. *Public and Private Life of the Soviet People: Changing Values in Post-Stalin Russia.* New York: Oxford University Press, 1989.

Shlyakhov, Vladimir and Eve Adler. *Dictionary of Russian Slang and Colloquial Expressions.* New York: Barron's, 1995.

Shumov, K. E. "'Eroticheskie' studencheskie graffiti na materialakh studencheskikh auditorii Permskogo universiteta" ("Erotic" student graffiti: On the data of student auditoriums of Perm University). In *Seks i erotika v russkoi traditsionnoi kul'ture* (Sex and eroticism in traditional Russian culture) edited by A. Toporkov, 454–483. Moscow: Ladomir, 1996.

Silantiev, V. D. "Ne ot goloda liudi pogibaiut, ot edy." (It's not hunger that kills you. It's food.) *Argumenty i fakty* 51, no. 896 (December 1997): 21.

Simons, G. L. *Sex and Superstition.* New York: Barnes and Noble, 1973.

Sinyavsky, Andrey. *Ivan-durak: ocherk russkoi narodnoi very.* (Ivan the Fool: A sketch of Russian popular belief). Paris: Sintaksis, 1991.

Smetanin, V., and Donskaia, K., eds. and compls. *Eroticheskii anekdot* (The erotic joke). Moscow: DataStrom, 1992.

Smirnitsky, A. I., ed. *Russko-angliiskii slovar'* (Russian-English dictionary). Moscow: Russkii iazyk, 1992.

Smolitskaia, O. V. "Semantika mata i problema semanticheskogo iadra chastushki" (Semantics of foul language and the problem of semantic nucleus of chastushka). *Razguliai* (Play time), vol. 1. Moscow: Salang and Klen, 1990.

Sokolov, Y. M. *Russian Folklore.* Detroit: Folklore Associates, 1971.

Soloviev, D., ed. and compl. *Izbrannye anekdoty* (Selected jokes). 4 vols. Moscow: Reklama, 1992.

Solzhenitsyn, Alexander. "The Smatterers." In *From Under the Rubble* edited by Alexander Solzhenitsyn et al., 229–278. Boston: Little, Brown, 1975.

Sonin, A. I., ed. *Anekdoty: Kushat' podano. Sadites' zhrat', pozhaluista.* (Jokes: Dinner is served. Pig out please.") Moscow: Lana, 1995.

Spears, Richard A. *Slang and Euphemism; A Dictionary of Oaths, Curses, Insults, Sexual Slang and Metaphor, Racial Slurs, Drug Talk, Homosexual Lingo, and Related Matters.* New York: New American Library, 1982.

Specter, Michael. "Deep in the Russian Soul, a Lethal Darkness." *New York Times,* June 8, 1997, sec. 4: 5.

Spender, Dale. *Man Made Language.* London: Routledge and Kegan Paul, 1980.

Stafford, Peter. *Sexual Behavior in the Communist World: An Eyewitness Report of Life, Love and the Human Condition Behind the Iron Curtain.* New York: Julian Press, 1967.

Stanihurst, Richard. "The Commodities of Aqua Vitae." In *A Treasure of Irish Folklore* edited by Padraic Colum, 388. New York: Wings Books, 1992.

Stanley, Alessandra. "Russian Alcoholics Taste Freedom and Vodka," *New York Times,* July 3, 1996: 5.

Starinskaia, Natalia, ed. and compl. *Veseloe zastol'e: Tosty* (A jolly feast: Toasts). Minsk: Mezhdunarodnyi knizhnyi dom, 1996.

Starshinov, Nikolai. *Razreshite vas poteshit* (Let us entertain you). vols. 1 and 2. Moscow: Stolitsa, 1992a.

———. "Russkaia chastushka XX veka" (Russian chastushka of the twentieth century). In *Tri veka poezii russkogo erosa* (Three centuries of Russian erotic poetry) edited by A. Shchuplov and A. Iliushin, 129–157. Moscow: Piat' vecherov, 1992b.

Stern, Mikhail with August Stern. *Sex in the USSR.* New York: Times Books, 1980.

Tertz, Abram (Andrey Sinyavsky). *Mysli vrasplokh* (Thoughts off-guard) Munich: Ekho-Press, 1980.

Timroth, Wilhelm von. *Russian and Soviet Sociolinguistics and Taboo Varieties of the Russian Language (Argot, Jargon, Slang and "Mat").* Translated from German by Nortrud Gupta. Munich: Verlag Otto Sagner, 1986.

Tolstaya, Tatyana. "Notes from Underground," *New York Review of Books,* 37, no. 9 (May 31, 1990): 3–9.

Toporkov, Andrey. "Erotika v russkom fol'klore" (Eroticism in Russian folklore). In *Russkii eroticheskii fol'klor* (Russian erotic folklore) edited by A. Toporkov, 5–20. Moscow: Ladomir, 1995a.

———. ed. *Russkii eroticheskii folklor* (Russian erotic folklore). Moscow: Ladomir, 1995b.

———. ed. *Seks i erotika v russkoi traditsionnoi kul'ture* (Sex and eroticism in Russian traditional culture). Moscow: Ladomir, 1996.

Toth, Emily. "Forbidden Jokes and Naughty Ladies." *Studies in American Humor* N. S. 4, no. 2 (Spring-Summer 1985): 7–17.

Treml, Vladimir. "Alcohol Abuse and the Quality of Life in the Soviet Union" In *Quality of Life in the Soviet Union* edited by Horst Herlemann, 151–162. Boulder, CO.: Westview Press, 1987.

Uspensky, B. A. "Religiozno-mifologicheskii aspekt russkoi ekspressivnoi frazeologii (Semantika russkogo mata v istoricheskom osveshchenii)" (Religious and mythological aspects of Russian expressive phraseology [Semantics of Russian foul language in historical light]). In *Semiotics and the History of Culture: In Honor of Jurij Lotman* edited by M. Halle et al., 197–302. Columbus, Ohio: Slavica, 1988.

———. "'Zavetnye skazki' A. N. Afanas'eva" (Afanasiev's "Secret tales"). In *Ot mifa k literature* [From myth to literature] edited by S. Iu. Neklidov and E. S. Novik, 117–138. Moscow: Rossiiskii universitet, 1993.

Utechin, S. F. *Everyman's Concise Encyclopaedia of Russia.* New York: Dutton, 1961.

Utesov, Leonid. "Stikhi L. Utesova." (Utesov's verses). In Antonina Revel's *Riadom s Utesovym* (Being next to Utesov), 225–232. Moscow: Iskusstvo, 1995.

Vasilieva, O. V., and S. B. Giukhina "*Anekdot i chastushka (Slovesnyi tekst kak sposob povedeniia)* (The anecdote and chastushka [A verbal text as behavior]). In *Uchebnyi material po teorii literatury. Zhanry slovesnogo teksta: Anekdot* (Study material on theory of literature. The genres of a verbal text: A joke) edited by A. F. Belousov, 95–99. Tallin: Tallinskii Pedagogicheskii Institut, 1989.

Vasmer, Max. *Etimologicheskii slovar' russkogo iazyka v chetyrekh tomax* (Etymological dictionary of the Russian language in four volumes]. Moscow: Progress, 1986.

Vishnevskaia, Galina. *Galina: A Russian Story.* San Diego: Harcourt Brace Jovanovich, 1984.

Visson, Lynn. *Wedded Strangers: The Challenges of Russian-American Marriages.* New York: Hippocrene Books, 1998.

Volkan, Vamik D. *The Need to Have Enemies and Allies: From Clinical Practice to International Relationship.* Northvale, NJ: Jason Aronson, 1994.

Voronina, Olga. "Soviet Patriarchy: Past and Present." *Hypatia* 8, no. 4 (Fall 1993): 97–112.

Wenthworth, Harold, and Stuart Berg Flexner, eds., *The Pocket Dictionary of American Slang.* New York: Pocket Books, 1968.

White, Stephen. *Russia Goes Dry: Alcohol, State and Society.* Cambridge: Cambridge University Press, 1996.

Wierzbicka, Anna. "Soul and Mind: Linguistic Evidence for Ethnopsychology and Cultural History." *American Anthropologist* 91, no.1 (1989): 41–58.

Williams, Sarah. 1998. "Footbinding and Its Final Days: An Anthropological Perspective." *Honors Review* (Hunter College) (1998): 4–12.

Wilson, Christopher P. *Jokes: Form, Content, Use and Function.* London: Academic Press, 1979.

Wolfe, Tom. "Pornoviolence." In *75 Readings: An Anthology* edited by Susan D. Hurtt and Bernadette Boylan, 145–151. New York: McGraw-Hill, 1989.

Zakharova, L. D. "Russia nepristoinaia chastushka" (Russian indecent chastushka). In *Russkii mat: Antologiia* (Russian foul language: An anthology) edited by F. N. Iliiasov, 164–168. Moscow: Lada, 1994a.

———. "Kazhdyi drochit, kak on khochet" (Everyone masturbates the way he wants). In *Russkii mat: Antologiia* (Russian foul language: An anthology) edited by F. N. Iliiasov, 285–298. Moscow: Lada, 1994b.

Zhelvis, V. I. "Invektiva: muzhskoe i zhenskoe predpochtenie" (The invective: Male and female preferences). In *Etnicheskie stereotipy muzhskogo i zhenskogo povedeniia* (Ethnic stereotypes of male and female behavior) edited by A. K. Baiburin and I. S. Kon, 266–283. St. Petersburg: Nauka, 1991.

Zinik, Zinovy. "After the Third Glass." *Times Literary Supplement,* January 31, 1997: 7.

Zorin, A. "Legalizatsiia obstsennoi leksiki i ee kul'turnye posledtsviia" (Legalization of obscene lexicology and its aftermath). In *Antimir russkoi kul'tury* (Anti-world of Russian culture) edited by N. Bogomolov, 121–142. St. Petersburg: Ladomir, 1996.

Index